MANAGING
LEVIATHAN

FOR

Jesse, Matthew, Nicholas

Anna & James

MANAGING LEVIATHAN

ENVIRONMENTAL POLITICS
AND THE ADMINISTRATIVE STATE

edited by Robert Paehlke and Douglas Torgerson

broadview press

Cataloguing in Publication Data

Main entry under title:

Managing leviathan: environmental politics and the administrative state

Includes bibliographical references
ISBN   0-921149-54-9

1.   Environmental policy — Canada.   2.   Environmental policy —
United States. 3. Bureaucracy — Canada. 4. Bureaucracy — United
States. 5. Public administration. I. Paehlke, Robert. II. Torgerson,
Douglas, 1948-   .

HC120.E5M35 1990   363.7'056'0971   C90-093411-5

broadview press   in the US, broadview press
P.O. Box 1243   269 Portage Rd.
Peterborough, Ontario   Lewiston, NY
K9J 7H5   Canada   14092   USA

Acknowledgements

For financial support for parts of this work, the editors thank the Social Sciences and Humanities Research Council of Canada; the Frost Centre for Canadian Heritage and Development Studies, Trent University; and the Committee on University Aid to Research in the Arts, Trent University.

Some parts of this volume have been previously published: Robert Paehlke, 'Democracy and Environmentalism: Opening a Door to the Administrative State' is updated and revised from an article which appeared in *Environmental Ethics* 10 (1988), pp 291-308; Ted Schrecker, 'Resisting Environmental Regulation: The Cryptic Pattern of Business-Government Relations' is essentially new, though based upon an article which appeared in *Alternatives: Perspectives on Society, Technology and Environment* 13:1 (1985), pp. 9-21; Kernaghan Webb, 'Between Rocks and Hard Places: Bureaucrats, Law and Pollution Control' is updated and revised from an article which appeared in *Alternatives: Perspectives on Society, Technology and Environment* 14:2 (1987), pp 4-13; Robert B. Gibson, 'Out of Control and Beyond Understanding: Acid Rain as a Political Dilemma' is updated and revised from an article which appeared in *Alternatives: Perspectives on Society, Technology and Environment* 11:2 (1983), pp. 3-8; Robert Paehlke and Douglas Torgerson, 'Toxic Waste and the Administrative State: NIMBY Syndrome or Participatory Management?' is updated and revised from an article which appeared in *Public Policy and Administrative Studies*, Vol. 2, O.P. Dwivedi and R. Brian Woodrow, eds. (Guelph: University of Guelph, 1985), pp. 110-132.

Contents

PREFACE

The calm voice of the official assures the public that the proper administrative procedures are in place: all is under control, and environmental protection can be taken for granted. Yet just when the populace seems lulled again into a sense of security, another environmental crisis captures the focus of popular attention. One after another, an apparently unending series of household words enters the language: acid rain, dioxins, PCBs, sewage sludge, ozone depletion, nuclear meltdown. Also newly thrust into the everyday vocabulary are names of environmental trouble-spots: Love Canal, Three Mile Island, Bhopal, Chernobyl, Valdez. The official image of order is each time, at least momentarily, jostled aside by an image of a world running out of control.

Environmental politics is alive with these conflicting images. In political and economic life, administrative organizations want to define environmental troubles as manageable problems which can be subjected to rules and procedures consistent with established priorities. To see environmental problems otherwise is portrayed as irrational and socially irresponsible, as threatening disorder. Yet even as some environmental activists tone down their rhetoric and gain legitimacy in public debates governed by the administrative idiom, events often overtake everyone: official assurances and compromise proposals ring hollow whenever a new disaster becomes visible. And many environmental activists remain fully opposed to the administrative world, viewing state and economy—the present organization of public and private power—as requiring nothing less than a total and immediate transformation. The alternative is catastrophe. They will have nothing to do with Leviathan.

Although official imagery can become unsettled, there remains a certain reflex response which seems sure to restore popular faith in Leviathan—in the administrative state, or more broadly, the centralized, hierarchical administrative form that dominates advanced industrial society. For a prevailing bias sees this as the only possible administrative form, and the effective management of environmental problems thus appears to demand support for this order and its outwardly sincere and competent efforts. Democracy itself seems somehow at odds with proper environmental management.

While the conventional administrative viewpoint is comfortable with this latter conclusion, the idea has also been voiced by a type of environmentalism which has rather desperately reached out for an authoritarian solution. The opposite environmentalist position—the flat rejection of the prevailing administrative apparatus—has yet to offer more than a vague belief in principles of decentralization, participatory democracy, and natural harmony. This rejection of administration is easily ridiculed and dismissed because it has produced little as yet by way of a plausible approach to problems of environmental management. The hard-headed realism of the administrative mind seems to confront nothing more substantial than a naïve sentimentalism.

An exploration of environmental politics and administration, this book is designed to directly counter the conventional administrative bias of centralization and hierarchy by questioning the nature of administration and its relationship to democracy. This focus directs attention as well to the context and definition of environmental problems.*

Often, democracy and administration are thought to be necessarily at odds; the debate is over which of the two should be sacrificed. Any defence of democracy will, indeed, be feeble on these terms if humanity faces serious environmental problems requiring effective administration. The terms of debate may shift dramatically, however, if we consider the potential for democracy and effective administration to be mutually supportive: then principles of decentralization and participation themselves become relevant to managing Leviathan. If democracy is necessary for the successful resolution of environmental problems, the tables would indeed be turned on the conventional administrative bias.

Contemporary developments in administrative theory have already challenged this bias: the variability, complexity, and political character of administrative situations have all been recognized. Decentralization and participation are increasingly viewed as instrumentally—as well as morally—valuable. This volume builds upon this tendency with essays emphasizing the political character of environmental administration and probing the potential of decentralization and participation for defining and resolving environmental problems.

---

* The editors assume sole responsibility for the design and purpose of the volume as a whole. The authors are individually responsible for their particular articles.

To counter a prevailing bias, one need not offer a completed conception to replace it. At issue is a matter of orientation, and the task is to show the limits of a particular focus while identifying forces and interests which make that focus rigid, rendering it resistant to alternatives. By drawing attention to the resistances which sustain a bias, this effort promotes a reorientation but does not pretend to offer a neat and clear alternative. The goal of this volume is rather to help revise the agenda of inquiry and practice in environmental decision-making. This does not mean necessarily substituting one bias for another (as some might be eager to say): the point, rather, is to open up questions which have been closed or which have never been clearly posed and considered—to encourage a more flexible orientation, attentive to the context and the constraints that shape inquiry and practice.

While guided by both environmental and democratic concerns, this volume is deliberately designed to be exploratory—in a sense, inconclusive. For example, the full potential of decentralization, often a focus of environmentalists, has certainly been neglected in administrative thought and practice. To say this, however, is not to argue that centralization in environmental management should or could simply be replaced with decentralization. Within the general reorientation which we propose, it is indeed a key tenet that the definition and solution of problems must take account of the complexities of particular contexts. Further work along these lines is a task for ourselves and others.

Overall, in recognizing a complex array of environmental problems, the latter part of this century has come in for a considerable shock. Despite efforts to absorb this shock through administrative imagery and routine, the recognition of environmental problems has been unsettling to the expectations of order and progress which have guided industrialization and helped to construct the edifice of modern administration. It is at least questionable whether the outlook promoting this pattern of development is capable of grasping and effectively handling the incalculable environmental impact which the pattern inadvertently generates. A reexamination of the conventional approach to environmental administration is thus surely in order.

The essays in this book are relevant to questions of environmental politics and administration in advanced industrial societies generally, but there is a consistent, particular focus on North America. Cases and illustrations are largely drawn from environmental politics and administration in the United States and Canada. The authors are American and

Canadian, with some from each country writing about the other as well as their own. Although the volume as a whole is neither comparative nor international in intent, the essays do suggest notable similarities and differences between the two societies while serving as reminders of the importance of each for the other.

If the approach advanced here has any validity, then decentralization and participation have a potential to promote the effective handling of environmental problems. We do not know precisely what this potential is, but hope that it might serve to improve both environmental protection and the prospects of enhancing democracy. Moving in this direction would certainly affect the management of Leviathan. Whether it could ultimately mean moving beyond Leviathan is another intriguing question — one which requires first, however, a revision of the present agenda of inquiry and practice.

PART I

The Environment as an Administrative Problem

If there is a problem, better management is often assumed to be the solution. This assumption has deeply influenced the rise of advanced industrial societies and now guides much of the response to environmental problems. The environmental challenge demands effective administration, and some fear that this may force a sacrifice of democracy. The image of Leviathan thus reassures even as it threatens.

We find another way of looking at the situation, however, if we focus on the limits of administration as it is conventionally conceived and practiced. Administrative organizations have been especially effective in dealing with narrowly defined problems. By and large, conventional administration seems to work so long as there is no need to worry about side-effects. The difficulty, however, is that the environment has emerged as a major problem precisely *as* an accumulation and interaction of side-effects.

There are, of course, specific problems of the environment which current administrative activities help to mitigate. But, despite particular successes—and no matter how ingenious and dedicated individual administrators may be—it does nonetheless seem that conventional administration ultimately confronts insurmountable obstacles to effective environmental management. The articles in Part I focus on the nature of these obstacles and explore the prospect that they might be overcome through a revised, more democratic approach to administrative inquiry and practice.

ENVIRONMENTAL ADMINISTRATION:
REVISING THE AGENDA
OF INQUIRY AND PRACTICE

Douglas Torgerson and Robert Paehlke

Concern has often been voiced about the undemocratic tendencies of the administrative state. However, it has usually been thought that these tendencies must, to a large extent, be tolerated because of the administrative exigencies of an advanced economy and society. Complex problems are deemed to require a concentration of knowledge and power in centralized hierarchies. This alignment of knowledge and power has been considered unavoidable, albeit regrettable from a democratic perspective—an administrative necessity in the emergence of industrial civilization.

Now, we are told, industrialization faces a range of problems greatly exceeding in complexity those earlier confronted. The advent of environmental problems, in particular, poses difficulties which can be handled only through professional expertise and specialized organization. Notions of decentralization and public participation may have appeal but they should not be allowed to interfere with the really serious business of administration in an advanced industrial society.[1]

Continued orderly development would thus necessitate Leviathan in the form of the administrative state. Even if this is not precisely Hobbes's Leviathan, an order governed by a central power of absolute authority—even, that is, if the principle of popular sovereignty is maintained along with formal institutions of democracy—the administrative state still remains set in the basic order of centralization and hierarchy which Hobbes discerned and encouraged in the early emergence of the modern state. Hence, the hard, if sad, truth is that operating the administrative state—managing Leviathan—necessarily extracts sacrifices from democracy.[2]

We question the view that undemocratic measures are necessary for effective administration[3]—particularly given the advent of environmental problems. Even though there is now much discussion of the so-called NIMBY (not-in-my-back-yard) Syndrome and of popular resistance to necessary measures of environmental management, it was indeed a popular upsurge and sense of environmental crisis some two decades ago which gave rise to administrative reforms for environmental protection.

A landmark event in this regard was the establishment of the *National Environmental Policy Act* of 1969 in the United States. Passed in the midst of a fervor of environmental concern, this legislation required agencies of the federal government to prepare environmental impact statements for activities "significantly affecting the quality of the human environment." Against the backdrop of a burgeoning environmental movement, the proposed Trans-Alaska Pipeline was the first major project to be affected by the new legislation. By demanding that the requirements of environmental impact statements be rigorously observed and by initiating court action, environmental groups sought to slow governmental approval. While action in the courts was eventually undercut by what amounted to a Congressional exemption of the pipeline from the requirements of the legislation, the opposition of environmentalists did focus attention on a clear need: as industrialization expands into new territory—in both the technological and geographical sense—large projects require careful scrutiny even to accord with the interests of their proponents. In the case of the pipeline, environmentalists were able to demonstrate that the engineering plans first proposed were unsuited to Alaskan conditions: subsequent changes avoided a fiasco.[4]

The chances for effective environmental protection were clearly enhanced by public involvement—by challenges to the ensemble of public and private bureaucracies which would otherwise have been left to themselves to design, construct, operate, and regulate the pipeline. Here and elsewhere, indeed, it would seem that tendencies toward the effective handling of environmental problems come not because of bureaucracy, but in spite of it.

Do some problems arising in the aftermath of industrialization require significantly greater public participation and decentralized initiative than is normally allowed in the realm of the administrative state? Much evidence suggests an answer in the affirmative, but our point is not to offer a final answer to the question. What we recommend, instead, is simply for this question to counter prevailing presuppositions which promote a bias in favor of centralized hierarchy. In the context of these presuppositions, many possible initiatives which might simultaneously advance both democracy and effective administration appear implausible. For the possible to be discovered and rendered plausible requires a reorientation of administrative inquiry and innovation. What this volume as a whole presents is no general theory, then, but evidence and ideas which should encourage new hypotheses and a reframing of problems.

Conventional approaches to administration presuppose a central position of planning and control, a unified will privileged by superior knowledge. Politics presupposes differences in interests and perspectives along with a dispersion of power; and this is what conventional administration seeks to exclude in principle — or at least to keep to a minimum — collapsing a diversity of interests into a single, homogeneous interest.[5] Not only does this perspective miss the actual dynamics of organizational relationships: what is also overlooked is the way observations, insights, and ideas are influenced by interest and position. Knowledge is not something which can somewhere be insulated and enshrined, for — to be relevant — it depends always upon the context and dynamics of organizational activity. Those in a position to know (in significant part) are those involved in this activity who have an interest in inquiry — in clearly and continuously sorting out aspects of a developing process.

In practice, the positions and interests of central organizational actors screen out the perception of relevant features of situations and problems. Conventional orientations are thus limited, ironically, in the very realm which they take to be their own: knowledge. In particular, their sources of knowledge are inadequate to problems arising from new, complex, and dynamic situations; and these are the kinds of conditions which seem to arise with striking frequency now that much industrialization has run its course.

While our focus here is on environmental problems arising in this aftermath of industrialization,[6] limitations of the conventional administrative perspective have long been recognized in efforts to promote decentralization and participation in organizations. These efforts, of course, were typically contained within centralized hierarchies and served to reinforce the legitimacy of established administrative organizations; yet these same efforts also pointed to the potential effectiveness of alternative organizational forms. This potential, perceived even in the emergence of industrialization, now is often considered especially significant with the advent of post-industrial technologies which rely dramatically upon knowledgeable, committed, innovative, and flexible people in the organization. Beyond the context of manufacturing, moreover, public participation has been viewed as potentially important in the effective "co-production" and delivery of services.[7] Our approach to environmental policy and administration is intended to complement investigation and experimentation along these lines. We do not know how far this direction might fruitfully be explored, whether with regard to manufacturing, services, environmental problems or other areas. That is to say, we do not predict in advance how helpful decentralization and participation may prove to be in administration generally. Nor, we would add, do we suggest that such measures should necessarily be pursued only to the extent that they can prove themselves administratively effective: interest in democratic government and society would give further cause to move in this direction. We are convinced, however, that an interest in democracy is not the only reason to do so — and that the supposed conflict between democracy and effective administration is typically overdrawn.

What is it that lends plausibility to the way this conflict is usually treated? The short answer to this question is the spectre of disorder. The conventional bias in favor of centralized hierarchy has regarded alternative organizational forms not simply as potentially less effective, but as practically impossible — as illusions offering a short path to chaos and ruin. Since there can supposedly be no secure order without centralized hierarchy, the choice of organizational form is dictated by administrative necessity. We can see through this notion, however, if we recognize that we are never confronted with order as such, but always with a particular order — and that any particular order is bound up with particular interests. This recognition points to the hidden political dimension contained in claims that any particular order is administratively necessary.[8] Experiments with alternative organizational forms may well provoke disorder, but this is not necessarily because such forms are administratively impossible.

Different organizational forms bring to the fore different interests and thereby generate conflicts which are unsettling to the notion that administration must proceed from one legitimate will — a single, unified authority. Inasmuch as the agenda of administrative inquiry and practice presupposes this notion, changes which allow the entry of different legitimate interests into the decision process will threaten to provoke unpredictable changes to that agenda and the way it is set:[9] new issues then can be identified, and problems can be redefined in novel ways.

Resistance to such change can be expected even though innovations might contain features helpful to the interests of the established order. For the prevailing configuration of interests will both inhibit clear perception of potential advantages and promote considerable concern about an anticipated loss of control. The potential for a loss of control will be sensed as a definite threat to a particular order and its prevailing interests; and this loss will readily be both regarded and portrayed as the advent of chaos.

To protect a given order in the name of administrative necessity is thus to resist revisions in the agenda of inquiry and practice. But this resistance takes a toll: administrative capacity to learn is necessarily constrained as divergent interests and perspectives are excluded from serious consideration; ritual and routine tend to predominate in the definition and handling of problems. Indeed, it has been argued that administrative organizations should, in their own interests, recognize and deliberately allow the political processes which pervade them. Especially when organizations face complex and changing circumstances, explicit organizational politics serves to draw attention to the array of factors which need to be taken into account in defining and solving problems.[10] This argument, of course, challenges the conventional bias in favor of centralized hierarchy by raising the prospect of alternative forms of effective administration. In contrast, preoccupation with maintaining order rules out an open airing and resolution of the conflicts rooted in differing interests. Politics, rendered illegitimate, is thereby obscured and suppressed — though, of course, not eliminated. Administration conventionally proceeds with the idea that it is, or ought to be, entirely separate from politics.

Yet the idea that administration can be insulated from politics is no longer able to withstand scrutiny. The persistence of the idea is partly because of a general bias, but also partly because of particular interests and priorities. The conventional exclusion of politics from administration is, indeed, not strictly administrative, but broadly political; its *raison d'être* is to protect administrative organizations from the unwelcome change in established priorities which any questioning of the existing agenda threatens to create.

The organizations and procedures which the administrative state has developed for environmental protection often prove themselves to be dramatically ineffective. Of course, one does not have to look to the conventional bias of administrative thought and practice to find a reason for this ineffectiveness. Whether one's analysis is informed by pluralist, elite, or class models,[11] it is not difficult to conclude that environmental management has typically had a low priority, despite much rhetoric. Thus it could reasonably be argued that broad social and political forces, rather than administration, constitute the real problem in blocking effective environmental management. But we would maintain that the forms and practices of administration are interwoven with these social and political forces.

This complex of forces manifests itself differently in various socio-political contexts. For example, if we were broadly to compare capitalist and socialist societies, we would certainly find different patterns of socio-political forces. Generally speaking, however, we would also find a low priority placed upon effective environmental management compared to that placed upon effective industrial development.[12] The relatively low priority placed upon environmental protection, moreover, is not unrelated to the typical form of administration.

Bureaucracy, Weber maintained, is a reliable and effective instrument.[13] Yet Weber did not argue that bureaucracy is an instrument suitable for just any purpose. In broad historical terms, indeed, he saw bureaucracy as an organizational form reflecting and reinforcing a particular pattern of development: the rationalization and industrialization of the world. Bureaucratization thus contains an agenda of historical development: the salience of this form of centralized hierarchy has as a purpose the promotion of particular interests. The order serves a certain conception of progress and the socio-political forces promoting it.

To question the prevailing administrative form is unavoidably also to question prevailing priorities; for the two are interwoven. Beyond the question of priorities, moreover, is the issue of whether centralized hierarchy — particularly bureaucratic organization — could ever be sufficient for, or appropriate to, the task of effective environmental management. Can bureaucracy, in other words, deal effectively with the unanticipated consequences of the pattern of development which it promotes and in which it participates? From a conventional administrative viewpoint, this question might well appear nonsensical. Yet in the contemporary development of administrative theory, the basic idea has become commonplace: the appropriateness of an organizational form depends upon the task at hand. By putting a twist on the "contingency" approach to administration,[14] we thus suggest that the advent of environmental problems tends to challenge, rather than reinforce, the conventional presuppositions of administration, particularly those favoring centralized hierarchy and a closed process of decision-making.

The administrative state is often viewed through a focus which directs attention strictly to the organization of public government. However, the administrative state has emerged within a broader context; there has been a tendency for public and private bureaucracies — despite conflicts — to develop patterns of mutually supportive relationships which shut other potential participants out of the decision-making process. The context, more broadly considered, is one of rationalization, industrialization, and bureaucratization; and the administrative state thus plays a key part in a world largely dominated by an ensemble of great organizations.[15] Of course, the domination is by no means complete or perfectly coordinated: the task of managing Leviathan continually confronts and generates problems. Here a political dimension of this management becomes evident.

Environmental politics, in particular, holds up a mirror to the world of administration, showing its bias and limits. Concern for the efficient use of natural resources has, of course, long been expressed within the world of administrative organizations,[16] and the administrative state has considered resource management to be a province of its own. The emergence of environmental politics in the latter part of this century, however, is a token of the failings of the administrative state. Beyond pointing out shortcomings of the administrative state in its own terms, environmental politics at times also raises doubts about the fundamental thrust of industrialization, and — even more broadly — questions both the viability and morality of the human domination of nature.

The administrative state, of course, seldom seems moved by such critique, but rather — by virtue of organizational structures and priorities — seeks to absorb it, consistently reasserting the necessity of a conventional mode of administration. From this perspective, the advent of environmental politics is reduced to an expression of narrowly self-serving groups and individuals; hence the desire of people to keep environmental problems out of their own areas, out of their own backyards, is deemed a socially pathological response to a natural and necessary course of development — a response termed the NIMBY Syndrome. The task of administration is thus identified as one of containing and overcoming irrational resistance.

The not-in-my-backyard attitude was early identified as a problem by those involved in the emergence of environmental politics. Yet their definition of the problem varied dramatically from that promulgated from the conventional administrative perspective. For those attempting to mobilize environmental concern in society, NIMBY was typically seen as a necessary initial step in the development of an environmentally concerned and informed citizenry.[17] The development and participation of such a citizenry was regarded as necessary politically in giving salience to environmental concerns. Here environmental politics was to intervene in the management of Leviathan, promoting different priorities, interests which the conventional perspective tended to ignore.

Yet such a change of political priorities anticipates a change of administrative structures: at a minimum, the task of managing Leviathan can be viewed as one requiring more active involvement by various segments of the population at large. This prospect is, to a large extent, in accord with the vision of self-management in a participatory society.[18] Moving to a world beyond Leviathan, however, is difficult to accept as an immediate goal. The present concerns of environmental politics, indeed, cannot avoid the continuing problem of managing Leviathan.

Notes

1. This outlook represents a continuation of the early conservationist orientation, which accorded well with conventional administration and was challenged by the dramatic outburst of environmentalism in the 1970's. On this point, see Robert Paehlke, "Democracy and Environmentalism: Opening a Door to the Administrative State," in this volume. For an insightful discussion of democratic participation in the context of the administrative state, see R. W. Phidd, "The Administrative State and the Limits of Rationality," in O. P. Dwivedi, ed., *The Administrative State in Canada* (Toronto: University of Toronto Press, 1982). *Cf.* Emmette S. Redford, *Democracy in the Administrative State* (New York: Oxford University Press, 1969), ch. 8. Redford formulates a concept of "workable democracy" which takes as fixed the conditions which have produced the administrative state.

2. For further discussion and references to relevant literature, see Douglas Torgerson, "Obsolescent Leviathan: Problems of Order in Administrative Thought," in this volume.

3. Effectiveness and efficiency are sometimes clearly distinguished, sometimes implicitly conflated. Effectiveness here primarily means getting the job done—achieving a goal. Yet this notion of effectiveness cannot altogether exclude considerations of efficiency since some notion of reasonable or satisfactory cost is normally implicit in a goal. Efficiency also presupposes effectiveness since, obviously, a goal cannot be efficiently achieved without first actually being achieved. We acknowledge—though for purposes of the present discussion believe we need not discuss—the complex conceptual difficulties which arise from problems of implementation. We also do not believe it necessary here to discuss the economic concept of efficiency, which seems (if strictly followed) to require administratively (if not humanly) impossible calculations of universal costs and benefits. *Cf.* Herbert A. Simon, *Administrative Behavior: A Study of Decision-Making Processes in Administrative Organization* (New York: The Free Press, 3rd ed., 1976); Laurence H. Tribe, "Policy Science: Analysis or Ideology?" *Philosophy and Public Affairs* 2 (1972), pp. 66-110. Jeffrey Pressman and Aaron Wildavsky, *Implementation* (Berkeley: University of California Press, 3rd ed., 1984); Clarence N. Stone, "Efficiency versus Social Learning: A Reconsideration of the Implementation Process," *Policy Studies Review* 4:3 (1985), pp. 484-496.

4. It was concluded that a hot oil pipeline should not be buried in permafrost; hence a section was built above ground. See Mary C. Berry, *The Alaska Pipeline: The Politics of Oil and Native Land Claims* (Bloomington: Indiana University Press, 1975), pp. 103-107. *Cf.* Martin Stuart Baker, "Implication of the National Environmental Policy Act," in Wolfgang F. E. Preiser, ed., *Environmental Design Research* (Stroudsburg, PA: Dowden, Hutchinson and Ross, 1973), Vol. 2, pp. 89-92; Frederick R. Anderson, *NEPA in the Courts: A Legal Analysis of the National Environmental Policy Act* (Washington, DC: Resources for the Future, 1973), chs. 1, 8.

5. See Jeffrey Pfeffer, *Power in Organizations* (Boston: Pitman Publishing, 1981), esp. chs. 1, 3. *Cf.* Douglas Torgerson, "Limits of the Administrative Mind: The Problem of Defining Environmental Problems," in this volume.

6. Industrialization is not over, but neither is it new; and enough has passed to allow us to perceive previously unanticipated aspects of its aftermath. Indeed, the emergence and articulation of

widespread environmental concern may be taken as an historical event which has rendered this aftermath visible. This event, moreover, has converged with the now common notion that social and economic developments are ushering in a "post-industrial" era. This notion is by itself significant if the shaping of the future is somehow bound up with its perception. We make no bold predictions, but inquiry cannot dispense with implicit or explicit judgments constituting a form of historical orientation. See Douglas Torgerson, "Contextual Orientation in Policy Analysis: The Contribution of Harold D. Lasswell," *Policy Sciences* 18 (1985), pp. 241-261. For discussion of some relevant issues, see Timothy W. Luke and Stephen K. White, "Critical Theory, the Informational Revolution, and an Ecological Path to Modernity," in John Forester, ed. *Critical Theory and Public Life* (Cambridge, MA: The M.I.T. Press, 1985).

7. See, *e.g.*, Larry Hirschhorn, *Beyond Mechanization: Work and Technology in a Postindustrial Age* (Cambridge, MA: The M.I.T. Press, 1986); Richard Sundeen, "Coproduction and Communities: Implications for Local Administrators," *Administration and Society* 16:4 (1985), pp. 387-402. Mary Parker Follett, *Dynamic Administration: The Collected Papers of Mary Parker Follett* (New York: Hippocrene Books, 2nd ed., 1977) remains striking as a contribution along these lines from the 1920's.

8. For a case in point, see David Dickson, *Alternative Technology and the Politics of Technical Change* (Glasgow: Fontana, 1974).

9. On agenda setting, see, *e.g.*, Robert W. Cobb and Charles D. Elder, "The Politics of Agenda Building: An Alternative Perspective for Modern Democratic Theory," *Journal of Politics* 33:4 (1971), pp. 892-915.

10. See Pfeffer, ch. 9.

11. For a useful comparison of pluralist, elite and class models, see Robert R. Alford, "Paradigms of Relations between State and Society" in Leon Lindberg *et al.*, eds., *Stress and Contradiction in Modern Capitalism: Public Policy and the Theory of the State* (Lexington, MA: Lexington Books, 1975).

12. *Cf.* Donald R. Kelley *et al.*, *The Economic Superpowers and the Environment* (San Francisco: W.H. Freeman, 1976).

13. For further discussion of Weber, see Torgerson, "Obsolescent Leviathan."

14. For a succinct discussion of this approach in relation to others, see Fred Luthans, "The Contingency Theory of Management," *Business Horizons* 16 (1973), pp. 63-72.

15. *Cf.* Torgerson, "Limits of the Administrative Mind."

16. *Cf.* Samuel P. Hays, *Conservation and the Gospel of Efficiency: The Progressive Conservation Movement, 1890-1920* (New York: Anteneum, 1968).

17. By the early 1970's, there were explicit discussions along these lines in environmentalist circles. On the loose identity of public interest groups generally as a democratic social movement, see Michael W. McCann, "Public Interest Liberalism and the Modern Regulatory State," *Polity* 21:1 (1988), pp. 373-400. *Cf.* the concept of "new social movements" as discussed, *e.g.*, in Luke and White, pp. 40ff, 53 n. 46.

18. *Cf.* Carole Pateman, *Participation and Democratic Theory* (Cambridge: Cambridge University Press, 1975); C. B. Macpherson, *The Life and Times of Liberal Democracy* (Oxford: Oxford University Press, 1977). Benjamin R. Barber, *Strong Democracy: Participatory Politics for a New Age* (Berkeley: University of California Press, 1984); Gar Alperovitz, "Towards a Decentralist Commonwealth," in Howard J. Ehrlich *et al.*, eds., *Reinventing Anarchy* (London: Routledge and Kegan Paul, 1979).

OBSOLESCENT LEVIATHAN: PROBLEMS OF ORDER IN ADMINISTRATIVE THOUGHT

Douglas Torgerson

Canst thou draw out leviathan with an hook?…Canst thou put an hook into his nose?…Will he make many supplications unto thee? will he speak soft words unto thee? Will he make a covenant with thee? wilt thou take him for a servant for ever?

Job 41:1-4.

U*pon ascending to power, a new regime expresses grave concern about the condition of the public treasury. The profligate ways of the past will, it is announced, now have to end. Officials receive their orders and set quietly to work while the populace is left in suspense about the import of the announcement. Later is learned that — among other things — certain funds no longer will be available to help keep track of a spread of poisons in the earth, air, and water. Consternation and controversy follow among the public, and the decision even gives rise to complaints among officials, who say they were not properly consulted. A senior administrator meets with his staff and acknowledges their concerns: "A number of people have told me, 'if you had…consulted us, we program managers — we people who really know what is going on and what we are doing — we could have given you a better way out and we would have given you some different ways of cutting back.'" The administrator points to his own problems, to imperatives of speed and discretion which left him no real option, but he agrees with a principle which underlies the complaints: "when you don't act democratically, when you act from the top,…well you make mistakes." When these words mysteriously appear in the press, many members of the public express agreement; they say that they have thought much about the problem of spreading poisons — and* *that the government should consult the citizenry when deciding what is important.*

The senior administrator in this true story[1] implicitly recognized what has long been identified as a key question of administration — the problem of centralization versus decentralization.[2] Tight control at the center can undermine the pattern of communication needed to support decision-making by leaving out of the process those who really grasp an issue and know how to deal with it. This problem, often evident within the framework of an administrative apparatus, also pertains to the relationship between an organization and those outside its formal boundaries. More broadly, in the context of contemporary concerns, the problem involves the relationship between the administrative state and the citizenry of an advanced industrial society.

Centralization seems to be almost a natural reflex of administration. Indeed, early in this century, the first attempt to develop a general theory of administration portrayed centralization as part of the "natural order".[3] Even then, it was clear that decentralization was a necessary counterpart to centralization, and much subsequent administrative thought has labored with the question of how these opposing pulls should be balanced. Nonetheless, a prejudice favoring centralization has remained as a permanent fixture in the universe of administration. Especially in the face of emergencies, pressing problems, crises, the standard reflex has been to look for a central authority to take charge, to maintain or restore order.

Leviathan and Environment

This reflex certainly sprang into operation with the emerging perception of an environmental crisis in the latter part of this century. Sometimes bluntly and simplistically stated as the need for an "environmental dictator", the appeal to a central authority was at times also given careful formulations which sought ways to retain certain vestiges of democratic values. Nonetheless, the accent throughout clearly presupposed the effectiveness of centralized authority and reflected the traditional focus of administrative thought. In a sophisticated version of this approach, William Ophuls looked back to Hobbes and defined the problem as a question of "Leviathan or Oblivion?" Interpreting Hobbes as advocating "autocracy with power residing preferably in the hands of one man," Ophuls sought to preserve democratic values as much as possible, but nonetheless concluded that solving the environmental crisis required submission to "a higher power": "the tragic necessity of Leviathan."[4]

Hobbes proposed his Leviathan as an order of absolute authority, sanctioned by reason. Fear of disorder, Hobbes maintained, was sufficient for all rational individuals to invest their natural powers in a sovereign individual or group capable of maintaining control. A striking portrayal of Hobbes's view is presented in the famous 1651 frontispiece to *Leviathan*, in which a colossal monarch rises above and surveys the city below. With sword and sceptre in either hand, the monarch casts a gaze of serenity and benevolence; his body, upon inspection, appears moreover as a composite of the individual bodies of citizens, each distinct and all reverently facing him. Hobbes's Leviathan may seem, at first glance, itself to be the absolute ruler, but this is a misleading impression; for the sovereign is a distinct *part* of Leviathan — of this "mortal god" — and all citizens are, in turn, themselves distinct parts, incorporated into the whole. Yet the impression is only partially misleading; for the sovereign is the "soul" of Leviathan, the concentration of all powers and wills into a single power and will, the mainspring of action, so to speak. No power can approach the power of Leviathan because all powers constitute and participate in this being; its life depends not only upon the acquiesence of subjects to the sovereign, but — as well — upon the active transfer of their powers to him, by which they all individually place themselves at his disposal and forsake any action not authorized by him. In this manner, the citizens both support the sovereign and enact Leviathan, which — although their own creation — now appears as a power distinct from and above them, in essence represented by the sovereign.[5] Once established, the distinct power of the sovereign becomes the single legitimate source of direction in society; neither wisdom nor tradition has any independent authority:

> Would you have every man to every other man alledge for Law his own particular Reason? There is not amongst Men a Universal Reason agreed upon in any Nation, besides the Reason of him that hath the Soveraign Power. Yet though his Reason be but the Reason of one Man, yet it is set up to supply the place of that Universal Reason, which is expounded to us by our Saviour in the Gospel; and consequently our King is to us the Legislator both of Statue-Law and of Common-Law.[6]

For Hobbes the main question is not whether the sovereign is wise, but whether he is obeyed; for it is obedience which ensures order.

The appeal of Leviathan is, indeed, the appeal of order; and the problem of order appears to become salient as one contemplates various scenarios of environmental crisis. To look to Hobbes for a solution, however, is to ignore the sense in which he is part of the problem — how, indeed, the perception of environmental crisis may reflect the obsolescence of Leviathan. The organizational form contemplated in Hobbes is a rationally constructed artifice of centralized power, an instrument of order exercised through formal patterns of command and obedience. Historically, this is the form adopted in the emergence of the modern state as it arose from diverse, inconsistent patterns of medieval authority. By cutting through traditional bonds and entanglements, the modern state — in both absolutist and liberal versions — cleared an orderly, predictable space for increasingly abstract and standardized relationships in state, economy, and society. The formation and expression of public opinion fostered and guided these developments in a manner which Hobbes did not foresee, even though his own ideas exerted a seminal influence. As it happened, the main currents of public opinion were guided by notions of order and progress which reinforced trends of abstraction and standardization in state, economy and society even while advancing the principle — anathema to Hobbes — of popular sovereignty. The culmination of these trends, moreover, was curiously in tune with Hobbes in the sense that they fostered an order of formalized and centralized authority while depriving public opinion of its vitality and independence — a world of great organizations, in which the modern state emerged as an administrative state.[7] This is the world which Max Weber witnessed developing in the early part of this century. The future, he believed, would be cast in this mold. Although by no means personally enamored of this prospect, Weber provided a striking account of what we have come to know as the traditional approach to administration.

It is possible to discern a "problem of order" in Hobbes, but this is not simply because the presuppositions of his theory point to an essentially fragmented social universe. In the seventeenth century, he percieves a society which can be held together only if individuals, forsaking the thrust of their passions, rationally relinquish their personal powers and subjugate themselves to a single, overarching authority. Hobbes's presuppositions also serve to articulate salient characteristics of his age.[8] For Weber, in contrast, what impends in the early twentieth century is the "iron cage" of an economy and society cut to fit bureaucratic organization. The autonomy of the individual does not threaten to undo the prevailing order; indeed, the readiness of the individual to submit rationally to authority is so evident that it becomes possible to identify a source of authority typical of this age — one beyond either charisma or tradition, one which would have pleased Hobbes: the ground of authority which Weber called "rational". An order based upon such authority was one which Hobbes could identify as something in need of construction. For Weber, this order was one to be grimly acknowledged.[9]

The image of Hobbes's Leviathan is the image of an overarching authority enforcing order upon a naturally recalcitrant subject-matter. Fear of the implications of environmental crisis provides a motive to reassert this order by resurrecting Leviathan. Here the diagnosis takes the source of the crisis to be the "possessive individualism" which Hobbes attributed to human nature and which, in any case, has emerged as a distinguishing feature of human beings in the modern age.[10] Reliance upon Hobbes thus takes the possessive individual as given and tends to reinforce the notion that rationality demands quiescence and unquestioning obedience to a superior authority. What is thereby ruled out is the idea of a vital and informed public opinion capable of criticizing, shaping, and participating in authority. Indeed, the notion of resurrecting Leviathan ignores the extent to which Leviathan is alive and well, represented in the institutions which Weber saw emerging with the rationalization, bureaucratization, and industrialization of the world. For even though a culture of possessive individualism certainly contains a frightening potential, a mere reassertion of authority over individuals misses the mark: *viz.*, Leviathan itself. That is to say, a largely centralized mode of administration in state, economy, and society has performed key functions both in advancing industrialization and in generating those very problems which have elicited a perception of environmental crisis. If Leviathan, in this sense, has been a key tool in shaping the modern world, then the problems of that world lead us to ask whether the tool is not now obsolescent. For the very source of order now appears as a source of impending disorder.

Administration Reexamined

The traditional approach to administration endures today despite challenges in both theory and practice. Images of centralized hierarchy—such as Weber's bureaucracy or Hobbes's Leviathan—continue to profoundly influence organizational structure and conduct, together with the way problems are identified and handled. Yet this approach persistently encounters difficulties, and it has become apparent that these difficulties are themselves often generated by this very approach. While centralized hierarchy has demonstrated its effectiveness for certain purposes, this organizational form also often shows itself to be inept, or at least not as effective as possible alternatives.

The consideration of alternatives for industrial organization has been an important focus in the development of management thought at least since the late 1920s.[11] The intense focus on such alternatives today could well be viewed—as earlier interest in them has, indeed, rightly been seen—as part of a quest for more subtle means of manipulating the human factor in production. This interpretation cannot be dismissed, but the current focus is also informed by a recognition that new technologies are rendering the traditional approach to administration increasingly less effective.[12] Similarly, in such areas as service delivery, occupational safety, health care, rural projects, community planning, and urban development, decentralized initiative has been identified as often a vital component of effective administration. A key point which arises from the literature, implicitly and explicitly, moreover, is that the potentials of decentralization and participation are contingent—*i.e.*, context-dependent. Indeed, consistency on this point is not surprising because, as a counter to traditional presuppositions, the focus on decentralization and participation is necessarily at odds with a centralizing orientation typically insensitive to what is local and particular: the centralizing approach generally seeks to render its subject-matter homogeneous, hence manageable.[13]

Environmental problems are our particular concern here, and it is evident that they have largely been generated or magnified by centralized hierarchies. It thus seems at least questionable whether these problems can be identified and resolved through an extension of this organizational form. Indeed, the present situation provides grounds for a critical examination of the traditional prejudices of administration—and for an exploration of alternative approaches. Here Weber offers a point of departure.

The rise of the administrative state may, indeed, be considered in terms of Weber's description of the rationalization of the modern world. The essence of rationalization, for Weber, was a central "belief" of modern culture that "there are no mysterious incalculable forces...that one can, in principle, master all things by calculation." This belief both promoted and appeared to be validated by the emergence of industrialization, that "tremendous cosmos of the modern economic order." Central to these developments, moreover, was the advent of bureaucratization: the rising significance of formal organization in both the state and the economy. In both public and private organizations, the administrative apparatus was designed for calculability and efficiency through formal hierarchies of personnel with strictly delimited functions. The anonymity and formalization of relationships in bureaucracy made the organization a reliable instrument for those who controlled it and a predictable mechanism for those who dealt with it. Even resistance to bureaucratic control would fall prey to the logic of bureaucratic organization. "The whole pattern of everyday life is," Weber said, "is cut to fit this framework."[14]

What makes bureaucratic administration "rational", according to Weber, is that it exercises control through knowledge. This is mainly the knowledge of "the personally detached and strictly objective *expert*," who discharges responsibilities according to rules and calculations "without regard to persons." Exerted thus primarily through technical knowledge, bureaucratic control is also enhanced through "official secrets". Each organization typically reinforces its power by hiding "its knowledge and intentions" and excluding "the public".[15]

Bureaucratization would, in Weber's view, be a common feature of both planned and market economies, although he did allow for a difference. The "single hierarchy" of the planned economy would create a monolithic structure, in contrast to the parallel operations—with some potential conflict—typical of public and private bureaucracies in a market economy.[16] In either case, however, the welfare of the mass of the population would remain dependent upon an overarching "bureaucratic apparatus"—"upon the continuous and correct functioning" (in the case of the market economy) both of state administration and of the increasingly "bureaucratic organizations of private capitalism."[17]

It was long after Weber that the term "administrative state" came into use.[18] Yet Weber was early to perceive a concentration of power in the enclaves of administration: "In the modern state the actual ruler is necessarily and unavoidably the bureaucracy...." While Weber was concerned to identify ways of mitigating state bureaucratic power—keeping it in check primarily through the instrument of parliamentary review—he resigned himself to the extraordinary effectiveness of the organizational machine: "The future", Weber wrote in 1918, "belongs to bureaucratiza-tion...."[19]

In light of Weber, the rise of the administrative state appears as a necessary concomitant of the rationalization and industrialization of the world. What we witness is not, then, simply a change in the locus of state power, but the emergence of a more or less cohesive administrative sphere, upon which all social life is now largely dependent. The relatively recent concept of "bureaucratic symbiosis", moreover, seems simply an extension of Weber's thesis: "Organization...relates effectively to or-ganization. The various specialists of the private bureaucracy work readily with their opposite numbers in the public bureaucracy pooling information for a jointly achieved decision."[20] Despite apparent conflict, according to this conception, a largely closed administrative world now promotes, monitors, and regulates the industrial economy. This formulation may be a substantial exaggeration, but the advance of industrialization has certain-ly reinforced a tendency toward a closed process of administrative decision-making. For the rapid technological development of industrial society has been accompanied by an increased reliance upon the ad-ministrative sphere and its experts, deemed necessary to perform the calculations required to master an increasing range of complex, technical problems.

Here a conflictual relationship becomes collaborative; a mutual ac-commodation of interests and perspectives tends, in effect, to bring public and private organizations together in what becomes a largely cohesive administrative apparatus. Of course, there remain counter tendencies. Nothing said here is meant to deny the obvious fragmentation both within and among public and private administrative structures.[21] No monolith is being conjured up. What is doubtful, nonetheless, is whether this ad-ministrative sphere, this—partly coherent, partly fragmented—pattern of bureaucratic organizations, has the collective capacity to identify and regulate effectively the range of environmental problems which it generates. Can everything really be mastered by calculation?

An affirmative answer to this question is no longer generally taken for granted. Indeed, inasmuch as administrative thought has reflected the exigencies of administrative practice, significant doubts have been posed concerning the traditional presupposition of a detached mind capable of rationally governing a centralized hierarchy.[22] Even Hobbes, we may recall, did not hold that the sovereign reason should necessarily be wise, only that it should maintain order. For what both Hobbes and Weber knew was that order was a precondition for predictability; human affairs were not necessarily calculable — they were potentially chaotic — but they could be made calculable through the enforcement of order. A key problem increasingly recognized now in administrative thought is that of order generating disorder; here the presuppositions of hierarchy, centralization, and calculability are drawn into question.

In the technocratic orientation to administration, these presuppositions are retained in a modified form. While the centralized hierarchy is attenuated in favor of a systems approach capable of a more deliberate balancing of centralization and decentralization, this technocratic approach remains wedded typically to a single point of reference: an abstract "decision-maker" or a "controlling group" as the ultimate source of direction. Abstraction and formality remain central features of a style focused upon defining and treating administrative problems as matters suitable for calculation. Yet the problems must be cut down to manageable size.[23] Indeed, in what has been called the "neo-Weberian model",[24] we find the world of administration inhabited by "administrative man", one who deals not with the full complexity of things, but who (as described by Herbert Simon) remains "content" to follow a greatly simplified map since "he believes that the real world is mostly empty — that most of the facts of the real world have no great relevance to the particular situation he is facing and that most significant chains of causes and consequences are short and simple."[25] If Weber envisioned an administrative complex towering over an increasingly calculable world, the neo-Weberian model portrays a world which is at least manageable — that is, calculable enough for most administrative purposes. In either case, those within the administrative structure remain narrowly focused on what is directly relevant to their own particular functions. The final guarantee of both the traditional and technocratic approaches, moreover, remains a faith in the secure order of Leviathan. It can be taken for granted that no radical decentralization or expansion of participation has any place in the administrative sphere — that such moves could only pose a threat to order.

Yet the presuppositions of traditional and technocratic orientations have been challenged by the argument of Emery and Trist that a "gross increase in...*relevant uncertainty*"[26] has made environmental complexity a necessary focus of concern. The environment is now a problem which the traditional and technocratic approaches to administration themselves persistently exacerbate:

> The very success of the technocratic bureaucracy...has led to dysfunctional effects. For these immense organizations go it alone without regard to what others are doing, while interdependencies...are increasing.... Concentrated largely on their own short-term specific objectives, they have given only marginal attention to the longer-term, more general effects of their actions on wider systems. These effects have not been supposed to be their business. As a result, unintended consequences pile up...[27]

The upshot of this line of argument is that, far from becoming more calculable or unproblematic, the organizational environment has become so troublesome that the bureaucratic form itself has been thrown into question: "If to usher in this century Weber felt he could rightly unveil bureaucracy as a newly perfected organizational monument..., then our chances of reaching the year 2000 in reasonably good shape...would appear to entail our identifying and becoming skilled in practising, an alternative organizational principle."[28]

This conclusion is a culmination of various developments in administrative thought which have converged to draw into question reliance upon centralized hierarchy as the "one best way" to approach organization and administration. Here the focus on the salience and complexity of the "human factor" has combined with the recognition that different approaches to administration differ in their effectiveness depending upon the situation—*i.e.*, upon differences in contingencies such as the task at hand, the mechanical apparatus, the type of people involved, the material resources available, and the environment external to the organization.[29] The systems approach, moreover, has emerged as necessary in establishing a conceptual grasp of this multitude of variables. Even though such conceptualization has generally been sought as a means of reasserting order and control in a domain that threatened to become too complex and dynamic to manage, the systems approach does not in principle maintain the privileged position which the centralized hierarchy had traditionally been assigned. Indeed, in focusing upon the organizational environment, Trist and others have pressed the systems approach in a manner which explodes the typical technocratic framework.[30]

The concept of organizational environment here refers primarily to organizations interacting through the broader ensemble of social and economic conditions. It is a short step, however, to include the conditions of the natural environment. Indeed, this step has been taken in a systems-theoretic argument by Hooker and van Hulst which maintains that "massive, narrowly focused bureaucracies of 'experts'"—both public and private—exhibit "an incompetence to deal with the key holistic features of reality." There is, in other words, a mis-match between the prevailing form of human organizations and the systemic properties of the natural environment. With each organization oriented to the efficient performance of specific functions, the ensemble of public and private bureaucracies persistently generates a vast, complex array of unintended, unanticipated consequences which often eludes effective monitoring and control. Narrowly conceived organizational goals combine with highly restricted patterns of information flow to obscure the connection between particular organizational operations and the relevant totality of direct and indirect outcomes. Effective monitoring and control of environmental problems would thus require the information flows and "complex feedback patterns" which are obtainable only by matching the internal arrangement of organizational relationships to "the external system structure." "Meaningful public control," it is concluded, "...calls for decentralization and democratization." The exigencies of the administrative task themselves thus call for a "radical decentralization" of institutions[31]—a change which is, of course, political as well as administrative.

Conclusion

Once we recognize the prevailing form of order as generating disorder, we are at a point where the issue of centralization and decentralization can be recast. However, the pronounced centralizing bias typical of administrative thought continues to reassert itself in the very terminology which allows us to formulate the issue: de-centralization remains a variant upon the natural and normal. We have no easy way of expressing the notion of a pattern of organization which is at once radically decentralized and coherent—except, perhaps, the term "anarchy" (which, of course, carries the strong popular connotation of chaos).[32]

Hobbes formulated the modern conception of organization as an artifice, severed from tradition, which could be rationally designed upon the basis of calculable criteria. By the terms of Hobbes's argument, what was to be achieved was order as such: the sole secure order possible in light of human nature — a centralized hierarchy subordinated to a single, ultimate authority. Leviathan, for Hobbes the only reliable order which reason could construct from nature, was modified at the hands of his liberal successors — Locke to Bentham — and acquired a clear historical purpose: progress in the subordination of nature to human goals.[33] Here Weber remains illuminating because he portrays the apotheosis of centralized hierarchy — bureaucratization — as part of the wider processes of industrialization and rationalization. He describes bureaucracy as an effective instrument in the hands of those who control it. Yet his analysis shows bureaucratic organization to be effective for certain purposes, not necessarily for all. (Indeed, Weber could imagine the eventual collapse of the modern industrial cosmos from a constraint of energy resources.)[34] Bureaucracy has been effective in promoting industrialization, in both capitalist and socialist economies. Yet we have not generally witnessed bureaucracy handling effectively the serious problems which industrialization has generated. Indeed, the administrative sphere has — in either economic form — remained oriented toward industrialization.[35]

In the present historical context, a recourse to Leviathan would merely tend to reinforce the very order which has generated the problem. Yet, it is at least plausible to suggest that the prevailing administrative form needs to be challenged, not strengthened — that the sphere of administration should, indeed, be radically transformed. The point is not to advocate further reliance upon the economic "invisible hand" which the administrative sphere employs to a greater or lesser extent in different countries. Such a move would not necessarily alter the basic form or diminish the extent of the prevailing administrative apparatus.[36] Instead, to press the question as one of administrative form is to focus upon the distinctly political character of the issue. A radically decentralized and democratic alternative would necessarily open up the administrative world to the influence of interests which have generally been excluded or marginalized. To say this is also to suggest, of course, that the prevailing administrative form is not maintained simply because of some supposed "administrative" necessity; the administrative sphere resists even the serious consideration of alternatives because of the conjunction of ideological presuppositions, particular interests, and shared purposes which constitute that domain.[37]

Yet as the limitations of this administrative form become apparent in particular cases, there will be various pressures and piecemeal initiatives which will at least seem to anticipate broader innovations and a more sweeping redefinition of the problem. Already, the voice of marginal and local interests has been clearly significant both in warning the administrative sphere of major environmental dangers and in taking the initiative to mitigate environmental damages. The question now is the extent to which such interests will participate in, and perhaps transform, the management of Leviathan. At once administrative and political, the question is also historical—whether, in the aftermath of much industrialization, an alternative pattern of administration and development will emerge.

As one of the architects of modernity, Hobbes both reaffirmed and—despite himself—placed at risk the principle of absolute authority. For this authority was to be legitimated no longer by an unquestioned tradition, but by reason alone—as exercised by a multitude of possessive individuals all fearfully calculating and planning for their security. For Hobbes, reason demanded obedience by all to the dictates of a single authority—in effect, the abdication of the sovereign reason of each in favor of one sovereign reason representing all. In the emergence of modernity, political and administrative thought has repeated Hobbes's disposition by generally recognizing the "necessity" of centralized hierarchy, even while affirming the principle of popular sovereignty.[38] Since Hobbes, nonetheless, this disposition has expressly been founded upon argument. Even though both traditional and technocratic approaches to administration have taken the argument to be closed, current signs of the obsolescence of Leviathan provide an opportunity to re-open the question. The point is not simply to substitute a decentralizing bias for a centralizing bias; the balancing of the two remains an issue to be addressed. To re-open the question, however, means that traditional and technocratic fixations are to be challenged by a diversity of interests and perspectives previously excluded from serious consideration. Already in this questioning, then, we anticipate broader participation in inquiry and discussion: an institutionalization of discourse at odds with centralized hierarchy.

Notes

1. The story is that of the Conservative government which came to power in Canada in 1984. Considerable controversy arose over the budget cuts which the new government required of Environment Canada, especially those concerning the elimination of research programs to monitor levels of toxic chemicals in herring gulls in the Great Lakes region. In the midst of this controversy, a tape recording of a meeting between the Deputy Minister, Jacques Gérin, and his staff was leaked to the press. See Michael Keating, "More Environment Cuts Hinted," *The Globe and Mail* (December 12, 1984), p. 5. On the reaction of citizens groups, see Robert Gibson, "The Government Shows Its Colours," *Alternatives* 12:2 (1985), pp. 49-52.

2. See, *e.g.*, Herbert A. Simon, *Administrative Behavior: A Study of Decision-Making Processes in Administrative Organization* (New York: The Free Press, 3rd ed., 1976), pp. 234ff.

3. Henri Fayol, *General and Industrial Management* (London: Pitman Publishing, 1967 [1916]), p. 33.

4. William Ophuls, "Leviathan or Oblivion?" in Herman E. Daly, ed., *Toward a Steady-State Economy* (San Francisco: W. H. Freeman, 1973), pp. 219, 229. *Cf.* William Ophuls, *Ecology and the Politics of Scarcity* (San Francisco: W. H. Freeman, 1976); William Ophuls, "Technological Limits to Growth Revisited," *Alternatives* 4:2 (1975), pp. 4-11; William Ophuls, "The Politics of Transformation," *Alternatives* 6:2 (1977), pp. 4-8. The idea of an "environmental dictator" was explicitly discussed during the 1970's in some environmental organizations as an approach to the perceived environmental crisis. There is a significant literature on the "neo-Hobbesian" approach of Ophuls and others. See, *e.g.*, K. J. Walker, "The Environmental Crisis: A Critique of Neo-Hobbesian Responses," *Polity* 21:1 (1988), pp. 67-81.

5. Thomas Hobbes, *Leviathan* (Harmondsworth: Penguin Books, 1968 [1651]). For passages especially relevant to these points, see pp. 81-82, 150-151, 189-191, 289-290, 312-313, 375, 376ff. The frontispiece contains an explicit reference to *Job*. For Hobbes's discussion of this text, see p. 362. For an important discussion of Hobbes which draws attention to the frontispiece, see Sheldon S. Wolin, *Politics and Vision: Continuity and Innovation in Western Political Thought* (Boston: Little, Brown, 1960), ch. 8. My view of Hobbes has been significantly influenced by C. B. Macpherson, *The Political Theory of Possessive Individualism: Hobbes to Locke* (Oxford: Oxford University Press, 1964).

6. Thomas Hobbes, *A Dialogue between a Philosopher and a Student of the Common Laws of England* (Chicago: University of Chicago Press, 1971 [1681]), p. 67. The speech is by the "Philosopher".

7. *Cf.* Gianfranco Poggi, *The Development of the Modern State* (Stanford: Stanford University Press, 1978); Karl Polanyi, *The Great Transformation: The Political and Economic Origins of Our Time* (Boston: Beacon Press, 1957). Also *cf.* J. B. Bury, *The Idea of Progress* (New York: Dover Publications, 1955 [1932]), esp. p. 76.

8. See Macpherson, *Possessive Individualism*, ch. 2. The Hobbesian "problem of order" is a well-known theme in Parsons. For a discussion which draws upon unpublished sources, see William Buxton, *Talcott Parsons and the Capitalist Nation-State: Political Sociology as a Strategic Vocation* (Toronto: University of Toronto Press, 1985), pp. 20ff, 256ff.

9. Max Weber, *The Protestant Ethic and the Spirit of Capitalism* (New York: Charles Scribners' Sons, 1958), p. 181; Max Weber, *Economy and Society*, 2 Vols. (Berkeley: University of California Press, 1978), Vol. 1, p. 215; J.P. Mayer, *Max Weber and German Politics* (London: Faber and Faber, 2nd ed., 1956).

10. Macpherson, *Possessive Individualism*; *cf.* C. B. Macpherson, "Hobbes' Bourgeois Man" in his *Democratic Theory* (Oxford: Clarendon Press, 1973). Remarkably, the neo-Hobbesian literature presents an historically abstract concept of the "tragedy of the commons," ignoring the way in which the enclosures movement historically relied upon state intervention to end the regulation of common lands by tradition. See Garrett Hardin, "The Tragedy of the Commons," *Science* 162 (1968), pp. 1243-1248, and Garrett Hardin and John Baden, eds., *Managing the Commons* (San Francisco: W. H. Freeman, 1977) in contrast to Polanyi, *The Great Transformation*. This irony deserves greater attention.

11. Especially remarkable in this regard was the work of Follett on management during the 1920's. See Mary Parker Follett, *Dynamic Administration: The Collected Papers of Mary Parker Follett* (New York: Hippocrene Books, 2nd ed., 1977). Also see, *e.g.*, Elton Mayo, *The Human Problems of an Industrial Civilization* (New York: Viking Press, 1960 [1933]); Joan Woodward, *Industrial Organization: Theory and Practice* (London: Oxford University Press, 2nd ed., 1980 [1965]).

12. *Cf.*, *e.g.*, Larry Hirschhorn, *Beyond Mechanization: Work and Technology in a Postindustrial Age* (Cambridge, MA: The M. I. T. Press, 1986). Also *cf.* Reinhard Bendix, *Work and Authority in Industry: Ideologies of Management in the Course of Industrialization* (New York: Harper and Row, 1963); Frank Fischer, "Ideology and Organization Theory," in Frank Fischer and Carmen Sirianni, eds., *Critical Studies in Organization and Bureaucracy* (Philadelphia: Temple University Press, 1984).

13. See Adam W. Herbert, "Management under Conditions of Decentralization and Citizen Participation," *Public Administration Review* 32 (1972), pp. 622-637. John D. Montgomery, "When Local Participation Helps," *Journal of Policy Analysis and Management* 3:1 (1983), pp. 90-105, stresses the importance of differences in types of administrative activity; and Richard A. Sundeen, "Coproduction and Communities: Implications for Local Administrators," *Administration and Society* 16:4 (1985), pp. 387-402, emphasizes the importance of differences in types of locality. Both conventional administration and an approach reliant upon decentralization and participation, of course, involve difficulties. Curtis Ventriss and Robert Pecorella, "Community Participation and Modernization: A Reexamination of Political Choices," *Public Administration Review* 44 (1984), pp. 224-231, shows how the choice of difficulties—and potentials—is political: the perception that the current course of modernization is inevitable fosters the notion that following the conventional approach is somehow neutral, purely administrative. Also see, on some particular issues, David W. Orr, "U.S. Energy Policy and the Political Economy of Participation," *Journal of Politics* 41:4 (1979), pp. 1027-1056; C. A. Hooker and R. Van Hulst, "The Meaning of Environmental Problems for Public Political Institutions," (on energy and health systems) in William Leiss, ed., *Ecology versus Politics in Canada* (Toronto: University of Toronto Press, 1979); and (for complementary discussions of health problems in the workplace) Robert Sass, "The Underdevelopment of Occupational Health and Safety in Canada," *ibid.*, and Robert Paehlke, "Occupational Health Policy in Canada," *ibid. Cf.* Timothy W. Luke and Stephen K. White, "Critical Theory, the Informational Revolution, and an Ecological Path to Modernity," in John Forester, ed., *Critical Theory and Public Life* (Cambridge, MA: The M. I. T. Press, 1985); Gar Alperovitz, "Towards a Decentralist Commonwealth," in Howard J. Ehrlich

et al., eds., *Reinventing Anarchy* (London: Routledge and Kegan Paul, 1979).

14. Max Weber, "Science as a Vocation," in *From Max Weber: Essays in Sociology* (New York: Oxford University Press, 1958), p. 139; Weber, *Protestant Ethic*, p. 181; Weber, *Economy and Society*, Vol. 1, pp. 223-224; Vol. 2, pp. 874-975. *Cf.* Alfred Schutz, "The Problem of Rationality in the Social World," in his *Collected Papers*, Vol. 2 (The Hague: Martinus Nijhoff, 1964), p. 71.

15. Weber, *Economy and Society*, Vol. 1, p. 225; Vol. 2, pp. 975, 992. The knowledge of the public bureaucracy is exceeded only by that of the private bureaucracy since commercial enterprises are ever-mindful of the costs of miscalculation and since secrets are "more safely hidden in the books of an enterprise than...in the files of public authorities." (*Ibid.*, Vol. 2, p. 994.) Consequently, public administration often finds itself in a constrained and disadvantaged position when dealing with private business management.

16. *Ibid.*, Vol. 2, p. 1402; *cf.* Vol. 1, pp. 224-225.

17. *Ibid.*, Vol. 2, p. 988.

18. See Dwight Waldo, *The Administrative State* (New York: The Ronald Press, 1948).

19. Weber, *Economy and Society*, Vol. 2, pp. 1393, 1401. *Cf.* p. 1418: "There is no substitute for the systematic cross-examination (under oath) of experts before a parliamentary commission in the presence of the respective departmental officials." Also *cf.* pp. 992-993, 997-998, 1403, 1419-1431.

20. John Kenneth Galbraith, *Economics and the Public Purpose* (New York: Mentor Books, 1975), pp. 155-156.

21. For a penetrating analysis of a case of fragmentation in public bureaucracy, see Edgar J. Dosman, *The National Interest: The Politics of Northern Development 1968-75* (Toronto: McClelland and Stewart, 1975). However, for a neo-Marxian effort to demonstrate a wider systemic logic to this fragmentation, see Rianne Mahon, "Canadian Public Policy: The Unequal Structure of Representation," in Leo Panitch, ed., *The Canadian State: Political Economy and Political Power* (Toronto: University of Toronto Press, 1979). *Cf.* J129rgen Habermas, *Legitimation Crisis* (Boston: Beacon Press, 1975), pt. 2, chs. 4-5.

22. On this and related points, see Douglas Torgerson, "Limits of the Administrative Mind," in this volume.

23. *Cf.* Herbert A. Simon, "The Structure of Ill-structured Problems," (1973) in his *Models of Discovery* (Dordrecht, Holland: D. Reidel Publishing, 1977).

24. Charles Perrow, *Complex Organizations: A Critical Essay* (Glenview, IL: Scott, Foresman and Company, 2nd ed., 1979), ch. 4.

25. Simon, *Administrative Behavior*, pp. xxix-xxx.

26. F. E. Emery and E. L. Trist, "The Causal Texture of Organizational Environments" (1965) in F. E. Emery, ed., *Systems Thinking*, 2 Vols. (Harmondsworth: Penguin Books, rev. ed., 1981), Vol. 1, p. 254 (original emphasis).

27. Eric Trist, "A Concept of Organizational Ecology," *Australian Journal of Management* 2:2 (1977), p. 166.

28. *Ibid.*, p. 167.

29. See, *e.g.*, T. Burns, "Mechanistic and Organismic Structures" (1963) in D. S. Pugh, ed., *Organization Theory* (Harmondsworth: Penguin Books, 2nd ed., 1984); Paul R. Lawrence and Jay W. Lorsch, *Organization and Environment: Managing Differentiation and Integration* (Boston: Harvard University, 1967); Ph. G. Herbst, *Alternatives to Hierarchies* (Leiden: Martinus Nijhoff,

1976).

30. See, *e.g.*, C. West Churchman, *The Systems Approach* (New York: Dell Publishing, rev. ed., 1979); John D. McEwan, "The Cybernetics of Self-organizing Systems" (1963) in C. George Benello and Dimitrios Roussopoulos, eds., *The Case for Participatory Democracy* (New York: The Viking Press, 1972).

31. Hooker and Van Hulst, "The Meaning of Environmental Problems for Public Political Institutions," pp. 131-134.

32. On the achievement of "harmony" under anarchy, see Peter Kropotkin's 1905 *Encyclopedia Britannica* article "Anarchism," in Peter Kropotkin, *Kropotkin's Revolutionary Pamphlets* (New York: Dover Publications, 1970), esp. p. 284. Also see, Howard J. Ehrlich, "Anarchism and Formal Organizations: Some Notes on the Sociological Study of Organizations from an Anarchist Perspective," in Ehrlich *et al.*, eds., *Reinventing Anarchy*.

33. "The experience of what the royal authority could achieve encouraged men to imagine that one enlightened will, with a centralised administration at its command, might accomplish endless improvements in civilisation." Bury, *The Idea of Progress*, p. 76. *Cf.* Macpherson, *Possessive Individualism*, chs. 2, 5-6; C. B. Macpherson, *The Life and Times of Liberal Democracy* (Oxford: Oxford University Press, 1977), chs. 1-2. Also *cf.* Elie Halévy, *The Growth of Philosophic Radicalism* (Boston: Beacon Press, 1955). The role of Locke as an apostle of "progress" is emphasized in Victor Ferkiss, *The Future of Technological Civilization* (New York: George Braziller, 1974).

34. Weber, *Protestant Ethic*, p. 181.

35. *Cf.* Donald R. Kelley, *et al.*, *The Economic Superpowers and the Environment* (San Francisco: W. H. Freeman, 1976).

36. *Cf.* Torgerson, "Limits of the Administrative Mind."

37. *Cf.* David Dickson, "Limiting Democracy: Technocrats and the Liberal State," *democracy* 1 (1981), pp. 61-79; T. J. Schrecker, *Political Economy of Environmental Hazards* (Ottawa: Law Reform Commission of Canada, 1984).

38. *Cf.* Jean-Jacques Rousseau, "A Discourse on Political Economy" (1758) in *The Social Contract and Discourses* (London: Everyman's Library, 1966), esp. pp. 236-242.

DEMOCRACY AND ENVIRONMENTALISM: OPENING A DOOR TO THE ADMINISTRATIVE STATE

Robert Paehlke

Bleak political and economic conclusions have been drawn from contemporary environmental realities. Some theorists have lamented the possible demise of democratic practice on the shoals of an economic scarcity of "environmental" origin.[1] The suspicion has also been voiced that environmentalism itself, whatever its merits, in certain versions harbors a serious threat to democratic institutions.[2] While these concerns make some considerable sense and have been worked out in a theoretically cogent manner, the day-to-day practice of environmental politics has often had an opposite effect: democratic processes have been enhanced. The environmental movement itself, moreover, stands in contrast to the earlier conservation movement: now at odds with the administrative state, environmentalists characteristically distrust bureaucratic—and even some scientific—expertise.[3] Environmentalist organizations have often favored openness and participation in environmental administration, thereby reflecting deeply democratic impulses. My conclusion is that the resolution of environmental problems may well be more promising within a political and economic context which is more rather than less democratic.

Environmentalism and the End of Democracy: The Theory

A pessimistic case for the future of democracy has ben made in the largely complementary theoretical work of Williams Ophuls and Robert Heilbroner. Ophuls, a political theorist, might be seen as writing in a Hobbesian tradition; Heilbroner, an economist, as in some ways providing a modern update of the Malthusian dilemma. Unlike Malthus, however, both Ophuls and Heilbroner understood many of the complexities of resource scarcity. They did not characterize the problem as simply the product of excessive population growth. Unlike Hobbes, neither unambiguously welcomed increased authority as a necessary protector of commodious living; indeed they expressed profound regret regarding the undemocratic future they concluded was likely and necessary. Each came to gloomy economic and political conclusions after a quite careful review of future resource availability, food-growing capabilities, likely population growth, pollution and the general environmental impacts of human economic activities, and, most important perhaps, future energy options.

As Ophuls put it:

> Once relative abundance and wealth of opportunity are no longer available to mitigate the harsh political dynamics of scarcity, the pressures favoring greater inequality, oppression, and conflict will build up, so that the return of scarcity portends the revival of age-old political evils, for our descendants if not for ourselves. In short, the golden age of individualism, liberty and democracy is all but over.[4]

Similarly, Heilbroner drew this conclusion:

> ...given these mighty pressures and constraints we must think of alternatives to the present order in terms of social systems that offer a necessary degree of regimentation as well as a different set of motives and objectives. I must confess I can picture only one such system. This is a social order that will blend a "religious" orientation and a "military" discipline. Such a monastic organization of society may be repugnant to us, but I suspect it offers the greatest promise for bringing about the profound and painful adaptations that the coming generations must make.[5]

What both saw as inevitable in an era of resource scarcity was the need for severe political control, economic restraint, enforced discipline, and a social unity uncharacteristic of liberal-democratic societies.

Writing at about the same time as Heilbroner and Ophuls, but without being explicitly familiar with their particular arguments, John Passmore presents the following in seeming reply:

The view that ecological problems are more likely to be solved in an authoritarian than in...a liberal democratic society rests on the implausible assumption that the authoritarian state would be ruled by ecologist-kings. In practice there is more hope of action in democratic societies. In the United States, particularly, the habit of local action, the capacity of individuals to initiate legal proceedings, the tradition of public disclosure, are powerful weapons in the fight against ecological destruction.[6]

But elsewhere in his argument Passmore fears that the expansion of governmental responsibilities virtually implies the "gradual emergence of a bureaucratic police state."[7] Further, Passmore at several points characterizes environmentalists as possessing an enthusiasm for coercion, generally without granting the existence of a stronger tendency within the movement to precisely the opposite: popular empowerment with enhanced participation and openness.[8]

Passmore's argument, as well as those of Ophuls and Heilbroner, have in the ensuing years provided considerable fuel to those who would prefer virtually any form of economic growth to even a modicum of environmental protection. These critics and editorial writers have continuously told the public that environmentalists are anti-democratic elitists. A particular point of criticism is that environmentalists are comfortable and unconcerned about the loss of jobs implicit in the policies they espouse; and this point has been effectively countered elsewhere.[9] However, the general allegation that environmentalism is anti-democratic has not been clearly rebutted from an environmentalist perspective. Here I offer one response to this charge.

One might claim that Ophuls and Heilbroner simply over-reacted to the implications of exponential population growth, the energy crisis, and the seemingly sudden visibility of environmental degradation. Such a conclusion may well be valid in hindsight, but is far too easy. For example, while there are now signs that global population stabilization may be possible, it remains a very long way from achievement.[10] It is clear as well that grain producing capabilities can be, and indeed have been, radically expanded in most of the Third World.[11] However, this latter achievement rests in turn on radical increases in the use of water and fertilizer, and thus fossil fuel inputs. These latter increases may both be unsustainable in the long run.[12] Whether or not this change is temporary, it is not obvious that population stabilization will be achieved before the green revolution reaches full fruition. Nor, and this is more important, is it obvious that either environmental degradation or the declining availability of fossil fuels will not in and of themselves place real bounds on future economic growth. Finally, though there are now signs that the economic and political systems of many developed nations can stop growth in total energy demand, there is limited evidence that they can oversee any long-term reduction in that demand, however gradual.[13] Indeed, a more convincing case can be made that the future holds a long series of economic lurches created by energy supply problems similar to those of 1979-1983. Overall one might conclude, again with the advantage of hindsight, that the economic and resource arguments lying behind the frightening political visions of the 1970s were overstated, but nonetheless may yet prove an important dimension of our long-term future.

Yet a more serious error of Ophuls, Heilbroner and others is their underestimation of the capabilities of democratic political institutions. At least some nations may find an answer to future economic, environmental, and resource problems in *more* rather than *less* democracy. Democracy, participation and open administration carry not only a danger of division and conflict, but as well perhaps the best means of mobilizing educated and prosperous populations in difficult times. Indeed, the environmental issues of the 1970s have, in practice, often led to the revitalization and expansion of participatory opportunities.

Environmentalism and Democratic Practice: Opening a Door

Several important analysts of the environmental movement have noted a reasoned and principled inclination of many environmental organizations to the open administration of environmental and resource policies. To some extent this emphasis contrasts with the perspective of earlier conservationists, particularly with the faith they placed on expert administration and governmental bureaucracies as protectors of the public interest.[14] Richard Andrews has noted that conservationists assumed that there was a "single public interest" which "could be discovered or determined by experts."[15] In practice, however, it was found that the very private interests which were to be controlled by public servants (acting in the public interest) came themselves to dominate the resource management agencies. Those private interests in effect came to determine the public interest jointly with those in the employ of the public bureaucracies. In response to this pattern, "[t]he solution demanded by environmentalists was open access to administrative decision processes for all interested persons."[16] Thus, with this experience and perception, environmentalists typically urged greater openness and greater public involvement in administrative decision-making.

One can link this distinctive emphasis to some important academic perceptions of the 1950s and 1960s. In the 1950s, Grant McConnell and others linked the concept of the "captured" administrative agency to conservation issues. McConnell argued that administrative decisions regarding valuable resources are never exclusively technical in nature; they are political and value-laden. As he put it in a study of the U.S. Forest Service: "Any decision that will in fact be made will be in terms of the particular set of values held by the administrator, or perhaps, by the particular set of pressures that are brought to bear on him."[17] Similarly Lynton Caldwell, writing in 1963, observed that:

> Scientists may one day tell us what kinds of environment are best for our physical and mental health, but it seems doubtful if scientists alone will be able to determine the environmental conditions that people will seek. There will surely remain an element of personal judgement that cannot be relegated to the computer.[18]

In short, expertise is relevant to environmental decision-making, but it is not sufficient. Effective decision-making, from an environmentalist viewpoint, involves both expertise and the views of those who are most affected by the decisions at hand. All views, it has been argued, must be aired openly. Again, as Andrews put it, it has been the view of environmentalists that "in closed or low visibility arenas the power of highly organized private interests is maximized."[19] There has all along among environmentalists been a very strong sense of the public's right to know and to be involved in the decisions that affect their lives. Rachel Carson, whom many have called the founder of environmentalism, wrote in *Silent Spring* in 1960:

> It is not my contention that chemical insecticides must never be used. I do contend that we have put poisonous and biologically potent chemicals indiscriminately into the hands of persons largely or wholly ignorant of their potentials for harm. We have sub-

jected enormous numbers of people to contact with these poisons, *without their consent, and often without their knowledge.*[20]

The early statements of McConnell, Caldwell, Carson and the analyses of the origins of the environmental movement by Andrews, Hays, Schnaiberg and others suggest that there is a strong link between environmentalism and enhanced democratic openness and participation.[21] This link in principle, as we shall see, was generally carried through into the practice of environmental administration in the 1970s.

The development of participatory opportunities at the national level began in the United States with the Administrative Procedures Act of 1946. The anti-pollution bills of the 1960s revived this initial effort and a significant leap, in the view of some analysts, was made with the National Environmental Policy Act (NEPA) of 1969. NEPA, as is well known, required the preparation of environmental impact statements and open agency consideration of alternatives. Executive Order 11514, which followed, required timely public information and ("whenever appropriate") public hearings. The NEPA process also created an additional basis for litigation by environmental interest groups and citizens, and such activity increased considerably, especially in the early years of the bill.[22] More than a decade after its passage Lynton Caldwell wrote the following by way of a summary evaluation:

> The genius of NEPA lies in its linkage of mandatory procedure to substantive policy criteria and in the pressure it brings on administrative agencies to consider scientific evidence in their planning and decision making. NEPA is importantly, even though secondarily, a full disclosure or public participation law. Other statutes provide more explicitly for this procedural reform, although NEPA adds to their strength.[23]

Not all analysts of NEPA, however, have been so favorably disposed to its effectiveness, especially as a means of enhancing public involvement. The best critique of NEPA's effectiveness in this regard is probably still that of Sally Fairfax, published in *Science* in 1978.[24] Fairfax's argument, in brief, is that NEPA locks environmental activists into an unduly formal set of procedures and reduces the effectiveness of their participation in a sea of paperwork. "While it cannot be conclusively demonstrated, the public involvement that NEPA has induced is so formal, so predictable, and so proposal-oriented that it seems to have stifled meaningful dialogue between citizens and agencies."[25]   Indeed, in Fairfax's view, NEPA may well have stifled public participation in environmental decision-making which was developing well in any case prior to 1969.[26]   In expressing her doubts about NEPA, Fairfax makes clear that public participation regarding environmental protection was increasing in a variety of ways prior to NEPA and continued to expand after NEPA in ways Fairfax contends were unrelated to that particular bill. For example, Fairfax carefully documents the ways in which "standing" before the U.S. courts on environmental matters broadened independently from the provisions of NEPA. Although formally providing participatory procedures, she thus suggests, the new administrative mechanism served to contain rather than expand the impulses of popular participation.

For our purposes here we do not need to resolve the debate regarding the strengths and weaknesses of this particular bill. The reality doubtless lies between Fairfax's skepticism and Caldwell's general comfort. But no one questions that citizen participation was an important part of the early stages of the environmental era. More than that, environmentalists — Fairfax among them — have consistently pressed at every opportunity for more and more effective means of involving the educated and the general public in decision-making processes.

It is hardly surprising that agencies have sought to structure, and in effect control, public involvement. As Fairfax notes, they naturally want to promote the expansion of their attentive publics, their clientelle. But bureaucracies, almost by definition, seek silence, and if open to participation, prefer managed participation. Max Weber observed this early in the century as he described what we have come to call the administrative state:

> Every bureaucracy seeks to increase the superiority of the professionally informed by keeping their knowledge and intentions secret. Bureaucratic administration always tends to be an administration of "secret sessions": insofar as it can, it hides its knowledge and action from criticism.[27]

In effect, environmental organizations have sought to counter this tendency; indeed, the whole body of U.S. environmental legislation has been, in part, an important means of opening a door to the administrative state. The expansion of democratic practice has sometimes been consciously intended and sometimes has been simply the outcome of the fact of participation—of attempts to reverse or modify existing environmental policies by legal, democratic means. The participatory dimensions of environmental legislation both promote and place orderly bounds on participation. In so doing such legislation limits, but at the same time legitimizes, such participation. Limitation is particularly important to some in decision-making agencies. Legitimation can prove to be very important to environmentalists, especially in political contexts wherein environmentalism is less favored by the political leadership of the day, or of lesser interest to the public at large.

Throughout the 1970s new environmental legislation in the United States contained provisions assuring public participation.[28] Indeed, every major piece of U.S. environmental legislation in the 1970s allowed for public participation in environmental decision-making. Environmental legislation that did not add new channels for public involvement was rarely, if ever, proposed and never enacted in this period.

The Current Scene: Closing the Open Door?

The Reagan years in the United States showed how easily public sentiment can become tentative about environmental concerns. In such a context a political leadership hostile to environmental protection can roll back earlier gains very rapidly, even if there remains majority public support of a more subdued character. But public participation provisions built into legislation can be very important within a climate of relative indifference. Knowledge of what is going on and vehicles for comment and action can help to check a hostile bureaucracy. Such supports are also essential as particular issues jump into and then fade from the headlines, as the issue attention cycle continues its seemingly inevitable rhythms.[29] The Reagan administration sought to close the open door in environmental administration, but was never fully able to do so. The environmental movement grew in strength rather than faded, in part because there were windows into the administrative world and in part because those put in place to close the doors were either unappealing, or dishonest, or both.

In Canada, where the tradition of cabinet government has normally led to a more closed administrative process, environmental decision-making also led to a perceived need for enhanced public involvement. However, greater governmental caution regarding openness has led, for example, to an environmental assessment process, both federal and provincial, which is generally more limited. Nonetheless, there continue to be calls from environmentalists for more open and participatory procedures.[30] Similarly, decision-making regarding pesticides in Canada has been until very recently a closed and cautious process, cautious in the sense that there has been a general absence of significant challenges to the preferences of farmers or the agricultural chemical industry. The process most often simply followed the environmental challenges to pesticide use which were previously sustained in the United States. However, in the wake of the Industrial Biotest (IBT) scandals in the United States, Agriculture Canada, the responsible ministry, has undertaken to revise decision procedures significantly and to increase openness and opportunities for public inputs very significantly.[31]

The hesitation to encourage and promote ongoing public involvement in administrative and legal decision-making in Canada stands in contrast to the extent to which normal ad hoc participatory policy instruments have been applied to environmental issues. Specifically in Canada, as in Britain and Australia, Royal Commissions have in recent years frequently been appointed to deal with environmental matters. It has seemed at times as if this device of long-standing general use has been tailor-made for controversies of an environmental nature.

Far and away the most important single use of environmental Royal Commissions in Canada has been the federal government's Mackenzie Valley Pipeline Inquiry headed by Mr. Justice Thomas R. Berger.[32] The Berger Commission (1974-1977) was highly innovative as regards public involvement. Berger spent days and even weeks in each of very many, very small native villages in the remote and distant northern reaches of Canada. Hearings were as informal as necessary to make participants comfortable and television and media coverage of some of these meetings was extensive. Berger's more recent efforts in Alaska showed a similar approach and have elicited this comment:

> In the inquiry process Tom Berger has created what may well become the most important invention of the Twentieth Century. We could call it a "Cross-Cultural Hearing Aid". In his second northern inquiry, Berger journeyed to 62 villages all over Alaska to listen to Eskimos, Indians and Aleuts. The "hearing aid" quality of both efforts derived primarily from the media coverage (which differed considerably in the two cases), the provision of

interpreters in Native languages, and, in the case of the MVP Inquiry, the concurrent organizing work undertaken by Dene Nation field workers.[33]

The first Berger Commission set an example of effective public participation noted worldwide. It also, to some extent, reinforced the sense of caution in Canadian governmental circles about the political risks associated with the public inquiry process. Nonetheless, numerous other inquiries have followed the Berger inquiry, mostly within provincial rather than federal jurisdiction and including most notably, in Ontario, the Royal Commission on Electric Power Planning, the Royal Commission on the Northern Environment, and the Royal Commission on Matters of Health and Safety Arising from the Use of Asbestos. All of these inquiries have utilized an extensive public hearing process. In addition, at least three other provinces have had inquiries regarding the environmental and/or occupational health effects of uranium mining. In each of these cases, and many others, there has been extensive public involvement, often encouraged by intervenor funding, and generally involving participation from a wide variety of social groups.[34]

Public involvement in environmental decision-making has probably been most extensive in the case of nuclear power plants, uranium mining and nuclear fuel processing. This is true of Canada, the United States, Australia, and most Western European countries. In Canada the environmental impact assessment process has been extensively used, as have Royal Commissions. Regular Canadian channels for decision-making regarding nuclear safety have, however, been very closed indeed.[35] In the United States the public has been far more involved in the regular decision channels regarding nuclear power. In Britain and Australia large-scale special inquiries have been used. In Continental Europe large-scale public reviews, extraparliamentary dissent, and referenda have been commonplace in France, West Germany, Sweden, Austria, the Netherlands, Switzerland, and elsewhere. In Sweden a long process of special public discussions led, in 1979, to a halt to new reactor construction and a possible phasing out of nuclear power by 2010. Sweden previously was relatively heavily dependent on nuclear electricity.

As Nelkin and Pollack have written, following an extended study of participation in nuclear decision-making in several European jurisdictions:

...the participatory ideology has been "contagious." Demands for increased public involvement have spread from one sector to another; the experiments in the area of nuclear policy were but a natural extension of political reforms directed to democratization in the workplace...[and elsewhere].[36]

And:

The experiments to date surely represent more an effort to convince the public about the acceptability of government decisions than any real sharing of power. Yet even the limited increase in public discussion has influenced nuclear policies, at the very least encouraged greater caution. In the long run, the implementation of public policies concerning technology and the very legitimacy of the responsible authorities may depend on the politics of participation.[37]

These words take on new meaning in the realization that all of these inquiries regarding nuclear power preceded both Chernobyl and Three Mile Island. The doubts of a skeptical public seem to have been at least as reliable as the views of the "objective" experts in the employ of many governments. Future authorities, one assumes, may be even more wary of proceeding with nuclear or other high-risk technologies without some process of public involvement. Indeed the whole process of risk assessment, when seen as a technical (nonparticipatory) exercise, is increasingly facing heavy criticism as fundamentally anti-democratic.[38]

Much attention has been given to these processes of public involvement, even though they have rarely been considered collectively. There has also been significant attention to innovations such as environmental mediation. (See the essays by Douglas G. Amy, Robert Bartlett and John S. Dryzek in this volume.) These are (1) community right-to-know legislation, (2) internal responsibility systems regarding occupational health and safety, and (3) the use of referenda in environmental matters.

Community right-to-know and, as in New Jersey, for example, state right-to-know legislation has been increasingly popular in recent years.[39] These laws, by-laws, and ordinances can require the disclosure of all sites where certain hazardous chemicals are manufactured or stored and all routes by which they are transported. These disclosures are in some cases a complement to requirements on manufacturers and industrial users to inform their employees regarding chemicals to which those workers may be exposed. Community right-to-know is of great importance to residential and commercial property owners and to firemen, for obvious reasons. A right-to-know approach has also now been attempted at the federal level, in title three of the superfund amendments. At the very least, many citizens have by now concluded that they have a basic right to know the risks to which they are being subjected. We might recall at this point that it is now a quarter of a century since Rachel Carson argued, with regard to pesticides, that such a right existed.[40]

The occupational health and safety internal responsibility system has been established in several Canadian provinces, most notably Ontario, Quebec, Saskatchewan, Alberta, and British Columbia.[41] The system involves three basic rights: the right to know, the right to a union-management (or worker-management) health and safety review committee, and the right to refuse unsafe work. Here again is a legislated requirement of openness and participation, this time throughout the private sector as regards employer-employee relations in the health and safety field. The internal responsibility system provides a means whereby individuals can in principle achieve workplace safety without the need to resort to actions so drastic as plant-wide strikes. Katherine Swinton has noted that many believe that this system is superior to a system wholly dependent on either management initiatives or government inspection or both:

> Prevention is more likely to occur through an effective internal responsibility system and worker participation. Worker input into occupational health and safety regulation, whether in establishing programs to improve health in the workplace or in carrying out inspections utilizes the workers' experience and knowledge of the workplace. Those on the shop floor are likely to be aware of the unused machine guard or the clogged ventilation system....[42]

She goes on to argue that especially those managers who feel that more responsibility regarding health and safety must ultimately rest with workers appreciate the educative and peer-pressure aspects of the system. But Swinton also makes clear that many workers and union leaders

> ...see participation in regulating the workplace as a basic right. It is a worker's health and bodily integrity which are threatened by hazardous conditions, and he should be given sufficient informa-

tion to evaluate the risks, opportunity for questioning the existence of such hazards, and a voice in their control.[43]

An internal responsibility system has considerable potential as a device
for mobilizing industrial workers to a greater participatory role in
workplace decision-making. This is a prospect which has not been lost on
observers on the political left in the United States. Noble, in a recent
book, has concluded for this very reason that a system of this sort would
be preferable to the existing practice of the Occupational Safety and
Health Administration.[44]

The third in our list of techniques, the referendum, though less noted,
has been used extensively in many U.S. states for many years now, particularly as regards initiatives concerning refillable containers and nuclear
issues.[45] In 1986, for example, there were referenda regarding nuclear
power, toxic chemicals, urban growth, radioactive waste dumps, and toxic
waste treatment facilities in various states.[46] We might recall as well the
important use of the referendum on nuclear power in Sweden. Nonetheless, to my knowledge there have been few systematic reviews of the use
of the referendum in environmental decision-making.

The forms of public involvement discussed here are ones which
generally allow for intervention into the decision-making processes of
administrative organizations. As we review the current scene of public
participation in environmental administration, one final matter should be
considered. Weber pointed out that those who sought to challenge an
administrative apparatus were typically forced to adopt a similar administrative form. As mechanisms for the articulation of interests, political parties in particular have tended to follow the path of
bureaucratization. The issue which arises here, then, is the organizational
form adopted by environmentalists for the mobilization of environmentalism.

What we find among environmental organizations is ambivalence and
diversity: there is at times some amount of bureaucratization, but there is
also strong resistance to this tendency. Ironically, this resistance has
become especially clear when environmentalists have sought to organize
an effective political party. Here we can note in particular the matter of
party organization in the West German Green Party. The Greens have
made several notable participatory innovations. The party's federal assembly meets annually. Half of the membership of the party's federal
board of directors is newly elected each year and only one reelection to

the same position is permitted. There have even been efforts to rotate holders of elected office within their terms, but the party backed off from this as too destabilizing. Nonetheless, it is expected that few if any office-holders will seek reelection in order that the power of particular individuals does not become entrenched and so that many party members have the opportunity to serve. In general every effort is made to decentralize control of the party and to involve a maximum proportion of the membership in party governance. One exception to this rule, a rule which one must assume is an important principle for the Greens, is that party membership as a proportion of party votes has thus far been lower than that in most other West German parties.[47] This is important because it means that candidate selection has thus far drawn from a quite small group (it may well be the case that a larger membership will come only if and when the party achieves a share of power). Despite this problem with membership size, it is nevertheless notable that the Greens have emphasized membership participation within the party and enhanced public participation in the wider society.

Conclusion

In sharp contrast to the theoretical views noted at the outset, environmentalism has in practice widely and consistently led to (or at least sought) an expansion of democratic opportunities and an opening of administrative decision-making to public participation. Environmentalists have highly valued the protection and indeed the further development of democratic institutions. Even the emphasis on potential threats to democracy in the writings of Ophuls and Heilbroner can be interpreted as further evidence of such concern, however pessimistic their overall conclusions. With the advantage of hindsight, we might now conclude that both Ophuls and Heilbroner were looking too widely, and perhaps too early, to see the consistency of the pattern set out in this essay. It does not necessarily follow, of course, that the potential next wave of resource limitations on economic prosperity will not seriously weaken the democratic hopes and efforts of contemporary environmentalists.[48] What needs rethinking is the character of the relationship between the quality of democratic institutions and processes and the actuality of resource and environmental limitations.

One important dimension of this rethinking is the relationship between elites, masses, and economic growth. Volkmar Lauber and Mark E. Kann, without apparently being aware of each other's work, have argued that it is elites—particularly economic elites in the case of Kann and political elites in the case of Lauber—that pursue economic growth to the detriment of the environment.[49] The general public, both maintain, would be relatively more open to accepting restraints on such forms of economic growth. As Kann puts it: "There are no guarantees that people will make wise decisions, but they have an incentive to do so: they must live with the consequences."[50] This is, of course, too simple: some populations can export some of the environmental costs of their economic gains to other jurisdictions and/or to future generations. Nonetheless, Kann's central assertion may remain valid: "My thesis is that to the extent that the environment has been influenced in the United States it has mainly been influenced by elites who exercise concentrated power on their own behalf."[51] Lauber's proffered cure, moreover, is one with which both Kann and I would be comfortable: "power today is too closely linked with growth. Under those circumstances it seems more promising to restrain and limit power. For that purpose, liberal democracy is rather well fitted; it is one of the problems for which it was designed."[52]

Yet to what extent will future environmental protection mandate economic restraint? What sorts of economic restraints are likely in a world of limited resources? Will adequate environmental protection require economic restraints that a democratic majority could not be persuaded to actively insist upon? That is perhaps the heart of the dilemma which all societies may well soon face. This problem cannot be solved here, but it is important to recognize it.[53]

What can be ventured here are some limited observations. First, democracy may well be the best political tool humankind has developed for mobilizing populations, especially educated and at least moderately prosperous ones.[54] Environmentalists have, at least implicitly, sensed this point. Since they often call for significant changes in socio-economic organization, and even socio-economic goals, innovative democratic means may be the best, if not the only, means of achieving their goals.

One expression of appreciation of the relationship between resource limitations, environmentalism and democracy different from and superior to that of Ophuls, Heilbroner and Passmore, is that of Richard J. Barnet. Barnet, in *The Lean Years*, reviewed the same range of issues that Ophuls and Heilbroner considered. He came to similarly pessimistic conclusions regarding future resource prospects, but explicitly rejected both their neo-Malthusian and neo-Hobbesian conclusions: "In today's world," he first noted, "the heirs of Malthus preach what they call 'lifeboat ethics,' claiming the same monopoly on realism that fortified the dismal preacher when he pronounced his death sentence for the poor."[55] And he went on to add this: "Despairing of human altruism to subordinate the quest for personal enrichment to the common good, the heirs of Hobbes have seized upon the dangers of ecological catastrophe to legitimate the modern-day Leviathan."[56] In stark contrast to both these views, Barnet noted the importance of democracy as an educational and mobilizing tool:

> Democracy is under severe attack at the moment when gathering evidence suggests that popular participation is a survival value. Major structural changes cannot take place in any country without the mobilization of the whole people. The solution to the energy crisis in the U.S., for example, requires a degree of public understanding and participation which our political institutions do not know how to achieve.[57]

Even Barnet, however, may have underestimated to some extent existing political institutions and existing public sophistication. Goldrich's analysis of the process which followed on the Northwest Power Act of 1980 is a case in point, as are many of the examples already noted. Both the Northwest Power Planning Council, an official planning body, and the Northwest Conservation Act Coalition, a citizen body, sought "...to integrate the values of environmental enhancement, citizen participation in government decision-making, and economic development."[58] The point is that all things environmental do not necessarily involve bleak economic and political scenarios.

A wide variety of environmental measures, including mandatory reuse and recycling of containers, many forms of energy conservation, sustainable agriculture and forestry, pollution abatement requirements, and enhanced public transportation, involve, for example, more rather than fewer employment opportunities. Others, such as appliance and auto energy efficiency standards, in and of themselves involve few if any employment changes. However, most such measures do involve economic dislocations, economic costs for someone to bear, and, in some cases, induced inconveniences. But the general public, polls suggest, is not unwilling to make sacrifices to achieve environmental protection. Political participation can help make the attendant redistribution of costs and benefits fairer and more widely understood. Democratic mobilization is essential to the achievement of such policies in the face of the opposition of vested interests which such policies inevitably engender.

In conclusion, I would stress what I think is obvious: first, environmental politics, especially in North America, must be at its heart a majoritarian politics. Difficult economic times thus leave very little room for simple no-growth vanguardism. To the credit of the environmental movement much of this faded as we entered the 1980s. Environmentalists should continue to emphasize the positive side of their program — sustainable and decentralized economic development and employment opportunities.[59] Finally, environmentalism cannot be successful in the long run without a continuous enhancement of opportunities for democratic participation.

Notes

1. William Ophuls, *Ecology and the Politics of Scarcity* (San Francisco: W. H. Freeman, 1977); Robert L. Heilbroner, *An Inquiry into the Human Prospect* (New York: W. W. Norton, 1974). A thoughtful response to this literature from a perspective similar to that in this chapter is David W. Orr and Stuart Hill, "Leviathan, the Open Society and the Crisis of Ecology," in David W. Orr and Marvin S. Soroos, eds., *The Global Predicament: Ecological Perspectives on World Order* (Chapel Hill: University of North Carolina Press, 1979). I came upon this excellent article shortly after the original publication of an earlier version of this essay in *Environmental Ethics* 10 (Winter, 1988), pp. 291-308.

2. John Passmore, *Man's Responsibility for Nature* (London: Duckworth, 1974). Passmore's case was made against what he saw as dangerous tendencies within environmentalism; the arguments of Ophuls and Heilbroner focused on the political implications of environmental and resource scarcity. Passmore might well regard Ophuls and Heilbroner as examples of that which he feared. Passmore's work has, of course, been seen as problematic in several regards. See, *e.g.*, Robin Attfield, *The Ethics of Environmental Concern* (Oxford: Basil Blackwell, 1983); Val Routley, "Critical Notice of John Passmore, *Man's Responsibility for Nature*," *Australasian Journal of Philosophy* 53 (1975), pp. 171-85.

3. It is this environmentalist distrust of "established" science that seems to disconcert Passmore. Passmore concentrated perhaps too much on extreme statements of this distrust and did not appreciate that such doubts, rather than being a threat to democratic values, could support more participatory forms of decision-making. Further, one might add that the recognition that in some contexts science and values become inextricably linked can also result in better science.

4. Ophuls, p. 145.

5. Heilbroner, p. 161.

6. Passmore, p. 183.

7. *Ibid.*, pp. 193-194.

8. *Ibid.*, pp. 60-61, 96 and 99. To his credit Passmore does allow the possibility that environmentalism may turn out to be an "anti-bureaucratic" force (see p. 183 n.).

9. Regarding the net positive effect on employment opportunities associated with pro-environmental policies see, for example, the numerous studies cited in Frederick H. Buttel, Charles C. Geisler, and Irving W. Wiswall, eds., *Labor and the Environment* (Westport, CT: Greenwood Press, 1984) and in David B. Brooks and Robert Paehlke, "Canada: A Soft Path in a Hard Country," *Canadian Public Policy* 6 (1980), pp. 444-453. Also of interest here is Richard Kazis and Richard L. Grossman, *Fear at Work: Job Blackmail, Labor and the Environment* (New York: The Pilgrim Press, 1982).

10. The United Nations now projects that global population stability will be achieved over the next century at perhaps a total of ten billion souls, roughly twice the present population. However, given the fact that until the 1970s population growth had done little but accelerate for centuries this new projection is as much hope as certainty.

11. For an overinterpretation of this new reality see Peter Drucker, "The Changed World

Economy," *Foreign Affairs* 64 (1986), pp. 768-791.

12. That is, not only will it be difficult to achieve further increases, but those that have occurred may be at least in part temporary. Obviously we cannot count on long-term supplies of those fertilizers that are obtained from fossil fuels. Some irrigation water as well is drawn from nonreplenishing sources and most irrigation affects soil salinity. Biotechnology may find ways around some of these limits, but gains without costs can hardly be assumed.

13. That is, the early 1980s saw a halt to energy demand growth, but the mid-1980s have witnessed a considerable and unwarranted relaxation of attention to this issue.

14. I discuss this theme more extensively in "Participation in Environmental Administration: Closing the Open Door?" *Alternatives* 14:2 (1987), pp. 43-48. Indeed the conservation movement often seemed to assume that public bureaucracies could somehow objectively determine the "public interest."

15. Richard N. L. Andrews, "Class Politics or Democratic Reform: Environmentalism and American Political Institutions," *Natural Resources Journal* 20 (1980), p. 228.

16. *Ibid.*, p. 237.

17. Grant McConnell, "The Conservation Movement—Past and Present," *Western Political Quarterly* 7 (1954), p. 471.

18. Lynton K. Caldwell, "Environment: A New Focus for Public Policy?" *Public Administration Review* 23 (1963), p. 139.

19. Andrews, "Class Politics or Democratic Reform,", p. 237.

20. Rachel Carson, *Silent Spring* (Greenwich, CT: Fawcett Publications, 1962), p. 22.

21. Sources not thus far cited are Samuel Hays, "From Conservation to Environment: Environmental Politics in the United States Since World War Two," *Environmental Review* 6:2 (1982), pp. 14-41; and Allan Schnaiberg, *The Environment: From Surplus to Scarcity* (New York: Oxford University Press, 1980).

22. Lettie McSpadden Wenner, "The Misuse and Abuse of NEPA," *Environmental Review* 7 (1983), pp. 229-254; on this point see esp. pp. 229-231.

23. Lynton K. Caldwell, *Science and the National Environmental Policy Act* (Tuscaloosa: University of Alabama Press, 1982), p. 74. A quite effective, pro-NEPA, argument is also made by Serge Taylor in *Making Bureaucracies Think: The Environmental Impact Assessment Strategy of Administrative Reform* (Stanford: Stanford University Press, 1984).

24. Sally K. Fairfax, "A Disaster in the Environmental Movement," *Science* 199 (1978), pp. 743-748.

25. *Ibid.*, p.746.

26. For example, Fairfax dates the origins of greater participatory involvement in administration to the Administrative Procedures Act of 1946.

27. Max Weber, "Bureaucracy," in *From Max Weber: Essays in Sociology* (New York: Oxford University Press, 1946), p. 233.

28. This generalization holds for the Clean Air Acts of 1970 and 1977, the 1972 amendments to the Federal Water Pollution Control Act, the Toxic Substances Control Act (TSCA) of 1976, the Resource Conservation and Recovery Act (RCRA) of 1976 and the Comprehensive Environmental Response, Compensation, and Liability Act of 1980, the so-called "superfund" legislation.

29. *Cf.* Robert Paehlke and Douglas Torgerson, "Toxic Waste and the Administrative State:

NIMBY or Participatory Management," in this volume; and Walter A. Rosenbaum, "The Politics of Public Participation in Hazardous Waste Management," in James P. Lester and Ann O'M. Bowman, eds., *The Politics of Hazardous Waste Management* (Durham, NC: Duke University Press, 1983).

30. Regarding both the cautiousness and the call for reform see Robert B. Gibson and Beth Savan, *Environmental Assessment in Ontario* (Toronto: Canadian Environmental Law Research Foundation, 1986); G. E. Beanlands and P. N. Duinker, *An Ecological Framework for Environmental Impact Assessment in Canada* (Halifax: Dalhousie University Institute for Resource and Environmental Studies, 1983); Evangeline S. Case *et al.*, eds., *Fairness in Environmental and Social Impact Assessment Processes* (Calgary: University of Calgary Law School, 1983); and J. B. R. Whitney and V. W. Maclaren, eds., *Environmental Impact Assessment: The Canadian Experience* (Toronto: Institute for Environmental Studies, University of Toronto, 1985).

31. See *National Workshop on Risk-Benefit Analysis* (Ottawa: Pesticides Directorate, Environment Canada, 1985); and William Leiss, *The Risk Management Process* (Ottawa: Pesticides Directorate, Agriculture Canada, October, 1985). Regarding IBT see Samuel Epstein, *The Politics of Cancer* (San Francisco: Sierra Club Books, 1978).

32. See the final report of this commission, *Northern Frontier/Northern Homeland*, 2 Vols. (Ottawa: Supply and Services Canada, 1977); for a lucid commentary see Douglas Torgerson, "Between Knowledge and Politics: Three Faces of Policy Analysis," *Policy Sciences* 19 (1986), pp. 33-59.

33. Walt Taylor and Peggy Taylor review of Thomas R. Berger's *Village Journey: The Report of the Alaska Native Review Commission, Alternatives* 14 (1987), p. 35.

34. For a good overview of the use of the inquiry process see Liora Salter and Debra Slaco, *Public Inquiries in Canada* (Ottawa: Science Council of Canada, 1981).

35. See G. Bruce Doern, "The Atomic Energy Control Board," in G. Bruce Doern, ed., *The Regulatory Process in Canada* (Toronto: Macmillan Company of Canada, 1978).

36. Dorothy Nelkin and Michael Pollack, "The Politics of Participation and the Nuclear Debate in Sweden, the Netherlands, and Austria," *Public Policy* 25 (1977), pp. 333-357.

37. *Ibid.*, pp. 356-357. See also Dorothy Nelkin and Michael Pollack, *The Atom Besieged* (Cambridge, MA: The M.I.T. Press, 1981).

38. See Charles Perrow, *Normal Accidents: Living With High-Risk Technologies* (New York: Basic Books, 1984) and T. F. Schrecker, *The Pitfalls of Standards* (Hamilton, Ontario: Canadian Centre for Occupational Health and Safety, 1986).

39. Mary Louise Adams, "Right to Know: A Summary," *Alternatives* 11:3/4 (1983) pp. 29-36. For a discussion of the extent to which recent federal initiatives in this area have been an attempt to preempt state and local efforts see P.R. Tyson, "The Preemptive Effect of the OSHA Hazard Communication Standard on State and Community Right to Know Laws," *Notre Dame Law Review* 62 (1987), pp. 1010-1023, and Albert R. Matheny and Bruce A. Williams, "The Crisis of Administrative Legitimacy: Regulatory Politics and The Right-to-Know," in this volume

40. See 14 above. In that statement Carson went on to say, "If the Bill of Rights contains no guarantee that a citizen shall be secure against lethal poisons distributed by either private individuals or by public officials, it is surely only because our forefathers, despite their considerable wisdom and foresight, could conceive of no such problem."

41. See, e.g., G. B. Reshenthaler, *Occupational Health and Safety in Canada* (Montreal: Institute for Research on Public Policy, 1979) and Katherine E. Swinton, "Enforcement of Occupational Health and Safety Legislation: The Role of the Internal Responsibility System," in Kenneth Swan

and Katherine E. Swinton, eds., "Studies in Labour Law" (Toronto: Butterworths, 1982). T. F. Schrecker, *Workplace Pollution* (Ottawa: Law Reform Commission of Canada, 1986). The term *internal responsibility system* was first used by Dr. James Ham, head of the Ontario Royal Commission on the Health and Safety of Workers in Mines (1976).

42. Swinton, "Enforcement," p. 146.

43. *Ibid.*, pp. 146-147.

44. Charles Noble, *Liberalism at Work* (Philadelphia: Temple University Press, 1986).

45. See, e.g., William U. Chandler, *Materials Recycling: The Virtue of Necessity* (Washington, DC: Worldwatch Institute, 1983).

46. See *Environmental Action* 18:4 (1987), p. 6.

47. Gerd Langguth, *The Green Factor in German Politics* (Boulder, CO: Westview Press, 1986), pp. 47-49.

48. That is, how solid are the participatory structures that have been established? Would they withstand, for example, another wave of oil price shocks? Would we not see environmental impact analysis by-passed in any future "crisis" mentality? Or indeed would environmental protection itself stand up in the face of the economic fall-out that may yet result from the last price shock (namely the current debt crisis induced in large part by the flood of petrodollars)?

49. Mark E. Kann, "Environmental Democracy in the United States," in Sheldon Kamieniecki, Robert O'Brien, and Michael Clarke, eds., *Controversies in Environmental Policy* (Albany: SUNY Press, 1986), pp. 252-274 and Volkmar Lauber, "Ecology, Politics and Liberal Democracy," *Government and Opposition* 13 (1978), pp. 199-217.

50. Kann, p. 253.

51. *Ibid.*

52. Lauber, p. 217.

53. For further discussion, see Robert Paehlke, *Environmentalism and the Future of Progressive Politics* (New Haven: Yale University Press, 1989).

54. There has been an extensive literature regarding the relationship between democracy, socio-economic development and political mobilization—particularly work in the 1960s by J. P. Nettl, Karl Deutsch, Phillips Cutright, S. M. Lipset, Karl de Schweinitz, Jr., Lyle W. Shannon, and Deane Neubauer.

55. Richard J. Barnet, *The Lean Years: Politics in the Age of Scarcity* (New York: Simon and Schuster, 1980), pp. 297-298.

56. *Ibid.*, p. 302.

57. *Ibid.*, p. 313.

58. Daniel Goldrich, "Democracy and Energy Planning: The Pacific Northwest as Prototype," *Environmental Review* 10 (1986), p. 211.

59. By decentralization I do not mean to suggest that the geographic dispersion of populations is environmentally appropriate. On the contrary environmentalists, in my view, have significantly underestimated the technical and political links between environmental protection and urbanism. See Robert Paehlke, *Bucolic Myths: Towards a More Urbanist Environmentalism* (Toronto: Institute for Urban and Community Studies, University of Toronto, 1986).

PART II

TECHNIQUES AND PROCESSES OF ENVIRONMENTAL ADMINISTRATION

The administrative response to environmental problems has been ambivalent. Much of the response has been conventional, involving modest reforms to the established procedures and structures of an administrative apparatus historically dedicated to the advance of industrialization. Still, there have been innovations which do at least point toward a form of environmental administration that would entail a significant departure from this conventional orientation. But even as innovative techniques and processes raise the prospect of something radically new, they are simultaneously drawn back toward the sphere of standard operating procedures. This ambivalence draws attention to the inevitable interweaving of politics and administration and suggests that the future of environmental administration depends very much upon that of environmental politics.

The articles in Part II explore the nature and potential of environmental administration. Although the authors strike different and, at times, conflicting notes, they are all concerned with the potential for a mode of administration which would break through conventional boundaries. Questioning the nature of reason and examining the role of expanded public discussion, the articles may also be viewed as part of a larger methodological ferment which rejects the technocratic posture of a once-dominant positivism while seeking a fundamental re-orientation of administrative and policy studies.

DECISION TECHNIQUES FOR ENVIRONMENTAL POLICY: A CRITIQUE

Douglas J. Amy

In advanced industrial countries, much of the responsibility for protecting the natural environment has been handed over to administrative agencies. In the United States, after Congress passed such landmark pieces of environmental legislation as the *National Environmental Policy Act* and the *Clean Air Act*, environmental politics began to focus increasingly on administrative bodies like the Environmental Protection Agency which were given the important tasks of monitoring the quality of the environment, developing specific environmental regulations, and enforcing them. As a part of those efforts, administrative agencies have sought to develop environmental decision-making techniques. The hope has been that the use of these techniques would enable the government to manage and protect water quality, air quality, forests and wilderness in a rational and professional manner. This essay will critically examine three of these techniques: (1) environmental impact statements, an approach that originated in the 1970s; (2) cost-benefit analysis, the technique preferred by the Reagan/Bush administrations in the 1980s; and (3) environmental dispute resolution, a new technique that some believe will become common in the 1990s.

There is considerable academic literature that examines the advantages and disadvantages of these techniques. Much of this material has analyzed the intellectual and scientific validity of these approaches. Proponents of various techniques have celebrated the objectivity and rationality of their methods, while critics have pointed out their technical shortcomings and their normative and philosophical biases. These debates have been useful, but they leave out an important element that is necessary for a full understanding of these phenomena — they leave out the politics of these techniques. It is important to recognize that the development and utilization of decision-making techniques in the administrative state has as much to do with politics as it has with intellectual merit. In other words, the adoption of particular methods is often more a response to powerful political interests than the product of an intellectual search for the most rational technique. Thus to understand the evolution of decision-making techniques—why particular approaches have been preferred at different times—we must understand how these techniques have served the interests of powerful groups both inside and outside the state and how the distribution of power among those groups has changed over time. The story of environmental decision-making techniques concerns not simply their intellectual advantages and disadvantages, but also the political advantages and disadvantages such techniques offer to important groups in society.

Environmental Impact Statements

One of the main techniques that continues to inform environmental decisions is the environmental impact statement (EIS). The use of the EIS was first required of U.S. federal agencies by the *National Environmental Policy Act* passed in 1969. All agencies whose projects could have a substantial impact on the human environment were required to prepare an EIS. The report was to cover not only the potential environmental ramifications of the proposed project or program, but would also consider alternative options. A draft of the report would be circulated among other government agencies and public groups that might be affected by the project, and the final report was to include the comments of these groups and respond to them.

The reasoning behind the EIS requirement was simple and appealing. Too long had the nation been recklessly building highways, filling in wetlands, cutting down forests, and damming rivers with little concern for the long-range environmental effects. Now officials would be required to "look before they leap." And the hope was that now that officials were equipped with more information and more options they would be able to make better (*i.e.*, more scientific and rational) decisions that would minimize environmental damage. The logic behind this approach was so appealing that it quickly spread to state and local governments in the U.S. and was often expanded to include not only public development projects, but private ones as well. In this way, the EIS quickly became a widespread decision technique in the effort to protect the environment.

The emergence of the EIS requirement very much reflected the growing power of the environmental movement of the late 1960s. At that time, the movement was enjoying booming membership and the public showed increasing support for environmentalists' assertion that environmental values had for too long been neglected and must now be given more importance in government decision-making. Initially environmentalists had high hopes that the EIS requirement would be instrumental in ensuring protection for the environment. And, in fact, there have been some cases, as in real estate development in the Florida Keys and off-shore oil leasing, where the EIS process forced significant alteration in projects. However, much of the early enthusiasm for this technique has long since waned — and few environmentalists now believe that the EIS is the "revolutionary" approach some had portrayed it to be.[1] It has become clear that there are substantial problems with this technique. The problems are of two sorts: technical and political.

Technically, questions have arisen about the scientific validity of these reports. Identifying and assessing long and short-term environmental impacts is a complex scientific task. Enormous uncertainties often are present in the data and models used, a situation made worse by the unreasonable time constraints that typically are imposed on analysts. G.F. White has argued that because of the daunting complexity of the subject matter, assessors sometimes embrace simplified approaches and methods that obscure the real impacts and issues.[2] Other observers have complained that the authors of these reports often have questionable scientific credentials, use outmoded and inappropriate methodologies, and produce "large, diffuse reports containing reams of uninterpreted and incomplete descriptive data and in some cases construct 'predictive' models, irrespective of the quality of the data base."[3]

Of course, these technical problems are not necessarily intractable. Better training and better research techniques would no doubt go a long way toward improving the quality of these reports, and indeed there have been significant improvements from the early days of the 1970s. But even if these technical problems can be worked out, there still remain the political problems surrounding the use of the EIS, and these are much more serious and intractable. The main political problem is that decision-makers often do not use the EIS in the way it was intended, and so the EIS only rarely has a real effect on development decisions. Decision-makers usually make their project decisions first, then shape the impact statements to justify these decisions.[4] The result, as one critic pointed out, is that while a few projects have been altered or canceled through the EIS process, "there is a good deal of evidence that the overwhelming majority of projects go through the process unscathed."[5]

Part of the problem here is that some of the central political assumptions underlying the EIS process are quite naive. The EIS approach presumes, for example, that decision-making in bureaucracies is a rational process based on the detailed analysis of information and options. But in reality project decisions are usually more the product of politics than scientific analysis.[6] As H.P. Friesema and P.J. Culhane have pointed out: "The expectation that [the EIS] will cause federal agencies to produce scientific, holistic, optimising, evaluating, mitigating, and coordinating policy seems to be the latest manifestation of the rational decision-making perspective on bureaucratic behavior...[But] public administration behavior is not scientific management, it is politics."[7]

In this sense, the EIS process generally ignores the political context in which environmental decisions are made. In particular, it neglects the ever-present pressure on government agencies to promote and support economic growth and development. Much of the role of the administrative state in advanced capitalist societies consists of providing the infrastructure and resources for business activities — roads, dams, forests, oil reserves. And it is these pressures — not the lack of adequate impact information — that have often led to environmentally irresponsible decisions.

In the context of these economic pressures, the rational analysis mandated by the EIS requirement begins to serve a political purpose quite different from the one initially imagined by proponents. Instead of guiding decisions, the EIS becomes a way of retrospectively rationalizing and legitimating decisions made on other grounds. This need to legitimize decisions is a powerful one in the administrative state, and it is a need that must be appreciated to fully understand the role that decision-making techniques play in these bureaucracies. All administrators rely on decision-making techniques to help them legitimize their decisions and to forestall public opposition. Unlike legislators, administrators cannot claim that they are elected by the public and thus have the right to make policy decisions. Given this lack of democratic legitimacy, they must often fall back on technocratic forms of legitimation — claims that their decisions are legitimate because they are based on superior information and thorough analysis. For administrators, then, what is often politically useful about the EIS is not that it increases the rationality of their decisions — but that it enhances the *appearance* of rationality and thus serves to undermine environmental opposition to development projects. As one critic pointed out, decision-makers "have been quick to grasp the quickest way to silence critical 'eco-freaks' is to allocate a small portion of funds for any engineering project for ecological studies."[8] Thus, although administrators often chafe at the requirements of the EIS, those very requirements can prove politically useful to them.

Environmentalists have been quick to identify and condemn these political abuses of environmental impact statements. Some critics, like Sally Fairfax, have gone as far as to argue that the EIS process may be largely a waste of time for environmentalists.[9] Challenging the EIS of a project and developing alternatives often takes enormous amounts of time and energy on the part of environmental groups that are already understaffed and underfunded. And the result of all that work is often not to derail a project, but merely to require the agency to generate another EIS before it goes ahead. In this way, the EIS process may dissipate the energy of environmental forces and serve as a distraction from other more effective political activities.

But this evaluation of the political impact of the EIS may be too pessimistic. For although its impact on federal decisions may not have been as substantial as environmentalists have wanted, the EIS has in other ways served as a useful political tool. For example, one of the main reasons that economic development has gone largely unchallenged in capitalist societies is the fact that the social and environmental costs of that development often are indirect and hidden. The EIS process can bring many of these previously hidden environmental costs to light and this can serve as an important organizing tool for environmental activists.[10] The information and alternatives developed in these reports can be used to mobilize citizen opposition to development projects. In addition, the EIS process has served to give citizen and environmental groups the legal grounds to participate in these development decisions. The opportunity to comment on a draft EIS and the ability to gain access to the courts to challenge an inadequate one mean that new forms of citizen participation exist where they did not before.

To sum up, the environmental impact statement has had mixed results as a decision-making tool — but this is to be expected given the mixture of political forces in which it exists. Decision-making techniques function to serve powerful political interests both inside and outside of government, and there are a variety of interests at work here. On the one hand, environmentalists form a well-established political lobby that still enjoys strong public support, and the EIS has proved at least somewhat useful to the environmentalist cause. Despite all the shortcomings of the EIS, most environmentalists still believe it is better to require one than not. On the other hand, private corporations and government agencies concerned with encouraging economic development remain a strong political force. Although initially unhappy with the EIS requirement, they have learned to use it to further their own political ends and to undermine potential political opposition. In this way, the contradictory political effects of environmental impact statements very much reflect the dynamic clash of political forces that exist around environmental issues today.

Cost-Benefit Analysis

If the EIS was the technique of the 1970s, cost-benefit analysis was the technique of the 1980s.[11] In the U.S. it dominated the Reagan administration's approach to environmental decisions. But despite the claims of its proponents, the shift toward cost-benefit analysis was not due to its obvious intellectual superiority, but rather was primarily a product of a shift in power among those interests involved in environmental issues. As Thomas Edsall has documented quite well in his book *The Politics of Inequality*, the late 1970s witnessed a significant change in the distribution of political power in the United States.[12] Business interests had been put on the political defensive in the early seventies by environmentalists, consumer groups, and public interest lobbies. By the mid-seventies, business was making a concerted effort to regroup and develop new and more effective sources of political power. Besides expanding traditional lobbying efforts in Congress, business and other conservative groups began to pour tens of millions of dollars into political action committees in an effort to elect sympathetic legislators and presidents. They also began to sink millions into conservative and business oriented think-tanks, including the Heritage Foundation, the American Enterprise Institute, and the Mountain States Legal Foundation. These organizations were to develop the intellectual ammunition for the new conservative assault on liberal government.[13]

By the early 1980s this political offensive began to show significant results. The Reagan administration came to power and part of the intellectual ammunition it brought with it was cost-benefit analysis. This technique had long been used occasionally in the federal bureaucracy, to assess the feasibility of water projects, and so on. But it was now to become the centerpiece in the effort to deregulate the U.S. economy. Business interests and conservative economists had argued throughout the 1970s that federal regulations, including environmental regulations, were too costly for business and helped to account for falling corporate profit rates and an inability to compete with foreign producers. These interests urged the adoption of cost-benefit analysis to ensure that new regulations did not produce more economic harm than public good. While this approach began to gain some attention during the Carter administration, it was not until the Reagan administration rose to power in 1980 that cost-benefit analysis became the decision-making technique of choice in regulatory situations. Cost-benefit analysis began to be heavily promoted by James Watt in the Interior Department and Anne Gorsuch in the EPA as part of their environmental deregulation effort. In addition, in February of 1981 the Reagan administration issued Executive Order 12291 which designated the Office of Management and Budget to review all proposed new regulations to ensure that their costs did not exceed their benefits. Very quickly, cost-benefit calculations were being used to argue against a wide variety of environmental regulations including the control of acid rain, the safe disposal of dioxins, the control of disease causing cotton dust in the workplace, and many other concerns.[14]

But although cost-benefit analysis came to the fore largely because of political forces, its considerable intellectual appeal should not be underestimated. It portrays itself as the essence of economic rationality. It promises to systematically investigate and quantify the advantages and disadvantages of possible environmental decisions and then objectively choose the option that produces the most public benefit. In effect, cost-benefit analysis transfers the economic rationality of the marketplace from the private sector into the public sector; private firms wouldn't produce something unless they made a profit, so why should government? It is a difficult logic to refute. As one scholar has pointed out: "Cost-benefit analysis is perhaps the most intuitively attractive reform proposed for regulation. Nothing could make more sense than to issue regulations only if the regulation provided more benefits than costs."[15]

This kind of economic rationality had a political as well as intellectual appeal to administrators. As mentioned earlier, the late 1970s were a time of much criticism of regulators and regulation. Many conservatives argued (and some of the public agreed) that much of government regulation is arbitrary and excessive. Cost-benefit analysis seemed to be one way to restore "common sense" to government regulation. As Robert Zinke has observed, "cost-benefit analysis...gained acceptance on the basis that scientific objectivity and economic rationality in regulatory decision-making will restore administrative legitimacy." And one of the hopes was that this increased legitimacy would "reduce the level of unnecessary conflict surrounding regulatory and administrative processes."[16] Thus, like the EIS, part of the political appeal of cost-benefit analysis lies in the ability of beleaguered administrators to use it to legitimate their decisions.

However, this legitimation strategy has been only partially successful. With the increasing use of cost-benefit analysis by administrators there also has come increasing criticism by environmentalists and others who see serious technical, political, moral, and philosophical flaws in this decision technique. On the technical level, there are great difficulties in trying to put a price on all impacts of a policy — especially impacts for which there are no markets, as is usually the case with the social and environmental impacts of policy decisions. One result of this is a tendency to underestimate or ignore the environmental benefits of regulations. That which is intangible or unquantifiable is assumed to be unimportant. This was the case in the Reagan administration's approach to acid rain control. A great deal of effort was put into calculating the costs of acid rain control mechanisms (scrubbers, coal washing, etc.), but little effort was made to price the environmental benefits of those controls. Indeed, administration officials at the National Acid Precipitation Assessment Program canceled their only research project designed to assess the economic benefits of acid rain controls in June of 1987, citing substantial scientific uncertainties and an inability to quantify the damaging effects of acid deposition.[17]

Diligent analysts are always devising new strategies to put "shadow prices" on non-market impacts — a current favorite being the "willingness to pay" approach.[18] This is often seen as a way around the inherent bias against these elusive factors, but as critics have pointed out, "the accuracy of any given shadow price is almost always open to question."[19] Moreover, there are usually several competing ways to calculate these prices. For instance, there are now numerous techniques to calculate the value of human life — but they assume or produce different values. And since there seem few rational ways to choose between these various techniques, the value chosen is ultimately arbitrary, thus undermining the supposed objectivity and precision of the technique.[20]

The problem here is not simply that this technique is imprecise, but that imprecision allows the technique to be manipulated for political purposes. By manipulating analytic assumptions, analysts can easily devise cost-benefit reports that simply rationalize decisions made on other grounds. And indeed, this is one of the most common complaints about this technique.[21] The authors of one textbook on environmental law have observed that "agencies often engage in extremely slipshod cost-benefit analysis of their proposals, frequently biasing their results in favor of their projected course of action."[22] One of the easiest and most common ways to predetermine the conclusion of a cost-benefit report is to manipulate the discount rate — the figure used to calculate the worth of benefits and costs that occur in the future. The figure chosen for the discount rate can often be the most decisive factor in determining whether the benefits of a project outweigh the costs. The fact that there are multiple rationales for choosing a discount rate means that there is ample opportunity for outside considerations and biases to enter into the analysis.[23]

But the criticisms of cost-benefit analysis go far beyond the charge that it is imprecise or that it can be manipulated for political purposes. Some critics argue that even when it is used correctly and "objectively", it is based on a set of questionable moral and political assumptions. One common complaint is that the technique is anti-democratic — that instead of increasing public participation in environmental decision-making (as is the case with the EIS), cost-benefit analysis can serve to decrease it. John Byrne has contended that the cost-benefit approach not only fails to require public participation in decision-making, but may actually view that participation as undesirable because people may contaminate the objectivity of the process with their "subjective assessments of their idiosyncratic circumstances."[24] And indeed, one finds some supporters of cost-benefit analysis arguing that one major advantage of the approach is that it gets rid of the need for full public discussion and public consent to policy decisions. As Herman Leonard and Richard Zeckhauser have stated: "We believe that the benefit-cost criterion is a useful way of defining 'hypothetical consent' for centralized decisions affecting individuals with widely divergent interests: hypothetically, if compensation could be paid, all would agree to the decision offering the highest net benefits."[25] Thus it is with some reason that Byrne concludes that cost-benefit analysis "calls for the abandonment of rule by consent in favor of the rule of reason.... The replacement of consent with reason as the foundation of governance is intended to dispense with the inefficiency and irrationality of politics, but in fact it dispenses with democracy in favor of the administrative state."[26]

Of course, defenders of cost-benefit analysis argue that their technique is in fact very democratic — that its values are those of the public, expressed through their private choices in the market place. They believe that the use of market prices or the "willingness to pay" criterion are the best ways to gauge public opinion about the cost and benefits of policies and their ultimate desirability. There are, however, several problems with this line of argument. First, as mentioned above, many important impacts fall outside the marketplace and the shadow prices chosen may represent more the values of the analysts than those of the public. Second, one can seriously question the democratic nature of the market itself. The market is often compared to an election where people "vote" with their dollars. But it is an odd election where some consumers (the well-off) have many more votes (dollars) to express their preferences than others. In the market, then, there is a kind of economic ballot-box stuffing that results in some people's preferences being expressed more strongly than others — a situation that hardly seems fair or democratic.[27] Third, and perhaps most telling, there is reason to believe that the choices made by people as private consumers in the marketplace may be quite different, and less thoughtful, than the choices they make as political actors. As Mark Sagoff observes: "Not all of us think of ourselves simply as *consumers*. Many of us regard ourselves as *citizens* as well. We act as consumers to get what we want *for ourselves*. But we act as citizens to achieve what we think is right or best *for the community*."[28] And these two choices may often differ. As an individual, for example, I may sometimes choose to speed on the highway, but as a citizen I want the police to enforce the speed limit. Or to use an environmentally related problem, as a consumer I prefer the convenience of throw-away bottles, but as a voter I supported a referendum to outlaw them and mandate recycling. In short, the values embodied in private consumption behavior (and codified in the market and cost-benefit analysis) may be quite different than those arrived at through public debate and decision-making. In areas like environmental policy where the long term public interest may differ significantly from our short-term individual desires, it may be better to put our trust in people as citizens interacting in the political process than in people as consumers expressing their current individual preferences.

Finally, cost-benefit analysis can be criticized on ethical grounds. Most of these criticisms begin by pointing out that this technique is nothing more than an updated and quantified version of utilitarianism, and that while economists seem oblivious to the inherent problems of this kind of ethical system, moral philosophers have long been aware of its many pitfalls.[29] For example, like utilitarianism, cost-benefit analysis can easily foster distributional injustice; that is, it can sanction policies where the costs fall disproportionately on one group and the benefits on another. This is the case in nuclear power plants where those living close by must bear most of the risks while others enjoy the benefits of the electricity.[30] More importantly, one can also question the basic ethical logic underlying cost-benefit analysis itself — the utilitarian assumption that a project is desirable if the benefits outweigh the costs. As Steven Kelman has pointed out, even when benefits outweigh costs, other ethical considerations may lead us to conclude that an activity is wrong or undesirable.[31] For example, most of us would still consider rape to be ethically unacceptable even if it could be demonstrated that the pleasures of the rapist were considerably greater than the pain of the victim. Likewise, most of us would hesitate to apply cost-benefit criteria to the rights of free speech or freedom of religion. In other words, there are areas of policy delineated by rights and other ethical considerations that make a cost-benefit approach inappropriate. Kelman explicitly concludes that "in areas of environmental, safety, and health regulation, there may be many instances where a certain decision may be right even though its benefits do not outweigh its costs."[32]

As the foregoing discussion demonstrates, critics of cost-benefit analysis have shown that this technique is riddled with numerous flaws and biases. But what critics sometimes fail to appreciate is that merely demonstrating the presence of such deficiencies may do little to curb the use of this technique. Cost-benefit analysis prospered in the U.S. during the 1980s not because politicians and administrators were unaware of its flaws, but precisely because they were very aware of its flaws and how they could be used to help delegitimate and reverse the push for environmental regulation. The tendency of cost-benefit analysis to be arbitrary, to routinely underestimate the environmental benefits of regulation, and to discourage public participation may be exactly what made it appealing to those in the Reagan administration interested in promoting a pro-growth/anti-environmental policy agenda. Thus, as long as conservative economic interests remain in the dominant position of power, then it is likely that cost-benefit analysis will continue to be pushed as the environmental decision-making tool of choice.

Environmental Dispute Resolution

The new kid on the block in environmental decision-making is a process known as environmental dispute resolution, an approach that began to come into its own in the 1980s and which many proponents believe will have a major impact in the 1990s. Broadly speaking, environmental dispute resolution is an effort to use face-to-face negotiations and consensus building to resolve disputes over environmental issues.[33] Usually a neutral mediator brings together the various interests involved in a dispute (businessmen, environmentalists, citizens, government officials) and attempts to fashion a compromise upon which everyone can agree. Originally, this approach was used mostly on an ad hoc basis to address local or regional environmental disputes involving such things as mine reclamation, flood control projects, parks, or hazardous waste facility siting. More recently, a new form of environmental dispute resolution has emerged — regulatory negotiation (reg-neg). This is an attempt to introduce mediated negotiation sessions as part of the formal regulation-setting process in U.S. federal bureaucracies.[34] Because reg-neg is closely tied to administrative decision-making, it will be the primary focus here; but as will become clear, many of the arguments surrounding this technique apply to the more ad-hoc forms of environmental dispute resolution as well.[35]

In regulatory negotiation, instead of agency personnel developing a regulation on their own, the agency convenes a series of meetings with representatives of groups interested in the regulation. These meetings are often run by an independent mediator and their aim is to produce a consensus about the proposed rule or regulation. The consensus recommendation is then used by the agency as the basis for formulating the final regulation. The process then follows normal procedures, with the regulation being published, the agency accepting comments and holding public hearings, until the final regulation is issued. In the last few years, there have been a number of experimental reg-neg efforts within the EPA, and a piece of legislation authorizing the widespread use of this technique seems destined for approval by Congress in the near future.[36]

Regulatory negotiation differs in significant ways from the other approaches we have considered here. Most importantly, reg-neg is not a method of analysis, but rather a political procedure. Among other things, this means that its claims to legitimacy and effectiveness rest on very different grounds from the other two techniques. Its legitimacy rests not on claims to be scientifically or economically rational, but on claims to be procedurally neutral and democratic. Reg-neg assumes that if all affected parties agree on an environmental rule, then that rule is a legitimate and desirable one. This is essentially similar to the pluralist claim that if the policy-making procedure is fair and democratic, then whatever policy is produced is by definition a good one.

As with the other two techniques, it is this claim to legitimize administrative decisions that constitutes much of the appeal of reg-neg. Indeed, proponents of this approach point out that one of the main goals of reg-neg is to increase public acceptance of administrative decisions and to forestall potential court challenges.[37] This may be particularly advantageous in the case of environmental regulations, which seem to be constantly challenged in court either by environmentalists or by business. Of course, the idea of using participation to increase the legitimacy of administrative decisions is hardly entirely new with reg-neg. Comment periods and public hearings have long been used to give the aura of democracy and public participation. But it has also been long known that this kind of participation is largely symbolic and ineffective. Public hearings, for example, usually come too late in the process to have any real effect. Administrators have made up their minds about a rule at that point and are unlikely to change their approach in any significant way.

Regulatory negotiation, however, may be a step toward more genuine participation in the rulemaking process — largely because it takes place in the crucial early stages of that process, presumably before agency personnel have come to any firm conclusions. This could be particularly important for environmental groups. During the Reagan era, environmental groups had little, if any, input in the early stages of rulemaking at the EPA or Department of Interior. However, these agencies would routinely discuss proposed rules with corporations and business organizations.[38] While this kind of one-sided participation seemed particularly common in the Reagan administration, it is merely an extreme example of the problem of "capture" that afflicts most administrative agencies. As John Chubb has pointed out, one of the factors that contributes to the capture of federal bureaucracies by business lobbies is the lobbyist's constant informal contacts with agency personnel.[39] These contacts (which in some cases take place daily) give these lobbies early warning about proposed rules and regulations and provide the opportunity to shape the regulatory agenda early on in the process. It may be that reg-neg could work to undermine the one-sidedness of this capture process.[40] Because it attempts to include all interested groups — including environmentalists — reg-neg may provide a more equal opportunity for early influence.

But the political impacts of regulatory negotiation may not all be advantageous to environmentalists or the environment. To see why this might be the case, it is useful to examine the forces that brought environmental dispute resolution into being in the first place and which support it today. This approach had its origins in dissatisfactions with the confrontational style of politics employed by many environmentalists in the 1970s. Proponents of dispute resolution felt that the tactics of citizen activism and litigation had outlived their usefulness and were now simply creating useless stalemates that were impeding progress. They believed that one could find a "middle ground" between business interests and environmentalists that would not interfere with needed economic growth.[41] Not surprisingly, many elements in the business community were attracted to this idea and were among the earliest financial backers of this process.[42] They were naturally interested in a technique that could blunt environmental advocacy and distract environmentalists from the courtroom, the scene of many environmental victories in the 1970s. In this sense, the emergence of environmental dispute resolution in the early 1980s fit in quite well with what Samuel Hays has described as the business campaign to "neutralize" environmental activism:

> The idea of environmental mediation was strongly supported by the business community, as well it might be…. Its initial point of departure often was a focus on the litigation citizen environmentalists had generated, which was described as excessive. The atmosphere around environmental mediation continued to be one of criticism of citizen action rather than of the business community. On the whole it helped to bolster the corporate drive to discredit public environmental initiatives.[43]

It should be added that the philosophical and ethical assumptions underlying dispute resolution also had a great appeal to the business community. Particularly appealing was the assumption that there are no "right" or "wrong" sides in environmental disputes — that each side has interests that are equally valid and therefore some middle-ground compromise is the most desirable solution to a conflict. Naturally, environmentalists were suspicious of a process which automatically took away the moral stigma associated with polluting or destroying irreplaceable ecosystems. They viewed pollution as being wrong—not as merely an equally valid interest that must be respected. Moreover, if pollution is the problem and environmental regulation is the solution, then the predisposition for compromise contained in dispute resolution might only ensure that the problem will not be fully addressed.[44]

In the case of regulatory negotiation, some observers worry that the presumption of equally valid interests and the desirability of compromise may change the political role of environmental agencies. Many environmentalists believe that U.S. federal agencies such as the EPA and Interior Department should act as vigorous advocates for environmental values. In reg-neg, however, there is a tendency for the agency to act more as broker than as advocate. The agency may adopt a position of neutrality—favoring neither environmentalists nor business. Some environmentalists believe that this approach is not desirable and may result in weaker environmental regulations than might have come out of an agency acting more forcefully and independently. In this sense, it may not be a coincidence that reg-neg has been promoted by some elements within the Reagan administration. If this new process encourages environmental agencies to relinquish their traditional advocacy role, then it would fit in quite well with a neo-conservative inclination to the view that economic growth can be unshackled by reducing environmental regulation.

There are other environmental concerns as well regarding this new process. In particular, there is a concern that the unequal resources possessed by the various groups taking part in reg-neg efforts will in itself undermine the potential fairness and neutrality of the process—the very qualities that proponents celebrate. First of all, this inequality may limit who can take part in these efforts. Reg-neg can be a time-consuming and expensive process. It is very labor intensive, involving much by way of meetings, travel, and research. Some well-funded groups, especially business lobbies, would have little difficulty meeting these expenses. But many citizen and environmental groups may find these expenses very problematic and may for this reason be unable to participate in the negotiation sessions. Thus while reg-neg may open the door to early public participation in the regulatory process, not all groups may be able to afford to walk through that door.

In addition, even those environmental groups which can participate in reg-neg efforts will find that their relative lack of resources will put them at a disadvantage at the bargaining table. Groups like the Natural Resources Defense Council can rarely afford to devote the time of more than one staff attorney to a particular regulatory issue; in contrast, business groups often have a large and well-financed in-house staff for these efforts. Moreover, the economic resources of the business lobbies allow them to hire many outside experts and fund various kinds of analyses and studies that can be used to bolster their case at the bargaining table. In the administrative process, information is power, and it is business that usually wields this power most effectively in negotiation sessions.[45] Although regulatory negotiation cloaks itself in procedural neutrality—just as cost-benefit analysis cloaks itself in scientific neutrality—it may thus only reproduce the power inequalities that already exist in the outside political world.[46]

What is the likely future of regulatory negotiation? Will it become a major approach to environmental rulemaking in the 1990s? Chances of this seem dim, for several reasons. First, as many observers of this process have pointed out, reg-neg is only likely to produce consensus in certain kinds of situations. Among the conditions mentioned are: (1) the regulatory issue must involve no basic disagreement over basic values or principles; (2) there should be no legal precedents or fundamental policy issues at stake; (3) there should be substantial agreement among the parties as to the relevant facts of the case; (4) there should be only a small number of interests and affected parties involved; and (5) none of the parties should be able to benefit from delay or stalemate. But how many regulatory disputes would be characterized by these kinds of conditions? One could imagine a few. For example, reg-neg could be quite appropriate where there was already agreement between environmentalists and business about the basic goals of a given regulation and disagreement only on details, such as the timetable for implementation, the exact levels of pollution to be allowed, and so on. But how many regulatory disputes are of this nature? Indeed, most regulatory disputes become disputes precisely because they *do* involve basic disagreements over values and policies, substantial disagreement over the facts of the case, and numerous and varied affected parties. For these reasons, environmentalists like David Doniger of the Natural Resources Defense Council believe that this technique is only "good for a small class of cases."[47]

The second factor likely to limit the use of reg-neg is ambivalence on the part of many of the groups which would participate. Environmental groups have been slow to jump on the reg-neg bandwagon. As we have seen, this process has the potential to either help or hinder the interests of environmentalists, depending on the circumstances and character of its use. Thus it is not surprising that most environmentalists have approached it with suspicion and wariness.[48] There is also some reluctance on the part of career administrators to embrace this new process. Undoubtedly some welcome an approach that promises to divert political and legal challenges to agency decisions. But it is also clear that many administrators are content to continue making regulatory policy in the traditional manner.[49] And it would be natural for administrators to dislike sharing their power with outside participants and to resent the inclusion of yet another procedural requirement in the decision-making process. It is likely, then, that reg-neg will encounter administrative foot-dragging—in contrast to cost-benefit analysis, which fits well with most agencies' standard operating procedures and usually reinforces the power of administrators.

Whether administrative decision-making techniques prosper is, as noted, fundamentally a question of power. Regulatory negotiation has come this far largely because of its support from the business community and the energetic (though somewhat self-serving) lobbying of mediators and dispute resolution professionals. What remains unclear at this point is whether this will form a sufficient power base to ensure the widespread use of reg-neg in the U.S. federal bureaucracy in the 1990s.

Conclusion

The rise of environmental decision-making techniques in the 1970s coincided with the shift in the focus of environmental concerns from legislative to administrative bodies. As Samuel Hays has pointed out, it also coincided with the emergence of a community of environmental professionals who believed that neutral analytic techniques and planning skills were the preferred alternative to politics in the management of environmental concerns.[50] But as we've seen, the hope that decision-making techniques can escape from politics has been a false one, in several ways. First, these techniques usually have flaws and biases that render them far from neutral. Second, the choice of which techniques come to be used and exactly how they are used is a political matter, largely determined by how those techniques serve powerful political and economic interests both inside and outside environmental agencies. The primary lesson to be derived from all of this is that those concerned about the environment should not put too much faith in new decision techniques. The fate of the environment depends much more on such things as the pressures generated by our economic system and on which interests wield the most power in the policy-making system. Better environmental decision-making techniques, while a necessary step toward the most effective possible protection of our environment, are largely useless unless the distribution of power in society ensures that these techniques will be utilized properly in both the public and the private sectors.

Notes

1. Gladwin Hill, "Environmental Impact Statements, Practically a Revolution," *New York Times* (December 5, 1976), IV, p. 14.

2. G. F. White, "Environmental Impact Statements," *Professional Geographer* 24 (1972), pp. 302-309.

3. D. W. Schindler, "The Impact Statement Boondoggle," *Science* 192 (1976), p. 509.

4. Hill, p. 14.

5. Allan Schnaiberg, *The Environment: From Surplus to Scarcity* (New York: Oxford University Press, 1980), p. 319.

6. See Sally Fairfax, "A Disaster in the Environmental Movement," *Science* 199 (1978) p. 745.

7. H. P. Friesema and P. J. Culhane, "Social Impacts, Politics, and the Environmental Impact Statement Process," *Natural Resources Journal* 16 (1976), pp. 340-341.

8. Schindler, p. 509.

9. Fairfax, p. 747.

10. One example of how useful and insightful the EIS process can be when it is used in a diligent and creative way is the Mackenzie Valley Pipeline Inquiry headed by Mr. Justice Thomas R. Berger. See D. J. Gamble, "The Berger Inquiry: An Impact Assessment Process," *Science* 199 (1978), pp. 946-952.

11. For a good description of this technique and its uses, see E. J. Mishan, *Cost-Benefit Analysis* (New York: Praeger, 1976).

12. Thomas Byrne Edsall, *The New Politics of Inequality* (New York: W. W. Norton and Co., 1984), see esp. ch. 3.

13. For more on conservative approaches to policy analysis, see Frank Fischer, "Policy Expertise and the 'New Class': A Critique of the Neoconservative Thesis," in Frank Fischer and John Forester, eds., *Confronting Values in Policy Analysis* (Beverly Hills: Sage Publications, 1987), pp. 94-126.

14. For an insightful examination of the use of cost-benefit analysis in the cotton dust case, see Susan Tolchin and Martin Tolchin, *Dismantling America* (New York: Houghton Mifflin, 1983), ch. 4.

15. Robert C. Zinke, "Cost-Benefit Analysis and Administrative Legitimation," *Policy Studies Journal* 16 (1987), p. 63.

16. Zinke, pp. 63, 65.

17. See *New York Times* (June 9, 1987), p. A27.

18. For a good description of shadow pricing and the willingness to pay approach, see Peter G. Sassone and William A. Schaffer, *Cost-Benefit Analysis: A Handbook* (New York: Academic Press, 1978), ch. 5.

19. Peter Wenz, *Environmental Justice* (Albany: State University of New York Press, 1988), p. 221.

20. For more on this point, see Alasdair MacIntyre, "Utilitarianism and Cost/Benefit Analysis: An Essay on the Relevance of Moral Philosophy to Bureaucratic Theory," in Tom L. Beauchamp and Norman Bowie, eds., *Ethical Theory and Business* (Englewood Cliffs N.J.: Prentice-Hall,

1979), pp. 266-275.

21. Zinke, p. 72.

22. Roger Findley and Daniel Farber, *Environmental Law in a Nutshell* (St. Paul: West Publishing, 2nd ed., 1988), p. 50.

23. See Arnold J. Meltsner, *Policy Analysts in the Bureaucracy* (Berkeley: University of California Press, 1976), pp. 146-150.

24. John Byrne, "A Critique of Beauchamp and Braybrooke-Schotch" in Norman Bowie, ed., *Ethical Issues in Government* (Philadelphia: Temple University Press, 1981), pp. 202-205. See also, John Byrne, "Policy Science and the Administrative State: The Political Economy of Cost-Benefit Analysis," in Fischer and Forester, pp. 70-93.

25. Cited in Zinke, p. 67.

26. Byrne, 1981, pp. 204-205.

27. Wenz, p. 217.

28. Mark Sagoff, "At the Shrine of Our Lady of Fatima, or Why Political Questions Are Not All Economic," in Donald Scherer and Thomas Attig, eds., *Ethics and the Environment* (Englewood Cliffs, NJ: Prentice-Hall, 1983), p. 223.

29. See, *e.g.*, Wenz, chs. 8-10.

30. For more on the debate over cost-benefit analysis and distribution justice, see Wenz, pp. 215-219.

31. Steven Kelman, "Cost-Benefit Analysis: An Ethical Critique," *Regulation* 5 (1981), pp. 33-36.

32. *Ibid.*, p. 33.

33. For a good overview of this approach by a leading proponent, see Gail Bingham, *Resolving Environmental Disputes: A Decade of Experience* (Washington, D.C.: The Conservation Foundation, 1986).

34. For a good overview of this process and the case made for it, see Lawrence Susskind and Gerard McMahon, "The Theory and Practice of Negotiated Rulemaking," *Yale Journal of Regulation* 3 (1985), pp. 133-165.

35. For a more lengthy discussion of the various advantages and disadvantages of environmental dispute resolution, see Douglas J. Amy, *The Politics of Environmental Mediation* (New York: Columbia University Press, 1987).

36. See S. 1504, *Negotiated Rulemaking Act of 1988*, which was passed by the U.S. Senate in 1988.

37. See Rochelle L. Stanfield, "Resolving Disputes," *National Journal* (November 11, 1986), p. 2765.

38. See Jonathan Lash *et al.*, *A Season of Spoils* (New York: Pantheon Books, 1984).

39. John Chubb, *Interest Groups and the Bureaucracy* (Stanford: Stanford University Press, 1983), see esp. chs. 4 and 5.

40. It should be noted that informal contacts are not the sole cause of capture. Capture is a complex process with a variety of causes. See, for instance, Theodore Lowi's classic treatment of this problem in *The End of Liberalism* (New York: W. W. Norton, 2nd ed., 1979). Thus even if the process of informal contacts were made more "fair" by reg-neg, it is doubtful if this reform would eliminate the problem.

41. See Samuel P. Hays, *Beauty, Health, and Permanence: Environmental Politics in the United States, 1955-1985* (New York: Cambridge University Press, 1987), pp. 408-419.

42. See Amy, p. 98.

43. Hays, p. 417.

44. For more on the problem of compromise in environmental disputes, see Amy, ch. 6.

45. For more on power inequities in environmental dispute resolution, see *ibid.*, ch. 5.

46. These problems linked to financial inequities may not be intractable. A bill authorizing regulatory negotiation that is currently working its way through the U.S. Congress (S. 1504, *Negotiated Rulemaking Act of 1988)* contains a provision for the establishment of a fund that would enable groups that could prove financial need to participate in the process and to hire technical consultants.

47. See Doniger's comments in *Dispute Resolution Forum* (January 1986), pp. 10-11. Doniger also worries that over-eager mediators may push to use reg-neg on unsuitable issues.

48. See, *e.g.*, Doniger, pp. 8-11.

49. See Julia M. Wondolleck, "Resolving Forest Management Planning Disputes: Obstacles and Opportunities," *Resolve* 20 (1988), p. 11.

50. Hays, ch. 12.

ECOLOGICAL REASON
IN ADMINISTRATION:
ENVIRONMENTAL IMPACT ASSESSMENT
AND ADMINISTRATIVE THEORY

Robert V. Bartlett

All thinking worthy of the name must now be ecological, in the sense of appreciating and utilizing organic complexity, and in adapting every kind of change to the requirements not of man alone, or of any single generation, but of all his organic partners and every part of his habitat.[1]

Administrative Theory and the Environmental Problematique

Current administrative institutions are in no way adequate to the challenge presented by the modern environmental predicament. Still, accepting the administrative state as a permanent feature of the political landscape means accepting that, if environmental problems are to be solved, they must be solved in major part administratively — through more, different, somehow better administration. This is the point of departure for a majority of environmental reformers and policy analysts, who worry little about the fundamental structure of their political world. Yet deeper analysis of the capabilities of bureaucratic organizations and administratively dominated systems, both governmental and nongovernmental, leads other theorists to raise troubling questions about the real possibilities of effective environmental *administration*.

These concerns arise less from the myths of the tyranny or the incompetence of the bureaucrat than from a realization of the significance of a partial congruence between the underlying causes of environmental degradation and the underlying imperatives of large, modern, administrative organizations. The environmental problematique has, without question, given rise to an institutional crisis. And the converse is true as well: every identifiable primary and proximate cause of contemporary environmental degradation can be linked in myriad ways to the seemingly inherent ecological deficiencies, or pathologies, of the administrative state.

Thus the administrative state presents an unhappy conundrum for theorists of environmental politics. To accept the administrative state largely as it is is to accept severe limits on the structuring of the environmental problematique for analysis—limits so severe as possibly to exclude any truly attractive solutions. The risk always is one of treating symptoms, a strategy that may complicate and even prevent timely diagnosis and treatment of causes. Energies may be focused instead on critiques of the administrative state itself, analyses of improbable alternatives, and normative arguments for wholesale social and political restructuring. The risk here is that of irrelevancy, in both the action world of politics and the theoretical world of scholarship.

Indeed, the dilemma may have no satisfactory solution, although few, including me, would be willing to admit as much. Perhaps, then, more attention ought to focus on possible strategies that neither accept the administrative state for what it is nor require its dismantling before a replacement is erected. The "creative third alternatives" that may hold the most promise, for both action and analysis, are what might be called either "subversive" or "worm in the brain" strategies.[2] Such strategies involve dismantling or transmogrifying the administrative state from within—gradually and not entirely predictably—while remaking individual values and patterns of thinking and acting and, perhaps, while promoting "the preconditions for more substantial institutional innovation."[3] I argue that mandatory environmental impact assessment may often be, in potential and in realization, a policy strategy of this kind.[4]

Although impact assessment is one of the major innovations in policy making and administration of the twentieth century, so far it has received little attention from political or policy theorists, who have tended to underestimate and misread its power, complexity, and subtlety.[5] As "feed-forward" mechanisms, several variants of impact assessment such as technology assessment and social impact assessment are significant for environmental politics.[6] As a way of forcing explicit consideration to environmental concern, of course, the impact assessment approach that is of most interest is environmental impact assessment (EIA).

EIA is centrally important, not only because of its obvious relevance but also because, unlike other forms of impact assessment, its underlying logic is anchored in a distinctive rationality, namely ecological rationality.[7] On the surface, EIA, like other forms of impact assessment, appears as a straightforward strategy that seeks to mitigate the destructive potential of industrial society, to ameliorate impact by basing action on greater and more widespread knowledge, and, thus, to enhance the ordinary rationality of policy and decision.[8] But by requiring, fostering, and reinforcing ecological rationality, both inside and outside of government, environmental impact assessment may well be subversive of the traditional administrative state. If so, it may have a far greater significance for environmental politics than heretofore has been recognized.

Ecological Rationality and the Administrative State

Ecological rationality is a rationality "of living systems, an order of relationships among living systems and their environments."[9] As such, ecological rationality is a form of practical reason that can be distinguished from other prominent forms, such as technical, economic, social, legal, and political rationality.[10] Technical rationality seeks efficient achievement of a single goal. Economic rationality entails the maximum achievement of a plurality of goals. Underlying technical rationality and economic rationality is the principle of efficiency; both are based on an order of measurement, comparison of values, and production. Social rationality seeks integration in social relations and social systems, an ordered social interdependence that makes social action possible and meaningful. Legal rationality refers to the reason inherent in any clear, consistent, and detailed system of formal rules for preventing disputes and providing solutions. Political rationality is a rationality of decision making structures, of a practical intelligence capability for solving problems facing a society. Its principle of order is that of facilitating arrival at effective collective decisions.

All of these forms of reason are relevant to an analysis of politics in the administrative state. The narrowly instrumental character of administration and administrative organizations makes technical and economic rationalities dominant; indeed, the dominance of these rationalities is the defining feature of modern industrial societies.[11] The concept of rationality itself in such societies is often identified exclusively as technological and economic rationality. As Max Weber was only the first to argue, the growth and spread of bureaucracy is explained by its inherent instrumental rationality — in other words, its peculiar legal and political rationality enhances its technical and economic rationality. Many post-Weberian critiques of bureaucracy focus on the pathologies or dysfunctions deriving from its flawed social rationality.[12] And the administrative state exists in and must make use of a nonsocial environment with which it must be at least minimally compatible. The ecological rationality of any social system, over the long run, must substantially coincide with the ecological rationality of its supporting physical environment.

The various forms of rationality are at least partly incompatible, and they may fundamentally conflict.[13] Nor are they all of the same order of importance. According to Paul Diesing (who did not explicitly consider ecological rationality), political rationality has precedence over other forms "because the solution of political problems makes possible an attack on any other problem while a serious political deficiency can prevent or undo all other problem solving."[14] John Dryzek argues persuasively, however, that ecological rationality is a still more fundamental kind of reason: "The preservation and promotion of the integrity of the ecological and material underpinning of society — ecological rationality — should take priority over competing forms of reason in collective choices with an impact upon that integrity."[15] The priority of ecological rationality, according to Dryzek, is lexical. That is, it has absolute priority over other forms of reason because long term, serious conflict between ecological rationality and other forms of rationality will result in the elimination of the other forms. This notwithstanding, ecological rationality does not fully preempt or supplant other forms of rationality: rarely is it completely determinative and it has little relevance to many dimensions of human activity.[16]

Each of these forms of reason can be reflected at three different levels of rationality: functional, substantive, and procedural. Functional rationality is the rationality inherent in the functioning of systems, societies, or organizations. The functional rationality of a system is the degree to which system behavior is organized according to particular principles and can be understood by reference to principles of order.[17] Functional rationality does not necessarily imply that a system is engaged in the process of thinking or reasoning. Nor does it imply that the principles underlying a given functional rationality must be known by any individual person — only that they be knowable.

Substantive rationality applies to individual decisions or actions.[18] It is an attribute of the behavior itself and refers to whether behavior is "appropriate to the achievement of given goals within the limits imposed by given conditions and constraints."[19] Substantive rationality is a standard for judging and labeling behavior — a behavior is substantively rational if it is appropriate or correct (if it *appears* to be rational).

Procedural rationality, in turn, refers to the actual processes of reasoning, the cognitive procedures used to choose actions.[20] It describes an intelligent system's ability to discover appropriate adaptive behavior.[21] Rationality in this sense is not an attribute of an action or behavior but an attribute of a deliberative, intellective process — synonymous with the common sense use of the term "reasoning".

The relationships among functional, substantive, and procedural rationality are problematic. Some individual actions may be nonrational (substantively) in the context of a society or organization that is highly rational (functionally). That is, even though some behaviors of some individuals cannot be labeled rational — they are not appropriate to the achievement of the individual's goals within the limits of conditions and constraints — the social system of which these individuals are a part may still exhibit a high degree of functional rationality. A functionally rational economy, for example, may in large part be based on predictable nonrational behavior by individuals. Likewise, individual behaviors may be rational (substantively) even though no reasoning (procedural) was employed by the individual in choosing the behaviors. And, as mentioned earlier, a system may be rational (functionally) without any individual understanding (procedural rationality) its principles of order.

Linkages among these levels of rationality can be found, although they are not all fixed and they seem to be in one direction only. Functional ecological rationality does not require substantive ecological rationality, but substantive ecological rationality across all individual behaviors should almost always result in functional ecological rationality.[22] Likewise, substantive ecological rationality does not require procedural ecological rationality, but the probability that behaviors will be substantively rational is always greater to the extent that humans and human systems reason ecologically before acting.

Linkages among functional, substantive, and procedural rationality are especially important in relating ecological rationality to the environmental predicament of the administrative state. The ultimate concern, of course, is with functional ecological rationality. Does a social system or organization, or do such systems collectively, exhibit ecological rationality? That is, is behavior organized according to ecological principles of order?[23]

Remember, it is not *necessary* that ecological principles be understood, or even that reasoning occur, to achieve functional ecological rationality. Ecosystems completely devoid of humans have somehow managed. And the only known examples of functionally rational human societies have been certain traditional cultures lacking formal scientific understanding of ecological relationships.[24] Each and every action or behavior need not be ecologically rational either—the functional ecological significance of individual behaviors depends on the homeostatic and adaptive capabilities of particular ecosystems and the consequences of exceeding those capabilities. Traditional human societies tended to exhibit functional ecological rationality because those societies that failed to do so did not long survive—the punishment for ecological unreasonableness imposed, sooner or later, by an indifferent universe.

Thus functional ecological rationality may provide an indispensable standard for evaluating human systems, but alone it provides rather weak guidance for action. For humans, trial and error is a less-than-desirable approach to design when choices are irreversible and errors are extraordinarily costly. The only other routes to functional ecological rationality may be through substantive and procedural ecological rationality.

The problem is one of meta-design and meta-policy. John Dryzek has thoroughly analyzed and evaluated seven major existing social choice mechanisms—markets, administered systems, law, moral persuasion, polyarchy, bargaining, and armed conflict—according to a functional ecological rationality standard. His standard comprises five criteria: negative feedback, coordination, flexibility, robustness, and resilience.[25] His assessment of these major social choice mechanisms is at best mixed: "Any 'winner' among the seven types of social choice would, then, be little more than the best of a poor bunch."[26]

The design problem Dryzek clearly spells out is one of identifying forms of social choice (1) that will perform better than existing institutions with respect to the functional ecological rationality standard and (2) that facilitate their own critical examination and, if necessary, modification and supersession. Dryzek finds only a very limited number of alternatives that meet these conditions. His agenda for institutional reconstruction includes only local autonomy, self-sufficiency, and radically reducing or eliminating hierarchy, thus to facilitate collective decision making through discussion — "practical reason" — and limited bargaining.

Whatever the merits and ultimate political feasibility of his "broad strokes" set of proposals (space limitations preclude a detailed critique), Dryzek is not specific about how to get from here to there (although, to his credit, he does acknowledge the problem). The difficulty is that existing, ecologically irrational social choice mechanisms will not just fade away:

> Any piecemeal introduction of innovative forms of social choice into a world of ecologically irrational mechanisms is perilous. For example, markets "imprison" governmental social choice; a legal system formalizes social interactions beyond its bounds; and the existence of administrative prerogatives and polyarchical imperatives can undermine discursive innovations.... Systems have a remarkable capacity to frustrate structural change....[They] therefore compound their ecological irrationality by securing their own perpetuation.[27]

If the necessary preconditions for institutional redesign do not reside in existing social choice mechanisms, how can a process of institutional innovation ever be initiated, and what hope is there that it would be allowed to proceed to fruition? Dryzek is uncertain.[28] His answer is to call for piecemeal introduction of alternative social choice mechanisms that may "promote the preconditions for more substantial innovation," even though such piecemeal innovation likely would be completely frustrated, given his argument.

Dryzek does not discuss piecemeal modification of, or tinkering with, the seven major existing social choice mechanisms, only their replacement. He dismisses as implausible the possibility that ecological rationality in social choice could be achieved by some combination of the seven mechanisms; all actively obstruct ecological rationality in some degree and all tend to displace rather than to resolve ecological problems. Moreover, he argues, exhaustive evaluation of all possible combinations would be impractical.[29]

His objections to the consideration of combinations of social choice mechanisms are not fatal. Evaluation need not be exhaustive to be fruitful. The potential for productive experimentation with existing mechanisms increases as our understanding of them increases. Experimentation and evaluation need not be limited to particular combinations, but might entail creatively tinkering with the imperatives of a given mechanism or grafting onto it entirely new but compatible mechanisms. In addition to marginally enhancing functional ecological rationality, such tinkering might also promote "the preconditions for more substantial institutional innovation," thus complying with Dryzek's two major design criteria.

Nor must the design and evaluation of alternative mechanisms be haphazard and unguided. As noted earlier, there are two routes to achieving functional ecological rationality: trial and error, or through institutionalization of substantive and procedural rationality. If the decentralized and discursive social choice structures that Dryzek recommends are ever to prevail, it will be because they turn out to be the kinds of structures that best institutionalize substantive and procedural ecological rationality *and* because predecessor mechanisms had paved the way, transforming (subverting) older established structures and mechanisms through earlier efforts to institutionalize substantive and procedural ecological rationality.

Environmental impact assessment, I argue, is perhaps the most significant example yet of such tinkering with the basic structures and mechanisms of the administrative state;[30] it represents a beachhead of ecological rationality that opens the way to further development. It certainly is not the only possible way of forcing ecological rationality into the administrative state, but it may be one of the most insidious. Indeed, there is some reason to think it may prove to be a particularly virulent kind of "worm in the brain."

Ecological Rationality Through Impact Assessment

Environmental impact assessment does not establish ecological rationality through some magic spell achieved either by technique or by incantation and ceremony. The impact of EIA on behaviors and processes is not automatic. Nor is it simple. Elsewhere I have presented the case for interpreting the U.S. National Environmental Policy Act, wherein modern EIA originated, as an experiment in institutionalizing ecological rationality in government and in a whole society.[31] NEPA does this in several ways; among others, by statutorily endorsing criteria of functional and substantive ecological rationality; by changing the legislative authorization of every federal agency; and by requiring that all federal agencies use procedural ecological reasoning in all planning and decision making. To assure the practice and political efficacy of this kind of ecologically based pre-decision assessment (EIA), NEPA mandates a justiciable disclosure document, the environmental impact statement, for all actions that would significantly affect the human environment.

EIA as established by NEPA is not an end in itself. Moreover, the logic of EIA is more sophisticated than merely that of making government more like science, or of naively legislating rational comprehensive decision making, or of enhancing rationality in the policy process through systematic generation and dissemination of knowledge.[32] Such simplistic interpretations have been common not only among the critics of EIA but among many of its advocates as well. In fact, many subsequent EIA systems at initiation have been superficially imitative programs, "based on a misreading of how the EIS [environmental impact statement] process works, and almost always on a misunderstanding of what is necessary if an impact statement system is to change agency policy."[33] Even so, there is at least a slight tendency for EIA to export its imperatives into other social choice mechanisms.[34] The twenty year history of EIA is sprinkled with stories of intendedly ineffectual EIA systems that unexpectedly have been consequential.[35]

In twenty years we have only begun to understand with some depth how and why EIA works. Serious analyses of EIA as a policy making strategy or as a mechanism for social choice have been amazingly few, even as EIA has developed, evolved, and spread to every part of the globe. There have been some impressive theoretical advances and penetrating analyses even though, as Geoffrey Wandesforde-Smith argues, "New questions about the meaning of the EIA process have always run ahead of the availability of definitive answers to earlier questions about how the process works and why it works the way it does."[36]

We know that EIA certainly can exist merely as symbolic window dressing, with little or no real influence on choice processes. It can be "frozen out" from any real policy or institutional effectiveness if it is not sufficiently linked, formally and informally, to the ways problems are defined, structured, and addressed. Because of its limited applicability and capacity, rarely does EIA have the potential to replace wholly other social choice mechanisms. But we know that EIA can be appended to, and integrated with, most other major social choice mechanisms, to some effect. The dynamics of markets can be altered, the coordinative capabilities of bargaining and mutual adjustment can be enhanced, the rigidity of law can be lessened. In spite of inherent tensions between the logic of EIA and the values of participatory democracy, most theorists find the two compatible and mutually reinforcing.[37] And EIA is most certainly good medicine for the administrative state, improving its effectiveness, increasing its coordinative capabilities, and enhancing its legitimacy while, ironically, making it less bureaucratic and less amenable to unified direction.[38]

The many possible variations of EIA systems or strategies can be (must be) tailored to particular political and cultural contexts, and as such will have differing consequences. Leonard Ortolano, Bryan Jenkins, and Ramon P. Abracosa explain the differential impact of different EIA systems by reference to six categories of formal controls.[39] Reviewing EIA in North America and Western Europe, William V. Kennedy concludes that

> EIA works best when it is instituted in a formal-explicit way. That is to say, it works when there is a specific legal requirement for its application, where an environmental impact statement is prepared, and where authorities are accountable for taking its results into consideration in decision-making.[40]

Other analysts find special significance in the ways that "formal structures can tap the powerful, informal incentives that operate inside every administrative agency, and which link it to the external world, so as to produce agencies that continuously and progressively think about environmental values."[41] Most notable in this regard is Serge Taylor's work analyzing successful EIA institutionalization as a virtually self-sustaining and self-regulating interplay of internal and external agency variables.[42] More than any other theoretical contribution to understanding EIA, Taylor establishes the potential for real advance in the comparative evaluation of impact assessment as a policy strategy. He also establishes the potential of EIA as a mechanism for social discovery of viable new political arrangements and for learning new ways of thinking about problems.

Thus, EIA can be adapted to a changing political and economic climate, and can be an active agent in changing that climate. This capacity for evolutionary policy change in a politics of EIA is further evaluated by

Wandesforde-Smith, who explores a key engine driving EIA as an adaptive, learning process: "individual entrepreneurial and strategic responses to a changing political world."[43] EIA offers opportunities and incentives for political individuals to "put their imprint on policy change by inventing and building coalitions, by making the case for change on the merits, and, above all, as Lynton Caldwell (1970) first imagined they would, by developing and affirming in EIA their environmental values."[44]

Thus, EIA can be a very powerful mechanism for influencing social choice, but not through coercion. Rather, EIA is a "catalytic" control:

> Catalytic controls require the bureaucracy to act and direct the bureaucracy towards certain goals but do not rob it of the capacity for creative problem-solving....They prod, stimulate, and provoke bureaucrats but also allow them to be both innovative and efficient.[45]

As I have argued elsewhere, the theorist or analyst who looks only for dramatic impacts or only for obvious direct effects is likely to be unimpressed.[46] Comprehending the significance and potential of EIA requires appreciation for the complexity of ways that choices are shaped, channeled, learned, reasoned, and structured before they are "officially" made. When EIA succeeds in making far-reaching modifications in the substantive outcomes of social activities, it does so by changing, formally and informally, the premises and rules for arriving at legitimate decisions.

By requiring and encouraging political actors, as individuals and as organizations, to think ecologically and to consider environmental values, EIA imbeds procedural ecological rationality in political institutions. By establishing, continuously reaffirming, and progressively legitimating environmental values and ecological criteria as standards by which individual actions are to be structured, chosen, and evaluated, EIA institutionalizes substantive ecological rationality. Although certainly not without weaknesses even as a strategy complementing other social choice mechanisms, EIA receives a positive evaluation with regard to all five of Dryzek's criteria of functional ecological rationality. It exhibits considerable potential as a device for negative feedback (as well as for "feedforward"). Its coordinative capabilities are substantial. It is modestly robust and is proving to be surprisingly flexible. Taylor's case for the resilience potential of EIA is persuasive. Moreover, unlike most other social choice mechanisms, EIA by its nature does not tend to displace rather than to confront ecological problems.

Successful EIA changes the criteria by which choices may be shaped and made. It requires consideration of particular sets of factual premises (ecological especially) and otherwise precarious values, and it demands the kinds of reasoning associated with those values and factual premises. It changes patterns of relationships among organizations and among individuals inside and outside of organizations. It creates powerful incentives, formal and informal, that thereafter force a great deal of learning and self-regulation upon individual and organizational actors. And it provides opportunities for individuals to develop and affirm environmental values and to press for innovative adaptation of structures and processes to a changing political world.

Options for extending and restructuring fundamentally the roles of EIA in various social choice arenas will remain available, and may even be adopted in foreseeable circumstances, paving the way for even more substantial, probably not yet imagined, institutional innovation. The co-evolution of politics and policy through EIA processes will likely continue nevertheless — restructuring environmental politics in the administrative state informally, subtly, and profoundly by promoting procedural and substantive ecological rationality.

Notes

I thank Walter F. Baber, Lynton K. Caldwell, John S. Dryzek, James N. Gladden, Robert Paehlke, Douglas Torgerson, and Geoffrey Wandesforde-Smith for their comments on an earlier draft of this article.

1. Lewis Mumford, *The Myth of the Machine: The Pentagon of Power* (New York: Harcourt Brace Jovanovich, 1970), p. 393.

2. Ecology is, of course, a subversive science. Paul B. Sears, "Ecology—A Subversive Subject," *BioScience* 14 (1964), pp. 11-13; Paul Shepard and Daniel McKinley, eds., *The Subversive Science: Essays Toward an Ecology of Man* (Boston: Houghton Mifflin, 1969). The worm in the brain metaphor was suggested to me by Richard Mitchell: "Quite insensibly, the *thing* creeps into your brain.... There it settles in and nibbles a bit here and a bit there...The very way you consider the world, or the very way in which the world is considered by you, is subtly altered." *Less Than Words Can Say* (Boston: Little, Brown, 1979), p. 10.

3. John S. Dryzek, *Rational Ecology: Environment and Political Ecology* (New York: Basil Blackwell, 1987), p. 247. See also William T. Gormley, "Institutional Policy Analysis: A Critical Review," *Journal of Policy Analysis and Management* 6 (1987), pp. 153-169.

4. Environmental impact assessment, of course, is not the only possible policy strategy of this kind. Another recent example of an apparently potent "subversive" strategy is California's Proposition 65 (the Safe Water and Toxic Enforcement Act). See Leslie Roberts, "A Corrosive Fight over California's Toxics Law," *Science* 243 (1989), pp. 306-309.

5. Robert V. Bartlett, "Impact Assessment as a Policy Strategy," in Robert V. Bartlett, ed., *Policy Through Impact Assessment: Institutionalized Analysis as a Policy Strategy* (Westport, CT: Greenwood Press, 1989).

6. On the concept of feedforward, see Herbert A. Simon, *The Sciences of the Artificial* (Cambridge, MA: M. I. T. Press, 2nd ed., 1981), p. 44; John S. Dryzek, "Policy Design in an Uncertain World," paper presented at Southern Political Science Association meeting, Atlanta, GA, 1982, p. 17; and Robert V. Bartlett, "Rationality and the Logic of the National Environmental Policy Act," *The Environmental Professional* 8 (1986), p. 107.

7. The concept of ecological rationality is developed in Dryzek, *Rational Ecology*; John S. Dryzek, "Ecological Rationality," *International Journal of Environmental Studies* 21 (1983), pp. 5-10; Robert V. Bartlett, "Ecological Rationality: Reason and Environmental Policy," *Environmental Ethics* 8 (1986), pp. 221-239. See also, Lynton K. Caldwell, "The Contextual Basis for Environmental Decisionmaking: Assumptions Are Predeterminants of Choice," *The Environmental Professional* 9 (1987), pp. 302-308.

8. See, *e.g.*, Dryzek, *Rational Ecology*, p. 189; Richard N. L. Andrews, *Environmental Policy and Administrative Change: Implementation of the National Environmental Policy Act* (Lexington, MA: Lexington Books, 1976); H. Paul Friesema and Paul J. Culhane, "Social Impact, Politics and the Environmental Impact Statement Process," *Natural Resources Journal* 16 (1976), pp.

339-356.

9. Bartlett, "Ecological Rationality," p. 229.

10. Paul Diesing, *Reason in Society: Five Types of Decision and Their Social Conditions* (Urbana: University of Illinois Press, 1962); also Dryzek, "Ecological Rationality," Dryzek, *Rational Ecology*, pp. 55-58; Bartlett, "Ecological Rationality."

11. Dryzek, *Rational Ecology*, p. 55; see also Mumford, *The Myth of the Machine*, and Jacques Ellul, *The Technological Society* (New York: Alfred A. Knopf, 1964).

12. *E.g.*, Robert K. Merton, *Social Theory and Social Structure* (Glencoe, IL: The Free Press, 1957) and Walter F. Baber, *Managing the Future: Matrix Models for the Postindustrial Polity* (University, AL: University of Alabama Press, 1983).

13. Conflict between ecological rationality and other forms of rationality is discussed at length by Dryzek, Bartlett, and Caldwell. See n. 7 above.

14. Diesing, pp. 231-232. Diesing did, however, anticipate ecological rationality as a prerequisite of social rationality: "Characteristic of a rational social system is its compatibility with the nonsocial environment..., to which it must be adapted if it is to continue in existence" (p. 88).

15. Dryzek, *Rational Ecology*, pp. 58-59.

16. For further discussion, see Bartlett, "Ecological Rationality," pp. 235-236; Dryzek, *Rational Ecology*, pp. 59-60.

17. According to Mannheim, functional rationality exists when "a series of actions is organized in such a way that it leads to a previously defined goal, every element in this series of actions receiving a functional position and role. Such a functional organization of a series of actions will, moreover, be at its best when, in order to attain the given goal, it coordinates the means most efficiently. It is by no means characteristic, however, of functional organization in our sense that this optimum be attained or even that the goal itself be considered rational as measured by a certain standard...." Karl Mannheim, *Man and Society in an Age of Reconstruction: Studies in Modern Social Structure* (New York: Harcourt, Brace, 1948), pp. 52-53. Max Weber referred to a similar concept as formal rationality.

18. Also called substantial rationality by Mannheim and Diesing.

19. Herbert A. Simon, "From Substantive to Procedural Rationality," in Spiro J. Latsis, ed., *Method and Appraisal in Economics* (Cambridge: Cambridge University Press, 1976), pp. 130-131.

20. Herbert A. Simon, "Rationality as Process and as Product of Thought," *American Economic Review* 68: 2 (1978), p. 9.

21. Bartlett, "Ecological Rationality," p. 224.

22. This is not to say that functional ecological rationality is ever a logical necessity or inevitable; it is always possible for something beyond controllable human behavior to intervene and vitiate the existing functional rationality of the relevant ecosystem.

23. See n. 7 above.

24. See, *e.g.*, Nicholas Wade, "Sahelian Drought: No Victory for Western Aid," *Science* 185 (1974), pp. 234-237; and Geoffrey Cowley, "The Electronic Goddess: Computerizing Bali's Ancient Irrigation Rites," *Newsweek* (March 13, 1989), p. 48. That is not to suggest, of course, that all or even most traditional societies were ecologically rational.

25. Dryzek, *Rational Ecology*, esp. pp. 25-54.

26. *Ibid.*, p. 181.

27. *Ibid.*, p. 245.

28. He is less uncertain, and less optimistic, in his companion article in this present volume, where he further considers the problem of challenging the administrative state from the outside in the face of the constraints and imperatives of the administrative state.

29. Dryzek, *Rational Ecology*, pp. 181-183.

30. Dryzek acknowledges as much (*ibid.*, p. 10), but does not further explore the potential of institutionalized EIA: "The policy process changes resulting from the passage of the U.S. National Environmental Policy Act (NEPA) in 1969 have restrained the actions of development-minded federal agencies and forced them to contemplate the environmental aspects of their proposals and decisions. The NEPA framework conditions policy outcomes without anyone presiding over it, and resists attempts by actors such as presidents and secretaries of the interior to downgrade environmental concerns. Social choice mechanisms do, in fact, generate (and are also, to a degree, the product of) convergent sets of expectations on the part of the actors involved in them, and so take on a life and momentum of their own."

31. Bartlett, "Rationality and the Logic of the National Environmental Policy Act."

32. Dryzek, *Rational Ecology*, p. 189; Bartlett, "Rationality and the Logic of the National Environmental Policy Act," pp. 108-109. See also, Paul J. Culhane, H. Paul Friesema, and Janice A. Beecher, *Forecasts and Environmental Decisionmaking: The Content and Predictive Accuracy of Environmental Impact Statements* (Boulder, CO: Westview Press, 1987), pp. 13-18.

33. Serge Taylor, *Making Bureaucracies Think: The Environmental Impact Statement Strategy of Administrative Reform* (Stanford, CA: Stanford University Press, 1984), p. 7.

34. *E.g.*, in the U.S. voluntary EIA is now undertaken by both private actors and local governments when acquiring real estate, as a preemptive defense against possible future liability for hazardous waste site cleanup costs.

35. See, *e.g.*, Ramon Abracosa and Leonard Ortolano, "Environmental Impact Assessment in the Philippines: A Case Study of the San Roque Water Resources Development Project," and Peter Wathern, "Implementing Supra-National Policy: EIA in the United Kingdom," in Bartlett, ed., *Policy Through Impact Assessment*,- pp. 65-72, 27-36; also Peter Wathern, "Containing Reform: The U.K. Stance on the European Community EIA Directive," *Policy Studies Review* 8 (1988), pp 94-104.

36. Geoffrey Wandesforde-Smith, "EIA, Entrepreneurship, and Policy Change," in Bartlett, ed., *Policy Through Impact Assessment*, pp. 155-166.

37. See, *e.g.*, Walter F. Baber, "Impact Assessment and Democratic Politics," *Policy Studies Review* 8 (1988), pp. 172-178; and Robert Paehlke, "Democracy, Bureaucracy, and Environmentalism," *Environmental Ethics* 10 (1988), pp. 291-308.

38. Robert V. Bartlett and Walter F. Baber, "Bureaucracy or Analysis: Implications of Impact Assessment for Public Administration," in Bartlett, ed., *Policy Through Impact Assessment*, pp. 143-153; and Robert V. Bartlett and Walter F. Baber, "Matrix Organization Theory and Environmental Impact Analysis: A Fertile Union?" *Natural Resources Journal* 27 (1987), pp. 605-615.

39. Leonard Ortolano, Bryan Jenkins, and Roman P. Abracosa, "Speculations on When and Why EIA is Effective," *Environmental Impact Assessment Review* 7 (1987), pp. 285-292.

40. William V. Kennedy, "Environmental Impact Assessment in North America, Western Europe: What Has Worked Where, How, and Why," *International Environment Reporter* 11 (April 13,

1988), p. 262.

41. Wandesforde-Smith, "EIA, Entrepreneurship, and Policy Change," p. 156.

42. Taylor, *Making Bureaucracies Think*.

43. G. Wandesforde-Smith and J. Kerbavaz, "The Co-Evolution of Politics and Policy: Elections, Entrepreneurship and EIA in the United States," in Peter Wathern, ed., *Environmental Impact Assessment: Theory and Practice* (London: Unwin Hyman, 1988), pp. 161-191.

44. Wandesforde-Smith, "EIA, Entrepreneurship, and Policy Change."

45. Gormley, "Institutional Policy Analysis," p. 160.

46. Bartlett, "Impact Assessment as a Policy Strategy."

DESIGNS FOR ENVIRONMENTAL DISCOURSE: THE GREENING OF THE ADMINISTRATIVE STATE?

John S. Dryzek

The fact that the Western world's environment is today somewhat safer, cleaner, and more securely protected than it was twenty or thirty years ago owes much to the efforts of the administrative state.[1] But despite any such accomplishments, the effects of the administrative state in environmental affairs today seem at best problematical, at worst nefarious. My intent here is to contemplate "greener" institutional alternatives to the administrative state, alternatives more likely to promote ecological values. Intelligent contemplation along these lines, be it of marginal reform or revolutionary transformation, requires that one first identify both the content and cause of any defects. Such diagnosis will help point not only to the qualities which institutional alternatives should possess, but also to the traps into which these alternatives may themselves fall. I shall suggest that these hazards are substantial enough to undermine many superficially attractive options. Yet I shall argue, nevertheless, that an institutional challenge to the administrative state, and to the broader political economy in which it moves, is a worthwhile project.

The Defects of the Administrative State

What, then, is wrong with the administrative state when it comes to environmental protection? At least three shortcomings may be identified. First, in terms of the basic criterion of environmental quality, administration is less than it once was. That is, despite any past achievements, the administrative state is running out of steam. While the early years of administrative regulation may be credited with some fairly obvious improvements in environmental quality, further achievements are hard to come by. A comprehensive survey of the evidence on this score is beyond the scope of this chapter—and in any case, many of the sources that one might cite are highly partisan, producing conflicting evidence. This much, it seems, is apparent: in the United States and elsewhere, the early years of environmental concern led to the adoption and implementation of policies with clear and obvious positive effects on environmental quality. In contrast, for the last decade or so the question of whether further policy efforts do or would produce benefits sufficient to justify their costs (irrespective of the metrics one applies) has become controversial.

Administration in the environmental arena thus confronts a problem also found in other areas of administration: diminishing marginal returns to effort. For example, the Soviet experience shows that central economic planning is an excellent device for rapid transformation of a static agrarian society into an industrial power—but thoroughly inept after that initial transition has been secured. In education, it is fairly easy for an administrative state to quickly convert an illiterate population to a literate one—but very hard thereafter to equalize educational opportunity, eradicate pockets of illiteracy, or otherwise promote educational achievement. Turning to social welfare, it is easy to virtually eliminate malnutrition, or provide a decent standard of public health—but hard to maintain and refine a system of welfare and health care that does not produce perverse and conflicting incentives, or generate attitudes of helplessness and dependency in clients. In short, as Charles Lindblom puts it, administrative systems have "strong thumbs, no fingers."[2]

A second shortcoming is that any achievements which can be credited to the administrative state may have been purchased at the cost of advancing bureaucratization and the instrumental rationalization or control of society more generally. This is Max Weber's scenario: *zweckrationalitat* triumphs precisely because it copes well with complex problems, but attendant upon this triumph is the demise of the more congenial features of human existence and association. Weber's fears are today echoed by everyone from conservative free marketeers to critical theorists and feminists.[3]

A third shortcoming stems from the fact that the state as a whole has priorities which have little to do with environmental quality, which may be overridden when it clashes with these other priorities. The precise content of state priorities is a matter of some dispute. But at a minimum, all states face the need to secure domestic order, to compete both strategically and economically in a hostile world, and to extract the finance for these activities.[4]   A corollary of this need for financial resources is that, in a market context, states are faced with the continual need to maintain business confidence in their activities, for otherwise they will be punished by economic downturn.   While inexpensive environmental programs producing clear and substantial benefits will have little impact here,[5] environmental policy may be a candidate for such punishment if and when diminishing returns of the sort discussed earlier set in.

The roots of these three defects of the administrative state lie in its epistemology and in its context. The *epistemology* of administration – its implicit theory of knowledge – is an instrumental-analytic one. That is, administration implicitly regards rationality as the capacity to devise, select, and effect good means to clarified and consistent ends. In the context of complex problems, this capacity also requires breaking such problems down into simpler components. As Weber pointed out long ago, bureaucracy is a device for the task decomposition and allocation which is necessary whenever problems overwhelm the information processing capabilities of a single individual (or small group of individuals). For all their protestations about matrix organization (espoused, for example, by the United States Environmental Protection Agency), task forces, organic structures, mosaics, and the like, and despite the best efforts of organization theorists over the years, just about all large organizations are still Weberian – that is, hierarchical and pyramid-shaped. Both authority and – implicitly – knowledge are centralized at the apex of the pyramid. The apex is assumed to know better than the lower levels, at least to the extent it is assigning and coordinating tasks among them, thereby ensuring that overall solutions to problems will be constructed in harmonious and effective fashion.

Now, Weber himself regarded this instrumental-analytic epistemology as an effective one, at least in terms of a capacity to resolve complex problems, if not in terms of the unfortunate byproduct of a loss of meaning in human existence. But it is now abundantly clear that there are limits to the capacity of bureaucratic forms of organization – and to the instrumental-analytic notion of rationality undergirding them – when it comes to truly complex problems. The reason is this: effective problem decomposition must be intelligent rather than arbitrary. And intelligent decomposition in turn requires that the sets and subsets into which a complex problem is divided should be relatively autonomous – that is, with a minimum of interactions across their boundaries. As complexity grows, then so will the number and variety of such interactions, until at some point the analytical intelligence at the center of the decision system is overwhelmed. The result is that time produces not a convergence on less problematical conditions, but endless displacement across the boundaries of sets and subsets.[6]

To what extent does this kind of administrative incapacity apply to environmental affairs? Ecological systems are indeed highly complex; as Barry Commoner puts it in crude but effective fashion, the first law of ecology is that "everything is connected to everything else."[7] One consequence is that attempts to resolve one environmental problem (for example, by building tall smokestacks to reduce local pollution) often simply create or exacerbate another kind of problem (for example, long-distance pollution such as acid rain).[8] The fact that most environmental agencies operate under the authority of a series of single-medium statutes (for example, the U.S. *Clean Air Act*, *Clean Water Act*, and *Resource Conservation and Recovery Act*) further exacerbates this situation, given that none of these statutes recognizes the possibility of cross-medium displacement.

The *context* of environmental administration can be as debilitating as its epistemology. As I have already noted, states in market systems are terribly constrained by their need to maintain the confidence of potential investors. Any state actions that threaten the profitability of industry and commerce are automatically punished by reduced investment followed by economic downturn.[9] If indeed we are witnessing diminishing returns to state effort on the environment, then it becomes increasingly likely that potentially effective environmental policies will in the future be vetoed by the anticipation of market punishment. The acid rain issue may offer a taste of things to come. Any significant dent in the acid rain problem will require action that is fairly expensive not just to the polluters in question, but also to regional and national economies. The potential economic impact of acid rain controls may explain why real action on this issue has been very slow to come and not yet apparent in many countries. Apologists for polluting industry of all sorts (not just acid rainers) are of course well aware of the high financial and economic costs associated with acid rain control, which is why they have an interest in keeping this issue on the political agenda. For as long as acid rain remains at center stage public attention is distracted away from other environmental issues where the cost-benefit ratio may be less favorable to inaction.[10]

There are, then, a number of automatic constraints upon any administrative state that operates in a market economy. And, as Lindblom points out, this kind of automatic punishment applies in any kind of market system, be it capitalist, market socialist, or whatever.[11]

Just as market systems do not have to be capitalistic, so capitalistic systems can flourish without a free market. It is in such oligarchic or monopoly capitalist economies (or economic sectors) that less automatic, but no less effective, constraints upon the administrative state come into play. I have in mind the influence polluters and despoilers can exert in policy-making—especially when the stakes are high, and the costs of effective policy are concentrated. This influence can be exercised directly upon administrative agencies, as well as in legislative politics. Thus agencies purposely insulated from legislative oversight (in the U.S., the "New Deal" type, such as the Securities and Exchange Commission, or Nuclear Regulatory Commission) prove vulnerable to capture by the very interests they are supposed to regulate or control. To prevent this kind of capture, the US Environmental Protection Agency was established under the "action-forcing" authority of Congress.[12] But the events of the early 1980s demonstrated that this kind of deliberately politicized agency too can be deflected from its mission by determined businesses conspiring with zealots in the upper reaches of the executive branch. And despite some undeniable achievements, the earlier history of the EPA shows that politicization of an agency can lead to strange bedfellows and peculiar compromises. Along these lines, Bruce Ackerman and William Hassler chronicle the life and times of a coalition between Western environmentalists and Eastern coal producers which pressed for a policy of forced scrubbing for emissions from all coal-fired power stations.[13] This policy effectively discriminated against Western producers of relatively clean, low-sulphur coal, thus keeping the West pristine and the East polluted.

This last example shows that environmental interests are not without influence in the administrative state, especially, perhaps, when they can ally with non-environmentalists, such as the Eastern coal producers just mentioned, or fiscal conservatives opposed to government subsidy of nuclear power. But when all is said and done the struggle is not an equal one. Business starts from a "privileged" position in interest group policies.[14] Business has more (financially) at stake; it has more to spend on lobbying, litigation, and campaign contributions; and it has more with which to threaten administrators and politicians (including withdrawal of the cooperation necessary to implement many public policies).

Institutional Alternatives: Discursive Designs

An agenda for institutional change can be constructed by starting with the epistemological shortcomings of the administrative state. In direct contrast to the Weberian argument, let me suggest that institutions can be expected to resolve complex problems to the extent they embody principles of free discourse among equals. Institutions of this sort will have the added advantage of undermining the instrumental rationalization and domination attendant upon administration and the like. Later I shall suggest that such freely discursive institutions are themselves prone to subversion by some of the more insidious aspects of the very same context which constrains the existing efforts of the administrative state, but for the moment a focus on the positive is in order.

The principles of free discourse I have in mind are those elaborated by critical theorists and others who have attended closely to the linguistic aspect of political life. One of the more well-known of such statements is associated with Jürgen Habermas's exposition of the idea of communicative rationality (which in turn is informed by his earlier postulation of an "ideal speech situation").[15] To Habermas, an interaction is communicatively rational to the extent that it proceeds among equally competent individuals under conditions free from domination, deception, self-deception, and strategizing. All that remains is the "forceless force of the better argument," which can relate to both normative judgments and empirical conditions and relationships. Habermas himself says little if anything about connections to social problem solving, and there are reasons to suppose he would regard the latter as the domain of instrumental-analytic rather than communicative rationality. But let me suggest first, that the principles of communicative rationality also give us the conditions for effectiveness in the resolution of complex social problems (including environmental ones), and second, that intimations of these principles can already be found in environmental politics.

To begin with my first contention (and here I summarize an intricate argument), communicative rationality is conducive to social problem solving inasmuch as it enables the individuals concerned with different facets of a complex problem to pool their understandings and harmonize their actions in the light of reciprocal understanding of the various normative issues at stake. This process proceeds in nonhierarchical fashion, and so no cognitive burden is imposed on any decision center. The interaction between different facets of a problem that constitute complexity is matched by communicative interaction among the individuals who care about each facet. And of course, the conditions of these communicative interactions are crucial if they are to ameliorate rather than exacerbate complexity, which is why they must be regulated by the canons of communicative rationality. Ideally, the product would then be consensus spanning both the normative and empirical dimensions of problems.[16]

If my argument here holds, then one might anticipate institutional intimations of principles of free discourse — discursive designs — in the vicinity of complex social problems. Three such manifestations are worth noting in the environmental arena. In moving from the first to the third one finds increasingly less in the way of communicative purity, but more in the way of a problem-solving orientation.

The first category is that celebrated by critical theorists and other radical philosophers: new social movements (they are "new" in the sense that they are not clearly class-based, which is why Marxists are suspicious of them).[17] These movements include feminists, peace groups, radical social ecologists, anti-nuclear activists, and the Greens who combine these concerns. All are committed to communicatively rational interaction in both their internal workings and the larger political relationships which they enter. One might argue that this relative communicative purity is purchased at the expense of effectiveness; most such movements remain on the fringes of political life.

A more explicit problem orientation may be found in the second and smallest but (arguably) most significant of my three categories, discursively designed public inquiries. This category is exemplified by the efforts in both Canada and the U.S. of Thomas Berger, who has conducted a number of public commissions on policy issues. Two of these have some connection with environmental issues: his inquiry into proposals to construct pipelines to bring oil and gas from the Canadian Arctic to southern markets,[18] and his investigation of the condition of Alaska's Native peoples in the light of the 1971 *Alaska Native Claims Settlement Act*.[19] These inquiries could be loosely styled as social and environmental impact assessment, inasmuch as they involve scrutiny of the effects of past actions and contemplation of the consequences of alternative development strategies for a region and a people. In both these cases Berger created a forum in which concerned and affected individuals could state, create, and develop their positions (especially through their participation in community hearings). Both consisted of prolonged interaction between

Berger himself, relevant experts (at least in the pipelines case) and community members. Berger's reports contained recommendations for policy actions built upon these interactions. In the pipelines case, he recommended that no pipelines be constructed before the settlement of Native lands claims and the strengthening of the Northern renewable resource economy. In the Alaska case, he suggested dismantling the regional corporations established by the 1971 Act and the transfer of their assets to revitalized tribal governments, which would also exercise political control in Native Alaska. But in both cases he was summarising a consensus reached through discourse among participants who attained a degree of communicative competence made possible by the kind of forum Berger established.[20]

My third category covers discursive exercises more closely tied to state and capital than new social movements or discursively designed public inquiries. This category consists of procedures such as environmental mediation, regulatory negotiation, and alternative dispute resolution. These procedures have in common the idea that parties to a dispute can reason through their differences in pursuit of an action-oriented consensus under the auspices of a neutral third party. They are often proposed and undertaken as alternatives to more established forms of conflict resolution, such as litigation or even violence. In the case of environmental mediation, participants might include environmentalists, developers, polluters, community groups, and government officials. Most of the cases of environmental mediation carried out in the fifteen years since the technique was introduced have concerned domestic U.S. disputes.[21] Conflicts over local air pollution, mining, water supply system construction, highway siting, hazardous waste treatment and disposal, and land use have been mediated. In most cases a determinate outcome has been reached and eventually – though this is not guaranteed – embodied in public policy. The rise of mediation parallels and reflects an explosion of interest in informal dispute resolution in a variety of domains, international as well as domestic.

Discursive Designs in Context

The most glaring shortcoming of the agenda for institutional reconstruction intimated in the preceding section is its inattention to the more or less automatic constraints upon collective decisions discussed earlier under the heading of context. In other words, to the extent they become involved in actual policy-making, discursive designs might fall victim to exactly the same kinds of constraints and imperatives as the administrative state.

The extensive critique of environmental mediation developed by Douglas Amy merits attention here.[22] Amy argues that the fate and function of mediation is to co-opt potential troublemakers by extending to them the illusion of participation. Thus placated with symbolic rewards, environmentalists and others will acquiesce in "responsible" development or pollution, and capital will get its way no less than under more conventional political arrangements. Environmentalists and community activists will be seduced into becoming mere agents of the state and capital, perhaps even of the Weberian process of instrumental rationalization. More insidiously, the very fact of sitting down on equal and reasonable terms with capitalists implies devaluation of *moral* concerns (for example, on behalf of ecological integrity as a basic value) to the status of mere particular interests, fit for tradeoff against the profits of polluters and developers. At best, one can expect little more than the conspiratorial externalization of the costs of an agreement, which may benefit the parties at the table, but impose high costs on others (for example, consumers, or distant ecosystems). The coalition between Western environmentalists and Eastern coal producers mentioned earlier is indicative of this last possibility (though it should be stressed that this coalition had nothing to do with mediation or any similar procedure).

At present, environmental mediation and regulatory negotiation exist on the margins of environmental policy-making. If they were to become more central, then additional hazards in the form of the automatic constraint exercised by the market would loom larger. Policy-making discursive designs could not afford to upset market confidence any more than the administrative state could. How, then, may discursive designs be rescued from the state, capital, and market?

The critics of environmental mediation and alternative dispute resolution more generally are no help here, for all they ever recommend is a return to administration, litigation, or legislation.[23] In other words, they offer only a dubious conservatism in the form of a return to a discredited, costly, arbitrary, and ineffective *status quo*. If industry is advantaged in mediation, then it is no less advantaged in the courts.[24] Is there any alternative to this reactionary counsel?

The answer, it seems to me, is that discursive designs should seek immunity from the state – and so from capital and market. Such immunity may of course be found in complete withdrawal from practical, problem-solving concerns, which new social movements sometimes engage in.[25] But there is an alternative to such withdrawal. Discursive designs could be located within and help constitute an autonomous public sphere, separate from but confronting the state. A public space of this sort is created whenever individuals congregate to scrutinize their relationships with one another and with the wider relations of power in which they are located. The subject of the public sphere is, as the name implies, *public* affairs. Perhaps the best historical example of a public sphere occurs in connection with the early bourgeois challenge to the feudal state, which disintegrated as the bourgeoisie itself sought and gained state power.[26]

Today, an autonomous public sphere would be faced with the task of discursively constructing challenges to the state. What, then, are the prospects for the development of a public sphere from which corporations *qua* corporations and government officials *qua* government officials would have to be excluded? At present, the prospects might seem quite dim. For example, mainstream environmentalists prize their access to government, with the attendant complicity in the process and content of public policy. Radical environmentalists such as Earth First! and Greenpeace often reject both conventional strategic politics and the more discursive possibilities intimated here in favor of guerilla theatre.[27]

Some cause for optimism may be found in the efforts of Thomas Berger alluded to earlier. Let me suggest that his Alaskan inquiry in particular constitutes an exemplary instance of the creation and sustenance of a public sphere in and through which a coherent challenge to the state is constructed, and a community is reconstituted. This inquiry was concerned with public affairs in two senses. First, its target was public policy (especially that of the U.S. federal government). Second, and perhaps more significantly, its subject was the self-determination of the collective future of a particular public – Alaskan Natives. The inquiry excluded government officials (except from local governments, which the inquiry was not challenging). It was constituted under the auspices of the Inuit Circumpolar Conference, a transnational organization of Inuit from Alaska, Canada, and Greenland, and financed by churches, foundations, local government, and Native Regional Corporations. The result was a forum in which ordinary Natives could testify, and to this end hearings were held in cities, villages, and fish camps throughout Alaska, at which 1450 individuals spoke. These individuals presented viewpoints, debated them, and argued with one another and with Berger, all in a context rendered meaningful by the existence and prior deliberations of the inquiry. Thus the commission did not just collect and collate individuals' positions; it also constructed a community position on land, economy, and governance, transforming sporadic protests by individuals and groups into a coherent challenge on behalf of a community and its way of life.

The establishment of a public sphere of this sort does not, of course, bring with it the abolition of the administrative state. However, this establishment does mean that the pressures upon the state from its capitalist and/or market context would be counterbalanced by the challenge from the public sphere. A cynical observer might claim that, no less than before, the interests of capital and market would always prevail in this unequal struggle. If so, then the public sphere would prove but a minor irritant, irrelevant in the larger political-economic structure. But other outcomes are conceivable. Berger's pipelines inquiry represents a challenge from the public sphere which eventually contributed to a state decision to overrule the interests of corporations; though the relative importance of this contribution compared to other influences on the decision (for example, a competing corporate proposal) remains unclear. And the public sphere created by new social movements does occasionally exert some influence (for example, in halting the headlong rush toward nuclear power); though the extent to which this influence is a matter of public sphere pressure rather than more conventional interest group activity often remains an open question.

Despite the possibilities associated with the idea of a public sphere, one should not underestimate the obduracy of the market, capitalism, and the administrative state itself. Moreover, it is hard to undermine these three obstacles to freely discursive public life simultaneously. Eliminating the free market is conceivable — but all such elimination usually produces is either monopoly capitalism and corporatism, with a concomitant enhanced capacity to exert direct pressure on the state, or a command economy which exacerbates the epistemological problems of administration discussed earlier. Abolishing capitalism might give us market socialism of some sort, which is as capable as a capitalist market of inflicting automatic punishment on government actions that threaten profitability, or, again, an economic system administered by state bureaucrats. Limiting the administrative state might produce only more of the market or monopoly capitalism (as in recent Chinese and Soviet economic reforms).

As things stand, then, discursive designs are not in and of themselves blueprints for an alternative political-economic system. What they do offer is a challenge to dominant institutional forms, which might contribute to a reconsideration of the way we order collective life. But in maintaining this challenge, proponents of and participants in discursive designs should be careful to avoid complicity in the complex *status quo* to which discursive designs offer the hope of an alternative.

Notes

1. I take the term "administrative state" to cover both administrative agencies and the statutory context in which they operate.

2. Charles E. Lindblom, *Politics and Markets: The World's Political-Economic Systems* (New York: Basic Books, 1977).

3. For a free marketeer critique along these lines, see Milton Friedman and Rose Friedman, *Free to Choose* (New York: Harcourt Brace Jovanovich, 1979); for a critical theorist's account, see Ralph Hummel, *The Bureaucratic Experience* (New York: St. Martin's, 3rd ed., 1985); for a feminist angle, see Kathy E. Ferguson, *The Feminist Case Against Bureaucracy* (Philadelphia: Temple University Press, 1984).

4. See, for example, Theda Skocpol, *States and Social Revolutions* (New York: Cambridge University Press, 1979), pp. 24-33.

5. Indeed, if Gorz is right, then business may actually welcome anti-pollution efforts insofar as they improve the quality of some of its productive inputs. See Andre Gorz, *Ecology as Politics* (Boston: South End Press, 1980), pp. 4-6. A particularly murky example may be found in contemporary Poland, where water supplies are often too polluted to be used in many industrial processes.

6. For details on this general argument, see Christopher Alexander, "A City is not a Tree," *Architectural Forum* 122:1 and 122:2 (1965), pp. 58-61 and 58-62; Todd R. La Porte, ed., *Organized Social Complexity: Challenge to Politics and Policy* (Princeton: Princeton University Press, 1975); John S. Dryzek, "Complexity and Rationality in Public Life," *Political Studies* 35 (1987), pp. 424-442.

7. Barry Commoner, *The Closing Circle* (New York: Bantam Books, 1972), p. 29.

8. For details on this argument as applied to ecological problems, see John S. Dryzek, *Rational Ecology: Environment and Political Economy* (Oxford and New York: Basil Blackwell, 1987), pp. 16-20.

9. See Fred Block, "The Ruling Class Does Not Rule: Notes on the Marxist Theory of the State," *Socialist Revolution* 7:3 (1977), pp. 6-28; Charles E. Lindblom, "The Market as Prison," *Journal of Politics* 44 (1982), pp. 324-336.

10. See James L. Regens and Robert W. Rycroft, *The Acid Rain Controversy* (Pittsburgh: University of Pittsburgh Press, 1988), pp. 29-30.

11. Lindblom, "The Market as Prison."

12. See Bruce A. Ackerman and William T. Hassler, *Clean Coal/Dirty Air* (New Haven: Yale University Press, 1981), pp. 7-12.

13. *Ibid.*

14. Lindblom, *Politics and Markets*, pp. 170-188.

15. See, for example, Jürgen Habermas, *The Theory of Communicative Action*, Vol. 1, *Reason and the Rationalization of Society* (Boston: Beacon Press, 1984).

16. For much more extensive argument along these lines, see Dryzek, *Rational Ecology*, pp. 200-215;

Dryzek, "Complexity and Rationality"; and John S. Dryzek, "Discursive Designs: Critical Theory and Political Institutions," *American Journal of Political Science* 31 (1987), pp. 656-679.

17. See, *e.g.*, Ernesto Laclau and Chantal Mouffe, *Hegemony and Socialist Strategy: Towards a Radical Democratic Politics* (London: Verso, 1985).

18. Thomas R. Berger, *Northern Frontier, Northern Homeland: The Report of the MacKenzie Valley Pipeline Inquiry* (Toronto: James Lorimer, 1977).

19. Thomas R. Berger, *Village Journey: The Report of the Alaska Native Review Commission* (New York: Hill and Wang, 1985).

20. For further approval of Berger's efforts on this score, see John Dryzek, "Policy Analysis as a Hermeneutic Activity," *Policy Sciences* 14 (1982), pp. 324-325; Douglas Torgerson, "Between Knowledge and Politics: Three Faces of Policy Analysis," *Policy Sciences* 19 (1986), pp. 46-51; and John S. Dryzek, " Policy Sciences of Democracy," *Polity* 17 (1989).

21. For a survey, see Gail Bingham, *Resolving Environmental Disputes: A Decade of Experience* (Washington, DC: The Conservation Foundation, 1986).

22. Douglas Amy, *The Politics of Environmental Mediation* (New York: Columbia University Press, 1987).

23. See, *e.g.*, David Schoenbrod, "Limits and Dangers of Environmental Mediation: A Review Essay," New York University Law Review 58 (1983).

24. See Samuel P. Hays, *Beauty, Health, and Permanence: Environmental Politics in the United States, 1955-1985* (New York: Cambridge University Press, 1987), p. 483.

25. Such withdrawal also seems to be the solution of Jürgen Habermas and Hannah Arendt, both of whom seek freely discursive collective life in domains thoroughly divorced from social problems. See Habermas, *Theory of Communicative Action*, and Hannah Arendt, *The Human Condition* (Chicago: University of Chicago Press, 1958).

26. See Jürgen Habermas, *The Structural Transformation of the Public Sphere: A Inquiry into a Category of Bourgeois Society* (Cambridge, MA: The M.I.T. Press, 1989 [1962]).

27. A specific problem which arises in applying the idea of a public sphere to ecological matters should be mentioned. The concept of a public sphere—and its communicative rationality—are rooted in a philosophical tradition which claims there should be a radical discontinuity between human dealings with one another and human dealings with nature. This tradition encompasses Aristotle, latter-day Aristotelians such as Hannah Arendt, and the Frankfurt School of critical theory. Its members argue that collective human life should be so structured as to prevent it becoming like human interaction with the natural world, which can only be instrumental and manipulative. Today, this judgment is based on a fear that the scientific and technical attitudes which have proven effective in controlling nature are increasingly being turned to the control of people. An ecological critique of this tradition would argue two points. First, these scientific and technical attitudes are not as fruitful as they might seem, as contemporary environmental crises demonstrate. Second, there is a sense in which the natural world contains not just brute matter for human manipulation, but also *agency*. Recognition of this agency undermines the legitimacy of an instrumental, manipulative attitude to the natural world, just as a recognition of human agency undermines the legitimacy of social control. Acceptance of agency in nature does not imply a regressive commitment to nature's reenchantment. It finds echoes in the works of some contemporary natural scientists; see, *e.g.*, James Lovelock, *Gaia: A New Look at Life on Earth* (New York: Oxford University Press, 1979), and Evelyn Fox Keller, *A Feeling for the Organism: The Life and Work of Barbara McLintock* (San Francisco: W. H. Freeman, 1983).

Thus there may be a sense in which natural entities can indeed participate in communicative practice. For a preliminary discussion of the implications of this recognition, see John S. Dryzek, "Green Reason: Communicative Ethics for the Biosphere," a paper presented at the Conference on Issues in Environmental Ethics, Bowling Green State University, 1988.

ADMINISTRATION AS AN
ENVIRONMENTAL PROBLEM

To see the environment as an administrative problem means, at first, cutting the environment down to size, making it manageable. This approach, however, quickly runs into trouble. In grappling with the environment, conventional administration betrays many inadequacies. These demonstrate the need for techniques and processes which will deal more sensitively and comprehensively with environmental complexities. The innovations so far developed offer an ambivalent potential, as suggested by the articles of Part II, either to reinforce or transform the boundaries of administration.

The single article in Part III reconsiders this potential by focusing upon the historical emergence and contemporary character of administration. From this perspective, administration itself appears as an environmental problem. Influenced by current methodological departures in administrative and policy studies, the article offers a critique of the "administrative mind" as an image which constrains the definition of environmental problems. The critique is, in the first instance, pointed at administrative ideology—an orientation which pervades the "administrative sphere" even if individual administrators may oppose that outlook and seek to escape it. However, the critique also turns upon elements of environmentalism, a counter-ideology which can itself ironically also come under the spell of the administrative mind. The essay suggests a theoretical re-orientation which anticipates the varied, complex world of environmental politics and administrative practice portrayed in Part IV.

LIMITS OF THE ADMINISTRATIVE MIND: THE PROBLEM OF DEFINING ENVIRONMENTAL PROBLEMS

Douglas Torgerson

"Out of the void comes the spirit that shapes the ends of men."

Chester I. Barnard, *The Functions of the Executive*, 1938

The world of administration projects itself, and often views itself, as rationally ordered and permanent. Its icon stands as the vast and anonymous, hard-edged office complex, replicated across the urban landscape; through this pervasive, towering presence, it displaces cathedral, palace, and parliament as the center of legitimate power. Supremely confident and authoritative, this world now constitutes the central, guiding intelligence of modern civilization. Notwithstanding functional differentiation and internal tension, the administrative world possesses a singular, overall coherence, which is at once obvious and obscure: "In the characterless office buildings that dominate the town centers, in the banks and ministries, the law courts and corporate administrations,...the private and public bureaucracies, one cannot recognize the functional relations whose point of intersection they form."[1] The complex of administrative organizations which directs contemporary society gathers its legitimacy from its central role in propelling a seemingly natural and necessary course of industrial progress—planning, anticipating problems, and overcoming obstacles which arise. In the process, the conventional distinction between public and private sectors, while ritually reaffirmed, becomes less functionally significant. A functionally integrated *administrative sphere* becomes increasingly suitable to a "whole society" viewed "as a firm intent on maximizing or optimising the ratio of its outputs to inputs."[2]

Yet the striking emergence of unanticipated difficulties—particularly those termed environmental problems—has challenged the administrative sphere. Its aura of certitude and stability has been unsettled not only by apparent shortcomings in responding to these problems, but also by the troubling sense that the administrative sphere has itself been the prime agent in generating the problems in the first place. My focus here is upon a particular issue with broad implications: how the administrative sphere *defines* environmental problems. The discussion is in the manner of a critique of ideology and draws attention to a "mobilization of bias".[3] A problem in defining environmental problems arises in the administrative sphere, I argue, largely because the task is seen to be one for the *administrative mind*. In considering the problem of definition, we must thus examine this perception and its context.

Those with an interest in resolving environmental problems must take the administrative sphere into account when themselves defining those problems and determining courses of action—either from inside or outside that sphere. Those on the outside are likely, with good reason, to conclude that an adequate definition and resolution of environmental problems calls for a transformation of the administrative sphere—not marginal changes. Yet any fundamental change of the administrative sphere must initially involve internal changes as well as changes in relation to society generally. A key issue which emerges in this regard, as we shall see, is the relationship between the administrative sphere and the public sphere.

The Administrative Sphere and the Human Condition

Despite pretensions of mechanized efficiency, the administrative sphere does not escape the human condition.[4] Throughout this century, and before, administrative thought and practice have proceeded with a sense of being central to the human task of mastering nature, of completing the industrial cosmos; but this very project has been hindered by the frequent recalcitrance of human nature itself—by failures to make needed sacrifices, to submit to a superior intelligence, to accept discipline. The progress of humanity has accordingly appeared to depend upon establishing and maintaining a strict order through the perfection of administrative control: the mastery of nature, that is, has depended upon a mastery of human nature.[5]

Managing Human Resources: Toward a Critique of Administrative Ideology

Enormous effort and ingenuity have been devoted to the problem of designing administrative techniques and processes which will achieve control of human beings through the methods of scientific investigation successfully applied to non-human nature.[6] To overcome the complexity of the human subject-matter, attention has thus focused on the problem of identifying and isolating manageable units—and thereby subjecting them to the control of an ascendant intelligence, an administrative mind. Yet this strategy of division and reduction, while exhibiting its power in the accomplishments of industrialization, has encountered repeated human resistance. Management thought has registered this resistance and has explored ways of eliciting cooperation so as to employ more fully the "human resources" potentially at the disposal of administrative organizations. This attention to the "human side" of organizations has coincided with an emerging conviction that there is no "one best way" to manage production—that the appropriate approach depends upon particular contingencies, such as task and environment, which confront an organization.[7] Especially when faced with situations of variety and complexity, both practitioners and theorists of management now stand less in awe of the administrative mind and rely significantly upon the initiative and problem-solving capabilities of subordinate personnel.

With this reliance, the old rationalistic imagery becomes less serviceable, and new attention is given to communication in organizations. Indeed, management theory is now able to focus more clearly on this imagery as something which, once taken for granted, could strangely obscure its own character by deflecting attention from certain irreducible elements of communication in human affairs: imagery, metaphor, symbolism. With organizational life recognized as humanly constructed and enacted—inescapably symbolic—rationalistic imagery, appealing to the reductionist fiction of a perfectly neutral language, at once loses some of its power: the imagery can no longer be accepted without question. In the context of varied and complex organizational situations, at least, attention has increasingly been given to developing new images, metaphors, and symbols which will prove effective in mobilizing the initiative and enhancing the problem-solving capacity of the organizational membership.[8]

This perspective contains key aspects of a critique of administrative ideology and can readily be pressed in a critical direction. Once seen for what it is, the old rationalistic imagery betrays a hidden association with — and dependence upon — the mythic: a bold vision of human progress culminating in a smooth and efficient industrial cosmos.[9] Although considerably downplayed, this mythic dimension remains as a distinct residue in a newer rationalistic imagery. This new imagery is associated with a technocratic conception of management which, employing an explicit systems approach, has been developed in recognition of variety and complexity in organizational problems. The logic of this approach is to avoid errors in problem-solving which arise from organizational differentiation and hierarchy — from splitting the overall structure into discrete sub-units according to such criteria as function, area, product; and from treating the implementation of plans as entirely subordinate to their formulation. Planning and control are thus predicated upon a management information system, consisting of multiple feedback loops which supply the relevant and timely data demanded by analytic tasks in sub-system decision centers.[10] Although a notable adaptation to organizational contingencies, this technocratic orientation ultimately remains both confident in the administrative mind and insensitive to the necessarily human character of itself and its context. The rationalistic imagery, in either case, participates in a style and mood, a range of associations, stereotypes, and clichés which fix attention and thereby systematically distort the identity and the context of analysts and administrators, while enhancing their legitimacy.

Focusing Attention: The Heuristics of Problem Definition

The rationalistic imagery seems most effective when most invisible, when left, that is to say, as a pervasive and unquestioned background of administrative activity. Fascination with the image of an administrative mind[11] remains a significant feature of contemporary culture, outside administrative organizations as well as within them; yet the image is seldom clearly recognized or named. Containing ambivalent, indistinct, even contradictory features, the image resists firm conceptualization; and this resistance is part of its power in shaping and directing the focus of attention. Central to the mythic dimension of modernity, the image of the administrative mind encourages a picture of mental activity as monological rather than dialogical, as involving impersonal cogitation rather than interpersonal communication. The image influences not only the formal structure, but also the informal relationships of administrative organizations; in particular, the image has an impact on how problems are approached — not simply on how they are solved, but as well on how they are initially identified and defined. Entwined in patterns of rationalistic imagery, founded upon a faith in order and progress, the administrative mind thus works a potent yet quiet effect on the way problems are handled in the administrative sphere. The image performs as a heuristic guide in problem-solving — one which, being typically unacknowledged, encourages a singularity of viewpoint that tends to exclude alternatives before they can be conceived.

Problem definition, I would contend, proceeds from a perspective, a way of seeing. Although perhaps trite as thus formulated, this contention gains significance if restated in terms of "contextual orientation" and "critical heuristics".[12] Problem definition proceeds from an orientation by which individuals and organizations understand themselves in relation to a context — *i.e.*, from an explicit or implicit image of "self-in-context".[13] This orientation guides problem definition because such a self-image carries with it at least tacit heuristic principles by which one identifies and deals with problems. These heuristic principles fix the focus of attention; particularly when they remain implicit and unquestioned, the heuristics of problem definition and solution restrict thinking to clichéd patterns. In contrast, an explicit focus on contextual orientation draws attention to an established way of seeing; this act is thus an exercise involving critical heuristics, whereby the principles which guide the handling of problems become open to question and change. A key feature of a project of deliberate contextual re-orientation is the examination and reformulation of "developmental constructs"[14] — a focusing on how to grasp the temporal dimension of one's context or, broadly conceived, on how to understand oneself in relation to historical change. When we consider the emergence of environmental problems, this issue becomes especially pointed; for here the recognition of problems was at odds with conventional expectations of order and progress.

Dominating Nature: The Promise of Order and Progress

As the increasing application of scientific investigation to non-human nature came to demonstrate its expected power in a panoply of technological success, the human domination of nature seemed nearly assured. All that was needed were techniques and processes of administration to deal with the troublesome human factor. Once the administrative apparatus had been properly designed—in accord with the imperatives of the administrative mind—the modern promise of progress could be entirely fulfilled. However, with the techniques and processes of administration developed over the past two decades to handle environmental problems, the domination of nature no longer is simply taken for granted. Now, in the aftermath of much industrialization, nature appears more complex and sensitive—in a sense, more recalcitrant to human designs. Unexpected failures in anticipating environmental problems have provided an impetus for administrative change. While still largely associated with a rationalistic imagery paying implicit tribute to the administrative mind, these changes also raise the prospect of a fundamentally different orientation of administrative theory and practice.

Inseparable from the administrative sphere and the emergence of its present problems, then, is the contextual orientation of those who have shaped that world and who now inhabit it. The predominant account of administration in this century has pictured a mechanical arrangement of personnel, with neatly specified functions, subject to a hierarchical order of authority—unified and directed by a single head. Not everyone has always believed that this account—this traditional conception—captured administrative realities fully, but it has at least provided a secure imaginary order. A complementary notion of order remains in the chief alternative to the traditional conception—that is, as noted above, the technocratic. In either case, an enduring sense of order serves to reinforce belief in modern administration as an historical agent of rationality while, at the same time, inculcating a sense of mission: identification with the cause of progress. Typically, that is to say, the contextual orientation—albeit largely implicit—involves a view of the individual and organization in terms of their historical significance. A central concern here is how this orientation enters into the definition of problems and constrains administrative capacity for problem-solving.

The Administrative Mind

The image of the administrative mind is one of an impartial reason exercising unquestionable authority for universal well being; it is an image which projects an aura of certain knowledge and benign power. The administrative mind presents itself as detached from mundane troubles, able in principle to master all things through calculation. Administration depends upon unity; there must be a single head to plan, organize, command, coordinate, and control. Anything else would not only be less than optimal; it would literally violate a law of nature—it would be a monstrosity. This notion, clearly stated in the first effort to formulate a comprehensive theory of administration,[15] reaches back to the early part of this century, but reflects as well the influence of early modern philosophy and medieval political theology.

The Authority of Mind: Rational and Magical

The exalted image of the administrative mind gathers authority from a distance posited between thought and action, mind and world, which largely rests upon a methodological solipsism—the presupposition of a self-enclosed mind whose thoughts are echoes of itself and are uncontaminated by mundane strife and error. What is excluded from this notion is the concept of mental activity being dependent upon interaction—upon the engagement of persons on the same plane in a common world. Indeed, the administrative mind is founded upon a principle of hierarchical division: mental over manual work, the "head" over the "hands".[16] The administrative mind thus rises as a central, ascendant figure, comprehending and ordering its domain.

The image of the administrative mind contains what a perceptive early writer on administration called an "illusion of final authority".[17] Evident in the clichéd notion that some *one* should be in charge, this illusion forms a backdrop to administrative routine, working a quiet effect on problem-solving through the suggestion that the strictly delimited functions and perspectives of organizational members are not part of an artificial arrangement, but are inscribed in the very nature of things. To accept the authority of the administrative mind is simply to accept what is natural and necessary—to recognize a superior, unifying intelligence. In an idealized organization, the membership accepts this authority continuously, as if by reflex bowing to the prestige of reason.

Given the overarching cause of order and progress, the administrative mind appears to operate on the basis of a broad, self-evident goal while establishing relatively narrow, short-term objectives and strategies. The immediate concern is with means, a technical question which can be divided up and parcelled out to a functionally differentiated staff for detailed analysis and calculation. No question should be raised by the staff about the point of the detailed work, for the task of directing individual efforts in a single, coordinated way is that of the administrative mind. Faith in order and progress tends, in any case, to preempt questions.

Yet in the imagery of order and progress, the solemn and authoritative mind of administration, while guided by methodical discipline in seeking solutions to problems, coexists with its apparent opposite: the miraculous. Fulfilling a grand historical vision, the administrative mind becomes strangely associated with the mind of the magus, which penetrates the mysteries of being and performs incredible wonders. However incongruous, this association seems to cast a potent spell by joining the lure of the mysterious to the authority of an austere reason. The relationship also recalls, indeed, the historical pattern whereby the attempt of modern technology and organization to master things through calculation emerges from and replaces the effort to gain mastery through magical enchantment.[18] What remains of old is not a method, but an aura, which envelops the image of rationality and obscures the limits of the administrative mind.

The Mystique of the Administrative Mind: Traditional and Technocratic

The paradoxical commingling of the rational with the irrational is most evident in the traditional concept of administration as command and obedience in a hierarchy of authority where the top position is occupied by a clearly identifiable executive decision-maker. This ultimate authority does not depend exclusively — or even mainly — on rationality; rather, with the authority of the executive accepted by virtue of tradition or charisma, decisions about organizational direction carry a promise of rationality but are allowed the privilege of an arbitrary quality. In this way, the ultimate authority remains strikingly free from the imperatives which shape and guide an otherwise unified structure. Nonetheless, as an administrative instrument, this structure itself is not freely chosen but manifests an imperative of historical development — order and progress — which no one can freely alter. The promise of rationality offered by arbitrary decision-making is thus to be redeemed by an historical pattern which is taken for granted — a pattern in which decisions remain unquestionable as long as the decision-maker succeeds in maintaining an image of successful mastery consonant with expectations of order and progress. Acknowledged perhaps by a wink and slightly embarrassed smile, irrationality does not become a relevant issue provided that power substitutes for reason: "Deep down, the mind feels that its stable dominance is no mental rule at all, that its *ultima ratio* lies in the physical force at its disposal. On pain of perdition, however, it must not put its secret into words."[19]

The dominance of rationality in the administrative sphere has been even further accentuated with the advent of a technocratic mentality which regards reason as the only genuine basis of authority. Here the "disenchantment of the world"[20] presses towards its completion in an apotheosis of rational decision-making which is both pure and anonymous. The reference to an identifiable decision-maker, necessary for traditional or charismatic forms of legitimation, is replaced by the assumption that a depersonalized mode of analysis operates as the guiding intelligence in a rationally ordered domain. Progress, that is to say, has reached a point where the work of construction is over and where bold initiatives, leaps of faith, are not only archaic but also threatening. Depersonalized, stripped of charisma and the trappings of tradition, the administrative mind reappears as the planning and controlling sub-system in a management information system:[21] a sub-system which, lacking a definite location at the top of a formal hierarchy, becomes elusive — a non-entity, a vanishing spirit, everywhere and nowhere. Although invisible, the administrative mind retains a presence, and the association of reason and myth, transfigured as the mystique of the administrative mind, is continually recalled by the symbols, icons, and rituals of administrative behavior. The technical terminology and algorithms of analysis, the organizational charts and diagrams, the institutional rules and procedures — these normal features of administration constitute a style and form of life which carry an implicit message of reassurance: there is an ultimate, objective, rational authority which oversees and cares for the whole. Even in the face of conflict, the typical techniques and processes of administration serve to pay homage — as a disillusioned technocrat has acknowledged — to the potent fiction of an "all-powerful, all-wise, all-loving" figure of authority.[22]

A Sacred Canopy: The Emergence of the Administrative Mind

The administrative mind is an image of unity, cohesion, order; excluded from it are division, difference, and conflict. From the medieval to the modern period, there is a recurrent idea that the visible world of appearances is contained within an invisible order, a cosmos, rationally ordered by an ascendant mind. Sheltered beneath a "sacred canopy",[23] the cosmos has essentially been monistic, designed in accord with a single plan, excluding plurality. For medieval political theology, the vision of a unified, hierarchical universe under one omniscient and omnipotent God constituted a hierocratic principle militating against the polytheistic and animistic traditions of diverse tribal communities. Divine revelation, moreover, was a necessary source for understanding the orderly plan of the universe; and the institution of the papacy came to provide a point of ascendancy, mediating between the mundane and the sacred, the earthly city and the heavenly city.[24] In early modern philosophy, the mind constituted a self-contained domain possessing a capacity to gain certain knowledge and control of the extended mechanical world. That is, humanity was seen to have the capacity, and right, to master nature by knowing nature; and this project was thought to be one best directed by a single master informed by reason.[25] Figures of the Enlightenment and early positivism would later regard the formulation of such ideas as a decisive moment in the "progress of the human mind"; and they would dismiss any association with magic in favor of science. Progress itself was considered the necessary unfolding of a cosmic order, a process in which humanity participated: first, by discovering the universal laws of nature and society through scientific investigation; and then, by organizing human activities in accordance with those laws. Clearing the path of progress meant harmonizing the direction of the human mind with that of a greater mind. Despite the increasingly secular formulations given to these ideas, they often retained an explicitly religious cast: appeals to rationality gained persuasiveness from a continuing association with the mythic. In the transition from the medieval to the modern periods, the cosmos became industrialized, conceived as a machine designed for human use; and apparently natural regularities in human society came to be regarded as components of this cosmic machine. The general task of administration was to direct human affairs through knowledge of the natural order; and this notion carried with it the more or less explicit suggestion of understanding and conforming to the universal plan of a transcendent mind — indeed, of sharing in the identity and purpose of that mind.[26]

For the medieval era, the divine order of the cosmos was represented in the form and proportions of the Gothic cathedral:[27] the harmony of Creation gained expression in this microcosm, and here humanity found a symbol of its common aspiration and intrinsic unity. Early in this century, however, another image was proposed to take the place of the cathedral — the skyscraper. Despite the rush and fragmentation of the times, one could imagine a fitting representation of the seemingly disparate yet coherent character of modernity: a single, mammoth building, encompassing at its base the whole center of a great metropolis and ascending to the clouds. Unlike the Gothic cathedral, the skyscraper was not content to symbolize or gesture to a transcendent realm; modernity sought to reach the heavens.[28]

Modern organization was even seen as replacing the heavens. Before the turn of the century, a prominent businessman and inventor advanced a proposal which — however curious — pressed to its limit the presuppositions of the age.[29] Centralization and concentration, as represented in the rise of great corporations, constituted a natural law which should be used rather than thwarted because this dynamic would produce *"a perfect civilization"*.[30] For this promise to be fulfilled, all that would be necessary would be for the "Aladdin's lamp"[31] of "unified intelligence" to light the way to a single "World Corporation" organized as a frictionless great machine, the "Embodiment of Millions of Minds, Centralized and Working in Harmony."[32] The wonder and beauty of it all could be brought about through the inherent law of enterprise which produced business consolidation. The perfect civilization of a single corporation would, moreover, mean that there would be "but one city on a continent, and possibly only one in the world." "Metropolis" would be the electrified center of the "vast machine", lit up like a "fairyland" and guided by the "genii" of unified human intelligence.[33] Once united into a single machine, one business corporation, humanity would shed "those shackles which now prevent it from moving serenely with the cosmic current."[34] Under the World Corporation, individuals would be born and would pass away, but the institution itself would be eternal: "this great Corporate Mind will live through the ages, always absorbing and perfecting, for the utilization and benefit of all the inhabitants of the earth."[35]

Problems of the Administrative State

The administrative sphere prides itself on order, but cannot control the consequences it generates. For persistent fragmentation accompanies coherence in this sphere; and the administrative mind is itself limited, especially by its focus on promoting the modern vision of progress. Various disorders arose early with industrialization, indicating the need for a central authority to regulate and promote the steady course of progress. Profound disagreements over the nature and scope of this need did not alter the fact that, whenever problems threatened to thwart the realization of the modern vision, hope was generally placed in the agency of a competent and detached administration[36]—in what has emerged as the *administrative state*.[37] Anticipated in a sense throughout the rise of the industrialization, the administrative state was clearly recognized in the twentieth century when rationalization—the disenchantment of the world—began to permeate economy and society with both industrial technology and bureaucratic organization. The formalized relationships impressed upon social life fell far short of producing overall coherence, and consequent problems of coordination—as they were viewed—placed demands upon the administrative capacity of the state. Problems were generally defined in terms of finding and pursuing the most efficient use of human and natural resources. The corresponding tasks of calculation, organization, and technological development called for a state administrative apparatus capable of functioning as regulator and promoter of an increasingly rationalized economy and society. These tasks necessitated a rationalized state able to formulate and implement policies based upon a sound assessment of what was required by the developing industrial order. In effect, this meant not only enhancing the administrative apparatus of the state, but also fostering and coordinating linkages throughout the administrative sphere as a whole.[38] Yet, while the administrative state can thus be regarded as a response to advancing industrialization and the spread of administrative organizations in society, the path for these developments was cleared earlier by state policies which already involved a centralization and expansion of state administrative capacity.

Mechanism and the Modern State: The Path of Rationalization

The administrative state gives particular shape to the generally centralized form of the modern state. In contrast to the diverse and multifaceted patterns of authority characteristic of the feudal era, the modern state arose as a single, central authority. It achieved the clear subordination of other social interests—typically, that is, with monarchial dominance over the landed aristocracy, the clergy, and the towns.[39] A key policy thrust of the emerging modern state, and one often in conflict with traditional interests, was to expand national wealth by fostering the development of markets. Initially, this was done through the mercantilist integration of insulated, particularistic trading patterns into a comprehensive yet controlled market; later, through the effort to erect the necessary framework for the market to stand, more or less, by itself — to operate as a self-regulating mechanism through a *lassiez-faire* regime. The deliberate design and institutionalization of this market mechanism was conceived as a harmonization of society with the natural order and proceeded through the removal of state and traditional restrictions on the production and exchange of commodities.[40]

Yet the removal of restrictions on commodity production and exchange meant not the diminution of the state, but its refocusing and expansion. The project was conceived under the image of the cosmos as a mechanism — one, indeed, rationally designed by the mind of the Diety. By aligning economic life with the eternal natural laws of this design, the state would perform its ordained function and allow the market mechanism to operate freely in the generation of wealth. Yet *laissez-faire*, as a rationalistic scheme, required a sweeping transformation of society and involved the division of social life into distinct public and private sectors.[41] A major administrative effort by the state was required in establishing this division, removing restrictions on market activities and maintaining the conditions necessary for the operation of the market: "The road to the free market was opened and kept open by an enormous increase in continuous, centrally organized and controlled interventionism.... Administrators had to be constantly on the watch to ensure the free working of the system."[42] In particular, major attention had to be given to three interrelated areas corresponding to the factors of production which were now to circulate freely as part of the exchange of commodities: land (*i.e.*, enclosing, or privatizing, the commons), labor (*i.e.*, promoting a mobile and disciplined workforce), money (*i.e.*, maintaining a currency standard).[43] These tasks involved an extensive reform, standardization, and rationalization of law, together with a centralization and transformation of traditionally dispersed and inchoate activities into functions of an ordered whole. Further expansion of state administrative capacity was prompted both by the social problems and disturbances of early industrialization and by the need for an infrastructure to promote continuing development. The market mechanism thus appears as a social instrument deliberately devised, produced, regulated, and maintained through the administrative apparatus of the state. The *laissez-faire* ideology provided a general prescription for harmonizing economy and society with the natural order; yet the implementation of corresponding policies generated social pressures and encountered exigencies not contemplated by the creed. The establishment of the market mechanism and the emergence of the administrative state constituted complementary, mutually reinforcing aspects of the same pattern of development — of a rationalized world increasingly under the influence of the administrative mind.

The Administrative State in Context: Administrative and Public Spheres

The administrative state should be viewed *not* as a vast apparatus of public administration, standing by itself. Rather, the administrative state should be seen as a distinctive historical phenomenon, coming into its own precisely when the state loses its stature as a single, overarching administrative structure. For an historical dynamic of the market mechanism, still largely unacknowledged from a *laissez-faire* perspective, was for that mechanism to undermine itself by promoting a concentration of enterprise and an enormous expansion of bureaucratic administration in the great private corporations. The administrative state thus constitutes a key feature, as suggested above, of a more comprehensive administrative sphere, in which the position of the state as a clearly distinct and independent apparatus becomes significantly attenuated.[44] As part of this administrative sphere, indeed, the state proved far less effective in its *laissez-faire* mandate of maintaining competition than in such tasks as facilitating industrial coordination and helping to assess and harness the dormant resources of the earth for efficient use.[45] The orderly appearance of the administrative sphere accords with the expectations of the administrative mind and depends upon the calculable characteristics of both formal organization and commodity exchange. Yet, in focusing upon its own orderly aspects, the administrative sphere insulates itself from awareness of the disorders which it generates outside the market mechanism and beyond formal structures of organization.

The emergence of the modern state as the central, ascendant organizational structure in society was accompanied by the advent of public opinion from a "public sphere".[46] This arena of intellectual culture and political discourse, supported by the increasing availability of books and newspapers and by the associations encouraged by urban life, constituted a communicative space in which the appropriate role and particular policies of the state could be debated and criticized. Such criticism did not, however, entail fundamental opposition. Indeed, for the Enlightenment *philosophes* under absolutism, monarchial authority appeared necessary for the transformation of the world which they envisioned: the task was essentially one for an "omnipotent" despot who could be "enlightened" by ideas generated in the public sphere — who, in other words, would listen to advice, would recognize the "natural laws" of political economy, and would accept the "rationalist conclusions" applicable to state policy.[47] While the potential of enlightened despotism fascinated key intellectual figures under constitutionally limited monarchy, parliament emerged as a significant forum for debating and shaping state policy.[48] Here, nonetheless, a basic homogeneity of viewpoint was ensured by strict limitations of the franchise to propertied men; the bourgeois class interest, in particular, provided determined support for policies aligned with the doctrines of early political economy. With the decline of absolutism and with the late nineteenth century expansion of the franchise, public opinion both expanded to incorporate more fully the articulation of socially subordinate interests and, paradoxically, tended to decline in significance. Confronted by an administrative sphere which could readily lay claim to the knowledge and expertise required for rational policy-making and implementation, the public sphere found itself increasingly pressed to the margins of the policy process. Indeed, the formation of public opinion itself came to be identified as an administrative problem to be accomplished through propaganda techniques, which often retained the form without the substance of rational discourse and which employed expanding, increasingly centralized media of communication.[49] While the public sphere came at times in this century to be viewed as thoroughly homogenized and manipulated, there have been opposing signs of independence and vitality.[50] These signs have become especially salient with the advent of problems generated but unanticipated by the administrative apparatus of advanced industrial society.

Unexpected Problems

Not long after the administrative state had been formed and named — in the mid-twentieth century — the seemingly inevitable advance of rationalization began to encounter unanticipated obstacles. The burgeoning of industrial technology and bureaucratic organization began to generate problems which had been unintended and indeed unimaginable. As certain flaws in technology and bureaucracy became widely apparent, the rationalization of the world became increasingly vulnerable to questions which before could — to the extent they were even possible to ask — be readily deflected. This unsettling development did not, of course, occasion the collapse of the administrative state; the result, if anything, was intensified reliance upon it as a coordinating mechanism to solve the new problems. The reflex was to expand the scope of measurement and calculation, to devise a comprehensive system of planning and control—a mode of accounting, in short, which would monitor, anticipate, and internalize the diseconomies of industrial expansion.[51] The emergence of present problems associated with resource constraints and pollution has not yet significantly altered this orientation. Nonetheless, on the fringes of administrative practice and in a thin public sphere[52] the monuments of administration have been called into question; and the emerging array of problems thus appears to contain a significant potential—that of promoting challenges both to the established pattern of development and to the conventional view of administration.

The administrative state responds by reflex to its emerging problems—and this, perhaps, is its most pressing problem. The celebrated lack of imagination characteristic of the bureaucratic mentality is no doubt part of the difficulty. Indeed, schooled in routines, their attention fixed by rules and conventions, administrative officials are, we have been told, at best predictable. For if deviations from normal procedures are regarded as irresponsible, then little innovation is to be encouraged or expected in the solution or definition of problems.[53] Yet such clichés about bureaucracy do not adequately portray the predicament of the administrative state: a paradox of this tedious institutional form is that it is invested with exalted imagery, the grand vision of order and progress ordained by the administrative mind—a vision which remains potent, even as present problems dramatically violate the expectations it fosters.

Problems of Defining Problems

Far from resting in calm certitude, actual administration is notoriously uncertain and fallible. The imposing image of an administrative mind thus competes with a less exalted, distinctly mundane, process. Yet while in everyday practice no one may fully and explicitly express faith in the administrative mind, the image is nonetheless potent, shaping perceptions, expectations, and viewpoints; while limiting the way problems are defined. The notion of administrative problem-solving as the exclusive domain of a detached and impersonal mind helps to orient a form of life characteristic of the administrative sphere.

Unquestioned Judgment

For problem-solving to be defined as a matter of calculation, all issues of problem definition would have to be thoroughly resolved; and a key issue is the identification of goals. Actual administrative practice of course violates the conventional imagery of unity under an administrative mind where all are committed to a common goal. For a collision and coalescence of particular interests, coming from outside and within, is a salient feature of the administrative sphere. In the very stress upon the necessity of unified authority one can detect an acknowledgement of potential disunity—the worry that internal or external conflicts might disrupt deliberations and thereby undermine the ability of administrators to establish and maintain a coherent order of operations.[54]

To suggest that problems can be solved by calculation is not only to express what might be a genuine conviction; it is also to assert the autonomy, and thus to promote the insularity, of administrative authority. The traditional divide between policy formulation and implementation has supplied a fiction which pays tribute to the inevitable role of judgment in decision; yet this dichotomy has, in effect, served to advance the insularity and unity of administrative authority as the seat of such judgment. Even though calculation may appear partially displaced in this traditional conception, a safe realm of cogitation has been preserved by excluding the troubles of interaction, discussion, disagreement. The judgments are to be unquestionable. If an appeal to reason must here be supplemented by appeals to traditional or charismatic sources of authority, all remains further supported by the mythic and rationalistic imagery of order and progress. In the technocratic conception, there is no longer any requirement for a distinct realm of unquestionable judgment, for what remains of judgment has been narrowed to the vanishing point. The administrative mind constitutes a framework for pure calculation through a management information system which defines problems according to self-evident axioms and uncontroversial postulates.[55] What may be regarded as self-evident or uncontroversial is readily established by the unquestioned presuppositions of the vision of order and progress. While in principle contradictory, these traditional and technocratic approaches readily co-exist in practice; for they are complementary in providing a flexible mechanism for deflecting efforts to question judgments of the administrative mind.

Conceptual Focus

To the extent that problem-solving is influenced by the image of the administrative mind, whether overt or tacit, the effect is to obscure the actual process. Even when a fundamental consensus upon goals can be taken for granted, the search for means generates oppositions and tensions which can provoke a revision of goals. The definition of problems, that is to say, is not simply a matter of choosing goals; there is a complex interplay of means and goals as new difficulties or opportunities become apparent. Consequently, it is possible to speak of solving the wrong problem. The definition of a problem turns upon what concept gains prominence in focusing attention; as long as one concept fixes attention, perhaps because its influence is not noticed, the nature of the problem appears obvious. With an interplay among alternative concepts, however, the definition of the problem is thrown into question. Significant even in contexts of fairly routine administrative matters, such questioning may involve the issue, for example, of whether an organization faces a problem of transportation or of inventory, of attitudes or of structure, of machinery or of people. Similarly, questions may arise concerning the fundamental identity and direction of an organization. Here the emergence and clarification of a leading concept appears as the key breakthrough to a solution — in effect, it appears that the essential step in solving a problem lies in defining it. To say this is to say that problem-solving is primarily concerned with how attention is focused.[56] To reveal an organizing concept which has gone unnoticed serves to refocus attention and to open up the possibility of play and flexibility among concepts.

Much recent innovation in management thought may be interpreted as an attempt — usually remaining marginal in practice — to break free of that fascination with the administrative mind which has guided the understanding of problem-solving in administrative organizations. Particularly in attempts to address the problem of problem definition, the accent has shifted from cogitation to interaction, from the remote operations of an austere mind to a communicative domain of multiple participants.[57] Indeed, it now becomes apparent that the practice of judgment necessary in defining and redefining problems involves an inescapable interplay of opposing ideas and perspectives — of difference, divergence, conflict.

Even in the case of a single individual, this process of positing positions and oppositions is not eluded, but internalized. Yet both for individuals and collectivities, the image of the administrative mind can still obscure and inhibit this process.

Concern with the problem of problem definition points to an opening, to a play and flexibility in conceptualization. By drawing attention, in particular, to the administrative mind as a guiding focus of conventional problem definition in administrative organizations, we render explicit what is often implicit; we draw to the forefront a typically ignored background. Such a move, that is, directs attention to context; orientation to context thus becomes something which need not be passively received, but might be consciously developed and refined. As we probe constraints on attention, moreover, we pass beyond the administrative mind to its fundamental rationale: the vision of order and progress. By focusing upon this vision and questioning it, we advance our deliberate project of contextual orientation to the point of a conscious elaboration of developmental constructs.

Defining Environmental Problems

Even to speak of environmental problems reflects some influence of the administrative mind. For the dramatic and widespread expressions of environmental concern, voiced some two decades ago, were animated by an idea which the administrative mind was not prepared to contemplate: that there was a fundamental flaw in the whole pattern of industrial development. Progress, as a quest to dominate nature, was seen to be itself a source of disorder, disrupting the natural systems upon which civilization and human life depended. The concern being voiced was one focused not only on separate problems, but on a whole pattern of problems — the collective consequence of which, it was feared, could be to throw humanity out of the balance of nature. The concern was not just with problems, but with a crisis.

Environmental Crisis and Administrative Vision

Although environmental concern achieved considerable acceptance and even popularity, the perception of crisis was resisted and rejected by the administrative sphere; indeed, to perceive a fundamental flaw in the whole project of industrialization would be to question the *raison d'être* of this institutional complex. Accordingly, those articulating this sense of crisis were ridiculed — and ridiculed fairly easily since the rationalistic imagery of order and progress was at hand to help in portraying as emotional and irrational those who perceived a crisis. An anomaly in the ideological universe, the perception of crisis was to be explained as an abnormality, as deviance stemming from social or psychological peculiarities, from some corruption of mental faculties. Those who spoke of crisis were the victims and purveyors of irrationalism because — it was charged with no hint of the irony — they lacked *faith* in technology and progress.[58] The exuberant industrial growth and rapid technological innovation of the post-war period encouraged an optimistic atmosphere and gave credence to the notion that the management of government and industry was safely in the hands of experts. During this period, moreover, the increasingly technocratic bent of the administrative mind was reinforced by the widespread adoption of a systems approach.

The perception of an environmental crisis involved seeing various impacts of post-war expansion as an interrelated, emerging whole.[59] Ironically, this very perception gained support not only from the systems-theoretic focus of ecology, but also from systems modelling techniques drawn from the new repertoire of technocratic management itself. With this appeal to rationalistic imagery, the perception of environmental crisis demanded a more measured response than name-calling. While this more considered response may itself have exposed some rather basic limits of technocratic systems management, the controversy became esoteric enough to implicitly encourage renewed reliance upon the administrative mind to resolve the question.[60] At the same time, the challenge which the perception of crisis posed to the administrative sphere — and its animating vision — was too fundamental to be faced directly. Not only the ideology, but also the apparatus of this sphere, rendered irrelevant any perception of a pervasive crisis; for this apparatus had been structured to promote industrialization, not to deal with the aftermath. With a comprehensive vision of order and progress taken for granted, the apparatus was structured so that its various parts would attend to specific, strictly delimited problems one at a time. Even rather routine difficulties were, of course, often complex enough to generate problems of coordination requiring policy adjustments and structural adaptations.[61] However, the structure had no capacity to respond to the perception of a crisis so pervasive and complex as potentially to strike at the foundations of the entire edifice — and to expose it as a house of cards. To be dealt with, the "crisis" had to be viewed and treated not comprehensively, as the product of a basic flaw in the whole project of industrialization, but in a manner which identified *manageable* problems. Although the problems could be regarded as somehow commonly "environmental", they had to be defined, in operational terms, as primarily separate, capable of being solved in a manner which matched the functional differentiation of the administrative apparatus.[62] This approach accorded not only with the established structure of administration, but also with a "commonplace" of the technocratic orientation: "that there is a high measure of certainty that problems have solutions before there is knowledge of how they are to be solved."[63] With this confidence and with environmental concern translated into discrete problems, faith in the established pattern of development could be maintained.

An Alternative Vision

The perception of environmental crisis and continuing confidence in the path of industrialization arose from competing visions of an emerging whole, each necessarily based upon fragmentary evidence. Each viewpoint, in other words, was part of a contextual orientation which contained a particular notion of the pattern of historical development, a notion which — again in each case — was articulated vigorously and lent a sense of future inevitability. Against the dream of an efficient and orderly modern millennium, the perception of environmental crisis posed the nightmare of an apocalypse in which nature would gain retribution for the violations of an arrogant humanity.[64] While continuing confidence in the path of industrialization was reinforced by prevailing cultural norms, the perception of crisis could also draw upon elements of the culture with imagery reviving the romantic reaction against modernity, recalling bucolic myths and old doubts about progress, appealing to populist sentiment, and reverently picturing nature as something essentially harmonious.[65] Humanity, as a matter of both ethics and survival, should seek to live in harmony rather than in conflict with nature. This, it was suggested, was a lesson of ecology. Since this lesson was unlikely to be learned well or quickly enough, catastrophe was in the offing. This accent of environmentalist thought conveyed the idea that nothing short of a total and immediate transformation of the established path would do. Futile gestures or withdrawal were thus the typical consequences.

Nonetheless, there were significant efforts to formulate a possible path of future development which would pose a distinct alternative to the established pattern—one accentuating ecological sensitivity, decentralized initiative, small-scale projects, "appropriate" technology, and community cooperation. This idea of an alternative pattern of development represented, in effect, an effort to promote a contextual reorientation by deliberately elaborating a developmental construct in sharp contrast to the received view. While perhaps promoted as necessary for continued human well-being, an alternative pattern of development was clearly not seen as inevitable; at most, it was a desirable possibility, one which could conceivably be pursued through concerted effort. Since it directly challenged the established administrative artifice and its expectations of order and progress, however, such an alternative could readily be rejected and ridiculed, portrayed as thoroughly unrealistic. Still, by addressing significant, concrete issues of administration and policy within the context of a comprehensively conceived alternative, this approach to development could at least unsettle the complacency of the conventional outlook and provide, by way of dramatic contrast, an intellectual space for questioning a prevailing conceptual framework.[66]

The Adminstrative Response

Yet these were questions which could not really be taken seriously by the administrative mind. Having defined environmental concern in terms of manageable problems, the administrative sphere responded in a piecemeal fashion—in effect, seeking initially to "clean up" problems left by industrialization. The chief strategy was state promulgation and enforcement of environmental standards which were designed with the announced purpose of keeping specific kinds of "pollution" within tolerable limits, while at the same time achieving a balance with established economic interests. These initiatives sometimes involved the revival or revision of existing regulations, sometimes the development of new ones. Even when effective on its own terms, however, this approach typically employed what—in retrospect—appear obviously to have been expedients and stopgaps: narrowly focused techniques which were insensitive to their own consequences, changing the location and character of emissions and wastes without eliminating them as a problem. Environmental regulation was thus designed with a focus on specific, existing problems.[67]

It was not necessary to admit to a pervasive environmental crisis for the administrative sphere to recognize, however reluctantly, that emerging patterns of technological innovation and economic expansion were bound to generate new problems. A concerted effort to advance an alternative pattern of development would have taken as its central focus the purpose and design of new projects, both individually and collectively; indeed, a chief element of this approach would have been to draw explicit attention to the *pattern* of development and to foster an alternative to it which would anticipate and avoid formerly unanticipated problems. The response of the administrative sphere did not countenance such a decisive change in the existing pattern of development; nonetheless, attempts were made to design more sensitive anticipatory mechanisms while promoting the continuation of the established course. These mechanisms took the shape of innovations in planning techniques — in particular, technology assessment, environmental impact assessment, and social impact assessment. Although generally advanced from a technocratic posture, accentuating the readily calculable while neglecting context, these planning innovations nonetheless implicitly acknowledged that difficulties had arisen with conventional expectations informed by the vision of order and progress. The application of these techniques was generally unenthusiastic; indeed, resistance by particular administrative organizations was often effective in preventing, curtailing, or circumventing anticipatory assessments. Still, this resistance itself suggests that the employment of these new techniques — however technocratically constrained — was worrisome for major interests involved in promoting the established pattern of development. For no matter how marginal the use of these techniques generally has been in the policy processes of the state and of corporations, their application nonetheless created a new factor which somehow had to be reckoned with and which, at important points, could affect the flow of decision-making. Indeed, if not tightly controlled, such assessments could not only direct attention to fundamental problems about specific projects, but could also lead to a questioning of the whole pattern of industrial development — of order and progress itself.[68]

The agencies responsible for environmental management — regulation, impact assessment, and related procedures — were at times developed from already established units with different primary mandates; at other times, new units were created, yet typically with a marginal position within the administrative sphere as a whole. These organizational realignments were in keeping with what would seem a measured response of treating environmental concern in terms of manageable problems.[69] In contrast, many who perceived the advent of a pervasive environmental crisis demanded a far more dramatic response—one which would effectively subordinate the entire administrative sphere and society as a whole under a single head devoted to environmental management.[70] Of course, this proposal was a futile reflex: one which sought simply to change the goal orientation of the administrative mind while ignoring the historical and political processes which, in shaping the apparatus of the administrative sphere, have also promoted ends suited to its form. In any event, both of these approaches shared a view of environmental management as a discrete function, something added on somewhere to an administrative edifice whose basic form was to be taken for granted.

Thinking in Another Direction

In conceptions of an alternative pattern of development, environmental management came to be viewed as potentially a characteristic of the whole, rather than a function of a part controlling the whole. Yet this view was itself—given its holistic focus—so sweepingly comprehensive that it seemed to deny itself any place to begin. Conceptually, the approach seemed capable of recommending only a total transformation—a change requiring a scope and magnitude of power which not only would be fantastic, but which would also violate principles of decentralization and participation that were generally seen as necessary features of an alternative path.[71] In practice, however, a focus on particular problems did emerge. In part, this focus tacitly acknowledged the rationale of administrative compartmentalization: that a problematic complex must, whether or not it constituted a "crisis", somehow be reduced to a set of simpler problems, each of which can become an object of separate attention. At the same time, however, the particular way in which the alternative orientation is decomposed into specific problems shows that how one cuts into a problematic complex is decisive for problem definition. What is distinctive about this orientation is that no problem is assumed, in analysis or design, to be entirely discrete; on the contrary, it is a guiding presupposition that efforts to solve a particular problem will affect efforts to solve other problems. Hence problem-solving designs are elaborated with, as it were, an open boundary; attention is permitted and encouraged to remain devoted to a broader context. From this perspective, the definition of one problem partly defines others; there is, indeed, mutual overlapping. Accordingly, administration must, in technique, process, and structure, match the complexity of these interrelated problems.[72] Although thought and organizations must somehow be bounded, in other words, this approach to problem definition and administration attempts to test and stretch these limits through deliberate contextual reorientation — and through designs informed by this effort.[73] This distinctive approach to contextual orientation, furthermore, promotes what is in effect a redefinition of conventionally defined environmental problems.

The problem of waste disposal, for example, becomes redefined as a problem of waste reduction and recycling. The problem of controlling pesticide pollution is redefined as a problem of developing agricultural patterns which require less pesticide input while, at the same time, utilizing organic nutrients which otherwise end up as waste. Health care expands its focus from cure to prevention, seeking to reduce pollution both in the workplace and beyond; and trying, moreover, to encourage healthful dietary patterns — which, in turn, are congruent with the agricultural patterns being developed. Air pollution control devices on vehicles are seen (at most) as part of the solution to a problem which also requires vehicle redesign to reduce fuel consumption, perhaps the use of different fuels, and even a reform of the entire transportation network — guided by a reconsideration of settlement patterns and work schedules. The problem of meeting increasing energy demand is redefined so that increases are no longer taken as given: the problem becomes one primarily of meeting energy needs through significantly greater reliance upon conservation and efficiency, an effort which complements and reinforces efforts regarding waste, pollution, health and so on.

What is generally common to environmental problems, as redefined, is that they and their proposed solutions are found by thinking in "another" direction. Such redefinition, indeed, appears risky; for although the new approaches may be insightful, even elegant, they also dispense with guarantees implied by the vision of order and progress, guarantees which depend upon the administrative mind as the coherent locus of comprehension and control. The problem-solving designs — the technical forms — here presuppose an emergent redesign and transformation of the administrative apparatus, anticipating a decentralization and diffusion of responsibility. The principle of design for the administrative form thus abandons the "illusion of final authority"; yet this does not mean that no elements of centralization remain. The point, rather, is that this orientation proceeds by throwing dramatically into question the conventional reflex of relying upon some central, superior authority as the sole agency and ultimate guarantor of direction and coordination. In sum, the guiding outlook is that a new balance needs to be struck between centralization and decentralization, generally favoring the latter. Intrinsic to the problem of defining environmental problems, then, is a problem of organizational design involving the prevailing form of the administrative sphere. But who is to define and undertake this tremendous task of redesign? Merely to pose the question is to suggest an answer, at least in the negative: no *one*.

Beyond the Administrative Mind?

Thinking in a different direction is the goal of various techniques which have been developed to enhance creative problem-solving capacity in administrative organizations. Here the primary focus is upon ways of thinking that will generate new perspectives and insights: that will identify a dominant concept, reverse the terms of a relationship, review a question in relation to an ambiguous image or statement, imagine a different context.[74] Yet the efforts of creative problem-solving have also been extended beyond these various techniques of shifting focus in a thought process. Attention has also been given to processes of interaction, especially in the dynamics of small groups, but also with regard to overcoming the modes of "selective perception"[75] typically generated by differentiation among administrative units. Here organizational designs have been developed to draw differing units and perspectives into closer communication with one another in order to keep organizations attuned to the dynamics and complexities of external contingencies. For planning procedures, indeed, there are designs for encouraging argument and explicitly challenging conventional assumptions.[76] Such innovations—while typically contained within a rather conventional orientation—signal less reliance upon the style of thinking associated with the image of a unified and controlling administrative mind. Indeed, the reliance upon a greater diversity of perspectives points beyond thinking as the analytic activity of an independent mind (cogitation) and draws attention to communication among persons (a form of interaction).[77]

Discursive Designs: An Ambivalent Potential

In the administrative techniques and processes employed in environmental management, we witness some parallel movement from cogitation to interaction — from a monological, self-enclosed process to one which is more open, dialogical. Environmental management here involves "discursive designs"[78] such as participatory planning, regulatory negotiation, environmental mediation, and forms of public inquiry. These discursive designs are oriented to principles which implicitly challenge the administrative mind and thus are at least suggestive of different administrative forms. Of course these innovations do not arise in a vacuum, and within their historical and political context, their potential is ambivalent.

Discursive designs point beyond the administrative mind as the organizing principle for environmental management. The prospect is one of moving from a cloistered mode of problem-solving to an institutionalization of discourse which would encourage an interplay of differences in defining and resolving problems. While diverging from a rationalistic preoccupation with cogitation in problem-solving, such an institutionalization of discourse would itself be oriented to a concept of reason which is at once broader and more modest than that of the administrative mind — viz., a "communicative rationality", which becomes manifest in interactive contexts which promote a free creation and exchange of ideas. Such communicative contexts are of course not characteristic of the administrative sphere, for communication here is typically organized to absorb differences and block insights which might support the critical mode of contextual orientation that an institutionalization of discourse presupposes. The result is a distortion of communication.[79]

Distorted communication arises not only because of an uncritical fixation on misleading notions. Such fixation is itself part of a policy process which systematically renders certain priorities central and others marginal, thereby fostering a particular mode of problem recognition: a "mobilization of bias" which, as part of its operation, tends to deflect attention from itself. That is to say, this bias is not simply a particular point of view, but a way of seeing things which is mobilized organizationally to discourage the serious consideration of alternatives. Of the individual, group, and class interests which vie for a hearing in the policy process, those which receive most favored treatment are those which are at once most crucial to the stability of advanced industrial development and most capable of persistently organized expression in an idiom consistent with prevailing presuppositions.[80] These are predominantly interests of institutions in the administrative sphere which possess both the significant incentives and the resources required for advancing their cause effectively. With information a key resource in advancing particular interests, those central to the process have reasons to gain and control information, withholding or releasing it—as it suits their purpose—both from one another and from those on the margins of the process. The effect, as one participant-observer has termed it, is an *"unconscious* conspiracy" to maintain a closed policy process.[81] Broadly based interests, such as that of environmental concern, possess less clearly a potential for effective organization. They have fewer available resources and often speak a language at odds with that of the main idiom. Simply to squeeze in, to gain entry and a measure of legitimacy, they often find it necessary to reformulate, even censor, their message to accord with the established bias.[82]

Discursive designs, in principle, anticipate an institutional form which, with a distinctly more open, decentralized, and participatory orientation, would be conducive to ideas and innovations focused on an alternative pattern of development: an administrative sphere, that is, open to the influence of an active, critical public sphere. Yet as narrow openings in a generally closed world, discursive designs appear precarious, always under the threat of being squeezed shut. What weighs against this prospect is the clear message of environmental concern, voiced by people facing particular threats and by a more or less cohesive network of organizations sharing a broader focus. The administrative apparatus encounters pressure to accommodate these interests, to eliminate their potential for obstruction, to smooth over differences. While troublesome to the administrative mind, discursive designs thus also provide a convenient resource to promote the incorporation of divergent interests into a more stable consensus. At the same time, administrative units responsible for handling environmental problems find environmentalist pressures useful at various junctures in the policy process, so long as these pressures can be contained within acceptable bounds. Accordingly, support for the institutionalization of discursive designs—hence, a more open process—can come from within the administrative apparatus. However, this greater scope for the articulation of environmental concern carries a risk; if institutionalization promotes incorporation, a divergent message can be more or less subtly screened, softened, rendered compatible with the perspective of the administrative mind—or safely ignored. This occurs in an especially subtle—one could say pernicious—manner when the troubling message is translated into a technocratic idiom which deferentially approaches the administrative mind and implicitly presupposes its rationality. In this way, the articulation of environmental concern reenacts an administrative ritual of distorted communication which, if recognized, would be exposed as irrationality masquerading as reason. Those able simultaneously to master and see through the technocratic idiom can, indeed, make it perform their own tricks, with wit and irony exposing the ritual for what it is while propounding a dramatically innovative perspective designed to stretch the administrative mind.[83] Discursive designs thus remain ambivalent.

The potential to oppose and expand the administrative apparatus from within is always accompanied by another possibility — that the opposing perspective will be reduced and contained within the apparatus. Discursive designs, nonetheless, constitute an intrusion into the domain of the administrative mind. Increasing the salience of non-programmed features of administrative organizations, these designs loosen the grip of ritual and routine. This is not to predict a particular outcome, but to indicate that what happens becomes less predictable because the control of the prevailing regime becomes less secure. In other words, these innovations involve an accommodation of divergent interests which necessarily carries uncertain prospects for all parties. Plurality tends to displace unity with the unpredictable, unbounded, and inherently fragile character of human action;[84] and in the ensuing conflict and coalescence of perspectives, there is an enhanced potential for problems to be redefined beyond conventional bounds. Certainly, even in the most discursive of designs, the increased openness of discussion remains within obvious restrictions. But the openings, however narrow, come in response to actual or anticipated pressures — that is to say, within a context. It is thus misleading to think of discursive designs in terms of their *inherent* potential. A response to pressures from a larger context, discursive designs are points of intersection between the administrative sphere and the society at large; and as part of this relationship, discursive designs influence, and remain subject to, a pattern of influences which is susceptible to at least some change. The potential of discursive designs can be assessed only as part of the potential for broader changes to emerge — *i.e.*, only as affecting and being affected by developments in the overall alignment of social power.

Discursive designs could affect these developments in different ways — principally, by acting either to absorb pressures within conventionally accepted boundaries or to magnify and expand these pressures. The administrative sphere will typically seek to promote discursive designs on its own terms, and this establishes a tendency for the simple absorption of pressure. This obvious tendency can alert those groups and individuals articulating environmental concern to the prospect of cooptation in particular cases. Indeed, the record of discursive designs indicates that this prospect can be assessed with regard to procedural issues which often become matters of dispute: the concrete issues involve such questions as access to information, the availability of financial aid, timing, the form and sequence of presentations, and the relationship of the process to policy formulation and implementation.[85] Yet the specific issues all revolve about a common point. Unlike more strictly analytic techniques, discursive designs are *obviously* not neutral elements of an objectively given system. Hence their legitimacy — and even their capacity to absorb and control pressures — is predicated upon an appeal to norms of fairness and openness in communication. Consequently, discursive designs are directly exposed to the potential for critique in terms of these norms.[86] Such critique can inform decisions by potential participants in specific cases about whether to press for a particular discursive design, to call for procedural change, to withdraw involvement, to stage an alternative discourse, or to make some dramatic protest. In any event, the administrative capacity to absorb pressures through discursive designs is limited; for an achieved consensus can dissolve if the process is perceived to violate significantly the norms of fair and open communication.[87]

The potential for cooptation provides a rationale for a general environmentalist suspicion of discursive designs and for doubts (possibly to the point of outright resistance) concerning how they might be formalized and institutionalized. Yet such concern about cooptation becomes pressing primarily from a specific vantage point: one which seeks the organization, coordination, and direction of a comprehensive social movement — *i.e.*, implicitly from the viewpoint of an administrative mind which wants secure control over the course of developments, which seeks strategic and tactical unity. Indeed, it is ironic to note that the potential for cooptation might well increase to the extent that such unity is achieved; for a singular thrust runs counter to a less manageable diversity. Actually, the sources of environmentalist pressure are not generally cohesive; they are multifarious, cohering at times, but fragmenting at other times — either through a certain indifference or through conflicts, sometimes severe, over particular issues or general directions. This diversity restricts administrative capacity to promote consensus through discursive designs, especially when the procedures proposed are sharply at variance with normative expectations of fair and open communication. Hence protest and refusal to participate in a forum by some could tend to strengthen the position of participants seeking greater openness through procedural changes. The outcome is what no one plans.

Problems in Redefining Environmental Problems

To offer sound assurances, to provide a guarantee that everything will work out — this lends formidable support to any human artifice and its figures of authority: a promise of order, of protection from chaos, of a sacred canopy. Not hesitating to extend this offer, the administrative mind is no doubt cognizant that any adoration of its austere image is linked to a sense and hope that someone, somewhere, somehow must comprehend and be in control of things — *i.e.*, that the "illusion of final authority" is no illusion. The industrial cosmos has so far been fashioned with abiding confidence in the administrative mind; and the administrative definition of environmental problems remains marked by this confidence. Taking for granted the structure and exigencies of the existing administrative sphere, together with assumptions of order and progress, the administrative mind defines manageable problems and develops manageable solutions. Often the mind sets its "invisible hands" to work as reliable instruments of social control and development, hands whose work is manifest in the apparently lawful regularities of economic and political systems. The cogitation of the administrative mind thus calls forth interaction, but interaction which is largely anonymous and strictly strategic, blind to problems beyond immediate interests. The mechanisms of market economy and pluralist polity, to the extent that they actually operate, are of course not self-regulating; they in principle presuppose, but do not fulfill, the promise of order and progress.[88] Actually, the mechanisms are always subsumed within an administrative framework. With a proliferation of complex environmental (and other) problems generated both by these mechanisms and by the rest of the administrative apparatus, the administrative mind falls back upon cogitation, but is unable to perform the measurements and calculations needed to comprehend the problems, even on its own terms. Imperfectly hidden behind the administrative mind, masked by alternating images of reason and myth, lies the frailty of the human condition.

To conceive an alternative pattern of development is to view environmental problems in a manner which departs from the confident presuppositions associated with the administrative mind. Indeed, from this perspective, even to speak of *environmental* problems might risk obscuring their character: one must recognize that the relevant problem-complex is *ecological*. To speak of environmental problems fosters the connotation that the problems can readily be made manageable; it diverts attention from the need for comprehensive, integrated design based upon sound ecological principles. Such an approach could thus ignore the need for what has been called "ecological wisdom".[89] What we witness in this conception is both a humility which departs from prevailing administrative confidence and an attempt to find some ground for retaining confidence in a more sophisticated approach to design. In one type of formulation, this position advances scientific "laws" of ecology and attempts to specify thresholds of tolerance in eco-systems. The principles established by ecology thus provide an adequate ground, in principle, for comprehensive planning and control: it becomes possible to speak of a "blueprint".[90] A significantly different formulation reveals both deeper humility and greater confidence. Here a scientific conception of ecology is deemed inadequate; science, as conventionally understood, does not offer the whole of ecological wisdom. Ecological sensibility is required to grasp form in nature, to recognize its immanent *logos*. This recognition, moreover, is to guide humanity in restoring key elements of "organic society" as part of an emerging, collective effort to achieve an "ecological society" of harmonious form: natural-social-technical-human. Dissolving hierarchical conceptions of organization which have been imposed upon both nature and society, an ecological society would be founded upon interdependence: the pattern of development would involve conscious appreciation of the intertwining of nature-in-humanity and humanity-in-nature. Here both natural necessity and human domination would be replaced as guiding conceptions in favor of the idea of an integrated potential, of humanity and nature freely evolving. Ecological sensibility would ensure that social decisions generally would be both morally and technologically appropriate to human/nature as an evolving form.[91]

Both these approaches to defining and resolving the complex of environmental, or ecological, problems clearly run counter to modes of environmental management oriented to the image of the administrative mind; and the articulation of these positions throws dramatically into question the arrogant presuppositions of order and progress. The notion of ecological sensibility, in particular, throws into relief the "repugnance"[92] — the aversion culminating in willful ignorance — with which civilized humanity regards the human being as natural being, as animal; by recalling what has painstakingly been forgotten, ecological sensibility tends to unsettle the studied composure of the administrative mind. Such recollection, moreover, signals a change in self-definition and thus a contextual reorientation which involves a shift in the focus of problem definition. Still, these approaches themselves both presuppose a latent order in nature which humanity has the collective capacity to uncover and to actualize through designs for an alternative pattern of development — a presupposition which both restores confidence and provides again, in some measure, the shelter of a sacred canopy.

Any deliberate approach to problem-solving presupposes some combination of confidence and humility — confidence in seeking to overcome a problem, humility in recognizing one. The attempt to establish a secure foundation for some balance between these attitudes is, in effect, to try to fix in place a particular heuristic principle to guide problem definition. The vision of order and progress in an industrial cosmos has supported the promotion of industrialization with a confidence which now, after experiencing some of the aftermath, is difficult to accept in good faith. Alternative approaches to development take this experience into account and, to a significant extent, seek to shift the balance between confidence and humility. This move shakes the established concept and fosters an unpredictable interplay of ideas and perspectives. Yet the complex of pressures from which these different viewpoints emerge tends to inhibit the interplay, to promote a fixity of concepts. In the context of political conflict, indeed, one seeks a secure strategic position, inaccessible to opponents. This is the logic of the parties in pluralist competition; it is also the logic of domination and resistance.[93] Yet it is not the logic of open discourse.

Between Administrative and Public Spheres: Space for Redefining Problems

The administrative sphere offers little space for open discussion, for questioning — much less changing — problem definition. Under the sway of prevailing priorities, and with these reinforced through the image of the administrative mind, there is little internal impetus to think in a different direction, to break free of clichéd patterns of thought. Contained and organized under this mental framework, the interactive elements of this sphere are typically reduced to modes of interchange which are variously directive and strategic, depersonalized, even anonymous. Pressure for open discussion primarily comes from social movements, groups, and individuals articulating interests which are on the periphery of the administrative sphere — and these include environmental concerns.

The articulation of these interests signals a notable shift from the situation at mid-century when it was possible to portray a cohesive administrative sphere, operating smoothly on the basis of a broad consensus, restricting partisanship to "mutual adjustment" and servicing a quiescent mass society.[94] Subsequent social changes involved the emergence of elements — or, perhaps, fragments — of an active public sphere increasingly capable of monitoring, criticizing, and influencing the operations of the administrative sphere. Demands for openness and participation constitute efforts to overcome a mobilization of bias by pressing peripheral priorities onto and into the administrative sphere — in effect, changing its priorities and creating greater potential for problem redefinition. The administrative sphere, of course, responds by variously repelling, accommodating, and containing these pressures — typically, that is, by changing its mind as little as possible. Discursive designs emerge from the ambivalent pressures of this context, at a point of division and intersection between administration and society: at the boundary, so to speak, of the administrative sphere and the emergent public sphere.[95]

The apparent fragments of a public sphere may ultimately amount to no more than a development within interest group politics, an expansion of pluralist tendencies in society. Yet it remains significant that, as reflected in the case of discursive designs, activity is being focused on the administrative sphere, on the task of gaining access to perceived key centers of decision-making. This is a response to the realization that it would not be adequate to focus effort only on established legislative bodies or on influencing public opinion. In terms of organizational design, the creation of discursive bodies connected to the administrative sphere would tend to match internal and external complexity. To the extent that these bodies were not integrated within the flow of administrative decision-making, however, their tendency would be only to complicate things, proving variously annoying or irrelevant to administration. Integration within the flow of decision-making could, of course, mean absorption — a reduction of the potential complexity.[96] Yet an integration which retained difference would enhance internal complexity in response to the complexity of environmental (and other) problems arising in a wider context. What would be increased, in other words, would be administrative capacity to redefine problems. There would be an increase of "cogitation in interaction"[97] which would challenge the hold of prevailing concepts. The capacity to redefine problems, moreover, would amount to a shift in priorities—hence a decisive change in administrative outlook and practice, together with a move towards realigning the apparatus. Problem definition would step beyond the limits of the administrative mind.

Ironies of Order

Here the main problem in redefining environmental problems has been cast as a problem in organizational design. Of course, the problem is also political, and the prevailing shape of power in society can easily block the recognition—not to mention the solution—of the problem in these terms. Nonetheless, it is conceivable that further rents could develop in the sacred canopy supplied by the administrative mind. Then there would no doubt be temptations in many quarters to patch up the canopy or to replace it with a new one. Yet the necessary fabric is not readily available, not even in the principles of ecology—however important these might be in a project of contextual reorientation. Certainly, practical activity—in either changing or maintaining a structure—must find a balance of confidence and humility. But this does not require the solid faith which has inspired the industrial cosmos; another balance—likely more appropriate to environmental problems—can rely upon flexible principles which are deliberately and provisionally accepted. Indeed, open discourse both presupposes and fosters such principles, while allowing any faith to be questioned.

The sacred canopy of the administrative mind protects the world from chaos; it is a serious mind, relentless in demanding order in its domain. Yet, manifest in the administrative sphere of advanced industrial society, it persistently generates disorders, especially in a complex of environmental problems which it is unable to comprehend, much less control. To this mind, pressures from an emerging public sphere are troublesome, risky, unsettling; they are intrusions, likely to generate chaos, even when placed in the fairly orderly form of discursive designs. What the brooding administrative mind cannot grasp is the irony of the disorders which it creates through the operations of its own apparatus.

To see the irony requires an appreciation for the *comic*, for it is in the comic that humanity recognizes both its frailties and its capacity for flexible, resourceful creativity.[98] Commenting upon failures in a case of environmental discourse—upon the tacit rules, the self-censorship, the pretenses which blocked open and free communication—an insightful participant-observer nonetheless looked forward to a time when it would be common for there to be "more open, more self-critical, even more playful discourse."[99] This hope recognizes a further irony, the obverse of the other. Comedy, play among concepts, a relaxation of control—these can foster a coherent and effective handling of problems. To recognize this irony is to identify a key heuristic principle in defining problems: to engage in discourse—indeed, to elaborate discursive designs—while always keeping alternative directions in mind. Of course, there is no guarantee that this principle will always help to solve our problems, or even to define them well. But, then, the broken promises of progress, the unforeseen problems already generated through the administrative sphere, teach us that no such guarantee is worth the paper on which it is printed.

Notes

1. Jürgen Habermas, "Modern and Postmodern Architecture," in John Forester, ed., *Critical Theory and Public Life* (Cambridge, MA: The M.I.T. Press, 1985), p. 327. *Cf.* Harold D. Lasswell, *The Signature of Power: Buildings, Communication, Policy* (New Brunswick, NJ: Transaction Books, 1979), pp. 64-65.

2. Gianfranco Poggi, *The Development of the Modern State* (Stanford: Stanford University Press, 1978), p. 142. In attempting to discern broad patterns of development, Poggi tends to disregard national and regional variations. Yet a focus which disregards certain differences does not necessarily deny their potential importance for other relevant inquiries. What I examine here is a general intellectual and institutional background, against which such differences might stand out.

3. The phrase "mobilization of bias" was presented in E. E. Schattscheinder, *The Semisovereign People* (Hinsdale, IL: The Dryden Press, 1975 [1960]) and developed in Peter Bachrach and Morton S. Baratz, *Power and Poverty* (New York: Oxford University Press, 1970), pp. 8, 43, 58. The concept of a critique of ideology is, of course, central to critical theory. Here the work of Habermas is most significant. See, *e.g.*, Jürgen Habermas, *Legitimation Crisis* (Boston: Beacon Press, 1975). In Habermas such a mobilization of bias would be a form of systematically distorted communication. The complementary work of Offe helps in making this connection. See n. 80 below.

4. *Cf.* Hannah Arendt, *The Human Condition* (Chicago: University of Chicago Press, 1958), esp. pp. 220ff.

5. See William Leiss, *The Domination of Nature* (Boston: Beacon Press, 1974). On the distinctly masculine character of this "mastery", *cf.* Rosabeth Moss Kanter, *Men and Women of the Corporation* (New York: Basic Books, 1977), ch. 1.

6. For a survey, see Daniel A. Wren, *The Evolution of Management Thought* (New York: John Wiley and Sons, 2nd ed., 1979). For a more critical view, see Reinhard Bendix, *Work and Authority in Industry: Ideologies of Management in the Course of Industrialization* (New York: Harper and Row, 1963), esp. pp. 58ff.

7. The "human resources" approach draws upon the psychological theories of Abraham Maslow. See, *e.g.*, Douglas McGregor, *The Human Side of Enterprise* (New York: McGraw-Hill, 1960). On the "contingency approach", see Joan Woodward, *Industrial Organization: Theory and Practice* (London: Oxford University Press, 2nd ed., 1980 [1965]); Paul R. Lawrence and Jay W. Lorsch, *Organization and Environment: Managing Differentiation and Integration* (Boston: Harvard University, 1967).

8. Of a large literature, see esp. Gareth Morgan, *Images of Organization* (Beverly Hills: Sage Publications, 1986).

9. *Cf.* Douglas Torgerson, "The Paradox of Environmental Ethics," *Alternatives* 12:2 (1985), pp. 27-29.

10. For an introduction which can also be read as a critique by an insightful insider, see C. West Churchman, *The Systems Approach* (New York: Dell Publishing, rev. ed., 1979).

11. The concept of "the administrative mind" employed in this article anticipates the completion of a larger study on images of mental activity in the emergence of management thought.

12. See Douglas Torgerson, "Contextual Orientation in Policy Analysis: The Contribution of Harold D. Lasswell," *Policy Sciences* 18 (1985), pp. 241-261; Werner Ulrich, *Critical Heuristics of Social Planning: A New Approach to Practical Philosophy* (Bern: Haupt, 1983). *Cf.* Judith I. De Neufville and Stephen E. Barton, "Myths and the Definition of Policy Problems," *Policy Sciences* 20 (1987), esp. pp. 183-184, 202.

13. Harold D. Lasswell, *A Pre-View of Policy Sciences* (New York: American Elsevier Publishing, 1971), p. 155.

14. *Ibid.*, pp. 67-68; *cf.* Torgerson, "Contextual Orientation," pp. 247-248.

15. Henri Fayol, *General and Industrial Management* (London: Pitman Publishing, 1967 [1916]), pp. 24-26 and ch. 5 generally. *Cf.* Max Weber, *Economy and Society*, 2 Vols. (Berkeley: University of California Press, 1978), Vol. 1, pp. 217-226; Vol. 2, pp. 956-1005, pp. 1381-1469, esp. p. 1402: "An inanimate machine is mind objectified.... Objectified intelligence is also that animated machine, the bureaucratic organization...." At the top of the mechanized hierarchy, though, one encounters "[t]he 'directing mind', the 'moving spirit'" which is different from the "mentality of the official" (p. 1403). Weber's ideal-type of bureaucracy thus differs from technocratic administration guided by a systems approach. (See n. 55 below). *Cf.* Henry Jacoby, *The Bureaucratization of the World* (Berkeley: University of California Press, 1976), pp. 152ff. Also note the focus on "the mind" in the development of managerial ideologies, esp. the New Thought Movement. See Bendix, *Work and Authority in Industry*, pp. 259ff., 275, 292, 311; also pp. 278, 283, 286, 294, 296, 298f., 302, 305. With the movement from Weberian bureaucracy to technocracy, the directing mind itself tends to become viewed after the image of the mechanism which it directs. The organization first becomes an engineering problem: "The engineer's mind is that of industrialism in its streamlined form." Max Horkheimer, *Eclipse of Reason* (New York: Seabury Press, 1974 [1947]), p. 151. The next step is envisioned in the following: "With recent developments in our understanding of heuristic processes and their simulation by digital computers, the way is open to deal scientifically with ill-structured problems—to make the computer coextensive with the human mind." Herbert A. Simon and Allen Newell, "Heuristic Problem-solving: The Next Advance in Operations Research" (1957), in Herbert A. Simon, *Models of Bounded Rationality*, 2 Vols. (Cambridge, MA: The M.I.T. Press, 1983), Vol. 1, p. 388. *Cf.* Herbert A. Simon, *The New Science of Management Decision* (Englewood Cliffs, NJ: Prentice-Hall, rev. ed., 1977).

16. "Ever since mental and physical labour were separated in the sign of the dominant mind, the sign of justified privilege, the separated mind has been obliged, with the exaggeration due to a bad conscience to vindicate the very claim to dominate which it derives from the thesis that it is primary and original—and to make every effort to forget the source of its claim, lest the claim lapse." If one looks at such effort beyond the "magic circle" of philosophy, one uncovers "a society unaware of itself." Theodor W. Adorno, *Negative Dialectics* (New York: Continuum Publishing, 1987 [1966]), p. 177. A *monological* concept of mind can be contrasted with a *contextual* one, and these are indeed the two key concepts underlying the two basic approaches to the philosophy of mind. See Guttorm Floistad, "Introduction" to Guttorm Floistad, ed., *Contemporary Philosophy: A New Survey*, Vol. 4, *Philosophy of Mind* (The Hague: Martinus Nijhoff, 1983), p. 2. *Cf.* C. West Churchman, *The Design of Inquiring Systems: Basic Concepts of Systems and Organizations* (New York: Basic Books, 1971). On "methodological solipsism", see Karl-Otto Apel, "The A Priori of Communication and the Foundation of the Humanities,"

Man and World 5:1 (1972), pp. 3-37.

17. Mary Parker Follett, "The Illusion of Final Authority" (1926) in *Dynamic Administration: The Collected Papers of Mary Parker Follett* (New York: Hippocrene Books, 2nd ed., 1977).

18. See Leiss, *Domination of Nature*, ch. 2. Faust is of course a key figure in this regard. Also see Edward Chase Kirkland, *Dream and Thought in the Business Community, 1860-1900* (Chicago: Quadrangle Books, 1964), pp. 9ff, on an intertwining of spiritualism, myth, religion, and science; and H. V. Nelles, *The Politics of Development: Forests, Mines and Hydro-electric Power in Ontario, 1849-1941* (Toronto: Macmillan of Canada, 1975), ch. 6, "Hydro as Myth." The phrase "order and progress" was the motto adopted by the early positivist Auguste Comte. See Raymond Aron, *Main Currents of Sociological Thought*, Vol. 1 (Garden City, NY: Anchor Books, 1968), ch. 2, "Auguste Comte." On the self-contradiction of the positivist notion of historical progress, see Jürgen Habermas, *Knowledge and Human Interests* (Boston: Beacon Press, 1971), pp. 71ff. *Cf.*, generally, Max Horkheimer and Theodor W. Adorno, *Dialectic of Enlightenment* (New York: Seabury Press, 1972 [1944]).

19. Adorno, *Negative Dialectics*, p. 177. Weber's distinction among three sources of legitimation (traditional, charismatic, and rational) was formulated at the level of ideal-types. He had no doubt that attention to particular contexts would reveal complex interconnections and variations. Weber's concepts of rationalization and bureaucratization do clearly anticipate the increasing salience of the rational mode; yet the top of the bureaucratic structure is not subsumed by the machine. See Weber, *Economy and Society*, Vol. 1, pp. 216, 222; Vol. 2, pp. 1403-1404. *Cf.* Jeffrey Pfeffer, *Power in Organizations* (Boston: Pitman Publishing, 1981), chs. 1, 6.

20. Max Weber, "Science as a Vocation," in *From Max Weber: Essays in Sociology* (New York: Oxford University Press, 1958), p. 139.

21. See Henry Mintzberg, "The Myths of MIS," *California Management Review* 15:1 (1972), p. 94: "the manager can be described as a sophisticated management information system."

22. Douglas Hartle, *The Expenditure Budget Process in the Government of Canada* (Toronto: Canadian Tax Foundation, 1978), p. 95. *Cf.* Langdon Winner, "Cybernetics and Political Language," *Berkeley Journal of Sociology* 14 (1969), pp. 3-17.

23. Peter Berger, *The Sacred Canopy: Elements of a Sociological Theory of Religion* (Garden City, NY: Anchor Books, 1969).

24. See Walter Ullmann, *Medieval Political Thought* (Harmondsworth: Penguin Books, 1975), ch. 4; Ian G. Barbour, *Issues in Science and Religion* (New York: Harper and Row, 1971), pp. 16-23.

25. Descartes was, of course, the key figure in this regard. See *Discourse on Method* (1637) in *The Philosophical Works of Descartes*, 2 Vols. (Cambridge: Cambridge University Press, 1975), Vol. 1, p. 119 for the famous promise of mastery over nature; pp. 87-88 for suggestions regarding the advantages of a single master. *Cf.* generally, E.A. Burtt, *The Metaphysical Foundations of Modern Physical Science* (Garden City, NY: Anchor Books, rev. ed., 1954). On associations with magical traditions, see Leiss, *Domination of Nature*, ch. 2 and pp. 60, 74-75. For a relevant discussion of Hobbes, see Douglas Torgerson, "Obsolescent Leviathan: Problems of Order in Administrative Thought," in this volume.

26. See J. B. Bury, *The Idea of Progress* (New York: Dover Publications, 1955 [1932]); Peter Gay, *The Enlightenment: An Interpretation*, 2 Vols. (New York: Alfred A. Knopf, 1966, 1969); A. L. McFie, *The Individual in Society: Papers on Adam Smith* (London: George Allen and Unwin, 1967), esp. pp. 69, 109ff, 117; William Coleman, "Providence, Capitalism, and Environmental Degradation: English Apologetics in an Era of Economic Revolution," *Journal of the History of*

Ideas 37:1 (1976), pp. 27-44.

27. See Otto von Stimson, *The Gothic Cathedral: Origins of Gothic Architecture and the Medieval Concept of Order* (New York: Harper and Row, 1964).

28. The image was suggested by Harold D. Lasswell in a private letter of 1923. See Douglas Torgerson, "Political Vision and the Policy Orientation: Lasswell's Early Letters," a paper presented at the Annual Meetings of the American Political Science Association, Chicago, September 3, 1987, p. 27.

29. See James Gilbert, *Designing the Industrial State* (Chicago: Quadrangle Books, 1972), ch. 6, "King Gillette's Social Redemption." Gillette was of course the inventor of the safety razor and the founder of the Gillette Safety Razor Company.

30. King C. Gillette, *The Human Drift* (Delmar, NY: Scholars' Facsimiles and Reprints, 1976 [1894]), p. 84 (original emphasis).

31. *Ibid.*, p. 75.

32. Gillette quoted in Gilbert, p. 174.

33. Gillette, *Human Drift*, pp. 87, 89, 93.

34. Melvin L. Severy, a disciple of Gillette, quoted in Gilbert, p. 170.

35. Gillette, quoted in Kenneth M. Roemer, "Introduction to Gillette," *Human Drift*, p. xviv.

36. See Karl Polanyi, *The Great Transformation: The Political and Economic Origins of Our Time* (Boston: Beacon Press, 1957), ch. 12; Robert Pinker, *Social Theory and Social Policy* (London: Heinemann Educational Books, 1973), ch. 2, "The Origins of Social Administration"; Kirkland, *Dream and Thought in the Business Community*, ch. 5.

37. Dwight Waldo, *The Administrative State* (New York: The Ronald Press, 1948).

38. In addition to Weber, see Samuel Haber, *Uplift and Efficiency: Scientific Management in the Progressive Era, 1890-1920* (Chicago: University of Chicago Press, 1964); Samuel P. Hays, *Conservation and the Gospel of Efficiency: The Progressive Conservation Movement, 1890-1920* (New York: Antheneum, 1969); Robert B. Reich, *The Next American Frontier* (Harmondsworth: Penguin Books, 1984), Part 2, "The Era of Management, 1920-1970"; John Kenneth Galbraith, *The New Industrial State* (New York: Mentor Books, rev. ed., 1972); Arthur S. Miller, "Legal Foundations of the Corporate State" and Daniel R. Fusfeld, "The Rise of the Corporate State in America," in Warren J. Samuels, ed., *The Economy as a System of Power*, 2 Vols. (New Brunswick, NJ: Transaction Books, 1979), Vol. 1.

39. See Poggi, *Development of the Modern State*, chs. 2-4.

40. See Polanyi, *Great Transformation*, chs. 5-6.

41. *Ibid.*, pp. 71-75.

42. *Ibid.*, p. 140.

43. *Ibid.*, chs. 16, 15, 17, respectively.

44. See Poggi, *Development of the Modern State*, ch. 6. *Cf.* Gerhard Lehmbruch, "Liberal Corporatism and Party Government," in Philippe C. Schmitter and Gerhard Lembruch, eds., *Trends Toward Corporatist Intermediation* (Beverly Hills: Sage Publications, 1979), esp. pp. 148, 154. I am suggesting that the administrative state should be viewed in this manner because doing so draws attention to relationships which one might neglect by taking the conventional boundary between public and private as an ontological given. I do not deny that the conventional boundary remains an important consideration in analyzing concrete relationships; nor would I rule out in

principle other conceptualizations which might reveal further neglected relationships. The problem of conceptualizing the state may, indeed, be viewed as involving the same problem, writ large, as that of defining an organizational boundary. See, *e.g.*, Raymond E. Miles *et al.*, "Organization-Environment: Concepts and Issues," *Industrial Relations* 13:3 (1974), pp. 244-264; the controversial conception of customers as part of a business organization, seen as a "cooperative system", in Chester I. Barnard, "Concepts of Organization," in his *Organization and Management* (Cambridge, MA: Harvard University Press, 1948); and the proposal for a "figure-ground reversal" in Eric Trist, "A Concept of Organizational Ecology," *Australian Journal of Management* 2:2 (1977), pp. 161-175. The identity, hence boundary, of the state—the realm of the "political" as distinct from the "economic"—emerged as a significant issue in the exchange between Miliband and Poulantzas. See esp. Ernesto Laclau, "The Specificity of the Political: The Poulantzas-Miliband Debate," *Economy and Society* 4 (1975), pp. 100-101; Nicos Poulantzas, "The Capitalist State: A Reply to Miliband and Laclau," *New Left Review* 95 (1976), pp. 81-82.

45. *Cf.* Hays, *Conservation and the Gospel of Efficiency*, the new Preface and ch. 13.

46. Poggi, *Development of the Modern State*, pp. 68-85, 104, 112, 124-125. The "public sphere" is a key concept in Habermas. For a general discussion, see Peter Uwe Hohendahl, "Critical Theory, Public Sphere, and Culture: Jürgen Habermas and his Critics," *New German Critique* 16 (1979), pp. 89-118. Also see Jürgen Habermas, *The Structural Transformation of the Public Sphere: An Inquiry into a Category of Bourgeois Society* (Cambridge, MA: The M.I.T. Press, 1989 [1962]).

47. Georges Lefebvre, "Enlightened Despotism," in Heinz Lubasz, ed., *The Development of the Modern State* (New York: Macmillan, 1964), p. 52.

48. On Bentham in this connection, see Elie Halévy, *The Growth of Philosophic Radicalism* (Boston: Beacon Press, 1955), p. 375. This study of utilitarianism as a form of rationalism is useful in portraying a texture of intellectual relationships stretching back to Hobbes. *Cf.* C. B. Macpherson, *The Life and Times of Liberal Democracy* (Oxford: Oxford University Press, 1977).

49. *Cf.* Harold D. Lasswell, *Propaganda Technique in World War I* (Cambridge, MA: The M.I.T. Press, 1971 [1927]), an early attempt to examine propaganda as "a concession to the rationality of the modern world," p. 221.

50. See, generally, Forester, ed., *Critical Theory and Public Life*.

51. See, *e.g.*, A. Myrick Freeman III *et al.*, *The Economics of Environmental Policy* (New York: John Wiley and Sons, 1973). On the externalization of costs as "intrinsic" to the market system, see Donella Meadows, "Equity, the Free Market, and the Sustainable State," in Dennis Meadows, ed., *Alternatives to Growth—I: Toward a Sustainable Future* (Cambridge, MA: Ballinger, 1977), p. 143.

52. *Cf.* Benjamin R. Barber, *Strong Democracy: Participatory Politics for a New Age* (Berkeley: University of California Press, 1984), ch. 1; Alan Wolfe, "Inauthentic Democracy: A Critique of Public Life in Modern Liberal Society," *Studies in Political Economy* 21 (1986), pp. 57-81.

53. *Cf.* Herbert A. Simon, "The Changing Theory and Changing Practice of Public Administration," in Ithiel de Sola Pool, ed., *Contemporary Political Science* (New York: McGraw-Hill, 1967), p. 99; Robert K. Merton, "Bureaucratic Structure and Personality," in his *Social Theory and Social Structure* (New York: The Free Press, rev. ed., 1957).

54. This anxiety is evident in Hobbes. A paradox of the administrative mind, moreover, is that it seeks to unify through a strategy of division; this suggests that only a rather forced unity is possible and that a troubling crack remains in the foundations.

55. The more traditional "decisionistic" model is distinguished from the increasingly salient "technocratic" model in Jürgen Habermas, "The Scientization of Politics and Public Opinion," in his *Toward a Rational Society* (Boston: Beacon Press, 1971), pp. 63ff. Within this technocratic frame one observes the transition from an earlier focus by technical experts (in scientific management) on achieving efficiency through standardized procedures to a reliance on a more sophisticated systems orientation (in management science). See Churchman, *Systems Approach*, chs. 2-3. For an important effort to refine the concept of technocracy, see Wolf V. Heydebrand, "Technocratic Corporatism," in Richard H. Hall and Robert E. Quinn, eds., *Organizational Theory and Public Policy* (Beverly Hills: Sage Publications, 1983). *Cf.* Laurence H. Tribe, "Policy Science: Analysis or Ideology?" *Philosophy and Public Affairs* 2 (1972), pp. 66-110; Christopher Nash *et al.*, "Criteria for Evaluating Project Evaluation Techniques," *Journal of the American Institute of Planners* 41 (1975), pp. 83-90; John Byrne, "Policy Science and the Administrative State: The Political Economy of Cost-Benefit Analysis," in Frank Fischer and John Forester, eds., *Confronting Values in Policy Analysis* (Beverly Hills: Sage Publications, 1987).

56. See Donald A. Schon, *Displacement of Concepts* (London: Tavistock Publications, 1963). Also see Ian I. Mitroff, "Systemic Problem-solving," in Morgan W. McCall Jr. and Michael M. Lombardo, eds., *Leadership* (Durham, NC: Duke University Press, 1978); Edward de Bono, *Lateral Thinking: A Textbook of Creativity* (Harmondsworth: Penguin Books, 1971); Rollo May, *The Courage to Create* (New York: Bantam Books, 1976), esp. ch. 5; James G. March, "The Technology of Foolishness," in James G. March and Johan P. Olsen, *Ambiguity and Choice in Organizations* (Bergen, Norway: Universitetsforlaget, 1976); Jeffrey Pressman and Aaron Wildavsky, *Implementation* (Berkeley: University of California Press, 3rd ed., 1984); David Dery, *Problem Definition in Policy Analysis* (Lawrence: University Press of Kansas, 1984).

57. Much work along these lines is conceived in explicitly dialectical terms, influenced in particular by Churchman, *Design of Inquiring Systems*. *Cf.* Ian I. Mitroff and Louis R. Pondy, "On the Organization of Inquiry: A Comparison of Some Radically Different Approaches to Policy Analysis," *Public Administration Review*, 43:5 (1974), pp. 471-479; Ulrich, *Critical Heuristics*. Also *cf.* Pfeffer, *Power in Organizations*, ch. 9. Aspects of this orientation were anticipated in the early work of Follett—*e.g.*, "Constructive Conflict" (1925) in *Dynamic Administration*—the very style and texture of which manifests a dialectical play of concepts.

58. For further characterization of the dispute, see Gideon Rosenbluth, "Economists and the Growth Controversy," *Canadian Public Policy* 11:2 (1976), pp. 225-239. Of course, this controversy had a precursor during the early development of economics as certain doubts were raised about progress. Here the miserable conditions of early capitalist industrialization were viewed against the dismal idea of a natural law in which famine would continually return as food production failed to keep ahead of population growth. Yet this was not to deny progress altogether, for hunger was a "divine sanction": "Malthus...had his own version of the gospel of progress.... Without the stimulus and pressure of surplus numbers of people, progress might end and technology stagnate." Donald Worster, *Nature's Economy: The Roots of Ecology* (Garden City, NY: Anchor Books, 1979), p. 151. What this suggests is that the vision of progress was not always a happy one; certainly this was the case even with Bentham, the apostle of happiness as "utility". The early dispute divided pessimistic and optimistic doctrines of progress; progress itself was not questioned. See Halévy, *Growth of Philosophic Radicalism*, pp. 268-276; *cf.* pp. 492-493.

59. See, *e.g.*, Barry Commoner, *The Closing Circle: Man, Nature and Technology* (New York: Alfred

A. Knopf, 1971).

60. See Donella H. Meadows *et al.*, *The Limits to Growth* (New York: Universe Books, 1972); also see H. S. D. Cole *et al.*, *Thinking About the Future: A Critique of the "Limits to Growth"* (London: Chatto and Windus Ltd. for the University of Sussex Press, 1973).

61. The formal matrix structure is one device which has been adopted by administrative organizations to balance competing demands from a complex environment. This device violates the principle of unity of command and often elicits resistance; nonetheless, explicit commitment to this traditional principle often coexists with tacit adaptations in the informal structure. See Stanley M. Davis, "Two Models of Organization: Unity of Command versus Balance of Power," *Sloan Management Review* 16 (1974), pp. 29-40; Ph. G. Herbst, *Alternatives to Hierarchies* (Leiden: Martinus Nijhoff, 1976), ch. 3; Pfeffer, *Power in Organizations*, pp. 356-363.

62. See Geoffry Wandesforde-Smith, "The Bureaucratic Response to Environmental Politics," in Albert E. Dutton and Daniel H. Henning, eds., *Environmental Policy* (New York: Praeger Publishers, 1973); *cf.* Lynton K. Caldwell, *Man and His Environment: Policy and Administration* (New York: Harper and Row, 1975). Some central environmental agency was often to perform a coordinating role, but this task was made difficult by a marginal position in the administrative apparatus and a restricted definition of what constituted "environmental" problems. See, *e.g.*, O.P. Dwivedi, "The Canadian Government Response to Environmental Concern," in O.P. Dwivedi, ed., *Protecting the Environment* (Vancouver: Copp Clark Publishing, 1974), esp. p. 176; Michael J. Whittington, "Environmental Policy," in G. Bruce Doern and V. Seymour Wilson, eds., *Issues in Canadian Public Policy* (Toronto: Macmillan of Canada, 1974), esp. p. 208. For a case study which stresses resulting jurisdictional disputes in the state and discusses the establishment of environmental units within corporations, see Douglas Pimlott *et al.*, *Oil Under the Ice: Offshore Drilling in the Canadian Arctic* (Ottawa: Canadian Arctic Resources Committee, 1976), chs. 2, 9 and esp. p. 133. A recent official document follows the Brundtland Report in recognizing the typical "Western reaction to problems: the analysis, sorting, classification and compartmentalization of 'hard' information, and then the creation of an institution to deal with each." William J. Couch, Federal Environmental Assessment Review Office, ed., *Environmental Assessment in Canada: 1988 Summary of Current Practice* (Ottawa: Supply and Services Canada, under the auspices of the Canadian Council of Resource and Environment Ministers, 1989), p. 9. Of course, it is an oversimplification to call the reaction a Western one. *Cf.* the Brundtland Report: World Commission on Environment and Development, *Our Common Future* (Oxford: Oxford University Press, 1986), pp. 310ff.

63. Galbraith, *New Industrial State*, p. 37. *Cf.* Thomas B. Nolan, "The Inexhaustible Resource of Technology," in Henry Jarrett, ed., *Perspectives on Conservation* (Baltimore: The Johns Hopkins Press for Resources for the Future Inc., 1961), esp. p. 66.

64. *Cf.* David Ehrenfeld, *The Arrogance of Humanism* (New York: Oxford University Press, 1978).

65. *Cf.* Theodore Roszak, *Where the Wasteland Ends: Politics and Transcendence in Postindustrial Society* (Garden City, NY: Anchor Books, 1973).

66. Bookchin's was an early and insightful contribution. See Murray Bookchin, "Ecology and Revolutionary Thought" (1965) and "Toward a Liberatory Technology" (1965) in his *Post-Scarcity Anarchism* (San Francisco: Ramparts Press, 1971). Also see E. F. Schumacher, *Small Is Beautiful: A Study of Economics as if People Mattered* (London: Abacus, 1974); David Dickson, *Alternative Technology and the Politics of Technical Change* (Glasgow: Fontana, 1974); Victor Ferkiss, *The Future of Technological Civilization* (New York: George Braziller, 1974); Herman E. Daly, ed., *Toward a Steady State Economy* (San Francisco: W. H. Freeman, 1973). For

approaches with a particular focus on energy, see Amory B. Lovins, *Soft Energy Paths* (Cambridge, MA: Ballinger Publishing, 1977), David B. Brooks, *Zero Energy Growth for Canada* (Toronto: McClelland and Stewart, 1981). Thinking along these lines in Canada came to focus on the concept of a "conserver society", which was given a quasi-official formulation in Science Council of Canada, *Canada as a Conserver Society* (Ottawa: Science Council of Canada Report No. 27, 1977).

67. See the discussion of "problem displacement" in John S. Dryzek, *Rational Ecology: Environment and Political Economy* (London: Basil Blackwell, 1987), pp. 16ff.

68. See Douglas Torgerson, *Industrialization and Assessment: Social Impact Assessment as a Social Phenomenon* (Toronto: York University, 1980).

69. See n. 62 above.

70. See, *e.g.*, William Ophuls, "Leviathan or Oblivion?" in Herman E. Daly, ed., *Toward a Steady-State Economy* (San Francisco: W. H. Freeman, 1973); William Ophuls, *Ecology and the Politics of Scarcity* (San Francisco: W. H. Freeman, 1977). The idea of an "environmental dictator" was discussed in some environmental groups in the 1970's.

71. This tension is evident in Ophuls. *Cf.* Charles Taylor, "The Politics of the Steady State," in Abraham Rotstein, ed., *Beyond Industrial Growth* (Toronto: University of Toronto Press, 1976).

72. See Dryzek, *Rational Ecology*, chs. 3-5; John S. Dryzek, "Complexity and Rationality in Public Life," *Political Studies* 35 (1987), pp. 424-442; C. A. Hooker and R. Van Hulst, "The Meaning of Environmental Problems for Public Political Institutions," in William Leiss, ed., *Ecology versus Politics in Canada* (Toronto: University of Toronto Press, 1979); Gareth Morgan, "Cybernetics and Organization Theory: Epistemology or Technique?" *Human Relations* 35:7 (1982), pp. 251-237.

73. See Eric Trist, "A Concept of Organizational Ecology," in contrast with Simon's focus on "bounded rationality"—*e.g.*, Herbert A. Simon, *Administrative Behavior: A Study of Decision-Making Processes in Administrative Organization* (New York: The Free Press, 3rd ed., 1976), esp. pp. xxix-xxx, 82; Herbert A. Simon, "The Theory of Problem-solving" (1972) in his *Models of Discovery* (Dordrecht, Holland: D. Reidel Publishing, 1977).

74. See n. 56 above.

75. *Cf.* Herbert A. Simon and DeWitt C. Dearborne, "Selective Perception," in Simon, *Administrative Behavior*.

76. See, *e.g.*, Richard O. Mason and Ian I. Mitroff, *Challenging Strategic Planning Assumptions* (New York: John Wiley and Sons, 1981); Ian I. Mitroff and Richard D. Mason, *Creating a Dialectical Social Science* (Dordrecht, Holland: D. Reidel Publishing, 1981); Churchman, *Systems Approach*, ch. 7; Pfeffer, *Power in Organizations*, ch. 9.

77. The contrast between "interaction" and "cogitation" is made in Aaron Wildavsky, *Speaking Truth to Power: The Art and Craft of Policy Analysis* (Boston: Little, Brown and Company, 1979). For a critique which discriminates between qualitatively different forms of interaction, see John Forester, "The Policy Analysis-Critical Theory Affair: Wildavsky and Habermas as Bedfellows?" in Forester, ed., *Critical Theory and Public Life*, esp. pp. 266ff. The distinctions which Forester makes are crucial to "discursive designs"; see n. 78 below and corresponding text.

78. See John S. Dryzek, "Discursive Designs: Critical Theory and Political Institutions," *American Journal of Political Science* 31 (1987), pp. 656-679. My discussion here also draws upon the articles by Dryzek, Douglas Amy, and Richard Bartlett in the present volume. Discursive designs would be central to what I have called a "third face" of policy analysis. See Douglas Torgerson,

"Between Knowledge and Politics: Three Faces of Policy Analysis," *Policy Sciences* 19 (1986), pp. 33-59.

79. The concept of "communicative rationality" is developed in the work of Habermas. For a convenient and well-informed summary, see Stephen K. White, *The Recent Work of Jürgen Habermas* (Cambridge: Cambridge University Press, 1988), pp. 28ff. For a discussion of distorted communication influenced by Habermas, see Douglas Torgerson, "The Communicative Context of Policy Analysis: The Problem of Strategic Interaction in the Policy Process," Ph.D. Thesis, University of Toronto, 1984. A brief summary of some key points is contained in Douglas Torgerson, "Interpretive Policy Inquiry: A Response to Its Limitations," *Policy Sciences* 19 (1986), pp. 397-405. This is not the place to go into the important issues raised by postmodernism and related approaches. *Cf., e.g.*, Michael Ryan, "New French Theory in New German Critique," *New German Critique* 22 (1981), pp. 145-161.

80. See Claus Offe, "Political Authority and Class Structures: An Analysis of Late Capitalist Societies," *International Journal of Sociology* 2:1 (1972), pp. 73-108; Habermas *Legitimation Crisis*, pp. 59-68, 136-138. Also see Robert R. Alford, "Paradigms of Relations Between State and Society," in Leon N. Lindberg *et al.*, eds., *Stress and Contradiction in Modern Capitalism: Public Policy and the Theory of the State* (Lexington, MA: Lexington Books, 1975). For a discussion of environmental policy framed by the concept of "mobilization of bias", see T. F. Schrecker, *Political Economy of Environmental Hazards* (Ottawa: Law Reform Commission of Canada, 1984). The bias renders some issues "manifest", others "latent", to follow a point developed in William Leiss, "The Political Aspects of Environmental Issues," in Leiss, ed., *Ecology versus Politics in Canada*, pp. 261ff. A general discussion of "the logic of a policy system" is presented in Torgerson, "The Communicative Context of Policy Analysis," ch. 7.7. *Cf.* n. 3 above.

81. Hartle, *Expenditure Budget Process*, p. 122 (original emphasis). For further discussion, see Torgerson, "The Communicative Context of Policy Analysis," esp. pp. 63-65.

82. See Robert H. Socolow, "Failures of Discourse: Obstacles to the Integration of Environmental Values into Natural Resource Policy," in Laurence H. Tribe *et al.*, eds., *When Values Conflict: Essays on Environmental Analysis, Discourse, and Decision* (Cambridge, MA: Ballinger Publishing, 1976), pp. 4-7, 20-22.

83. See, *e.g.*, Amory B. Lovins, "Cost-Risk-Benefit Assessments in Energy Policy," *George Washington Law Review* 45 (1977), pp. 911-943. Lovins presented this article (still in galleys) as background for his participation in the Debate Stage Hearings, Royal Commission on Electric Power Planning, Toronto, Ontario, October 19, 1977 (RCEPP, Exhibit 233). Later the Commission thanked Lovins for the "insights" which he generated in both closed and open sessions. See Arthur Porter, Chairman, *The Report of the Royal Commission on Electric Power Planning*, (Toronto: RCEPP, 1980), Vol. 1, p. 210, n. 7. The present article is written in conjunction with research on the historical emergence of the definition of the energy problem in Ontario. The problem of problem definition appears distinctly in this case as part of a problem in organization design. Some relevant background is presented in Douglas Torgerson, "From Dream to Nightmare: The Historical Origins of Canada's Nuclear Electric Future," *Alternatives* 7:1 (1977), pp. 8-17.

84. *Cf.* Arendt, *The Human Condition*, ch. 5; Michel Crozier and Erhard Friedberg, *Actors and Systems: The Politics of Collective Action* (Chicago: University of Chicago Press, 1980).

85. See Torgerson, "Between Knowledge and Politics," pp. 46ff.

86. *Cf.* Ray Kemp, "Planning, Public Hearings, and the Politics of Discourse" in Forester, ed.,

Critical Theory and Public Life.

87. On some problems of consensus formation and maintenance, see Lehmbruch, "Liberal Corporatism," pp. 153-154, 170-172, 180-181.

88. See Dryzek, "Complexity and Rationality," pp. 432f. Also see Dryzek, *Rational Ecology*, chs. 7, 9.

89. This term is used by Brian Tokar, "Exploring the New Ecologies," *Alternatives* 15:4 (1988), p. 31. See the preference for "ecology" instead of "environment" expressed by Murray Bookchin, *The Ecology of Freedom: The Emergence and Dissolution of Hierarchy* (Palo Alto, CA: Cheshire Books, 1982), pp. 21f. But *cf.* Worster, *Nature's Economy*, p. 37.

90. See the discussion of the "laws of ecology" in Commoner, *The Closing Circle*, pp. 31ff. *Cf.* Ted Spearing, "Thresholds of Tolerance in Environmental Management: An Area of Uncertainty," M.E.S. major paper, Faculty of Environmental Studies, York University, Toronto, 1980. Also note Edward Goldsmith *et al.*, *Blueprint for Survival* (Boston: Houghton Mifflin, 1972).

91. See Murray Bookchin, "Freedom and Necessity in Nature: A Problem in Ecological Ethics," *Alternatives* 13:4 (1986), pp. 29-38; Bookchin, *Ecology of Freedom*, esp. p. 11 and chs. 2, 12. Also see John Rodman, "Four Forms of Ecological Consciousness Reconsidered," in Donald Scherer and Thomas Attig, eds., *Ethics and Environment* (Englewood Cliffs, NJ: Prentice-Hall, 1983). *Cf.* Torgerson, "Paradox of Environmental Ethics," esp. pp. 33ff. For the viewpoint of "deep ecology", see Bill Devall and George Sessions, "The Development of Natural Resources and the Integrity of Nature," *Environmental Ethics*, 6 (1984), pp. 293-321. While at times insightful, this approach is at best unclear about its political and administrative implications: faith in the administrative mind seems to be rejected, yet also is implicitly maintained at crucial points. On the conflict between deep ecology and the social ecology of Bookchin, see Toklar, pp. 30-43.

92. Sigmund Freud, "A Difficulty in the Path of Psychoanalysis," in *The Standard Edition of the Complete Psychological Works of Sigmund Freud* (London: The Hogarth Press, 1955), Vol. 17, p. 140.

93. *Cf.* Douglas Torgerson, "Domination and Liberatory Politics," *Canadian Journal of Political and Social Theory* 2:1 (1978), pp. 137-157.

94. See, *e.g.*, Charles E. Lindblom, *The Intelligence of Democracy: Decision Making Through Mutual Adjustment* (New York: The Free Press, 1965). The fundamentally settled world presupposed and reflected in that book stands in contrast to the world "headed for catastrophe" invoked in the opening of Charles E. Lindblom, *Politics and Markets* (New York: Basic Books, 1977), p. 3. His examination of "politico-economic mechanisms" is thus explicitly aimed at finding means of averting an environmental catastrophe. For a further development along these lines, see Dryzek, *Rational Ecology*.

95. The discussion here of the administrative sphere and the public sphere is partly influenced by the treatment of "lifeworld" and "system" in Habermas. See, for a concise discussion, White, *The Recent Work of Jürgen Habermas*, ch. 5; for a brief, pertinent critique, see pp. 140ff. My view is that elements of the lifeworld "penetrate" the system more fundamentally than Habermas allows—hence the term administrative "sphere" in this article. Moreover, Habermas locates the "administrative system", as he calls it, too readily in the state. See Jürgen Habermas, *The Theory of Communicative Action*, 2 Vols. (Boston: Beacon Press, 1984, 1988), esp. Vol. 2, pp. 311, 343f. *Cf.* Torgerson, "Between Knowledge and Politics," p. 51.

96. See Socolow, "Failures of Discourse."

97. Dryzek, "Complexity and Rationality," p. 433.

98. See Joseph W. Meeker, *The Comedy of Survival* (New York: Charles Scribner's Sons, 1974). For a suggestive discussion of a flexible and adaptive approach to environmental management, see Daniel L. Dustin and Leo H. McAvoy, " Toward Environmental Eolithism," *Environmental Ethics* 6 (1984), pp. 161-166. Also see Henry S. Kariel, *Open Systems: Arenas for Political Action* (Itasca, IL: F. E. Peacock Publishers, 1969). *Cf.* Daniel Goodman, "The Theory of Diversity-Stability Relationships in Ecology," *The Quarterly Review of Biology* 50:3 (1975), p. 261: "although the hypothesis may be false, the policies it promotes are prudent."

99. Socolow, p. 32.

PART IV

THE POLITICS OF
ENVIRONMENTAL ADMINISTRATION

Environmental administration exists not in the calm, ordered world of the management textbook, but in a world of rough edges. Here environmental problems are defined at the intersection of diverse interests, of forces rife with complexity and variation. This world resists smooth conceptualization and ready comprehension, however much we orient ourselves through inquiry and practice. No general theory or set of specific cases provides an exhaustive and reliable map. Along the corridors of public administration, officials work amid a tangled web of legality, typically forced to respond to well-funded private initiatives while constrained, among other things, by the fingers which hold the public purse-strings. The difficulty is exacerbated because environmental problems often elude the available tools of analysis and management. Turning to concrete issues in the politics of environmental administration, the articles of Part IV focus on particular concerns such as acid rain and toxic waste, along with questions involving corporate power, environmental law, right-to-know, scientific uncertainty, and participatory management. Any effort to revise the agenda of inquiry and practice must keep in view the complexities, dilemmas and uncertainties of a world where politics and administration meet.

RESISTING ENVIRONMENTAL REGULATION: THE CRYPTIC PATTERN OF BUSINESS-GOVERNMENT RELATIONS

Ted Schrecker

Environmental protection as a political concern has decisively confounded skeptics like Anthony Downs—who, almost 20 years ago, predicted that "ecology" would succumb to the vagaries of what he called the issue-attention cycle.[1] Today's intensified mass media coverage of environmental issues was exemplified by *Time* magazine's departure from its usual personalized version of history in selecting endangered Earth as the Planet of the Year in January 1989. The major issues had a familiar ring: growing numbers of endangered plant and animal species; environmental effects of increasing global fossil fuel combustion; the intractable problem of disposing of ever-expanding volumes of household, commercial and industrial waste; and (of course) the population problem.[2] Perhaps not surprisingly, a national opinion poll taken in October 1989 found that respondents most frequently picked environmental issues as the most important problem facing Canada.[3]

This article began as an attempt to update earlier work on the nature of business power in environmental politics.[4] That work was based on the premise, which is still valid, that environmental regulation constitutes a challenge to the priorities of business because it inherently requires investments on pollution control or waste treatment which, other things being equal, would not be made. In all but exceptional cases business would avoid such "unproductive" uses of capital, since they fail to generate a return comparable to that available on investments in production technology, marketing, or product development (to give just a few examples). There are, in fact, at least two more subtle dimensions of the challenge. The first of these is suggested by the comment of one business executive interviewed in a landmark 1976 study of the political attitudes of U.S. business: "In the marketplace, every person gets a vote every day. The market is more democratic than the government."[5] This view is only slightly more extreme than that of a great many people in the business community. Environmental regulation implicitly, at least, counterposes the proposition that some kinds of resource allocation decisions should not be entrusted to the market but should be the product of collective choices about the kind of society we want, rather than the consequence of aggregating individual purchasing decisions.[6]

Environmental regulation also represents governmental interference with the entitlement of managers and shareholders to run their businesses as they see fit. The resulting shift in power away from corporate owners and managers has been perceived by business as threatening in much the same way, and for the same reasons, as workers' demands in an earlier period of industrial capitalism for union recognition and labor standards legislation. Yet just as collective bargaining rights and controls on hours and conditions of work have become entrenched in legislation, so too have environmental controls become a part of the political landscape to a degree which few people would have predicted two decades ago (or, perhaps, even five years ago).

In order to understand this superficially improbable outcome, I first review very briefly the nature of contemporary (*i.e.*, roughly post-1969) business resistance to environmental regulation, necessarily on an anecdotal rather than a comprehensive basis. (To my knowledge, no comprehensive treatment of this topic has yet been published.) I then explore some tentative explanations for the persistence of environmental concern among the public and restrictive environmental policies on the part of governments. For the most part, these represent productive directions for future research rather than properly tested (or even fully formulated) hypotheses. I have used both American and Canadian examples, to suggest both the similarities and the fundamental differences between the two countries.

Resisting Regulation: The Resources of Business

The demands for union recognition referred to earlier were bitterly resisted by business — in many instances, especially in the United States, by the use of armed force.[7] Business resistance to environmental regulation has at least on some occasions been similarly bitter, albeit without (at least in North America) the degree of violence associated with the labor struggles of the late nineteenth and early twentieth centuries. Firms charged with offences under environmental statutes have fought long and expensive court battles both to avoid conviction[8] and to intimidate political opponents. For instance, the Reserve Mining Company spent ten years defending its practice of dumping 67,000 tons of asbestos-laden mine tailings daily into Lake Superior from an iron ore refining plant against prosecutions and civil suits launched by both federal and Minnesota regulators.[9] In the early 1970s, the Canada Metal Company responded to concern on the part of area residents and municipal health officials about the effects of its emissions from its secondary lead smelter in a working-class Toronto neighborhood by subjecting journalists covering the story to aggressive legal harassment; lawyers for the smelter operators tried to have the courts forbid members of the Board of Health from considering the question of lead pollution because of their alleged "bias" on the issue.[10] Canada Metal was on the defensive again in 1981, when Canada's federal Department of the Environment charged that the firm's Winnipeg secondary lead smelter had violated regulations under Canada's federal *Clean Air Act*. A constitutional challenge to the regulations launched by the firm was not resolved until December 1982 (their constitutionality was upheld), and the case was finally thrown out of Provincial Court in February 1985 because of deviations from the air sampling procedure prescribed in the regulations.[11]

Reserve Mining, Canada Metal and any number of other firms in similar situations enjoyed the advantages available to any defendant with millions of dollars to spend in a court case involving quasi-criminal statutes under which every element of an offence must be proved beyond a reasonable doubt. In other words, the advantages of business in such contexts are corollaries of the financial resources at its command, and of the magnitude of cost savings from continued violations of the applicable law. One economist has noted with respect to enforcement of environmental requirements that the "benefits of delay are typically so great in comparison with the costs of complying that...a regulatory agency faces the possibility not of a handful of violators that it could reasonably handle, but of tacit noncompliance by large segments of an industry."[12] Such corporate recalcitrance can present obvious problems for regulatory departments or agencies with limited investigative and legal resources. It is, of course, often even more attractive for large firms to invest in trying to prevent the making of new and potentially costly regulations, both by lobbying and by litigation. As noted below, business lobbying against U.S. environmental regulation became much more widespread and intense during the 1970s. And on the litigation front, "industry has come to regard nearly every clause of each environmental protection law as a potential ally. Every guideline and regulation written by the EPA [U.S. Environmental Protection Agency] to implement the pollution control laws has been challenged by each industry involved, most often by multiple representatives of the same industry, and in many cases, simultaneously in several jurisdictions of the federal judiciary."[13]

However, the political resources of business in general, and of large corporations most particularly, are not just quantitatively superior to those of other parties to environmental conflicts; they are qualitatively distinct as well.[14] The most dramatic illustration of this fact involves what Kazis and Grossman have called "job blackmail": direct threats of plant shutdowns, disinvestment or capital strikes in response to regulatory initiatives.[15] Members of the business community are sometimes quite candid about job blackmail as a tactic for dealing with government. Said one executive in the 1976 study cited earlier: "We need political sophistication. We have to tell a state considering additional restrictions on business: 'The next plant doesn't go up here if that bill passes.'"[16] Three cases will suffice to illustrate the uses of job blackmail in environmental politics.

The mining and forestry operations of Noranda, Inc. account for much of the economic activity in northwestern Quebec. At the start of the 1980s, Noranda's Rouyn copper smelter accounted for 30 percent of Canadian sulphur dioxide emissions from non-ferrous smelters as well as dumping tons of arsenic, cadmium, lead and other contaminants on the surrounding area. Epidemiological research suggests that people living around the smelter have an unusually high chance of developing lung cancer.[17] (Sulphur dioxide, as well as being responsible for localized destruction of vegetation, is one of the two principal precursors of the acid precipitation which is blamed for destroying aquatic life in lakes throughout eastern Canada, the other being oxides of nitrogen whose most significant single source is motor vehicle emissions.) In May 1984, the president of Noranda, Adam Zimmerman, claimed that the firm "could find itself caught between the 'politically unacceptable' choice of closing a smelter that employs 1,200 people" or investing in modernization which would have the added effect of reducing sulphur dioxide emissions.[18] Looking back on this episode in 1989, Zimmerman said, "If it had come to a choice between spending $200 million and closing down the plant, I'd have closed down the plant. We didn't have the money. Is that bargaining for jobs? Maybe. But it wasn't done maliciously. I was just being realistic."[19] Yet during the same year, Noranda risked further deterioration of an admittedly weak balance sheet by borrowing more than $90 million to pay dividends to preferred shareholders. The principal beneficiary? The Bronfman family, one of Canada's richest, which indirectly controls Noranda and literally dozens of other Canadian firms.[20]

In Ontario, Kimberly-Clark of Canada Ltd. resisted provincial government attempts to enforce a 1986 pollution control deadline at its Terrace Bay plant by claiming that the plant was already only marginally profitable, and threatening to shut down the operation with a loss of 1200 jobs. Perhaps predictably, the provincial government backed down even though Kimberly-Clark's U.S. parent company was the most profitable firm in the U.S. forest products sector in 1985, earning $267 million (U.S.) on operations in 22 countries around the world.[21] The Kimberly-Clark confrontation was only the latest example of a pattern dating back more than a decade, in which pulp and paper firms both in Ontario and elsewhere have consistently failed to meet pollution control deadlines which they themselves have often negotiated with provincial governments.[22]

A third case is particularly striking in terms of its reflection of the ability of business to circumscribe the range of political choices open both to citizens and to government. In 1983 the U.S. EPA responded to threats by Asarco Inc. to shut down its Tacoma, Washington copper smelter if the agency pursued tougher restrictions on the firm's arsenic emissions by soliciting the views of area residents on whether they were willing to accept the (estimated) additional cancer risks associated with existing emission levels in return for the 500 jobs and associated indirect economic benefits the smelter provided. (In 1984, Asarco shut down the smelter for economic reasons not directly connected to pollution control requirements.[23])

Job blackmail is a particularly effective tactic for firms which are the major source of direct or indirect employment within a community or region. Consequently, environmental regulation in Canada[24] has generally been pursued reluctantly in provinces other than Ontario:[25] much of Canada outside the Quebec-Windsor corridor, which contains much of Canada's population and most of its manufacturing industry, is directly reliant on the economic health of resource-based industries (whether agriculture, mineral industries or forest products) for its economic survival. As illustrated by numerous examples from both Canadian and U.S.

contexts, the negative impacts on local and regional economies associated with the threat of plant shutdowns or layoffs enable affected firms or industries to appeal to a constituency far broader than their own workers.[26]

As noted below, the structure of Canada's electoral system augments the power of business effectively to hold local economies hostage in such situations. Even when such geographical considerations do not reinforce the power position of business, firms within industries whose profitability may be adversely affected by environmental regulation are uniquely well placed to create coalitions with those latent groups or existing organizations which might be indirectly affected as a result. In the U.S., a particularly effective effort of this type was the automobile industry's opposition to 1975 *Clean Air Act* amendments tightening emission standards; the three firms which dominate the industry were able to win support not only from the United Auto Workers but also from national organizations of auto dealers and parts manufacturers.[27] In Canada, similar coalitions have formed at the local level among forest industry firms, their workers and local retailers to oppose environmentalists arguing for more extensive protection of wilderness areas. A more sinister coalition involves Quebec asbestos mining firms and the Quebec and national governments under the umbrella of the Canadian Asbestos Information Centre, formed to promote domestic and (especially) export markets for the carcinogenic fibre.[28] Specific cases and conflicts, however, only tell part of the story.

The nature of capitalist economies means that conflicts characterized by overt job blackmail are exceptional, rather than routine. Since both governments and affected communities are aware of the economic consequences, overt threats of disinvestment are often unnecessary. Governments in all capitalist or mixed economies rely heavily on an ongoing flow of private investment to sustain the economic growth which both provides income and employment for their citizens and finances the provision of state services of various kinds. Thus, public policy in various areas must operate in a context of more or less continuous latent tension between the state's various other mandates, such as eliminating the damaging effects of economic activity on the environment, and the need to sustain the conditions for capital accumulation — that is, to maintain a favorable business climate. The effect on the range of policy choices which are considered feasible is summarized by Charles Lindblom's statement that "even the unspoken possibility of adversity for business operates as an all-pervasive constraint on governmental authority."[29] Lindblom thus refers to "the business executive as *public* official in the market system."[30] Carl Friedrich characterized the mechanism by which such constraints operate as a "law of anticipated reaction,"[31] and Claus Offe has elaborated by noting that "[t]he power position of private investors includes the power to define reality"[32] by their investment decisions. In other words, a tradeoff between jobs and the environment exists when the president of Noranda says it does. This is what he means by realism. Some of the conceptual implications of such uses of economic power to circumscribe both individual life chances and political choice are briefly discussed in the final section of this article.

The Persistence of Regulation: Explanations Needed

Despite the inescapable centrality of their position in the public life of a capitalist or mixed economy,[33] business and its managers in both Canada and the United States felt their political position threatened during the late 1960s and early 1970s. In the U.S. context, David Vogel has argued that environmental concern was not the only source of such a threat: the civil rights, consumer, and women's movements also contributed to a situation in which "the business community found itself fighting its political battles primarily on terrain defined by those who wanted to reduce its prerogatives."[34] Whether or not this was the case, business leaders undoubtedly *perceived* themselves as being on the defensive.[35] Institutionally, the resulting increase in the class consciousness of business was manifested in the formation of the Business Roundtable, an organization promoting the direct involvement of the CEOs of major corporations in political action around issues of broad concern to its members. Similarly, the Chamber of Commerce was transformed into an organization which took a much more active political role.[36] There was also a dramatic increase in the use of corporate wealth to finance lobbying, to swell the treasuries of business-oriented Political Action Committees (PACs), to provide support for academic researchers intellectually sympathetic to the business community, and to engage in extensive (and expensive) advocacy advertising campaigns.[37] Tactically, the result was a "sizeable increase in the number of *ad hoc* coalitions formed to lobby on specific issues."[38] According to Vogel, the result was "the end of a decade of reform" as business succeeded "in restoring its influence over the direction and substance of the political agenda itself."[39]

In Canada, the impetus for the growing politicization of business came less from the perceived excesses of social regulation and more from a combination of union wage demands, fears of inflation and a general perception that the Liberal government of the day was insufficiently responsive to business.[40] Similar corporate responses were evident in the formation of the Business Council on National Issues,[41] although Canadian business has not, so far, mobilized on a national level in response to social regulation in the same way it has on other economic issues like inflation and free trade. Nevertheless, a restoration of business influence has clearly occurred in both Canada and the United States—with the election of President Reagan in 1980 and 1984 and of the majority Conservative government of Prime Minister Mulroney in 1984 and 1988. The direct contribution of business political activity to these outcomes is perhaps questionable,[42] but this issue is not central to my argument here.

As one might expect, environmental regulation in North America subsequently underwent some substantial reversals. One of President Reagan's first acts in office, for example, was to give effect by Executive Order to the long-standing demand from industry for cost-benefit analysis of most new federal environmental, health and safety regulations.[43] Especially under Reagan's first appointee as Administrator of EPA, Anne Gorsuch (Burford), enforcement efforts were substantially decreased in favor of a more accommodating relationship with the regulated firms.[44] Prime Minister Mulroney was less explicitly committed to social deregulation, partly because there was (and is) little such regulation at the federal level.[45] However, the Mulroney government's general commitment to business priorities has been reflected both in such macro-level events as the successful implementation of a free trade agreement with the United States (an agreement whose implications for environmental policy and resource management the government refused to discuss or even acknowledge), and in such micro-level phenomena as the 1987 appointment as a senior advisor to Canada's Minister of the Environment of an executive on leave from Imperial Oil, Canada's largest oil company and a subsidiary of Exxon Inc.[46]

Yet in many respects, the predictable reversals have *not* occurred, and the victories achieved by business have been tactical rather than strategic. For instance, despite having successfully delayed the imposition of some emission reduction deadlines, the North American automobile industry has been transformed over the past two decades into a highly regulated area of economic activity,[47] and even its staunchest supporters now only propose incremental changes in the extent of regulation. Indeed, at this writing the Canadian government is actively advocating a new set of exhaust emission standards, considerably stricter than those currently in effect and modelled on standards already adopted by California. As another example, until the start of the present decade, prosecutions for violations of environmental laws in Canada were infrequent; fines, even after the difficult path to conviction had been trod successfully, were often trivial when compared with the cost savings associated with the commission of the offence; and enforcement, when it occurred at all, was generally characterized by protracted bargaining between polluting firms and regulatory agencies in which sanctions of any sort were invoked only as a last resort.[48] In many Canadian provincial jurisdictions, like Quebec, this is still true[49] by virtue of the underdevelopment of most of Canada's regional economies and the consequent unwillingness of government agencies to engage in conflict with locally or regionally important employers.[50] However, a countertrend has emerged in Ontario, Canada's richest and most industrialized province. Now there is increasingly aggressive prosecution for violating environmental statutes, provision for much higher maximum fines in legislation, and a pattern of higher actual fines on conviction.[51] A lawyer for Ontario's Ministry of the Environment has aptly characterized this pattern as one in which "media and scholarly attention upon the importance and fragility of the environment now finds its reflection in the courts."[52] On the national level, former Conservative Environment Minister Thomas McMillan condemned pollution as "the most serious white-collar crime in Canada" and the country's "record of enforcement and compliance" as "appalling".[53] Although the government of which McMillan was a part[54] did remarkably little to change this situation, the point is that such thoughts would have been politically unspeakable (especially by a Conservative!) a decade earlier.[55]

Even more surprising is the major expansion under the Reagan administration of the use of federal criminal investigations and prosecutions to enforce environmental requirements — a development which has included the establishment of an Environmental Crimes Unit (ECU) within the Department of Justice as well as an increased emphasis on criminal sanctions within the enforcement sections of EPA.[56] The head of ECU from 1981 (when it was founded) until 1988 said in 1989 that "the level of apprehension" on the part of corporate polluters "is not yet at a healthy level"[57], despite the $13 million in fines and 200 years in prison terms which the courts had imposed following conviction under the criminal provisions of federal environmental laws.[58] This is something one might have expected to hear during the Carter administration rather than at the end of the Reagan era.

These examples are necessarily anecdotal in nature, for it would be difficult if not impossible to develop an uncontentious indicator of the extent and severity of environmental regulation. They do suggest, at a minimum, that the ability of business to define or circumscribe the environmental policy agenda may be less extensive than many people (myself included) would have argued until very recently. The relevant literature suggests at least two themes which are worthy of pursuit by way of explanation. The first theme is cultural,[59] focusing on the connections among changing class structure, people's position within that structure, and the values and perceptions engendered by that situation. The second theme, which is derived from the work of Theda Skocpol and other neo-institutionalists, focuses on the connections among the distinctive character of national state institutions, the nature of state action and the content of the conflicts which characterize political life.[60] These are *not* competing or mutually exclusive explanatory frameworks; neither does their exploration imply a rejection of class conflict as a determinant (if not necessarily *the* determinant) of political outcomes.

Post-Materialism and the Social Construction of Environmental Problems

In numerous published works, Ronald Inglehart has suggested that many patterns of political activity in the so-called advanced industrial societies are usefully explained in terms of the emergence of "post-materialist" (as distinct from materialist) values.[61] "These societies," he argues, "are a remarkable exception to the prevailing historical pattern: the bulk of their population does *not* live under conditions of hunger and economic insecurity."[62] Inglehart links the growth of post-materialism to the process and content of socialization associated with the postwar generation's experience of growing up in this environment of relative affluence.[63] Less contentiously, he notes the growing proportion of the population of many industrial societies whose values could be characterized as post-materialist, and the fact that post-materialist value orientations are particularly prevalent among the expanding stratum of well educated, salaried managers and professionals in both public and private sectors.[64] (To provide one striking example of the expansion of that stratum: the number of people employed in education in the United States more than quadrupled in absolute terms, and more than doubled as a percentage of public employment and of the total labor force, between 1952 and 1982.[65])

This last set of observations provides the basis for a considerably more convincing explanation than Inglehart's for the spread of public environmental concern, one rooted in the changing occupational (and consequently class) structure of the societies in question. Many people in the occupational categories most congenial to post-materialism are not, as the experience of the 1980s makes clear,[66] unconcerned with material goods. Rather, the nature of their occupations (especially in the case of public employees) means they do not have to worry about them in the same way as do factory workers, miners and others whom Nicholas Watts refers to as being within the industrial "production core".[67] Thus the variable predisposing people to post-materialism at the individual level is not pre-adult socialization, but *adult* occupation, affluence and economic security.[68] Support for this approach is found in Inglehart's own finding that in the European Community countries late in the 1970s, "young technocrats may be Post-Materialistic, but young self-employed business people definitely are *not*." Neither (predictably) were manual workers, farmers, or the unemployed.[69] If economically secure post-materialists comprise both an expanding segment of the population and a portion of the electorate influential out of proportion to its numbers (as one would expect given their relatively high levels of income, education, and discretionary time[70]), that fact may help to explain the persistence of environmentalism and, in part, political responses to it.

The most striking contemporary manifestation of post-materialism is probably the rise of the West German Green Party: "the Greens have prospered particularly within postindustrial, new middle class segments of [West] German society," such as teachers, civil servants and those with media occupations.[71] Indeed, one of Inglehart's most intriguing findings, based on survey data, concerns the large size of the potential electorate for ecology parties in the European Community.[72] However, as will be noted below, the political impact of the Greens is a consequence not only of their value orientation, but also of a particular institutional framework that allows its direct translation into electoral representation. In other countries, it is necessary also to look for subtler mechanisms of post-materialist influence.

One of these is, of course, the conventional appeal to public opinion and its presumed influence on the range of policy positions considered acceptable by politicians. Particularly in the environmental field, the explanatory power of this approach with reference to policy outcomes which impose significant real costs on business (or on government!) is limited by the amenability of environmental questions to symbolic government action with little substantive effect. Thus the real distribution of resources and power can be left relatively undisturbed, if governments wish to leave it that way. Another approach, suggested by Inglehart, is to look for direct penetration of post-materialist values and their bearers into the centers of state power:

> By 1980, a Post-Materialist outlook had become more common than a Materialist one among young technocrats, professionals and politicians of Western countries. As experts, congressional staffers and members of ministerial cabinets, Post-Materialists had direct access to the command posts of the sociopolitical system.... The impact of Post-Materialism was no longer symbolized by the student with a protest placard, but by the public interest lawyer, or the young technocrat with an environmental impact statement.[73]

Obviously, the applicability of such broad generalizations, like that of generalizations concerning the prevalence of post-materialism itself, is limited by differences among countries in class structure, political culture, and political institutions. It is nevertheless at least plausible to suggest that post-materialist elements in the value structures of public officials, whether due to socialization, occupational status or (most probably) some combination of the two, are at least partly responsible for the persistence of government commitments to environmental protection. In this regard, Eric Nordlinger has made a persuasive argument for closer examination of the ways in which public officials shape the policy agenda to reflect their own political preferences, rather than merely responding to the strongest sets of class or interest group demands.[74] Inglehart's research has the potential to address a crucial omission in Nordlinger's work: his indifference toward the *genesis* of those officials' preferences. But the source of post-materialist preferences in another sense, one having to do with their internal cognitive structure, still eludes Inglehart; to understand it, a different approach is needed.

In the U.S. context, Samuel Hays has argued that the postwar trend toward larger-scale industrial technology and the rising standards of living which were accompanied by increased concern for the local environmental impacts of industrial activity generated resentment which was eventually transformed into a political movement.[75] One of the major defects of Hays' analysis as applied to the contemporary situation is that it implies that the roots of environmental concern lie predominantly in people's own first-hand perceptions of local environmental degradation. In a way, Hays is here echoing the assumptions of many economists like Lester Thurow, who view environmental quality as a good which individuals may purchase, individually or collectively (*i.e.*, as a public good), like any other good or service. Demand, according to Thurow, is highly income-elastic. In other words, as people and classes of people grow wealthier, they are more concerned with "goods" (clean air, water free from chemical contaminants, recreational amenities) which can only be "purchased" collectively, by way of support for political measures that reassign priority with respect to the use of the relevant resources. Thurow consequently claims that: "Environmentalism...is thoroughly economic. It is simply a case where a particular segment of the income distribution wants an economic good — a clean environment — that cannot be achieved without coercion" in the form of land use restrictions or effluent discharge limits.[76]

However, in many instances the environmental issues with which citizens appear to be most directly concerned are ones geographically and in other respects remote from their local experience: the preservation of northern Canadian wilderness areas; the destruction of the Amazonian rain forests. And citizen attitudes toward environmental degradation wherever it occurs are changing. In the early 1980s, R.A. Kagan identified the "moral ambiguity" of regulatory offences as one of the reasons for lackadaisical enforcement and the substitution of negotiation for the formal sanctions (like prosecution) which were legally available.[77] Over the past few years the way at least some citizens think about pollution has changed in quite a fundamental way. Environmental damage which was previously regarded as "largely the result of otherwise legitimate and socially desirable activities carried on by respectable enterprises"[78] is now widely regarded as not only avoidable but morally culpable.

Environmentalists tend to describe this phenomenon in terms of the emergence of an environmental ethic which at least partly transcends self-interest. Although emphasizing the point that environmentalists are not just amenity-seekers, as the conventional economic wisdom would have it, such descriptions still fail to address the question of why such an ethic (if indeed it is one) should emerge, and why it should emerge so conspicuously among some people but not others. The explanation of this phenomenon can best be sought using a social constructionist method of analyzing social problems. This method concentrates on "the claims-making activities and structuring practices that...constitute the *sine qua non* of a social problem."[79] In other words, the focus is on who defines a particular set of phenomena as a problem, on why it is perceived as a problem, and on the determinants of success and failure in conflicts over problem definitions. Social constructionist analysis has recently been usefully applied to the treatment of intoxicated driving by police, the public and the courts.[80] The change in the social (and legal) construction of relevant actions in this field has been analogous in many respects to the change which has occurred in the environmental field. The change in the case of pollution has, so far, been far less complete, and consequently less consistently reflected in policy outcomes.

There is little mystery to this. Redefining at least some categories of environmental degradation as culpable, or even criminal, conflicts with the neoconservative infatuation with private enterprise and confronts political opponents powerful by virtue of their economic clout, despite the receptive audience provided by the expanding proportion of the population whose values are at least partly post-materialist. Conversely, the policy changes which have been associated with growing punitiveness toward drunk drivers "were ideologically harmonious with the policy rhetoric of the Right," particularly in their insistent focus on individual responsibility and their expansion of police powers.[81]

Further research on the social construction of environmental problems will be extremely valuable in terms of clarifying the specific mechanisms by which post-materialist values and public concern are manifested in policy outcomes. One particularly useful focus, as in the case of drunk driving, will involve the mass media and the reasons for change in their treatment of environmental issues. Some of the consequences of intensified mass media coverage are readily apparent, such as the tendency to turn local issues into national or even international *causes célèbres*. Without national media coverage of the plight of residents of the Love Canal area in New York state, for instance, the disposal of hazardous industrial waste would probably have taken much longer to become a genuinely national political concern in either Canada or the United States.

The current spate of articles and programs on the plight of the Amazonian rain forest is an even more striking case in point. The question which remains, of course, is why media coverage should change and intensify when and as it does.

Politics Matters

Another observation which follows from the preceding discussion is that politics matters, not only within what Skocpol has referred to as the "(extremely flexible) outer limits" inherent in capitalism "for the kinds of supports for property ownership and controls of the labor force that it can tolerate"[82] but also, at least over the longer term, as a process of defining those limits. Within polities conforming to the colloquial ideal of democracy there is nothing like a one-to-one correspondence between the extent and intensity of public concern with environmental quality and its reflection in official policy. Policy outcomes are contingent upon not only the relative strength of particular groups such as business and labor, but also on the institutions and forms of organization characteristic of a particular political system. These factors can, themselves, affect the strength and efficacy of constituencies for a particular policy. This is the point made by Schattschneider about the "mobilization of bias" within political systems[83] and, more recently, by Skocpol:

> States and political parties within capitalism have cross-nationally and historically varying structures. These structures powerfully shape and limit state interventions in the economy, and they determine the ways in which class interests and conflicts get organized into (or out of) politics in a given time and place.[84]

Skocpol's observations are part of an argument against both Marxist and conventional interest-group theories of the state. The former focus on the state's responsiveness to class interests, the latter on the significance of a variety of group pressures, but both (she argues) pay insufficient attention to political institutions themselves. The validity of her argument can be demonstrated in the environmental policy field with reference to two examples.

The first example involves electoral systems. The structure of property rights characteristic of market economies lends credibility to job blackmail and threats of disinvestment or capital flight. However, from the point of view of politicians the sanction of most immediate significance is probably not the long-term delegitimation associated with slowed economic growth, but (especially in much of Canada) the more immediate one of vote losses which follows from popular fears of shutting down the town. Canada's electoral system rewards concentration on issues with strong regional winners and losers, and penalizes emphasis on policy positions (like many having to do with environmental protection) characterized by dispersed national support.[85] In the United States, the difficulty of forging a congressional majority committed to controls of emissions of the industrial pollutants which produce acid precipitation has been attributed to a very similar process of electoral arithmetic.[86]

Alternative electoral systems weight potentially competing sets of voter preferences in different ways. For example, the success of the Green Party in the Federal Republic of Germany is crucially linked to the country's system of proportional representation in which Bundestag representation corresponds to a party's percentage of the national popular vote once the threshold of 5 percent has been crossed. By contrast, the British Greens won 15 percent of the national vote in the 1989 European elections, yet (because of the country's plurality system of single-member constituencies) failed to gain a single seat.[87] In Canada, a Reform Party candidate for Parliament, appealing to strong regional resentments, recently won office in an Alberta by-election with fewer than 12,000 votes; a national Green Party might garner ten or twenty times as many votes without winning a single seat.[88]

The second example involves the exercise of administrative discretion in specific environmental policy fields, where comparative study of policy outcomes strongly reinforces Skocpol's line of argument. Differences in patterns of toxic chemical regulation between the United States on the one hand and France, West Germany, and Britain on the other are closely linked to the fusion of executive and legislative powers in the European states and their separation in the U.S. Regulatory decisions are not exposed to judicial scrutiny by way of litigation in the European countries, leaving executive agencies far freer to negotiate accommodations with industry without significant public involvement.[89] These differences have important consequences for the content of regulation, the treatment of scientific evidence and the deference accorded to "expertise".[90] Even more conspicuously, in countries like France where political authority is highly centralized, governments committed to nuclear power have been able to ignore extensive citizen opposition since there were virtually no political channels for its articulation.[91] At the other extreme, despite strong promotional efforts on the part of the United States government and the nuclear industry, the accessibility of the regulatory decisions provided by public hearing procedures, by judicial review of reactor licensing decisions and by the rate-setting procedures of state utility commissions has seriously limited the diffusion of nuclear power.[92]

An important corollary of these findings is that state institutions also affect *citizens'* capacities or political resources. Frances Zemans has pointed out that the ability of citizens to mobilize legal institutions in the United States is a form of political participation which "mitigates some of the problems inherent in representative government, including the limits of collective action and the difficulty of measuring intensity of subjective interest."[93] At least since the passage of the *National Environmental Policy Act* (NEPA) in 1969, the U.S. legal system has provided extensive and distinctive opportunities for citizens to intervene in the policy process, and (indirectly) in the organization and decision-making priorities of the national government.[94] The availability of these opportunities at least partly explains the persistence of environmental regulation in a hostile political climate. Within a few years after passage of NEPA, citizens' organizations were able to use litigation under its environmental impact statement provisions temporarily to halt the Trans-Alaska Pipeline pending completion of a more extensive environmental impact statement and development of various measures to mitigate its impacts. Such groups were also able to secure a court order requiring much more attention to environmental impacts on the part of the U.S. Atomic Energy Commission in nuclear reactor licensing.[95] NEPA also had the effect of changing the scale of political conflicts; because of its application to federal spending decisions like those associated with housing developments and highways, it transformed local political issues (literally) into federal cases.[96] In this respect, its impact has been similar to that of mass media coverage of environmental questions.

NEPA has also substantially altered the internal decision-making priorities of federal government agencies.[97] Some observers saw Supreme Court decisions at the end of the 1970s as seriously weakening the Act, yet it continued to be used in the 1980s to force administrative (and political[98]) consideration of environmental and social impact in such politically strategic and privately lucrative activities as pesticide spraying on federal forest lands and the issuance of oil, gas and mineral leases.[99] In a similar development, as enforcement activity by EPA declined substantially in the early 1980s, environmental organizations filed increasing numbers of citizen suits (explicitly provided for in most federal pollution control laws) to take up at least some of the slack.[100] Administrative authority is circumscribed in the U.S. context in other ways as well. For instance, in 1983 the Natural Resources Defence Council successfully sued the EPA to challenge both its use under the Reagan administration of secret meetings with pesticide industry representatives as the basis for evaluating the health risks of pesticides, and its relaxation of its guidelines for acceptable cancer risks from pesticides without providing an opportunity for public comment. These practices were alleged to violate the *Administrative Procedures Act*, which sets out requirements for public input into the making of federal regulations. In October 1984, EPA settled out of court by agreeing to review all the decisions made in closed meetings and to make public a complete record of the information leading to regulatory decisions about reevaluation of existing pesticides.[101]

This outcome could not have occurred in Canada, where decisions about pesticide approvals are routinely (and legally) made by secret meeting and press release.[102] Indeed, by late 1989 Canada still had no environmental impact assessment legislation at the federal level, but rather a widely criticized set of administrative guidelines for the federal Environmental Assessment and Review Process (EARP). These guidelines were applied to federal undertakings, until 1989,[103] at the absolute discretion of the initiating government department.[104] This does not necessarily mean that Canadian environmental law is weaker than that of the United States. It does mean that Canadian national governments are far freer than their U.S. counterparts to pursue accommodations with industry and to balance regional economic objectives (often achieved through extensive federal subsidies for energy and mineral development) against the achievement of broader environmental goals with less clearly defined and politically effective constituencies.

Environmentalists, understanding the importance of the political resources created by "environmental rights", have consistently argued for their entrenchment in legislation.[105] However, Canadian business understands the danger presented for its accommodations with government by the wild card of judicial intervention; likewise, as an "autonomy-enhancing strategy" (to use Nordlinger's term[106]), Canadian political leaders generally avoid any environmental law reforms which would provide an increased role for litigation. As just one example, when the draft legislation that became the *Canadian Environmental Protection Act* (essentially a consolidation of a number of weak existing environmental protection statutes) was released for public discussion in 1986, the Minister of the Environment who introduced it claimed that it embodied "in effect, if not technically, the country's first 'Environmental Bill of Rights'."[107] "Not technically" was a massive understatement; neither the draft legislation nor the final product contained provisions which would establish actionable rights even vaguely analogous to those existing under NEPA, U.S. federal pollution control or administrative procedure laws, or state legislation like Michigan's *Environmental Protection Act* (MEPA), a model widely cited by environmentalists.[108] During Parliamentary hearings on the legislation, numerous environmental groups advocated the addition of such provisions, as did (interestingly enough) the Canadian Labour Congress, a national umbrella organization of trade unions.[109] Similar arguments were made by the Minister's own advisory council.[110] Even the limited provisions for citizen-initiated action which the legislation did contain were challenged by some industry organizations.[111] More significantly, the Minister of the Environment attacked the concept of "environmental rights" on two separate occasions when he appeared before the Parliamentary committee examining the bill. "Inevitably," he said, "the interpretation is going to come from the courts, not from politicians who are accountable to the people. We would in effect abdicate to the courts decisions affecting the environment, and the courts are not accountable."[112] A few months later, he was to expand this argument, claiming that entrenching employees' rights, environmental rights, "and other bills of rights in areas of public policy...could very well undermine the capacity of elected and therefore accountable people to represent the public interest as they see fit."[113]

Some Speculations About the Future

The legal and administrative framework of environmental policy may help to explain the partial failure of deregulation in the U.S. This cannot be the case in Canada, where that framework would place few obstacles in the path of a national government (especially a majority government) bent on pursuing such a policy. However, the other explanatory approaches suggested so far remain at least potentially valid. In addition, the case of the *Canadian Environmental Protection Act* suggests an increasing degree of sophistication on the part of at least some politicians (and, we may well assume, the levels of the civil service concerned with policy development and legislation) about the importance of state autonomy. This sophistication is, in turn, shared by at least some of the beneficiaries of that state autonomy within the business community. Thus, we can expect increasingly frequent business defences of the ability of government regulatory agencies to do their job of environmental protection "responsibly".

A further hypothesis concerning the persistence of environmental regulation has to do, paradoxically, with the current strength of business influence on the overall political agenda. The political ascendancy of neoconservative ideas, and the practical reentrenchment of business definitions of political feasibility, probably makes business and its leaders less antagonistic toward environmental concerns. These concerns are not perceived, as they were in the 1970s, as one component of a more comprehensive threat to business priorities in the political agenda. One example which supports this hypothesis is the National Task Force on Environment and Economy, convened by the federal government under the auspices of the Canadian Council of Resource and Environment Ministers (CCREM) as part of a carefully choreographed response to the report of the World Commission on Environment and Development (the Brundtland Commission).

Both the Task Force and the Brundtland Commission are part of a more general pattern in which environmental concerns are taken seriously by corporate and governmental elites, at least for public consumption.[114] Providing what may turn out to be a preview of an environmental corporatism of the future, it comprised the federal Environment Minister and a number of his provincial counterparts, one academic, two representatives of non-governmental environmental organizations, the head of the Ontario Waste Management Corporation,[115] and business representation including senior executives with some of the worst polluters (and most aggressive opponents of environmental regulation) in Canada.[116] The Task Force completely excluded representatives of organized labor, thereby indicating the government's perception of their irrelevance. Its report endorsed "significant change in the way our economic initiatives are planned and supervised"; specific recommendations included more use of effluent charges and surety bonds to provide incentives for pollution reduction; incorporation of environmental review into "all government processes for screening, review and evaluation of economic development projects" and into all cabinet documents on economic developments; making government assistance to industry conditional on meeting environmental standards; "incorporating environmental assessment in all federal-provincial economic development agreements".[117]

Many of the Task Force's conclusions, as William Rees has pointed out, are so general as to be meaningless.[118] Others are reprises of familiar tunes, like its endorsement of "investment tax credits, credits for exceeding environmental standards, and reduced interest bonds" to finance pollution abatement. But several fall into neither category. Even if those have yet to be translated into action (which may or may not happen) a decade earlier it would have been unthinkable for many of the members of the Task Force, or the industries they represent, even to pay lip service to the worth of many of its policy recommendations.

A cynic might suggest that the participation of the corporate elite in such an exercise may be simply a way of avoiding the more serious impacts which might otherwise occur if politicians feel they must respond to intensified environmental concern by choosing policy instruments which will result in a genuine internalization of costs.[119] Alternatively, corporate involvement may be aimed at securing government subsidies for investments in modernization and pollution abatement. This would represent continuation of an existing pattern; above and beyond the favorable tax treatment accorded to pollution control investments in Canada, joint federal-provincial expenditure programs paid out more than $700 million in subsidies to upgrade lead smelters in British Columbia and pulp mills in eastern Canada during the early 1980s.[120] Firms like Noranda and Inco have been explicit in demanding such subsidies (in the interests of keeping their prices competitive on international markets) as the price of environmental responsibility.[121] In either case, and despite the continuing use of job blackmail as a bargaining tactic, the fact that some of the largest and most economically powerful firms in Canada have changed their tune on environmental questions suggests the extent of contemporary limits to raw economic power even within the context of a set of political institutions favorable to its exercise.

This observation leads to a tentative conclusion about the two distinct respects in which environmental politics is class politics. The first respect has to do with the ways (exemplified by job blackmail) in which business defends its ability to impose costs on citizens in the name of continued prosperity. A decade ago, Claire Nader challenged "the tenaciously-held view that government regulations equal coercion" and asked why "regulation of society authorized by the private power of the corporation" is not viewed as similarly coercive.[122] She went on to claim that "a pattern of systematic negligence," exemplified by the dumping practices of Reserve Mining, "is a form of deliberate regulation" no less coercive, and perhaps more so, than the actions of governments which attempt to protect citizens from the consequences of such action.

Citizens confronted with the tradeoff of jobs versus environment may well (and quite understandably) prefer the former, but the specific terms of the choice are the products of a power relationship sustained by a particular system of property rights and the differential mobility and time structure of capital and labor. This is why job blackmail works; "realism" in this context is, as noted earlier, defined in terms of the realities of the company president.[123] In the context of environmental policy, redressing this imbalance of power would involve changing the relations of production, and the basis for productive activities themselves, in quite a fundamental way. Few proposals for actually doing this have yet become part of serious political discourse in North America.

This is class politics at the level of theory, of the classroom. The second respect in which environmental politics is class politics is exemplified by the case of the Rafferty-Alameda dam, a Saskatchewan government project designed to provide power plant cooling water, irrigation and flood control which enjoyed widespread support among workers, businessmen and farmers (and even local members of the province's Wildlife Federation) in the area of its construction. After a Federal Court of Canada injunction sought by the Canadian Wildlife Federation temporarily halted the project,[124] one journalist characterized local reaction as blaming "a handful of naturalists, easterners, yuppies, New Democrats and Liberals for interfering in the town's economic future."[125] This is probably an accurate statement of local perceptions, and the controversy typifies a number of similar situations[126] in which the protagonists are clearly divided along class lines, but *not* as would be expected according to the conventional model of class politics. Workers, corporate managers and local businessmen tend, with some exceptions, to line up on the same side of such issues. The other side is overwhelmingly dominated by post-materialists or, as some have called them, members of the new class or the partly overlapping "professional-managerial class."[127] They are often from outside the immediate area, and their immediate livelihoods are conspicuously *not* at stake. Thus, the conventional class oppositions are redefined at a conflict-specific level, as Inglehart has suggested is happening at the level of national politics.[128] However this redefinition does not reflect a lessening of the significance of class cleavages in politics, but a change in the nature of the class-related demands of one set of protagonists. In Offe's words: "New middle class politics...is typically a politics *of* a class but not *on behalf of* a class."[129]

Not all site-specific environmental conflicts fit this model, of course. But many do, at least in Canada, and herein lies an important point. I have so far discussed post-materialism as though it were, within nations, a more or less evenly distributed phenomenon. This supposition is highly unlikely in the Canadian context given the structure of the Canadian economy. Post-materialism is likely to be concentrated in relatively affluent, economically diversified urban areas.[130] One of the corollaries of this observation is that in the event of economic recession, the political discourse on environmental issues would probably lead to the exacerbation of regional cleavages. Both the business community and local or provincial governments might be tempted to exploit the geographical dimension of polarization between materialists and post-materialists in a form of job blackmail which has the added power of long-standing regional economic grievances. Since it is highly unlikely that governments have succeeded in doing away with the business cycle, and since Canada's economy is strongly affected by slumps in those of its trading partners, it is worth speculating about a few other consequences of recession for environmental politics.

The associated squeeze on both corporate profits and government revenues would lead governments to be even more eager than they presently are to promote projects and resource management policies promising short-term gains in employment and tax revenues. Current policy commitments to sustainable development, such as they are, would probably not survive. A more likely scenario involves attempts by both business and government to persuade the attentive public of the need to minimize the unproductive costs of pollution abatement, and to abandon the careful planning of development projects which is essential to sustainable resource management. Having failed to reduce its budget deficit substantially even after several years of strong economic growth, the federal government might in times of recession be affected less by direct business pressure (although the deficit certainly increases its vulnerability in this respect) than by its own crippling financial predicament.[131]

North American environmental politics, then, emerges as a new and distinctive form of class politics, but its class content does not enable us to predict policy outcomes without acknowledging the importance of nationally distinctive political institutions. A more significant point is that the class conflicts which characterize environmental politics are deeper and more divisive than the disputes over shares of the national product which constitute class conflict in the familiar Marxian sense. The conflicts are also about the changing conceptions of what is worth doing (as individual economic actors and as a society) which come with economic security. Whether or not post-materialists espouse a genuinely distinctive environmental ethic, they *are* making judgments about how other people conduct their lives which are, in a broad sense, moral judgments (rather than just differences in consumer preferences and aesthetic tastes). This cultural dimension, and the fact that the gap between the economically secure and the rest of us is widening, lend added urgency to the task of determining whether any political space exists for integrating the two dimensions of class politics in ways which do not amount merely to the further entrenchment of privilege.[132]

Notes

1. A. Downs, "Up and Down with Ecology—The 'Issue-Attention Cycle'," *The Public Interest* 28 (1972), pp. 38-50.

2. "Planet of the Year: What on Earth Are We Doing?" *Time* (January 2, 1989), pp. 18-65.

3. H. Winsor, "80% of Canadians Opposed to New GST," *The Globe and Mail* (October 23, 1989), pp. A1, A2.

4. T. Schrecker, *Political Economy of Environmental Hazards* (Ottawa: Law Reform Commission of Canada, 1984); "Resisting Regulation: Environmental Policy and Corporate Power," *Alternatives* 13: 1 (1985), pp. 9-21.

5. L. Silk and D. Vogel, *Ethics and Profits: The Crisis of Confidence in American Business* (New York: Simon and Schuster, 1976), p. 49.

6. To give an obvious example, even if virtually all consumers might prefer cheaper, higher-powered cars at the cost of higher pollutant emissions, our collective choices as citizens may well favor requiring auto manufacturers to meet strict emission or fuel economy standards at the expense of interfering with consumer choice. To give a less obvious one, even though our decisions as consumers may favor intensely commercialized recreation, we may collectively choose as citizens to support policies which prohibit such developments. This argument is most closely associated with the work of Mark Sagoff, and it should be emphasized that there is nothing necessarily inconsistent or "irrational" about such choices. See Mark Sagoff, "Can Environmentalists be Liberals?" *Environmental Law* 16 (1986), pp. 775-796; "Economic Theory and Environmental Law," *Michigan Law Review* 79 (1981), pp. 1393-1419; "We Have Met the Enemy and He is Us, or, Conflict and Contradiction in Environmental Law," *Environmental Law* 12 (1982), pp. 283-315.

7. P. Taft and P. Ross, "American Labor Violence," in H. Graham and T. Gurr, eds., *The History of Violence in America: A Report to the National Commission on the Causes and Prevention of Violence* (New York: Bantam, 1969), pp. 281-395.

8. See J. DiMento, *Environmental Law and American Business: Dilemmas of Compliance* (New York: Plenum, 1984), pp. 1-18, 77-102.

9. Note, "Reserve Mining—the Standard of Proof Required to Enjoin an Environmental Hazard to the Public Health," *Minnesota Law Review* 59 (1975), pp. 893-926; J. Molloy, "Federal Environmental Statutes: The Adversarial Rulemaking Process," in *Environmental Enforcement*, Selected Readings Prepared in Conjunction with the Seventh Annual Conference on the Environment (Washington, DC: Division of Public Service Activities, American Bar Association, 1978), p. 6.

10. C. Lax, "The Toronto Lead Smelter Controversy," in W. Leiss, ed., *Ecology versus Politics in Canada* (Toronto: University of Toronto Press, 1979), pp. 50-62. Canada Metal was then, and until recently, part of the multi-billion dollar Canadian Pacific corporate empire.

11. "Long-drawn Trial of Lead Company Adjourned Again," *Winnipeg Free Press* (October 18, 1984); "Lead-emission Case Goes to Judge," *Winnipeg Free Press* (December 4, 1984); *R. v. Canada Metal Company Ltd.* (1982), 11 *Canadian Environmental Law Reports* 130; *Re the*

Canada Metal Company Ltd. and R. et al. (1982), 12 *Canadian Environmental Law Reports*; "Reasons for Decision" (February 28, 1985), *R. v. Canada Metal Company Ltd.*, Norton, J., Prov. Ct. (C. D.), Province of Manitoba, unreported.

12. F. Anderson, *Environmental Improvement Through Economic Incentives* (Baltimore: Johns Hopkins University Press for Resources for the Future, 1977), p. 16.

13. L. Wenner, *The Environmental Decade in Court* (Bloomington: Indiana University Press, 1982), pp. 172-173.

14. Andrew Blowers has discussed this distinction in terms of one between "pluralist" and "political economy" perspectives on business influence. The pluralist approach, reflecting the focus on interest groups which characterizes most U.S. and (especially) Canadian political scientists' discussions of influences on the outcomes of public policy, "argues that business is an interest group competing with other interests for access to decision makers in a relatively open political framework." The political economy approach, on the other hand, recognizes "business as a dominant force engaged in the control of large sectors of economic and political life." A. Blowers, "Master of Fate or Victim of Circumstance," *Policy and Politics* 11 (1983), p. 393.

15. R. Kazis and R. Grossman, *Fear at Work: Job Blackmail, Labor and the Environment* (New York: Pilgrim Press, 1982).

16. Silk and Vogel, *Ethics and Profits*, p. 66.

17. *Still Waters*, Report of the Sub-Committee on Acid Rain, House of Commons Standing Committee on Fisheries and Forestry (Ottawa: Supply and Services Canada, 1981), pp. 19-24; S. Cordier *et al.*, "Mortality Patterns in a Population Living Near a Copper Smelter," *Environmental Research* 31 (1983), pp. 311-332.

18. K. Noble, "Noranda Mines Links Pollution Control Costs to Fate of its Smelter," *The Globe and Mail* (May 31, 1984), p. B1.

19. R. Collison, "The Greening of the Boardroom," *Report on Business Magazine* 6: 1 (1989), p. 55.

20. B. Jorgensen, "Noranda Will Stick it Out Despite Debt," *The Globe and Mail* (June 29, 1985), p. B1.

21. K. Noble, "Pulp Mill Test of New Pollution Policy," *The Globe and Mail* (January 26, 1987), pp. B1, B2; S. Oziewicz, "1600 Jobs Preserved as Terrace Bay Mill Gets Pollution Reprieve, *The Globe and Mail* (January 31, 1987), p. A4; "Premier Sidesteps Bradley on Terrace Bay Mill Plan," *The Globe and Mail* (January 16, 1987), p. A12; "The Fortune 500," *Fortune* 113: 9 (April 28, 1986); *Who Owns Whom 1985 (North America)* (London: Dun and Bradstreet, 1985).

22. A 1985 study found that "approximately half" of Canada's 148 operating pulp and paper mills, and 36 of the country's 38 newsprint mills, did not meet effluent objectives specified under *Fisheries Act* regulations in 1970. Perhaps predictably, compliance rates were lowest in Quebec and the Atlantic provinces. IEC Beak Consultants Ltd., *Costs to Meet Federal Water Pollution Control Regulations in the Pulp and Paper Industry*, report to Environmental Protection Service, Environment Canada (Mississauga, May 1985; obtained by the author under the *Access to Information Act*), pp. 6.1-6.2. On Ontario, see P. Victor and T. Burrell, *Environmental Protection Regulation, Water Pollution and the Pulp and Paper Industry*, Regulation Reference Technical Report No. 14 (Ottawa: Economic Council of Canada, 1981); on B.C., G. Fraser, "Big Polluters not Prosecuted, Fisheries Memo Indicates," *The Globe and Mail* (December 5, 1989), pp. A1-A2.

23. P. Davis, "Arsenic and Jobs Trade-Off," *Nature* 304 (1983), p. 200; P. Dorman, "Environmental Protection, Employment and Profit: The Politics of Public Interest in the Tacoma/Asarco

Arsenic Dispute," *Review of Radical Political Economics* 16 (1984), pp. 151-164; B. Kalikow, "Environmental Risk: Power to the People," *Technology Review* 87 (1984).

24. Such regulation in Canada is, to a much greater degree than in the United States, a matter not of national jurisdiction. Constitutionally and politically the field is left to the individual provinces.

25. Trezise, "Alternative Approaches," pp. 408-409.

26. See H. Enchin, "Happily Paying the Price in Noranda's Abitibi Empire," *The Globe and Mail* (August 8, 1989), p. A1; L. Tataryn, *Dying for a Living* (Ottawa: Deneau and Greenberg, 1979), pp. 61-105 (on local resentment of journalists' and workers' concerns about the occupational and environmental health impacts of uranium mining in Elliot Lake, Ontario). For similar examples from the U.S. context see D. Jordan, "The Town Dilemma," *Environment* 19 (1977), pp. 6-15 (on PCB emissions in Bloomington, Indiana); A. Miller, "Towards an Environment-Labor Coalition," *Environment* 22: 5 (1980), pp. 32-39.

27. D. Vogel, "A Case Study of Clean Air Legislation 1967-1981," in B. Bock *et al.*, eds., *The Impact of the Modern Corporation* (New York: Columbia University Press, 1984), pp. 339-354.

28. M. Scales, "Canada Backs Asbestos Use, Third World Provides Markets," *Canadian Mining Journal* 103 (July 1982), pp. 19-23; "Canadian Asbestos: Export and Die?" *The Economist* (September 26, 1987), pp. 82-83. The Quebec government expropriated the province's largest private asbestos producer in 1978 (to fulfil a long-standing policy commitment of the then-ruling Parti Quebecois) and is hence directly involved in the industry.

29. Lindblom, *Politics and Markets*, p. 178; see generally pp. 170-221.

30. *Ibid.*, p. 171 (emphasis added). Clearly, it is predominantly the executives of large corporations who occupy this role, as distinct from the small businesspeople beloved of neoclassical economic theory and neoconservative political rhetoric. On the public nature of the power exercised by large corporations, see R. Dahl, *After the Revolution? Authority in a Good Society* (New Haven: Yale University Press, 1970), pp. 115-140; M. Nadel, *Corporations and Political Accountability* (Lexington, MA: D. C. Heath, 1976), esp. pp. 107-118.

31. C. Friedrich, *Constitutional Government and Democracy* (Boston: Ginn, rev. ed., 1946), pp. 589-591.

32. C. Offe, "Some Contradictions of the Modern Welfare State," in *Contradictions of the Welfare State* (Cambridge, MA: The M. I. T. Press, 1984), p. 151.

33. Lindblom refers to this situation in terms of the "privileged position of business" in political life. See his *Politics and Markets*, pp. 170-188; Charles Lindblom, "The Market as Prison," *Journal of Politics* 44 (1982), pp. 324-336.

34. D. Vogel, "The Power of Business in America: A Re-Appraisal," *British Journal of Political Science* 13 (1983), p. 23.

35. Silk and Vogel, *Ethics and Profits*; for an academic argument, sponsored by the Trilateral Commission, reinforcing this perception see S. Huntington, "The United States," in M. Crozier *et al.*, *The Crisis of Democracy* (New York: New York University Press, 1975), pp. 59-118.

36. P. Burch, "The Business Roundtable: Its Make-up and External Ties," *Research in Political Economy* 4 (1981) pp. 101-127; T. Edsall, *The New Politics of Inequality* (New York: Norton, 1984), pp. 121-125; Vogel, "Power of Business," pp. 34-37.

37. E. Drew, *Politics and Money* (New York: Macmillan, 1983); Edsall, *New Politics of Inequality*, pp. 130-137; Vogel, "Power of Business," pp. 33-38. On corporate advocacy advertising, see S. Sethi, *Up Against the Corporate Wall* (Englewood Cliffs, NJ: Prentice-Hall, 4th ed., 1982), pp.

162-205 (case study of such a campaign by Bethlehem Steel aimed at affecting both environmental and trade policy).

38. Vogel, "Power of Business," p. 36.

39. *Ibid.*, p. 39.

40. J. Laxer, *Canada's Economic Strategy* (Toronto: McClelland and Stewart, 1981), pp. 9-43.

41. *Ibid.*; D. Langille, "The Business Council on National Issues and the Canadian State," presented to the Canadian Political Science Association annual meeting (Ottawa: Carleton University, mimeo, 1985).

42. I would argue that a far more important factor was the changing class structure of the societies in question, coupled with (generally accurate) individual voter perceptions of their relative gains and losses from the existing direction of social and economic policy. For some explorations of this point of view, see T. Edsall, "Republican America," *New York Review of Books* (April 24, 1986), pp. 3-6; C. Offe, "Democracy Against the Welfare State?" in J. Moon, ed., *Responsibility, Rights, and Welfare* (Boulder, CO: Westview, 1988), pp. 189-228.

43. R. Andrews, "Economics and Environmental Decisions, Past and Present," in V. K. Smith, ed., *Environmental Policy under Reagan's Executive Order* (Chapel Hill: University of North Carolina Press, 1984), pp. 43-85; S. Tolchin, "Cost-Benefit Analysis and the Rush to Deregulate," *Policy Studies Review* 4 (1984), pp. 212-218; D. Whittington and W. Grubb, "Economic Analysis in Regulatory Decisions: The Implications of Executive Order 12,291," *Science, Technology and Human Values* 9 (1984), pp. 63-71. For a review of the ways in which cost-benefit analysis builds business priorities into the policy decision-making process, see T. Schrecker, "Risks versus Rights: Economic Power and Economic Analysis in Environmental Policy," in D. Poff and W. Waluchow, eds., *Business Ethics in Canada* (Scarborough: Prentice-Hall, 1987), pp. 265-284.

44. R. Brownstein and N. Easton, *Reagan's Ruling Class* (Washington, DC: Presidential Accountability Group, 1982), pp. 205-216 (see generally pp. 107-221 on the Reagan administration's early efforts to remake environmental and resource management policy in a radically different image); S. Hays, *Beauty, Health and Permanence: Environmental Politics in the United States, 1955-1985* (Cambridge: Cambridge University Press, 1987), pp. 491-526; H. Kenski and H. Ingram, "The Reagan Administration and Environmental Regulation," in S. Kamieniecki *et al.*, eds., *Controversies in Environmental Policy* (Albany: SUNY Press, 1986), pp. 284-293.

45. This low-key approach may also have something to do with the fact that the strongly business-oriented Economic Council of Canada, an advisory group to the federal Cabinet, had in a major study of regulation in Canada conspicuously failed to call for such measures, and indeed called for strengthening some areas of environmental regulation. See Economic Council of Canada, *Reforming Regulation* (Ottawa: Supply and Services Canada, 1981), pp. 83-108. Similar conclusions were reached a few years later by the Royal Commission on Economic Union and Development Prospects for Canada (the MacDonald Commission), which in its other recommendations provided the impetus for the Conservatives' promotion of free trade with the United States as a key element of economic strategy. See the Commission's *Report* (Ottawa: Supply and Services Canada, 1985), vol. 2, pp. 505-534. Thus, the ideological support the government could have called upon to legitimize a call for even less demanding environmental regulation was largely lacking.

46. L. Diebel, "Top Oil Man Calling Environment Shots, Lawyer Charges," *Toronto Star* (September 14, 1988), p. A11.

47. Vogel, "Power of Business," p. 27; E. Seskin, "Automobile Air Pollution Policy" in P. Portney,

ed., *Current Issues in U.S. Environmental Policy* (Baltimore: Johns Hopkins University Press, 1979), pp. 68-104. It could be argued, of course, that despite its overt public opposition to this transition the industry secretly welcomes it, because of the high cost of demonstrating compliance with emission standards and the associated barriers to market entry and incentives for exit. (Many European automakers withdrew from the U.S. market during the late 1970s and early 1980s because of the combined costs of meeting safety and emission standards.) However, there is little evidence for this supposition.

48. R. Gibson, *Control Orders and Industrial Pollution Abatement in Ontario* (Toronto: Canadian Environmental Law Research Foundation, 1983), esp. pp. 90-93; A. Picard, "Quebec Pays Price for Wealth in Industry," *The Globe and Mail* (August 15, 1989), pp. A1, A9. M. Rankin and P. Finkle, "The Enforcement of Environmental Law: Taking the Environment Seriously," *University of British Columbia Law Review* 17 (1983), pp. 35-57; J. Swaigen, "Sentencing in Environmental Cases," in L. Duncan, ed., *Environmental Enforcement: Proceedings of the National Conference on the Enforcement of Environmental Law* (Edmonton: Environmental Law Centre, 1985), pp. 94-99; A. Thompson, *Environmental Regulation in Canada* (Vancouver: Westwater Research Institute, University of British Columbia), pp. 33-36, 46-51.

49. A. Picard, "Polluters Get Off Lightly in Quebec, Study Finds," *The Globe and Mail* (March 20, 1989), p. A4.

50. The Kimberly-Clark case, cited earlier, is one example; for another, see Enchin, "Happily Paying the Price in Noranda's Abitibi Empire."

51. L. McCaffrey, "The Ontario Special Prosecution Team," in Duncan, ed., *Environmental Enforcement*, pp. 80-83; D. Saxe, "Fines Go Up Dramatically in Environmental Cases," *Canadian Environmental Law Reports* 3 (New Series) (1988), pp. 104-121.

52. Saxe, "Fines Go Up," p. 105.

53. T. McMillan, speech to graduates of Atlantic Policy Academy, Charlottetown, PEI, October 1986, as cited in "From the Horse's Mouth," *Alternatives* 14: 2 (1987), p. 59.

54. Although the Conservatives were returned with a majority, McMillan lost his own Parliamentary seat in the 1988 federal elections.

55. *Cf.* Law Reform Commission of Canada, *Crimes Against the Environment* (Ottawa: Law Reform Commission of Canada, Working Paper 44, 1985), which recommended the criminalization of some categories of acts which result in serious environmental harm. The Commission is an advisory body which reports to the Department of Justice.

56. R. McMurray and S. Ramsey, "Environmental Crime: The Use of Criminal Sanctions in Enforcing Environmental Laws," *Loyola of Los Angeles Law Review* 19 (1986), pp. 1136-1144; J. Abramson, "Government Cracks Down on Environmental Crimes," *Wall Street Journal* (February 16, 1980), pp. B1, B7.

57. Abramson, "Government Cracks Down," p. B7.

58. *Ibid.*

59. In the sense in which the term is used by A. Wildavsky, "Choosing Preferences by Constructing Institutions: A Cultural Theory of Preference Formation," *American Political Science Review* 81 (1987), pp. 3-22.

60. The best overview of this body of theory and research is T. Skocpol, " Bringing the State Back In," in P. Evans *et al.*, eds., *Bringing the State Back In* (Cambridge: Cambridge University Press, 1985), pp. 3-37. For an illustration of this approach see T. Skocpol, "Political Response to

Capitalist Crisis: Neo-Marxist Theories of the State and the Case of the New Deal," *Politics and Society* 10 (1980), pp. 155-201.

61. R. Inglehart, "Post-Materialism in an Environment of Insecurity," *American Political Science Review* 75 (1981), pp. 880-900; "The Changing Structure of Political Cleavages in Western Society," in R. Dalton *et al.*, eds., *Electoral Change in Advanced Industrial Democracies* (Princeton: Princeton University Press, 1984), pp. 25-69; "New Perspectives on Value Change," *Comparative Political Studies* 17 (1985), pp. 485-532; R. Inglehart and J. Rabier, "Political Realignment in Advanced Industrial Society," *Government and Opposition* 21 (1986), pp. 456-479.

62. "Post-Materialism," p. 881.

63. *Ibid.*, pp. 881-890; Inglehart and Rabier, "Political Realignment," pp. 458-464.

64. "Post-Materialism," pp. 892-897.

65. G. Peters, "The United States: Absolute Change and Relative Stability," in R. Rose, ed., *Public Employment in Western Nations* (Cambridge: Cambridge University Press, 1985), pp. 228-249.

66. Exemplified, at least in Canada, by the spread and increased militance of unionization among members of those quintessentially post-industrial occupational groups, teachers and white-collar civil servants (including such professionals as Crown attorneys).

67. N. Watts, "From Consensus to Dissensus: The Role of Distributional Conflicts in Environmental Resource Policy," in A. Schnaiberg *et al.*, eds., *Distributional Conflicts in Environmental-Resource Policy* (Aldershot, Hants: Gower, 1986), p. 3.

68. *Cf.* C. Offe, "New Social Movements: Challenging the Boundaries of Institutional Politics," *Social Research* 52 (1985), p. 851.

69. "Post-Materialism," pp. 892-893.

70. Offe, "Changing Boundaries," pp. 832-838.

71. W. Chandler and A. Siaroff, "Postindustrial Politics in Germany and the Origins of the Greens," *Comparative Politics* 18 (1986), p. 305.

72. Inglehart and Rabier, "Political Realignment," pp. 465-567.

73. Inglehart, "Post-Materialism," pp. 894-895.

74. E. Nordlinger, *On the Autonomy of the Democratic State* (Cambridge, MA: Harvard University Press, 1981).

75. S. Hays, "The Structure of Environmental Politics Since World War II," *Journal of Social History* 14 (1981), pp. 720-724.

76. L. Thurow, "Clean Air, New Industry: Let's Compromise," *The New York Times* (November 16, 1980), p. 2F; see also L. Thurow, *The Zero-Sum Society* (New York: Penguin, 1980), pp. 103-121.

77. R. Kagan, "On Regulatory Inspectorates and Police," in K. Hawkins and J. Thomas, eds., *Enforcing Regulation* (Boston: Kluwer-Nijhoff, 1984), pp. 53-54.

78. Trezise, "Alternative Approaches," p. 410.

79. C. Reinarman, "The Social Construction of an Alcohol Problem: The Case of Mothers Against Drunk Drivers and Social Control in the 1980s," *Theory and Society* 17 (1988), p. 92.

80. See *ibid.*, pp. 91-120.

81. *Ibid.* pp. 104-113.

82. T. Skocpol, "Political Response to Capitalist Crisis," p. 200. I am not, incidentally, convinced

that those limits are as flexible as Skocpol suggests, at least not within any specific historical context, but the question cannot be explored here.

83. E. E. Schattschneider, *The Semisovereign People* (Hinsdale, IL: Dryden Press, 1975, [1960]), pp. 60-75.

84. *Ibid.* For a similar analysis, but one which is much more receptive to the use of Marxist categories, see C. Offe, "Some Contradictions of the Modern Welfare State," pp. 158-161.

85. For an explanation of the mechanics and consequences involved, see R. Landes, *The Canadian Polity: A Comparative Introduction* (Scarborough: Prentice-Hall, 1983), pp. 334-346, 351-355. The few thousand votes that a government might risk losing by calling an employer's bluff when a plant shutdown is threatened in response to wilderness protection initiatives or pollution control requirements *might* be offset, in terms of national or popular vote totals, by a larger number of votes supporting a party's attempt to be tough on the environment. In terms of seat standings in Parliament or a provincial legislature, the latter group of voters is unlikely to have any impact whatsoever; the former may well do so.

86. R. Crandall, "An Acid Test for Congress," *Regulation* 8 (September/December 1984), pp. 21-28.

87. "Europe: When the Vote Comes In," *The Economist* (June 24, 1989), pp. 45-52.

88. J. Howse, "Upset in the West," *Maclean's* (March 27, 1989), pp. 12-13; V. Lyon, "The Reluctant Party," *Alternatives* 13: 1 (1985), pp. 3-8.

89. R. Brickman, *et al.*, *Controlling Chemicals: The Politics of Regulation in Europe and the United States* (Ithaca: Cornell University Press, 1985), esp. pp. 74-128, 301-317.

90. *Ibid.*, pp. 129-186. For a discussion of how judicial review of regulatory decisions has affected (and in my view made more sophisticated) the treatment of scientific evidence by U.S. regulators, see B. Gillespie *et al.*, "Carcinogenic Risk Assessment in the United States and Great Britain," *Social Studies of Science* 9 (1979), pp. 265-301; H. Latin, "The 'Significance' of Toxic Health Risks," *Ecology Law Quarterly* 10 (1982), pp. 339-395.

91. I. Bupp, "The French Nuclear Harvest: Abundant Energy or Bitter Fruit," *Technology Review* 83: 2 (1980), pp. 30-39; J. Campbell, *Collapse of an Industry: Nuclear Power and the Contradictions of U.S. Policy* (Ithaca: Cornell University Press, 1988), esp. pp. 136-180; J. Fagnani and J. P. Moatti, "The Politics of French Nuclear Development," *Journal of Policy Analysis and Management* 3 (1984), pp. 264-275.

92. Campbell, *Collapse of an Industry*, pp. 50-109; D. Maleson, "The Historical Roots of the Legal System's Response to Nuclear Power," *Southern California Law Review* 55 (1982), pp. 597-640.

93. F. Zemans, "Legal Mobilization: The Neglected Role of the Law in the Political System," *American Political Science Review* 77 (1983), pp. 690-703.

94. The discussion which follows concentrates on citizens' use of the courts to influence environmental policy. However, institutions of direct democracy such as referenda are also important at least at the state level, as illustrated by California's Proposition 65 initiative requiring stricter control of toxic chemicals. See D. Mazmanian, "Toxics Policy in California: New Directions in Environmental Policy Making," *Environmental Impact Assessment Review* 8 (198), pp. 149-157.

95. F. Anderson, *NEPA in the Courts* (Baltimore: Johns Hopkins University Press, 1973), pp. 247-259; J. Handler, *Social Movements and the Legal System* (New York: Academic Press, 1982), pp. 48-56; U.S. Council on Environmental Quality, *Environmental Quality 1973*, 4th Annual Report (Washington, DC: U.S. Government Printing Office, 1974), pp. 228-230; U.S. Council on Environmental Quality, *Environmental Quality 1974*, 5th Annual Report (Washington, DC: U.S. Government Printing Office, 1975), pp. 375-378.

96. See, *e.g.*, D. Ackman, "Highway to Nowhere: NEPA, Environmental Review and the *Westway Case*," *Columbia Journal of Law and Social Problems* 21 (1988), pp. 325-384 (on a New York City freeway construction project stalled and eventually abandoned as a consequence of litigation under NEPA).

97. L. Caldwell, *Science and the National Environmental Policy Act* (Birmingham: University of Alabama Press, 1982), pp. 1-96; S. Taylor, *Making Bureaucracies Think: The Environmental Impact Statement Strategy of Administrative Reform* (Stanford, CA: Stanford University Press, 1984).

98. The importance of this point should be emphasized; *cf.* Caldwell, *Science and the National Environmental Policy Act*, pp. 71-72: "[NEPA] has made it less practical for [congressmen] to urge projects so environmentally 'bad' that exposure through the NEPA process would almost certainly cause their demise."

99. D. Donaghy, "NEPA's Worst Case Analysis Requirement," *Natural Resources Journal* 25 (1985), pp. 495-514; W. Freudenberg and K. Keating, "Applying Sociology to Policy: Social Science and the Environmental Impact Statement," *Rural Sociology* 50 (1985), pp. 578-605; M. Mansfield, "Through the Forest of the Onshore Oil and Gas Leasing Controversy...") *Land and Water Law Review* 24 (1989), pp. 85-129.

100. J. Austin, "The Rise of Citizen-Suit Enforcement in Environmental Law: Reconciling Private and Public Attorneys-General," *Northwestern University Law Review* 81 (1987), pp. 220-233; J. Miller, "Private Enforcement of Federal Pollution Control Laws, Part I," *Environmental Law Reporter* 13 (1983), pp. 10309-10317.

101. *Natural Resources Defense Council v. U.S. Environmental Protection Agency*, No. 1509, Complaint for Injunctive and Declaratory Relief (DC District, May 26, 1983) and Settlement Agreement (DC District, October 14, 1984); see also *Pesticides: EPA's Formidable Task to Assess and Regulate Their Risks*, GAO/RCED-86-125 (Washington, DC: U.S. General Accounting Office, 1986), pp. 109-119.

102. J. Castrilli and T. Vigod, *Pesticides in Canada: An Examination of Federal Law and Policy* (Ottawa: Law Reform Commission of Canada, 1987), pp. 41-98. The exception occurs only when a pesticide manufacturer wishes to challenge a government decision to cancel approval of a particular substance, as happened in 1986 following the cancellation of approval for Monsanto's alachlor.

103. Note, in this regard, the 1989 decision of the Federal Court of Canada in the case of the Rafferty-Alameda Dam. The federal government initially granted the licence needed under the *International River Improvements Act* for this Saskatchewan government project as part of a deal with the provincial government to get its agreement with a proposal for a new national park in the days leading up to the 1988 federal election. It did so without conducting an environmental assessment under the guidelines for the federal Environmental Assessment and Review Process (EARP). The court ruled that the administrative guidelines setting out EARP procedures, which had first been published as a federal regulation in 1984 (Environmental Assessment and Review Process Guidelines Order, SOR/84-467, *Canada Gazette*, June 22, 1984) created a judicially enforceable obligation on the part of the Minister of the Environment to comply with the guidelines in all cases. (Reasons for Order, Canadian Wildlife Federation *et al.* v. Minister of the Environment and Saskatchewan Water Corporation (Federal Court of Canada, Trial Division, T-80-89, Cullen, J.) Previously, the federal government had treated their application as entirely discretionary. Despite protests from an outraged Saskatchewan government, the federal Minister of the Environment, Lucien Bouchard, announced that the decision would not

be appealed, and subsequently issued a new licence for the dam based on the government's own, internal environmental reviews (but not the public hearings called for under the EARP guidelines). This is an oversimplification of a complex legal battle, but it suffices to indicate its political significance.

104. For analysis of the many weaknesses of the EARP procedure, see among others Canadian Environmental Advisory Council, *Preparing for the 1990s: Environmental Assessment, an Integral Part of Decision Making* (Ottawa: CEAC, 1988); R. Cotton and D. P. Emond, "Environmental Impact Assessment," in J. Swaigen, ed., *Environmental Rights in Canada* (Toronto: Butterworths, 1981), pp. 266-272; "Improvements to the Environmental Assessment and Review Process," Discussion Paper (Ottawa: Government of Canada, mimeo, February 1983); W. Rees, "EARP at the Crossroads: Environmental Assessment in Canada," *Environmental Impact Assessment Review* 1 (1980), pp. 355-377; W. Rees, "Environmental Assessment of Hydrocarbon Production from the Canadian Beaufort Sea," *Environmental Impact Assessment Review* 4 (1983), pp. 539-555.

105. P. Muldoon, "The Fight for an Environmental Bill of Rights," *Alternatives* 15: 2 (1988), pp. 33-39.

106. Nordlinger, *On the Autonomy of the Democratic State*, pp. 90-143.

107. T. McMillan, "Notes for a Statement at a News Conference Announcing the Proposed *Environmental Protection Act*" (Ottawa: Environment Canada, mimeo, December 18, 1986), p. 1.

108. *E.g.*, J. Swaigen and R. Woods, "A Substantive Right to Environmental Quality," in Swaigen, ed., *Environmental Rights in Canada*, pp. 195-241.

109. *E.g.*, Canada House of Commons, Legislative Committee on Bill C-74, *Minutes of Proceedings* 5 (December 10, 1987), pp. 5-14 (Energy Probe), pp. 14-23 (Société pour Vaicre la Pollution); *Minutes of Proceedings* 7 (December 16, 1979), pp. 23-36; *Minutes of Proceedings* 9 (January 19, 1988), pp. 5-20, A1-A33 (Canadian Environmental Law Association) and pp. 50-59 (Greenpeace); *Minutes of Proceedings* 10 (January 20, 1988) pp. 4-19 (Pollution Probe).

110. Canadian Environmental Advisory Council, *Review of the Proposed Environmental Protection Act* (Ottawa: CEAC, 1987), pp. 27-28.

111. *E.g.*, Canada House of Commons, Legislative Committee on Bill C-74, *Minutes of Proceedings* 3 (December 3, 1987), pp. 5-18 (Asbestos Institute; see esp. p. 12); *Minutes of Proceedings* 7 (December 16, 1987), pp. 12-23 (Conseil du patronat du Quebec). The objections of the Canadian Chemical Producers' Association and the Canadian Manufacturers' Association, which are national rather than regional organizations, focused instead on the perceived punitiveness of the legislation, the treatment of confidential business information and the search and seizure powers of inspectors. See *Minutes of Proceedings* 6 (December 15, 1987). The differences in emphasis are intriguing, but unfortunately cannot be explored here in the detail they deserve.

112. Canada House of Commons, Standing Committee on Bill C-74, *Minutes of Proceedings* 1 (November 24-25, 1987), p. 25.

113. Canada House of Commons, Legislative Committee on Bill C-74, *Minutes of Proceedings* 14 (February 3, 1988), p 16; see generally pp. 14-16.

114. The report of the Brundtland Commission represents an elite consensus forged (not, one may well assume, without considerable friction) among leaders of the world's richest and poorest nations on such questions as the importance of ecology-economy linkages and the need for sustainable development, whatever that may mean. See *Our Common Future* (New York:

Oxford University Press, 1986). The President of the World Resources Institute, a heavily corporate-funded organization with ongoing cooperative relationships with the World Bank and numerous national development assistance administrations, is J. G. Speth, a former head of the U.S. Council on Environmental Quality appointed by then-President Carter. In December 1985, he told a colloquium on environmental issues sponsored by the Economic Council of Canada that the implications of environmental degradation for economic growth and national security constituted nothing less than "a new agenda for OECD countries." J. G. Speth, "Environment, Economy, Security" (Ottawa: Economic Council of Canada mimeo, December 1985).

115. Donald A. Chant, university professor and one of the founders of the environmental organization Pollution Probe in 1970, accepted the chairmanship of OWMC in 1981. This is a Crown corporation established by the Ontario government to provide industrial waste treatment services supposedly unavailable through the private sector. Dogged by public opposition and administrative problems, OWMC's proposed facility will now not be operational before the early 1990s, although the urgency of the hazardous waste problem was often invoked as a justification for OWMC's establishment and for the vagueness which surrounded (and still surrounds) the level of subsidy to be provided by Ontario taxpayers.

116. Canadian Council of Resource and Environment Ministers, *Report of the National Task Force on Environment and Economy* (Downsview, Ontario: CCREM, 1987). Members included senior executives of Inco Ltd., Dow Chemical Canada Inc., Noranda Forest Inc. (the same Adam Zimmerman whose defence of job blackmail was quoted earlier in this chapter), and Alcan Aluminum; also included was the President of the Canadian Petroleum Association, many of whose members had (for instance) actively opposed federal initiatives to eliminate the addition of tetraethyl lead to gasoline.

117. *Ibid.*

118. W. Rees, "A Role for Environmental Impact Assessment in Achieving Sustainable Development," *Environmental Impact Assessment Review* 8 (1988), pp. 279-280.

119. Roy Aitken, Inco's representative on the Task Force, has said that: "If you sit on the sidelines you'll eventually end up with the regulations you deserve. And those, typically, will be punitive with multi-million-dollar fines and jail terms." Collison, "The Greening of the Boardroom," p. 44. In response to Ontario government regulation, Inco at the end of 1988 finally submitted plans for a major rebuilding of its Sudbury nickel smelter complex which will have the effect of reducing sulphur dioxide emissions by 60 percent from 1985 levels. See S. McGee, "Inco Program to Cut Acid Rain," *The Globe and Mail* (December 31, 1988), pp. B1, B2. After refusing to make such a commitment for more than a decade, the firm has turned the decision into a major public relations coup.

120. J. Hunter, "B.C. to Help Cominco Modernize Smelter," *The Globe and Mail* (August 26, 1986), p. B1; K. Noble, "Forest Industry Attempts to Kick the Grant Habit," *The Globe and Mail* (December 31, 1985), pp. B1-B2.

121. Collison, "Greening of the Boardroom," pp. 53-54; for earlier examples see K. Noble, "Cutting Sulphur Dioxide Output a Question of Who Foots the Bill," *The Globe and Mail* (February 16, 1985), pp. B1-B2.

122. C. Nader, "Controlling Environmental Health Hazards: Corporate Power, Individual Freedom and Social Control," in E.C. Hammond and I. Selikoff, eds., *Public Control of Environmental Health Hazards, Annals of the New York Academy of Sciences* 329 (New York, 1979), p. 215.

123. For a magnificently succinct analysis of this process from the standpoint of Marxian economics

see Claus Offe, "Reflections on the Welfare State and the Future of Socialism," in *Contradictions of the Welfare State*, p. 284.

124. For discussion of the circumstances surrounding this injunction, see 103 above.

125. G. York, "Dam Workers, Residents Baffled by Court Ruling on Rafferty Project," *The Globe and Mail* (April 17, 1989), p. A8.

126. *E.g.*, the continuing conflict surrounding logging in the Temagami region of northern Ontario (see D. Henton, "Fight on to Save Temagami's Pine Giants," *Toronto Star* (June 11, 1989), pp. A1, A16-A17) and in the Queen Charlotte Islands of British Columbia (see A. Grzybowski, "The Fate of the Queen Charlottes," *Alternatives* 12:3/4 (1985), pp. 56-61). For an overview of such situations, see J. Dunster, "Forestry Conflicts in Canada," *Ambio* 16 (1987), pp. 59-63.

127. B. Ehrenreich and J. Ehrenreich, "The Professional-Managerial Class," in P. Walker, ed., *Between Labor and Capital* (Boston: South End Press, 1979), pp. 5-45.

128. Inglehart, "Changing Structure of Political Cleavages"; Inglehart and Rabier, "Political Realignment."

129. Offe, "New Social Movements," p. 833.

130. This is a fatal weakness in one recent attempt to apply Inglehart's approach to Canadian political culture, which relied on a national sample with no attempt at regional or intra-regional differentiation: H. Bakvis and N. Nevitte, "In Pursuit of Postbourgeois Man: Postmaterialism and Intergenerational Change in Canada," *Comparative Political Studies* 20 (1987), pp. 357-389.

131. The federal government is already using the need to finance new environmental programs as a justification for additional taxes. See G. Fraser, "Environmental Clean-up Linked to Higher Taxes," *The Globe and Mail* (August 25, 1989), p. A8.

132. I elaborate on these concerns in "Environmentalism and Lifestyles of the Affluent," in P. Findlay and S. Rosenblum, eds., *Debates within Canadian Social Democracy* (Toronto: Lorimer, forthcoming 1990).

BETWEEN ROCKS AND
HARD PLACES:
BUREAUCRATS, LAW AND
POLLUTION CONTROL

Kernaghan Webb

They can be viewed as faceless purveyors of state policy, as benevolent servants of society or as pawns manipulated by the capitalist power elite. No matter how they are perceived, there can be no doubt that government bureaucrats occupy a pivotal role in the pollution control process. Behind every piece of environmental legislation, behind every Minister of Environment lies a bureaucrat, and it is largely in his or her hands that the instruments of government policy are wielded.[1]

Surprisingly, however, the bureaucrats' perspective on environmental protection has not received much attention, with the result that the role of the bureaucrat is often not well understood. In the absence of this understanding, bureaucrats and indeed the entire pollution control process risk being misperceived. For example, it is all too easy to assume that once environmental protection legislation has been passed, implementation will automatically ensue. As a number of recent studies have revealed,[2] implementation rarely proceeds in so straightforward a manner. Legislation is often unrealistic and ambiguous, and courts may be inconsistent in their verdicts; Environment Ministers may lack clout in Cabinet; funding for programs is often insufficient; regulatees can be uncooperative and public interest groups, unsympathetic.

Faced with this less-than-ideal situation, bureaucrats may engage in compromises—with their political masters, with other departments, with industry and with the public. Although sought with the best of intentions, these compromises may, in the final analysis, satisfy no one. In this sense, bureaucrats may become the fall guys caught in the middle, the easy targets clearly visible between the many rocks and hard places which riddle the pollution control process.

Because of their central position in the process, bureaucrats frequently possess a considerably different understanding of the capabilities and limitations of instruments, institutions and actors involved in environmental protection than does the average citizen. The discussion which follows represents a legally trained observer's interpretation of how bureaucrats view legal instruments, the courts, regulated industries, the public, their political masters and other governments and bureaucrats. It is hoped that this description of the process "from the trenches", so to speak, will help inform future efforts to improve environmental protection. The focus is on Canadian legislation and practice, but much is applicable to other settings. Canadian environmental regulation would provide an interesting counterpoint, for example, to the comparative analysis of "national styles" in the United States and Great Britain.[3] The article closes with a number of suggestions for reform.

Bureaucrats and Legal Instruments

The bureaucrat typically has two major types of legal instruments to control pollution: command-penalty measures and incentives. How these instruments are described in law and how they actually operate are often two markedly different things.

Command-Penalty Instruments

Canadian legislators[4] have adopted a hybrid approach to pollution control: waste discharges are prohibited outright, restricted through effluent standards set in regulations, or authorized subject to certain conditions through a licencing or permit regime.[5] Breach of established standards or conditions can result in licence suspension or revocation, prosecution, or both.[6]

The legislation which establishes command-penalty measures is typically drafted in what can only be described as "bare bones", minimalist style. It usually sets out a series of offences, the authority to issue and restrict licences and to promulgate regulations, and a few basic enforcement powers. A reading of this legislation would suggest that the pollution control process operates in a rather mechanical manner—supply and revoke licences, detect violations and prosecute. Except in the case of isolated "spill" incidents, actual administration is considerably more complicated. In the case of continuous pollution discharges, there is no simple negligent behavior to be corrected or stopped; long term (and expensive) design and equipment changes are usually in order. In such circumstances, bureaucrats often prefer less formal methods of inducing compliance, such as negotiations, warnings and persuasion. Reasons for decisions not to resort to licence revocation and prosecutions run the gamut from perceived inadequacies in the formal procedures, to lack of faith in the value of such drastic measures, and apprehensions about the formal and public nature of legal proceedings.

The terms of command-penalty legislation usually do not admit to the substantial amount of informal negotiation which takes place in conjunction with enforcement activities.[7] These negotiations can concern everything from immediate term, "stopgap" measures, such as the installation of clarifiers and scrubbers, to complete process overhauls which improve efficiency while simultaneously reducing harmful emissions. From an operational standpoint, negotiation is often an extremely difficult task, because of the technical, scientific and economic uncertainties which surround the various abatement options and the political issues underlying these factors (*e.g.*, pressure from environmental groups, riparian landowners and fishermen for immediate effective control *versus* demands from company officials, employees whose jobs are threatened, local politicians and businessmen to move slowly and thus maintain the economic viability of the operation).

Negotiations can be time-consuming, expensive (as options are explored) and frustrating. Lawyers might feel more comfortable with an arm's length, "me-talk, you-listen" adversarial stance to pollution control, but a closer, sleeves-rolled-up relationship is often unavoidable:

> Although the Ontario Ministry of the Environment prefers to approach an industrial pollution problem by setting out the extent of abatement required and leaving to the company decisions about methods of achieving the abatement targets, the need, in the face of appeal rights, to set compliance targets that can be shown to be reasonable forces Ministry officials either to develop an understanding of technological options or to accept blindly the company's position on these matters.[8]

Legislators have not been entirely successful in creating a legal regime which reflects the give-and-take relationship of the negotiation process and yet is quick, inexpensive and fair at attaining environmental objectives. Typically, legislation does not explicitly authorize bureaucrats to consider competing resource uses, and to take into account technical, financial and socio-economic factors in reaching pollution control decisions.[9] A formal negotiation process such as the Ontario control order process or the British Columbia permit system, is fraught with pitfalls for the unwary. Are the terms of the control order or permit sufficiently clear and unambiguous so that, in the event of violation, enforcement is possible?[10] Will the company, at the end of negotiations, decide to appeal the terms as unreasonable?[11] Will the negotiation process subsequently be challenged by the company or third parties as being unfair?[12]

Because of the unwieldiness of formal legal mechanisms, bureaucrats have frequently been tempted to enter into informal, voluntary compliance arrangements with polluters. But the dangers here are also great: informal agreements, although quicker and less expensive, operate in an ambiguous, murky world without clear structure and rules, and can understandably raise the suspicions of those not involved in the negotiations. Informal arrangements are at least partially the result of a simplistic or inadequate legislative framework for implementation. In effect, bureaucrats and industry officials are left to work out the "real rules of the game" by themselves. These informal arrangements appear to be unenforceable in court.[13] The result is a secretive implementation environment, since bureaucrats cannot explicitly justify their actions in law.

If the terms of negotiated agreements (be they formal orders and permits or informal arrangements) are breached, bureaucrats have the option of re-negotiating, or of resorting to formal enforcement measures such as prosecutions. In Canada, unless legislation specifically compels enforcement through imperative language, there is no legal necessity for bureaucrats to resort to prosecutions every time a transgression is detected.[14] Instead, bureaucrats usually have discretion as to when and how to apply legislation.[15]

To the outsider, a government agency constantly engaging in prosecutions might appear to be tough, to be doing its job. However, there are numerous reasons bureaucrats might decide not to prosecute.[16] They may feel that courts lack the necessary technical knowledge in pollution matters, and that this fact reduces the likelihood of a conviction or significant penalty. The outcome of prosecutions is uncertain: at one extreme, judges can find dischargers not guilty or levy nominal fines. The complex nature of many ongoing pollution situations, and the continuous attention frequently needed to adjust processes and equipment to meet changing circumstances, do not mesh well with the formal rules of procedure and the orientation of the judicial process to making single, discrete decisions about single, discrete events. Bureaucrats may find prosecutions to be a slow and expensive process. As one commentator succinctly described it, prosecutions "...shift expertise and resources from pressing investigatory work, rarely lead to immediate environmental benefits or deterrent sentencing, and tend to harden adversarial attitudes."[17] Bureaucrats may even be explicitly warned in training manuals of the drastic consequences of enforcement actions which could result in shutdowns.[18]

To a bureaucrat who has been negotiating with a discharger, prosecutions can be considered an admission of failure: responsibility for pollution control at the mill or plant slips out of the hands of Ministry or Department of Environment technocrats and into the hands of lawyers. The role of the bureaucrat may be perceived as primarily conciliatory, with prosecutions only an option of last resort. Initiating a prosecution may be viewed as jeopardizing otherwise harmonious and constructive relations.[19] Prosecutions entail formalism and publicity. Bureaucrats may not have faith in the knowledge, commitment and capabilities of governmental counsel. They may be wary of injuring the sensibilities of other jurisdictions; where jurisdiction is shared, there may be informal agreements between departments not to prosecute.

The decision whether or not to prosecute rests on many factors, including the behavior and attitude of the alleged violator, his or her current efforts to correct the problem, the receptiveness of the court toward convictions for offences of this or a similar kind, the strength of the evidence, and the probability of—or preference for—prosecution by another enforcement authority. To take an example, in the case of *Fisheries Act* prosecutions of pulp and paper firms,[20] federal bureaucrats may consider the following factors:

☐ courts often appear reluctant either to convict industrial polluters or to levy substantial penalties;

☐ it is difficult to prove sublethal deleterious effects of effluent;

☐ the provinces have water pollution legislation of their own in place and by administrative arrangement are usually considered the lead enforcement authorities;

☐ rivalries exist among federal institutions as to who should bring the prosecution;

☐ many pulp mills are currently receiving federal and provincial funding for mill modernizations which should remedy major water pollution problems; and

☐ many pulp mills have entered informal "compliance agreements" with the federal government, allowing short-term violations of the legislation in return for commitments to long-term compliance.[21]

Legislation often provides minimal guidance for the enforcement of offence provisions. The *Fisheries Act*, for example, contains no indication of how to resolve the "jobs versus fish" dilemma. Read literally, all violations would appear to be worthy of prosecution, regardless of competing resource uses.[22] A few Canadian statutes have adopted a more sophisticated approach; they explicitly require administrators to consider other resource uses,[23] or authorize and structure federal-provincial administrative arrangements.[24] Where the statute provides a relatively detailed statement of policy and a structure for policy implementation, bureaucrats get a much clearer idea of how offence provisions are to be enforced, and can therefore carry out their activities confident that their actions are supported by law.

One innovation which has recently been adopted by the federal Department of Environment with respect to the new *Canadian Environmental Protection Act*[25] is the publication of a "Compliance and Enforcement Policy" which accompanies the Act. As the name suggests, the policy describes how the Department of the Environment intends to administer the legislation. The policy was drafted after extensive consultations with members of the public, environmental groups and the private sector. Promulgation and wide public dissemination of such policies "fleshes out" minimalist legislation, and gives bureaucrats, the private sector and the public some much needed guidance on how legislation will work in practice.

Financial Incentives

Although many may find it objectionable for government to assist polluters financially, the use of incentives is widespread, and can in certain circumstances result in quicker and more effective environmental protection than command-penalty measures. Financial incentives to abate pollution have taken a variety of forms, including grants,[26] tax subsidies[27] and loans.[28] Each type has distinctive legal and operational characteristics; indeed, within each incentive category, there can be many distinct examples.

Because the subject of abatement incentives is so rarely discussed in pollution control literature, a brief description of two recently available incentive programs is provided below. Following this, the bureaucrat's perspective on incentives is described.

The Pulp and Paper Modernization Program.[29] The federal-provincial Pulp and Paper Modernization Program was first established in 1979, following recognition that many Eastern Canadian pulp mills were using less than state-of-the-art production processes and in the face of stiffening competition from abroad. Pursuant to the Modernization Program, the federal and participating provincial governments offered to pay up to 25 percent of the capital costs of modernizations, providing those modernizations met with government approval. Financial assistance would be provided where government was satisfied the projects would not occur otherwise, would significantly improve the economic efficiency of an existing operation, and would meet government environmental objectives.

The Modernization Program offered government the opportunity to integrate pollution control improvements with production improvements. This holistic approach to environmental protection avoided the tendency toward end-of-pipe pollution control measures, in favor of more reliable in-plant solutions. At least in theory, the Modernization Program overcame the understandable resistance of pulp mill operators to the installation of new pollution devices on obsolescent production equipment.

If the legislative structure underlying command-penalty environmental protection measures is minimalist, the legal basis for grants can be even more ephemeral. In the case of the Modernization Program, the federal legislative origins can be traced to one long, ambiguous statement buried in the schedule to an Appropriation Act. The actual description of the program is contained in federal-provincial subsidiary agreements. Even in these subsidiary agreements, eligibility criteria for grants are described in vague terms, leaving wide discretion in the hands of bureaucrats. This discretion gives bureaucrats flexibility in bargaining, but it also means that potential applicants and third parties have little advance indication of what types of projects will be approved.

Negotiations leading to the awarding of a grant are highly technical and often lengthy, involving bureaucrats from departments in both the federal and participating provincial governments. Third parties are not involved in these negotiations. Neither legislation nor subsidiary agreements set out methods of recourse for rejected applicants. There are no provisions for third party participation at the negotiation or enforcement stages. Bureaucrats treat grant applications as confidential, and successful grant agreements as contracts, to which normal rules of privity of contract apply.

Since 1979, 94 grants to 54 companies in seven provinces have been distributed, at a cost to participating governments of $613 million generating a claimed $5.5 billion in capital investment.[30]

The Accelerated Capital Cost Allowance (ACCA) for Pollution Abatement Equipment.[31] Under federal and certain provincial tax legislation,[32] taxpayers can deduct from their income the capital cost of certain properties. The ACCA for pollution abatement equipment provides the taxpayer with a faster "write-off" for pollution equipment than for certain other properties. To be eligible for this form of subsidy, a property must be "primarily for the purpose of preventing, reducing, or eliminating"[33] pollution.

Tax deductions such as the ACCA are expenditures in the sense that, were the deductions not in place, government would normally collect money from the taxpayer: put simply, government is giving by not taking. This is a considerably less obvious method of providing assistance than is the direct act of disbursing funds: once a tax deduction has become law, the amount of government expenditure (revenue foregone) is not revealed in the regular budgetary process. It is not necessary for Parliament to approve the appropriation of government monies for a tax deduction; moreover, there is no "ceiling" on the amount which may be expended by government pursuant to a tax subsidy. Thus, from an accountability or visibility standpoint, tax expenditures are neither accounted for in the budget nor accorded the periodic parliamentary scrutiny which direct expenditures receive.

Usually, for a tax subsidy to be an incentive for changed behavior by a polluter, that polluter must be in a position to offset the amount of the tax subsidy against his or her income or profit for a year. (This may not be the case where "tax credits" are used: tax credits allow the recipient to "save" the amount owing from government for a future year, when she or he has income to offset the subsidy.) Consequently, the ACCA for pollution abatement is attractive only to those pulp mills which are in a profit-making position. Ironically, it is those pulp mills in poor financial shape (that is, the old, non-modernized mills) which need abatement equipment the most and on which the ACCA for pollution abatement equipment has least effect.

The tax system is considered to operate in a self-assessing manner. Deductions are claimed by the taxpayer, but may be subject to verification on audit. In the case of "low-volume" programs such as the ACCA pollution abatement initiative, the bureaucrats will approve abatement projects in principle prior to their actual installation. Tax subsidy programs tend to operate in an automatic or mechanical manner, with discretion structured through regulations, interpretations bulletins and advance rulings.

Generally speaking, tax subsidies do not require bureaucrats to assess the quality of a taxpayer's actions. A pulp and paper mill operator could install abatement equipment which, although eligible for a subsidy, was not the most effective method of reducing the pollution discharged by the mill. Moreover, the ACCA tax subsidy provides no continuing incentive to use the abatement equipment, once installed. The tax system is geared to expenditure of the taxpayer, not day-to-day actions. Tax matters are typically treated in strict confidence, so that information disclosure beyond the immediate parties concerned is unusual; as a result, it is difficult for members of the public to determine who is getting what, and why.

Command-Penalty vs. Incentive: The Bureaucrats' Perspective

Despite the brevity of the foregoing descriptions, and the wide number of differences which distinguish one incentive program from another, a few general observations can be made concerning the bureaucrats' perspective on incentives.

Because incentives do not threaten individuals with the loss of their life, liberty, or property, they have not attracted the public or legal attention garnered by command-penalty measures. To the bureaucrat, this has both advantages and disadvantages. On the positive side, bureaucrats can be relatively confident that incentive administration will proceed relatively unencumbered by court "interference". This is important to the bureaucrat concerned with getting things done, because administration geared towards courtroom appearances can easily become more preoccupied with evidentiary requirements, legal burdens of proof and the attendant high media profile associated with court appearances than with the primary objective of distributing incentives so as to achieve policy goals.

On the other hand, bureaucrats undoubtedly benefit from the legal rigor instilled by the involvement of courts and lawyers. For example, even though bureaucrats might prefer unfettered discretion, a court's insistence that rules be set out in advance can, when not taken to extremes, make the jobs of bureaucrats (and others) easier. Bureaucrats need the guidance provided by fully articulated legislative regimes so that they can confidently administer incentive programs as they are intended. The Pulp and Paper Modernization Program is a good example of an incentive initiative which cried out for a more elaborate legislative foundation and structure. As matters currently stand, the legal character of a Modernization grant is unclear, and the legal recourse of rejected applicants, unsatisfied recipients and concerned third parties is unknown. No one benefits from this amount of operational uncertainty.

Properly conceived, an incentive program can greatly enhance the bureaucrat's ability to induce changed behavior. Whereas command-penalty measures compel bureaucrats to play the heavy, incentives allow more of a "good guy" role, and can overcome industry resistance to installation of abatement equipment. The Pulp and Paper Modernization Program, for example, complemented the federal and participating provincial governments' command-penalty pollution control regimes in the sense that the program was primarily directed at reducing pollution by a segment of the pulp and paper industry (the older mills) which had generally not responded to command-penalty techniques. It operated in a non-confrontational, positive manner, and encouraged government and industry to look at pollution abatement in a holistic fashion.

On the other hand, should government be financing the pulp and paper industry to meet its command-penalty standards? From an operational standpoint, does the existence of a modernization grant agreement between government and industry affect prosecutorial decision-making?

The apparent incongruity in combining command-penalty measures with incentives high-lights the distinction between the ideal world and the real world of implementation. For many of the older pulp mills operating in Canada, compliance with effluent standards was not possible without major mill reconstructions. The modernization program provided impetus for these mills to modernize their facilities; by doing so, they may come into compliance with the command-penalty effluent standards. In effect, a modernization program grant can ease the transition from the old to the new rules, to the reality of modern environmental protection.

Other incentive programs can have only a negligible, symbolic effect on compliance. For example, it is doubtful that the ACCA tax subsidy is a major factor in decisions by polluters to reduce or not to reduce harmful discharges; rather, it gives bureaucrats "a spoonful of sugar to help the medicine go down" by offering polluters assistance once the decision to reduce pollution has been made. In this sense, the ACCA tax subsidy for abatement equipment may be used more for its symbolic value – as an indication that government will help industry meet its pollution standards – than as a practical catalyst for changing behavior.

Bureaucrats and the Courts

Bureaucrats may not always hold courts in high esteem. This can be explained in part as nothing more than institutional rivalry, but there is more to it.

The courts' role in the pollution control process can be roughly divided into two major components. One function is that of an enforcer of anti-pollution legislation, by way of the process of determining guilt or innocence in offence prosecutions, and levying sentences upon conviction. The court's second function is as a check against arbitrary and unfair actions of government. To a regulatee who feels hard done by as the result of a bureaucratic decision (or occasionally, to an environmental group shut out of the pollution control decision-making process) the courts offer an opportunity for a (comparatively) open and impartial airing of issues.

Courts as Enforcers of Legislation

In the 1970's, courts[34] (and some legislatures[35]) introduced the notion of the "strict liability" pollution offence, a half-way house between criminal offences (where the intention of the accused must be proven in order to secure a conviction) and absolute liability offences (where only proof of the act is necessary for a conviction).[36] With this new "strict liability" category of offence, prosecutors must prove beyond a reasonable doubt that the act of pollution has occurred, but not that the accused intended to pollute (as with criminal offences). The accused then can escape conviction by demonstrating to the court, on a balance of probabilities, that he had exercised "due diligence" — that he had done everything that reasonably could be done to avoid contravening the law. This defence is not available with absolute liability offences.

In one sense, the introduction of the strict liability offence greatly eased the job of the bureaucrat, because it reduced a great deal of confusion surrounding the legal nature of many pollution offences and eliminated the need to prepare evidence establishing that the accused intended to pollute (a particularly difficult task in the case of corporate wrongdoing). On the other hand, judicial recognition of the due diligence defence meant that, to secure a conviction, bureaucrats had to compile the evidence necessary to establish that the preventative systems in operation at the accused's mill or plant were insufficient. As one commentator noted, the introduction of the due diligence defence made the inspector's role considerably more difficult:

> Pollution inspectors trained to take samples of toxic materials and trace a pollution trail to its source, will now also have to establish who gave the orders that led to the pollution, who carried them out, what supervision was provided, how the equipment was maintained, and many other matters....[37]

This means that bureaucrats must know almost as much about the accused's operation as the accused person does. Preparation for prosecutions has become a major and difficult task.

To the bureaucrat, resort to prosecutions means relinquishing responsibility for a pollution problem to technically unqualified persons. The formal and adversarial nature of the judicial process is not seen as an ideal forum for resolving scientific and technical issues; bureaucrats may feel that their own implementation practices are as much on trial as the accused.[38] The media profile can be much higher, and constructive communication between bureaucrats and company officials may be disrupted.

Court proceedings can drag on for months, and be enormously expensive.[39] In short, except in straightforward cases of unrepentant acts of pollution, bureaucrats may wish to avoid resort to the courts.

Courts as Checks on Administration

In the traditional criminal enforcement model, the relationship between police and suspects typically begins with police reaction to a complaint or call for help, and ends shortly thereafter with a decision to prosecute or not to prosecute. The relationship between police and suspected criminals is kept short because the behavior in question usually stops as soon as or before police arrive on the scene: police usually deal with isolated incidents rather than engaging in ongoing efforts to correct unacceptable behavior.

Pollution control often cannot be achieved overnight. Long term, negotiatory relationships between bureaucrats and polluters are frequently unavoidable, as solutions are gradually worked out. The opportunity for allegations of administrative unfairness increases with the increased contact between bureaucrats and polluters.

The courts play an important role in ensuring that administrative discretion is not exercised in an arbitrary or unfair fashion through their judicial review function. The two legal doctrines embodying notions of fairness which are most directly relevant to pollution control decision-making are procedural fairness and abuse of process. Both doctrines have undergone significant developments in the past few years, and have been applied in environmental contexts. The doctrine of procedural fairness applies most clearly to administrative decision making (*e.g.*, negotiation and implementation of permits, licences, control orders, program approvals, etc.), while the abuse of process doctrine is of particular relevance to prosecutorial decision making.

As an example of courts' "check function", a regulatee successfully argued before the Ontario Divisional Court[40] that when Ontario Ministry of Environment (MOE) officials reject a request for amendment to a control order, this in itself amounts to a new control order, and thus can be appealed to the Ontario Environmental Appeal Board. From the perspective of the bureaucrat, the effect of the court's decision was to give regulatees a method of delaying enforcement of control orders, because appeals of rejected MOE requests for amendment defer control order implementation pending the decision of the Environmental Appeal

Board.[41]

To the bureaucrat, "judicialization" of the pollution control process formalizes negotiations, thus slowing down administration and stultifying give-and-take bargaining. Although there is obviously an element of self-protection underlying bureaucrats' ambivalence towards the courts, their position should not be dismissed too lightly. The courts' conception of justice is based on the judicial model, with all its formal and adversarial trappings. The informal arrangements and compromises which bureaucrats sometimes enter into may not meet courts' expectations of a fair process, but, they usually "get the job done". The effect of court challenges to bureaucratic actions would appear to be a "tightening up" of administrative practice, including greater care in who negotiates with polluters, in what is said and how it is said.

Bureaucrats and the Minister

In spite of all the media attention it receives, environmental protection often has a relatively low priority in government. Unlike other restricted or prohibited activities, pollution is usually a by-product of an activity otherwise encouraged by society. The extraction and refining of raw materials, the manufacturing of new chemicals and commercial products are activities which are intended to improve the quality of life, and are generally welcomed as such. In addition to the benefits received by society at large, such activities bring many rewards to government by way of personal and corporate tax revenues and the political benefits which flow to governments seen as being responsible for the continued growth of income and employment.

In Canada, government and industry often have an extremely close relationship, wedded by common objectives,[42] common attitudes,[43] and more concrete ties such as government loans, grants, and subsidies. Governments are hungry for revenue and employment-generating projects: in this broader context of government-industry partnerships, environmental protection generally does not receive a high priority. Environment has until very recently been considered a junior portfolio within Cabinet; in times of government spending cutbacks, environmental programs have often been the first to hit the chopping block.[44]

For all the fire and brimstone of legislation, it takes the political willpower of Cabinet and the Minister of Environment to make pollution control regimes work. Paul Pross notes that "...public opinion and political will are by far the most powerful constraining forces on bureaucratic action":[45]

> An official who believes that the government is not firmly committed to the policy he is mandated to implement will be all too aware of the sanctions that may be imposed on him if he interprets his orders too literally. Quite apart from personal considerations, he must weigh the possibility of reprisals in the form of budgetary constraints, perhaps even the emasculation of his unit.[46]

A strong-willed and articulate Environment Minister who has the ear of Cabinet can make the job of the bureaucrat immeasurably easier. With this support, the bureaucrat has the confidence that his or her actions will be backed up by superiors, and not traded away in Cabinet. Resources are magically made available to implement programs, and rumors of stiffer penalties and even stricter enforcement are rampant. This is an atmosphere of which pollution control bureaucrats usually can only dream.

Because environmental protection issues are almost invariably intertwined with other issues, the pollution control bureaucrat from the Ministry or Department is often in more or less constant contact with bureaucrats from other departments.

Bureaucrats and Other Bureaucrats

At the federal level, for example, although in practice the Environmental Protection Service (EPS) of the Department of Environment is the lead federal actor involved in industrial pollution control, in law the programs which EPS bureaucrats administer are the responsibility of other departments. Thus, EPS may administer the pollution control provisions of the *Fisheries Act*, but the *Fisheries Act* is nominally the responsibility of the Department of Fisheries and Oceans. An informal administrative arrangement between EPS and the Department of Fisheries and Oceans allows EPS to carry out its command-penalty functions. EPS also administers the Pulp and Paper Modernization Grant Program through its membership on interdepartmental committees, even though nominally the program is an initiative of the Department of Regional Industrial Expansion. EPS certifies the equipment which qualifies for an ACCA tax subsidy for pollution abatement, although the Department of National Revenue has responsibility for administering the federal income tax legislation.

Shared responsibilities can be a source of administrative problems. When EPS and the Department of Fisheries and Oceans adopt different interpretations of their legislative mandate, regulatees and the public simply think that government does not have its act together. On the other hand, EPS involvement in the Modernization Program of the Department of Regional Industrial Expansion enables EPS to have its concerns carried forward by another department, without dipping into the Department of Environment's meagre budget.

Generally speaking, although informal arrangements among departments perform a basic structuring and allocation function, their informality presents at least two drawbacks. First, they carry no official status, and thus their terms can be violated without any real likelihood of reprimand. Second, regulatees and the public may find it considerably more difficult to become aware of informal *ad hoc* and often unpublished arrangements.

The fact that both federal and provincial governments have constitutional heads of power upon which environmental protection legislation can be based is a mixed blessing. The existence of at least two levels of government, each with its own pollution control legislation, tends to ensure that even if one level of government is somehow prevented from responding to a pollution problem, other authorities should be able to take corrective action. Yet, where the authorities do not share the same opinion on how a pollution problem should be addressed, the potential for conflict and confusion is greatly increased.

Both the advantages and drawbacks of a multi-level authority system have been experienced in the Canadian context. There have been occasions, for example, where the federal government has enforced pollution legislation where no provincial action has been forthcoming;[47] and the opposite has also happened.[48] There have also been occasions when federal and provincial authorities have openly disputed the handling of a pollution problem,[49] with the waste dischargers, affected community and the general public caught in the middle.

Over the years, the federal and provincial governments have attempted to respond to the problem of duplication and overlap in a variety of ways. In the early 1970's, following the first major push of environmental legislation, informal accords[50] were negotiated between the federal and most provincial environment departments. The general thrust of these accords is to give provincial authorities and legislation a "lead" role, with the federal government as a back-up. However, there are three problems with this approach. (1) Because the accords are only informal agreements, their terms can be breached with relative impunity.[51] (2) The informal nature of the agreements also means that their existence is not widely known except among the key government and private sector actors regularly involved in environmental protection. For example, there is no mention in the federal *Fisheries Act* of provinces assuming lead enforcement roles. Finally (3), the existence of informal arrangements calling for co-ordinated action between the two levels of government may decrease the likelihood of uncoordinated *government* action, but this is no guarantee that *private citizens* will pay heed to them. Thus, private prosecutions have been launched under the *Fisheries Act* in spite of the fact that federal and provincial governments had agreed between themselves that no enforcement action would be taken.[52]

In short, while the existence of different layers of command-penalty legislation and administration tends to ensure that pollution problems are addressed, governments need to synchronize their legislation in formal, visible ways in order to prevent conflict and confusion which can bring legislation and administration into disrepute. The Canadian governmental response to the problem of transportation of dangerous goods (TDG) is an indication that improved co-ordination of federal-provincial action is in the offing. The federal and provincial TDG statutes are expressly designed to operate in a cooperative manner, to create a unified national response. In this legislation, there are express provisions allowing delegation of administrative and enforcement responsibilities from one jurisdiction to another.[53] A statutorily co-ordinated and unified approach to transportation of dangerous goods could, if successful, be the forerunner for similar legislative initiatives concerning other areas of environmental protection.

Bureaucrats and the Regulated

As noted earlier, the ongoing nature of pollution control and the scientific, technical and economic uncertainty surrounding the various abatement options frequently make long-term negotiations between bureaucrats and company officials unavoidable. The pollution control bureaucrat must be prepared to deal with a wide variety of regulatee types. These include responsible corporate dischargers, marginally profitable operators desperately in search of methods to cut costs, and openly unrepentant polluters willing to do anything to frustrate pollution control authorities.

The bureaucrat's best hope is a wide variety of legal responses: tax subsidies and grants to help offset costs, as well as regulatory and criminal command-penalty measures to reinforce the environmental protection message. Successful pollution control requires the right combination of cajoling and threats. A number of Canadian governments have been experimenting with the use of special enforcement squads,[54] whose sole purpose is to bring prosecutions. The advantage of these squads is that the problem of bureaucrats simultaneously acting as negotiators and enforcers (the so-called "white-hat, black-hat"[55] syndrome) is reduced. Front-line negotiators are relatively insulated from the enforcers.

Bureaucrats and the Public

In the face of constant pressure by members of the public demanding informed participation in environmental protection decision-making, the role of the citizen has become increasingly important and central to the pollution control process.[56] Environmental groups have developed considerable expertise in pollution control matters, and have cultivated direct lines of communication with government officials and the media. Often, it is apparent that citizen groups have not been satisfied with existing legislation and what they perceive to be bureaucratic inaction: this is evidenced by increases in citizen-launched court attempts at participation in government environment-related decision-making,[57] and an associated increase in private prosecutions.[58] Pollution control legislation of the 1960s, which included little if any explicit recognition of the important role played by citizens, is giving way in the late 1980s to a new generation of legislation which expressly commits government to informing and involving the citizen at virtually every stage of the process.[59]

This rise in citizen participation can be attributed, at a very general level, to the fact that citizens are less trusting of government than they once were:[60] the traditional "manager-client" relationship between government departments and resource users is less tenable in an age where the "public good" is no longer easily equatable with the unchecked growth and expansion of the private sector.[61] Citizens have, moreover, seized the legal tools available to them and are beginning to take their concerns to the courts. Courts offer citizens both the possibility of a public, high profile, fair hearing, and a way to circumvent bureaucratic quagmires. Probably the best example of a legal tool which has been championed by public interest groups is the *Penalties and Forfeitures Proceeds Regulations*[62] promulgated pursuant to the federal *Fisheries Act*. The regulations provide that a private citizen who initiates an action under the *Fisheries Act* which results in a fine will receive half of any penalty imposed. The regulations or earlier variations of them have existed since 1868, but had essentially lain dormant until they were rediscovered in the 1980's. The fact that prosecutions pursuant to the *Fisheries Act* prosecutions have been used to spark both federal and provincial action[63] has made private *Fisheries Act* prosecutions eminently attractive to environmental groups.

At times, bureaucrats can view private prosecutions as unnecessary, as when both federal and provincial officials are satisfied with the progress made by a discharger.[64] However, frustrated pollution control bureaucrats have also "set up" private prosecutions, in cases where political and departmental obstacles have prevented in-house enforcement.[65]

Above all, good relations between bureaucrats and the public depend upon the free flow of information. Freedom of information legislation represents a last ditch method for citizens to gain disclosure of administrative data. A more fruitful approach would be for government freely to involve citizens at every opportunity in the pollution control process.

Recent statutory initiatives at the federal and provincial levels suggest new legislative recognition of the important role that can be played by the public in pollution control. The Manitoba *Environment Act*[66] which was promulgated in 1987, and the federal *Canadian Environmental Protection Act*,[67] passed in 1988, both contain specific obligations to inform and involve the public in environmental decision-making.[68] The new Manitoba legislation includes mandates that the Minister regularly publish a "State of the Environment Report,"[69] and provides for public access and participation provisions at virtually every stage of the pollution control process, from the drafting of regulations[70] and licences[71] to enforcement.[72] The federal *Canadian Environmental Protection Act* also specifically requires public dissemination of information[73] and participation in the drafting of new regulations.[74] In addition, where any two persons are of the opinion that an offence has been committed, they may apply to the Minister for an investigation of the offence.[75] The Minister must then investigate the offence, and report back to the persons who originated the investigation within 90 days.[76] If the Minister discontinues the investigation, he must prepare a report explaining his actions, and provide it to the persons who originated the investigation.[77] In the short term, the type of commitments to an open, publicly accessible pollution control process contained in these new statutes will put additional burdens on the bureaucracy. But in the final analysis, a fully informed and involved public will both improve the quality of government decision-making in the environmental area and enhance the legitimacy of those decisions.

Conclusion

The perspective of pollution control bureaucrats deserves greater attention because, in the final analysis, it is they who wield the legal instruments and thus make the wheels go 'round. Bureaucratic action is influenced by such factors as the realism and thoroughness of legislation; the availability of appropriate legal instruments; the formality, expense and utility of court procedures; the political will of Environment Ministers; the informality of the governmental context; the cooperation of regulatees; and the stimulation of the public.

The bureaucrat's perspective should, in some respects, be taken with a grain of salt: there can be no denying, for example, that the enforcing and checking functions of courts are necessary and useful, and are not simply "interference" with bureaucratic action. Often, moreover, there is very little that can be done in law to make the bureaucrat's position more tolerable: political willpower, for example, can disappear with a change in governing party or a downturn in the economy, and no amount of legislation can guard against its disappearance.

Still, there are concrete reforms which could be undertaken. Command-penalty legislation would benefit from more realism and less ambiguity, including recognition of competing resource uses and of technical, scientific and economic uncertainties. Incentive legislation could provide clear indications of the legal character of the incentives, eligibility criteria, and methods of recourse for rejected applicants, unsatisfied recipients, and concerned third parties. Statutory commitments requiring informed public involvement could enhance government decision-making. Finally, publication of compliance and enforcement policies could elaborate upon how minimalist legislation is to be administered, explicitly providing for administrative arrangements among departments and governments. The bureaucrat will always be caught between the rocks and hard places which riddle the pollution control process. Nevertheless, careful attention to the perspective of the bureaucrat can lead to better environmental protection.

Notes

1. The terms "government bureaucrat" and "bureaucrat" here refer to those officials of government charged with the responsibility of policy implementation, and includes negotiators, inspectors, enforcement officers, analysts, and investigators.

   This article draws substantially on the following: K. Webb, *Industrial Water Pollution Control and the Environmental Protection Service*, (Ottawa: Law Reform Commission of Canada, Background Paper, 1983); K. Webb, "Environmental Law and its Enforcement—Comment," in P. Finkle and A. Lucas, eds., *Environmental Law in the 1980's: A New Beginning* (Calgary: Canadian Institute of Resources Law, 1981), pp. 197-201; J. Clifford and K. Webb, *Policy Implementation, Compliance and Administrative Law*, (Ottawa: Law Reform Commission of Canada, Working Paper 51, 1986); K. Webb, *Pollution Control in Canada: The Regulatory Approach in the 1980s*, (Ottawa: Law Reform Commission of Canada, Administrative Law Project Study Paper, 1988; and K. Webb, "Taking Matters Into Their Own Hands: The Increasing Role of the Public in Canadian Pollution Control," a paper presented to a meeting of the Law and Society Association, Windsor, Ontario, June 7, 1988 (publication forthcoming).

2. See, *e.g.*, A. R. Thompson, *Environmental Regulation in Canada: An Assessment of the Regulatory Process* (Vancouver: Westwater Research Institute, 1980); R. Gibson, *Control Orders and Industrial Pollution Abatement in Ontario* (Toronto: Canadian Environmental Law Research Foundation, 1983); P. Finkle and M. Rankin, "Environmental Law and its Enforcement", in Finkle and Lucas, eds.; see also sources in n. 1 above.

3. See D. Vogel, *National Styles of Regulation: Environmental Policy in Great Britain and the United States* (Ithaca, N.Y.: Cornell University Press, 1986).

4. For compendium of Canadian pollution control legislation, see R. Franson and A. Lucas, eds., *Canadian Environmental Law* (Toronto: Butterworths Looseleaf Service, revised continuously). For illustrative pollution control provisions see, *e.g.*, Part II of the Ontario *Environmental Protection Act*, R.S.O. 1980, c. 361, as amended; Part 2 of the British Columbia *Waste Management Act*, S.B.C. 1982, c. 41, as amended; and sections 34-43 of the federal *Fisheries Act*, R.S.C. 1985, c. F-14, as amended.

5. Needless to say, what is being presented here is a considerable oversimplification of how control regimes actually operate. In addition, the names and details of control techniques vary from one regime to another; for example, the Ontario *Environmental Protection Act* authorizes use of "certificates of approval" (s. 8), "program approvals" (s. 9), as well as "control orders" and "stop orders" (s. 11). The British Columbia *Waste Management Act* refers to "permits", "approvals", "orders", "regulations", and "waste management plans" (s. 3).

6. In addition to basic permitting or licensing powers, administrators often possess additional ordering powers, permitting them to impose new restrictions (*e.g.*, through "control orders"), to shut down operations (*e.g.*, through "stop orders"), and even to order clean up action (*e.g.*, through emergency remedial action orders).

7. As described in Thompson, Gibson, and Webb, *Pollution Control in Canada*.

8. Gibson, p. 90.

9. "Pressured by significant publics to address themselves to important but divisive issues, governments have found it necessary to draft minimal legislation which leaves out the regulatory provisions which precision would arouse opposition. Such legislation appeases all and satisfies none, least of all the officials who must develop regulations and negotiate their application. Frustrated at the mixed results of their efforts, we attribute their failure to bureaucratic bungling. In reality, however, the constraints they are working under are political rather than bureaucratic." Paul Pross, "Water and Environmental Law: Bureaucratic Constraints," in S. Guppy *et al.*, eds., *Water and Environmental Law* (Halifax: Institute for Resource and Environmental Studies, Dalhousie University, 1981), pp. 139-176, esp. p.167.

10. See, *e.g.*, A. Ackerman and B. Clapp, "Fraser River Task Force Report," British Columbia Ministry of the Environment, unpublished, July 30, 1980, and Gibson, p. 58, respectively, for the situations in B.C. (1980) and Ontario (1983).

11. See, *e.g.*, the description of lead industry challenges to control order standards in C. C. Lax, "The Toronto Lead Smelter Controversy," in W. Leiss, ed., *Ecology versus Politics in Canada* (Toronto: University of Toronto Press, 1979), pp. 57-71. See also the description of events surrounding issuance of an amended control order to Inco in Gibson, pp. 74-78.

12. See, *e.g.*, *Re: MacFarlane and Anchor Cap & Closure Corp of Canada Ltd.*, (1981) 33 O.R. (2d) 317 (Div. Ct). This case is discussed in greater detail below.

13. See, *e.g.*, *R. ex rel Howe v. Cyanamid Canada Inc.* (1981) 3 Fisheries Pollution Reports 151 (Ont. Prov. Ct.), discussed in greater detail in Webb, *Industrial Water Pollution*, pp. 286-292. In this case, informal federal approval of a provincial control order did not prevent a private prosecution pursuant to federal legislation.

14. Glanville Williams, in his article "Discretion in Prosecuting," *Criminal Law Review* (1956), p. 222, states:

    > It is completely wrong to suppose (as is sometimes done) that the institution of prosecutions is an automatic or mechanical matter. That is, indeed, the theory in some Continental countries, such as Germany, where the rule is that the public prosecutor must take proceedings for all crimes that come to his notice for which there is sufficient evidence, unless they fall within an exception for petty offences, in respect of which he is given a discretion.

    Williams' statement of the extent of prosecutorial discretion in England appears to be equally applicable to the Canadian situation. See, for instance, P. Burns, "Private Prosecutions in Canada: The Law and a Proposal for Change," *McGill Law Journal* 21 (1975), p. 293. For a more detailed discussion of all types of discretion but focusing on administrative discretion and judicial review of such discretion, see J. Evans, *et al.*, *Administrative Law: Cases, Text and Materials* (Toronto: Emond-Montgomery, 1980), chs. 10 - 11. For a more practical description of the situation, see Gibson, p. 65, regarding the Ontario Ministry of Environment prosecution policy: "A company that fails to meet the terms and deadlines of a control order may be prosecuted. But prosecution in the event of noncompliance is not mandatory."

15. S. Wexler, "Discretion: The Unacknowledged Side of Law," *University of Toronto Law Journal* (1975), p. 178, defines discretion as "...the right of a decision maker to act differently in two cases which the rules lump together...." See also the definition of discretion in J. DeSmith *Judicial Review of Administrative Action* (2nd ed., 1968), p. 264.

16. For a more complete discussion of reasons federal environment bureaucrats might wish to avoid *Fisheries Act* prosecutions, see Webb, *Industrial Water Pollution*, pp. 201-211.

17. Gibson, pp. 134-135. Gibson was speaking specifically of the Ontario Ministry of Environment as of 1983, and refers in footnotes to particular officials within MOE. Nevertheless, the thrust of his comments would appear to apply with equal force to other jurisdictions in Canada.

18. Federal Department of Environment bureaucrats are told: "The many small Canadian sulphite operations present a rather difficult dilemma. They are too small to even consider a recovery installation and yet are pressed by environmental authorities to reduce BOD loading and the toxic nature of the spent liquors. *Forcing the shutdown of such plants would be economically disastrous to many small communities.* The enforcement of recovery systems in the larger sulphite plants while leaving the smaller plants to function without recovery would be unfair from the point of view of affecting economic competition." *Training Manual on the Basic Technology of the Pulp and Paper Industry and its Waste Reproduction Practices*, prepared by A. J. Bruley (EPS 6-WP-74-3, revised April, 1975), p. 33 (emphasis added).

19. Keith Hawkins, in "Bargain and Bluff: Compliance Strategy and deterrence in the Enforcement of Regulation" *Law and Policy Quarterly* 5 (1983), p. 47 which describes the British environment officials' attitude (in part) as follows: "To 'use the big stick' or 'crack the whip' too zealously may well be counter-productive. For a field officer to be too eager or abrasive is to risk encouraging in polluters an unco-operative attitude or even downright hostility." Although Hawkins is describing the British bureaucratic attitude, some Canadian government officials clearly have similar attitudes.

20. Webb, *Industrial Water Pollution,*, pp. 201-211.

21. J. L. Betts (of the Environmental Protection Service, Environment Canada), "Regulations and Waste Characterization," *Proceedings of Seminars on Water Pollution Abatement Technology in the Pulp and Paper Industry* (Ottawa: Environment Canada, EPS Report 3-WP-76-4, 1976), p. 1.

22. This point was made quite strongly by the final report of the Inquiry on Federal Water Policy, which recommended amendment of the *Act* "to enable the habitat requirements of fish to be considered within the framework of integrated resource management of water systems." *Currents of Change*, (Ottawa: Environment Canada, 1985) p. 68.

23. See, *e.g.*, the *Ministry of Forests Act*, R.S.B.C. 1979, c. 272, 4(c).

24. *Transportation of Dangerous Goods Act* R.S.C. 1985, c. T-19, as amended, s. 25.

25. *Canadian Environmental Protection Act*, S.C. 1988, c. 22.

26. See, *e.g.*, Ontario *Environmental Protection Act,*, s. 3(g).

27. See, *e.g.*, the federal *Income Tax Act*, T.S.C. 1970, c. I-5, (Part I, Division B, subdivision b) and regulations S.O.R./54-62, s. 1100(1) (1) (Part XI).

28. See, *e.g., Ontario Environmental Protection Act, op.cit.*, s. 3(g).

29. Described in greater detail in Webb, *Industrial Water Pollution,*, ch. 9.

30. K. Noble, "Forest Industry Attempts to Kick the Grant Habit," *The Globe and Mail* (December 31, 1985). A comprehensive assessment of the value of the Modernization Program from an abatement perspective has not yet been made.

31. Described in greater detail in Webb, *Industrial Water Pollution,*, ch. 7.

32. See, *e.g.*, British Columbia *Municipal Act*, R.S.B.C. 1979, c. 290, s. 398(g).

33. Quoted from Schedule II, class 24 of the federal *Income Tax* Regulations, S.O.R./54-62.

34. *R.v. Sault Ste. Marie* (1978) 85 D.L.R. (3d) 161 (S.C.C.).

35. For example, s. 41(3) of the federal *Fisheries Act*, provides a due diligence defence so that "the common law is now substantially the same as this...provision." *R.v. Gulf of Georgia Towing Co. Ltd.* (1979), Fisheries Pollution Reports (Volume 2) 252 (B.C.C.A.), p. 254.

36. The constitutionality of many absolute liability offences is open to challenge following the Supreme Court of Canada decision in *Reference Re Section 94(2) of the Motor Vehicle Act* (1985) 2 S.C.R. 486. For more detailed discussion concerning the future of absolute and strict liability offences in light of the *Canadian Charter of Rights and Freedoms*, see Webb, "Regulatory Offences, the Mental Element and the *Charter*: Caution—Rough Road Ahead," *Ottawa Law Review* 21 (1990).

37. J. Swaigen, "Procedure in Environmental Regulation," in Finkle and Lucas, eds., *Environmental Law in the 1980's*, pp. 94-95.

38. See, *e.g.*, comments to this effect in Environmental Law Centre (Alberta) Society submission to the Government of Alberta, *Enforcement of Environmental Law in Alberta: A Critical Examination of Alberta Government Law, Policy and Practice with Illustration from the case R.v. Suncor Inc.* (Edmonton, 1983) pp. 13, 19-21.

39. Eugene Kupchanko, Assistant Deputy Minister of the Alberta Department of Environment estimated that the 1983 prosecution of Suncor for discharging oil and grease into the Athabasca River cost $2 million, and resulted in an $8,000 fine to Suncor, as reported in "Prosecuting Polluters is Effective Strategy, Ministry Lawyer Says," *The Globe and Mail* (May 24, 1984); but *cf.*, J. Swaigen, "Prosecution Can Be an Effective Method To Control Polluters," *Lawyers' Weekly*, (June 7, 1984).

40. See *Re: MacFarlane and Anchor Cap & Closure*.

41. See J. Swaigen, in "Procedure in Environmental Regulation," pp. 87-88: "Taken to its extremes "fairness" can totally frustrate government attempts to order a pollutor to cut back its emissions. The *Anchor Cap & Closure* case provides an illustration of a court decision which applies the fairness doctrine in such a way that it leads to the absurd result that a government order can never take effect since "fairness" allows the person subject to the order to ask for a revision of the order at any time and require a hearing before an independent tribunal if this revision is refused." But *cf.* Andrew Roman, "Comment," in Finkle and Lucas, eds. *Environmental Law in the 1980's,*, pp. 112-115, and Robert Franson "Comment," in *ibid.*, p. 124. By s. 122(3) of the *Ontario Environmental Protection Act* (enacted by S.O. 1983, c.52, s.17), the legislation has now been amended so that a decision to amend an order is not considered to be one capable of appeal.

42. For example, the Nielsen Task Force's concern with efficiency for the federal government strongly resembles private industry concerns in this regard. In fact, the Nielsen Task Force drew heavily on "expertise" from the private sector.

43. To reduce this to its simplest dimensions, for Canadian governments full employment is a major preoccupation; for industry, full employment means a more buoyant economy, with more money and consumers more apt to buy industry products.

44. Note, *e.g.*, at the federal level, cutbacks to the Canadian Wildlife Service, and to research and development staff.

45. Pross, p. 140.

46. *Ibid.*, p. 144. Pross goes on to note that officials are often too sensitive to the climate of public and governmental opinion, "often giving up far more than is necessary in anticipation of politically inspired criticism."

47. For example, in 1977, the federal Minister of Fisheries and Environment (as the post then was) used the "request for plans" and "restriction of operations" powers contained in (then) subsections 33.2(1) and (2) of the *Fisheries Act* to control the landfilling activities of a provincial Crown corporation (the British Columbia Development Corporation) at Tilbury Slough: *Approve Orders Prohibiting the Landfilling and Associated Construction in Tilbury and Deas Slough on the Fraser River in British Columbia*, P.C. 1977-2399. For more detailed discussion, see Webb, *Industrial Water Pollution*, pp. 195-197.

48. For example, in 1985 and 1986 in Ontario, the provincial Ministry of Environment took a number of enforcement actions against Dow Chemical regarding St. Clair river spills when no federal action was forthcoming.

49. For example, in the course of pollution control negotiations with the Irving Pulp and Paper mill at St. John, New Brunswick, the provincial environmental authorities sided with Irving against federal officials in proposing that Irving's air pollution problems be tackled before attempting to control its water pollution problems. (The Irving Mill in St. John is the subject of a case study in Webb, *Industrial Water Pollution*, pp. 377-393. See also the description of the Amax Mines case, *ibid.*, pp. 350-377.

50. As described in *ibid.*, pp. 173-194.

51. *R.v. Canadian Industries Limited* (1980) 2 Fisheries Pollution Reports 304 (N.B.C.A.) discussed in greater detail in Webb, *Industrial Water Pollution*, pp. 181-184.

52. See, *e.g.*, *R. ex rel Howe v. Cyanamid*, discussed in greater detail in Webb, *Industrial Water Pollution*, pp. 185-187.

53. See, *e.g.*, s.25 of the federal *Transportation of Dangerous Goods Act*, R.S.C. 1985, c. T-19, as amended.

54. In Ontario, a Special Investigation Unit has been created. A similar unit has been announced for Quebec: Francis Shalom, "Quebec Will Bill Polluters for Cost of 10-year Toxic-Waste Cleanup," *The Globe and Mail* (June 10, 1986).

55. See generally, E. Bardach and R. Kagan, *Going by the Book* (Philadelphia: Temple University Press, 1982).

56. See generally, J. Swaigen, "Introduction: The Emergence of the Public in Environmental Decision-making", in J. Swaigen, ed., *Environmental Rights in Canada* (Toronto: Butterworths, 1981), pp. 1-8; Webb, "Taking Matters Into Their Own Hands."

57. *Pim v. Ontario Minister of the Environment and the Lieutenant Governor in Council* (1979), 23 O.R. (2d) 45 (Ont. Div. Ct); *Canadians for the Abolition of the Seal Hunt & Harrison v. The Minister of Fisheries and the Environment* (1980) 10 C.E.L.R. 1; *Re SEAP and Atomic Energy Control Board* (1977) 74 D.L.R. (3d) 541 (Fed. Court Appeal Div.); *Croy v. Atomic Energy Control Board* (1979) 29 N.R. 14 (Fed. Ct. Appeal Div.); *Binbrook Anti-Dump Committee v. Regional Municipality of Hamilton-Wentworth* (1980) 10 C.E.L.R. 65 (Ont. Div. Ct.); see also *1981 Annual Report of the Ombudsman to the Legislative Assembly of British Columbia*, C.S. 81-063; see also *Energy Probe v. Atomic Energy Control Board* (1984) 8 D.L.R. (4th) 716 (Fed. Ct.), 15 D.L.R. (4th) 48 (Fed. C.A.); *Re Regional Municipality of Hamilton Wentworth and Hamilton Wentworth Save the Valley Committee Inc.* (1985) 19 D.L.R. (4th) 356 (Ont. Div. Ct.); *Re Ontario Energy Board* (1985) 19 D.L.R. (4th) 753 (Ont. Div. Ct.).

58. For example, there have been at least five private prosecutions pursuant to s. 33(2) of the federal *Fisheries Act* since 1981, and none previously.

59. See Webb, "Taking Matters Into Their Own Hands."

60. For example, Michael Adams, president of Environics Research Ltd. (a polling company) is reported as saying "Canadian voters have become considerably more well informed and critical, more cynical generally toward institutions and more self-reliant, and more pragmatic in their responses to political appeals and politicians." See Ross Howard, "Make Public Poll Results, Ottawa Told," *The Globe and Mail* (May 29, 1986).

61. This is paraphrased from P. Finkle, "New Approaches to Fairness: The Bureaucracy Responds," in E. Case *et al.*, *Fairness in Environmental and Social Impact Assessment Processes* (Calgary: Canadian Institute of Resources Law, 1984), pp. 31-34.

62. C.R.C. 1978, c. 827.

63. For example, *R. v. Crown Zellerbach Properties Ltd.* (Vendev) *et al.* (1981), 3 Fisheries Pollution Reports 84 (B.C. Prov. Ct.), as described in Webb, *Industrial Water Pollution.*

64. For example, in the *Cyanamid* private prosecution, described in greater detail in Webb, *Industrial Water Pollution.*

65. Confidential informational disclosed in interviews by federal officials.

66. S.M. 1987, c. 26, C.C.S.M. E125, proclaimed in force March 31, 1988.

67. S.C. 1988, c. 22.

68. Subsection 2(1) of the Manitoba Environment Act states that the goals of the Department of the Environment are "to protect the quality of the environment and environmental health...and to provide the opportunity for all citizens to exercise influence over the quality of the environment." Previous Manitoba legislation contained no such statement regarding public involvement. Subsection 2(d) of the *Canadian Environmental Protection Act* expressly obligates the Government of Canada to "encourage the participation of the people of Canada in the making of decisions that affect the environment," and ss. 2(g) requires the government to "provide information to the people of Canada on the state of the environment." No previous existing federal environmental legislation contained commitments of this kind. These provisions are more fully discussed in Webb, "Taking Matters Into Their Own Hands."

69. Manitoba *Environment Act*, ss. 6(1).

70. Manitoba *Environment Act*, ss. 41(2).

71. See, *e.g.*, s. 10 of the Manitoba *Environment Act*.

72. Pursuant to s. 38 of the *Environment Act*, any person may lay an information in respect of any offence, providing that it be laid within one year from the time when the subject matter of the proceedings arose or from the day on which the evidence came to the knowledge of the environment officer.

73. *Canadian Environmental Protection Act*, ss. 2(g), as discussed in note 68 above.

74. See, *e.g.*, s. 89 of the *Canadian Environmental Protection Act*.

75. Section 108 of the *Canadian Environmental Protection Act*.

76. Subsection 109 (2).

77. Subsection 109 (4).

THE CRISIS OF
ADMINISTRATIVE LEGITIMACY:
REGULATORY POLITICS AND THE
RIGHT-TO-KNOW

Albert R. Matheny and Bruce A. Williams

On the surface, "right-to-know" legislation appears to be straightforward.[1] Industries are required to reveal to affected parties — such as plant workers, local residents, and community officials — the nature of hazardous substances used in production. This way of seeing the issue is superficial, however, obscuring its deeper significance for understanding problems of social regulation in the United States which, as we shall suggest, involve a crisis of administrative legitimacy. "Right-to-know" is a political issue which, by uniting the interests of the residential community with the concerns of the workplace, runs counter to the historical separation of workplace and residence in American politics.[2]

To grasp the complex contours of power in right-to-know disputes, we employ a tripartite framework developed by Robert R. Alford and Roger Friedland in their approach to theories of the state.[3] Three distinct modes of analysis have traditionally been used in analyzing the state — "pluralist", "managerial", and "class". For Alford and Friedland, each of these "home domains" of analysis gives salience to a particular institutional dimension of state activity and thus reveals a distinct "logic of action". As we proceed from the home domain of pluralist analysis, we highlight a logic of democracy, the managerial perspective directs our attention to the logic of bureaucracy, and the class perspective focuses on the logic of capitalism.

Pluralism, to expand briefly, contains the familiar emphasis on open interest group participation in government, with politics defined as intergroup competition in a fair and rule-governed struggle, ultimately encouraging a consensus about the governmental process as a basis for state legitimacy. The *managerial* focus stresses elite decision-making based on technical expertise, the legitimacy of which depends upon the assumption that organizational entities can provide an objectively valid and efficient direction for the state. The *class* approach focuses on the reproduction of productive relations between labor and capital and the attendant crises of accumulation (declining profits) and legitimation (class struggle), with politics arising from mediation of these crises by the state. While each home domain of analysis suggests how the logics of democracy, bureaucracy, and capitalism are "contradictory logics", colliding in practice, each also tends to stress one logic over the others. Distinguishing and respecting the potential importance of each of these logics, however, provides for a more comprehensive framework and orients us for an empirical examination of the actual dynamics of social regulation.[4] The relevance of the different logics for our analysis is suggested in this passage from Alford and Friedland:

> Concrete social practices manifest the institutional logics of capitalism, bureaucracy, and democracy. Inside each institution, the activities of individuals are symbolically defined by a historically developed vocabulary of motives and beliefs. Interests that cannot be converted to a particular vocabulary within a logic of action are difficult to express or to handle within that institutional sphere.[5]

Our approach treats social regulation — particularly in the case of hazardous substances — as an issue which generates interests incompatible with the institutional realms traditionally associated with regulatory politics. The social regulatory process thus produces contradictions as interests seek articulation — or appeal to standards of legitimacy — outside of the conventional institutional vocabulary. Any solution to the crisis which would restore administrative legitimacy thus requires institutional restructuring.

Regulatory Politics: The Three Logics in Action

Working from a "class" perspective, Ira Katznelson argues that the early extension of suffrage in the United States was made less threatening to owners of capital by focusing workers' political energies toward their neighborhoods and the distributive policies characteristic of patronage party organizations. Redistribution of wealth and power across class lines was kept off the political agenda. In this way, newly enfranchised workers could participate in politics (thus legitimating the state) without challenging the power of capital through the ballot. Political participation developed as a complex, but fragmented, competition among neighborhood-based ethnic, racial, and religious groups over a limited range of benefits to be distributed by government. Thus, the "politics of residence" fragmented the potential of class voting in a decidedly "pluralist" way.

In the workplace, meanwhile, "workers were class conscious, but with a difference, for their awareness narrowed down to labor concerns and to unions that established few ties to political parties."[6] The advent of trade unionism cut across ethnic, religious, and even racial lines, but workers organized around the narrow issues of wages and job security in exchange for tacit recognition by management and the state of union legitimacy.[7] In effect, then, the obvious conflict between labor and capital at work was defined not in terms of class power, but in organizational terms of compensation and security, to be negotiated by elites in a "managerial" context which preserved the legitimate interests of organized labor and capital, as defined within the given form of industrial expansion.

The advent of the twentieth century witnessed the emergence of the Progressive movement in politics and its workplace equivalent, "scientific management". The movement was directly aimed at reducing the scope of residence-based partisan politics at the local level,[8] and, at the national level, Progressives transformed state institutions with their elite-oriented rhetoric of the "public interest".[9] At work, scientific management forced organized labor into even narrower pursuits by tying wages to efficiency. Control of the workplace became purely the province of management, as David Montgomery has argued:

> The essence of scientific management was a systematic separation of the mental component of commodity production from the manual. The functions of thinking and deciding were what management sought to wrest from the worker, so that manual efforts of wage earners might be directed in detail by a "superior intelligence"....Workers' happiness would come through an abundance of material goods, and that abundance was to be created through ever increasing productivity.[10]

The spirit of the Progressive movement limited the range of "pluralist" politics and shifted the balance of power in the "managerial" politics of the workplace precisely during the formative stages of administrative government in America. As a result, Progressives were able to influence the contours of economic regulation in terms of efficiency, and they supplied it with a "vocabulary of motives and beliefs" completely within the logic of bureaucracy. This logic was embraced and institutionalized in Franklin Roosevelt's New Deal. Somewhat reluctantly, the U.S. Supreme Court adopted the Progressive creed in its judicial review of administrative action by deferring broadly to agency expertise after 1937.[11] For the next generation, administrative government articulated itself within the "managerial" home domain. In this context, administrative decision-making ignored the "pluralist" emphasis on participation and process and the "class" emphasis on inequality and exploitation, on the assumption that the former was unnecessarily conflictual and partisan while the latter was merely the condition of an incompletely rationalized economy.

Criticism of administrative government began to surface consistently in the 1950s and 60s, as scholars from the left, right, and center attacked the legitimacy of the "managerial" home domain in agency decision-making.[12] Congress and the courts followed suit: the former by increasing agency oversight and establishing new regulatory agendas; the latter by developing new standards of judicial review.

Congress, in particular, developed agency mandates addressing new areas of regulation, specifically recognizing non-economic "externalities" (*e.g.*, pollution) and inequities (*e.g.*, discrimination) in the operation of the market. This "new social regulation",[13] unlike its economic predecessor, required a redistribution of values along nonmarket lines, and, in many cases, specified processes of agency decision-making which required greater public participation. Implicit in this latter requirement was a condemnation of the insulation of agency processes and a concession that "government failure"[14] should be as much the subject of regulation as market failure. An injection of the logic of democracy into administrative action was the favored remedy and was coincidentally reinforced by evolving standards of judicial review, which increasingly embraced a "pluralist" perspective of legitimate agency decision-making and also opened access to agency decision-making through liberalized rules of standing.[15]

Inspired at least in part by legitimation problems, the twin requirements of redistribution and enhanced participation have had an interesting effect on regulatory politics. Social regulation has not only had the unenviable political task of applying concentrated costs to well-organized interests, while distributing diffuse benefits over a general population;[16] the calculus of redistribution has also often been based on new, highly technical, and largely uncertain sources of information. Agency processes of elite negotiation have been replaced by more "pluralist", adversarial processes, in which cost-bearing interests and so-called "public interest groups" have new, but very different, incentives to participate.[17] Adversaries have typically clashed over the nature and sufficiency of evidence supporting an agency decision. The accumulated result of these evidentiary battles has been largely to discredit scientific and technical bases of agency policy whenever they are uncertain and to see agency decisions as arbitrary or, worse, "political". In effect, the whole managerial logic implied by bureaucracy has been called into question, and administrative government faces a crisis of legitimacy in social regulation.

Hazardous Waste Regulation as a Prelude to "Right-to-Know"

The delegitimation of social regulation can be briefly illustrated by the case of hazardous waste disposal facility (HWDF) siting.[18] Under federal legislation passed in the mid-1970s (the *Resource Conservation and Recovery Act*), the concentrated cost of proper disposal of hazardous wastes was imposed on identifiable industry sources for the diffuse benefit of the general population. Thus, at least in theory, a non-market redistribution was to occur, the specifics of which were to be determined by the U.S. Environmental Protection Agency. But, as states implemented the law, a second redistribution also appeared — the redistribution of risks associated with the siting of HWDFs. An intense minority of residents near a site and local governments providing services for the site were to bear concentrated risks, while the general population would benefit diffusely from the reduced risks associated with "safe" disposal of hazardous wastes.

The kind of redistribution occurring in HWDF siting is outside the bounds of conventional politics at the local level where political activity is typically organized around distributive issues. As a result, local political processes cannot handle the mobilization which occurs from the anticipated risks of redistribution.[19] Formerly passive local populations, already sensitive to the prospects of chemical accidents,[20] become aware, in the process of challenging HWDF siting, that "science" bends to the art of advocacy, that their site's designation is not simply a product of rational decision-making, and that resistance can be successful.

This kind of political awareness changes the nature of politics at the local level and thereby highlights a contradiction in the pluralist logic of democracy. Consensus in community politics is vital to the legitimacy of local political arrangements and is based on a long history of political competition over the distribution of public goods. The risks of redistribution reveal to the affected residents power relations disguised in the form of bureaucratic risk analysis and decision-making—and perhaps even reveal these relations as a "systemic" power which would force residents to accept those risks.[21] This realization can destroy the consensus surrounding local, distributive politics and can draw into question the efficacy of democratic processes in general.

"Right-to-Know" at Home and Work

The regulatory experience with hazardous waste—and chemical hazards in general—has resonated in communities across America to the extent that community concerns about chemical risks have invaded the workplace; together, labor and local activists have produced an impressive array of community and workplace "right-to-know" legislation. This is not to say that Love Canal and NIMBY predated concern about toxics in the workplace. In fact, such concern was a galvanizing factor behind the passage of the *Occupational Safety and Health Act* (OSHAct) of 1970.[22]

The Occupational Safety and Health Administration's (OSHA's) treatment of workplace toxics was inspired by and has consistently remained within the "managerial" home domain. Congress, as we have noted elsewhere, avoided the political (read: "class"-based) redistribution of risks, costs, and benefits between labor and capital in the regulation of toxics through a typically "pluralist" delegation of the task to agency expertise.[23] As a result, toxics regulation fit comfortably within the bureaucratic negotiations of organized labor and corporate capital. The potentially significant redistributive effects of OSHA's mandate—and particularly its Cancer Policy addressing the regulation of toxics—were blunted by bureaucratic delays and legal challenges, which ultimately in the 1980s left the agency and its politics in the hands of hostile administrators. As social regulation, the OSHAct hardly disturbed the *status quo.*[24]

In contrast, the source of "right-to-know" legislation has not been elite initiative. It appears to have grown from the grass-roots mobilization of citizens and rank-and-file workers who have broken down the barrier between residence and workplace in a two-fold political effort: (1) to reconstruct power relationships in both community and workplace and (2) to force the regulatory apparatus of the state to accept a democratically determined safety agenda. "Right-to-know" appears to have introduced "class" politics into the "pluralist" and "managerial" realms of community and workplace, respectively, by raising the long-dormant issues of democratic control of private property, on the one hand, and labor power in the control of the workplace, on the other.

Preemptive Federalism

The reaction of OSHA to local and state "right-to-know" legislation provides initial support for our suggestion that "right-to-know" represents a "class"-based challenge to the *status quo* of residential politics and to organized power in the workplace. In 1983, at the height of state and local legislative activity in the area, OSHA, with the explicit encouragement of industrial interests, promulgated the Hazard Communication Standard, to go into effect in May 1986 (29 C.F.R. sec. 1910.1200 [1986]). On the surface, OSHA's actions might be interpreted as a sincere agency response to its legislative mandate to protect workers from occupational hazards. By the remarkably candid admission of a well-placed insider, however, the standard was aimed at stopping community and state "right-to-know" initiatives in their tracks, largely through manipulation of the complex federal structure of occupational safety and health regulation in the U.S.[25]

OSHA has accomplished this manipulation with the following four moves: (1) by drafting the weakest possible disclosure provisions, largely granting management the power to determine which toxics to label; (2) by permitting the broadest possible exclusion of "trade-secret" substances from the labelling requirement; (3) by limiting enforcement of the standard to the manufacturing industry, in which similar labelling practices often already existed; and (4) most importantly, by pursuing the complete *preemption* of community and state "right-to-know" legislation from the field of enforcement, meaning not only state and local regulation of manufacturing industries, but also other industries untouched by the standard, and even state and local regulations involving industry disclosure to the community and/or its public safety officials.

The effect of the promulgation of the standard has been, first, to codify the *status quo ante* of workplace hazard disclosure, and then, through an extremely broad interpretation of the OSHAct's preemption provision (29 U.S.C. sec. 667(a) [1982]), to remove state and local "right-to-know" regulation from the field.[26] Of course, OSHA has been challenged in court (*United Steelworkers of America v. Auchter*, 763 F.2d 728 [3d Cir. 1985]; *New Jersey State Chamber of Commerce v. Hughey*, 774 F.2d 587 [3d Cir. 1985]), but the gist of these cases seems to assure that OSHA's watered-down version of "right-to-know" will at least preempt other workplace regulation, if not community "right-to-know" laws. Ultimately, the prospects of legal attack on OSHA's preemption strategy rest with a Supreme Court whose conservative majority has increasingly embraced a "neo-deferential" approach in reviewing administrative decisions.

The irony of using preemptive federalism to preserve established power relations is that, typically in social regulation, the opposite use of federalism—*i.e.*, delegating redistributive regulatory authority to the states—accomplishes the same end: nonenforcement and, consequently, protection of the *status quo*. States generally have a real disincentive to impose concentrated costs on industry for two reasons: (1) because states become less competitive *vis-a-vis* other states in attracting new industry and (2) because existing industry threatens to "exit", using "industrial blackmail" to ensure nonenforcement of redistributive regulations.[27]

Local and labor activists, when they mobilize beyond existing political and organizational structures in order to redistribute power in the community and the workplace, are "whipsawed" by the operation of the established regulatory structures. Such events lend credence to Alford and Friedland's assertion that the contradictory logics of the state are revealed when interests cannot be contained within one or another institutional logic. The resulting revelations delegitimize state action in general and social regulation in particular.

The Dilemma of Organized Labor

The role of organized labor in the development of "right-to-know" places unions in something of a dilemma. Insofar as "right-to-know" destabilizes the bureaucratic relationship between organized labor and capital, big labor may encounter, on the one hand, strong disincentives to pursue a "right-to-know" approach consistent with the grass-roots vision of the redistribution of power in the workplace. Yet big labor might also find it hard to resist placing this goal on its political agenda, both in principle and for less obvious practical reasons.

One commentator suggests that unions have driven a "soft bargain" in the advocacy of "right-to-know" at the state level — that is, organized labor gained toxic disclosure through the legislature rather than through "hard" negotiation with management at the bargaining table.[28] This approach has the dual advantage of limiting negotiations to bureaucratically established wage and productivity issues while shifting enforcement costs from dwindling union coffers to the state's administrative apparatus. On the surface, the "soft" approach may seem a strategic victory for organized labor, but it may also reveal union weakness or complacency — a recognition on the part of organized labor, in other words, that it has neither the organizational wherewithal to bargain directly for "right-to-know", nor the financial capacity to ensure meaningful enforcement of contractually established right-to-know provisions.

Either way, organized labor runs the risk of shifting the issue to the legislative and administrative arena, where capital has generally superior lobbying skills (particularly at the federal level, as attested by OSHA's Hazard Communication Standard). By involving the state in protecting workers' interests outside of the contract, moreover, organized labor weakens its already threadbare image as the workers' sole advocate — hence the case for union membership becomes less compelling for labor's rank-and-file.

The dilemma of organized labor — its contradictory position — could perhaps be explained by its origin as part of an administrative solution to class-based political conflict. In this sense, organized labor shares in the crisis of administrative legitimacy and might, consequently, have to take part in the only remedy which we can imagine: institutional restructuring with a new accent on democracy.

Conclusion: Restructuring Democratic Regulation

While "right-to-know" appears on the surface as a simple legislative directive, the issue actually goes deeper, as we have seen, bringing us to the heart of a crisis in social regulation. Quite simply, there has been a tendency for people to lose faith in conventional forms of democratic pluralism and — perhaps even more dramatically — in reliance upon expertise in public bureaucracies. This tendency becomes especially evident when — as is the case with the dangers of hazardous substances — the stakes are perceived to involve a significant redistribution of risks, costs, and benefits.

Experience thus suggests the need for new democratic forms for citizen involvement. In our larger critique of social regulation, we specifically address the contributions of democratic and critical theorists who are articulating these forms in concept. Citizens cannot participate effectually in government from a position of ignorance. In this light, "right-to-know" is about the profound effect that knowledge can have on one's political capacity: knowledge is power. "Right-to-know" demands can be seen as an attempt by workers to reestablish an equal footing with management in the control of the workplace. Such demands can be seen also as an attempt by citizens in general to come to grips with the hazards of their environment as they attempt to assert more control over their own lives.

Any solution to the crisis of legitimacy in social regulation, it would seem, must come from a fundamental restructuring of the politics of the workplace and the community. It is unlikely that "politics as usual" will be able to rely on the structural arrangements separating workplace from residence in the future. New structures will be required to accommodate the new and more challenging consciousness likely to emerge from the melding of worker and citizen. The contradictory logics of democracy, bureaucracy, and capitalism have been partially revealed in the process of social regulation, and, if we are correct, people have noticed. The politics of regulation may never be the same again.

Notes

1. The analysis in this chapter is based on the development of right-to-know in the United States. Generally in this area, Canadian developments have followed American precedents. Community right-to-know has not gotten very far in Canada—efforts in Toronto, for example, were put aside between 1985 and 1987 in favor of a less comprehensive provincial initiative. Occupational right-to-know, in contrast, is quite highly developed in nearly all provinces. See Canadian Centre for Occupational Health and Safety, *Community Right-to-Know Legislation in Canada: Implications for Public Health Units* (Hamilton, Ontario: C.C.O.H.S., 1987); Robert Paehlke, "Regulatory and Non-Regulatory Approaches to Environmental Protection," *Canadian Public Administration* 33 (1990), forthcoming; and Lee-Anne Jack, "Putting Safety in the Hands of Waters," *Occupational Health and Safety Canada* 5 (1989), pp. 52-61.

2. On this separation, see Ira Katznelson, *City Trenches* (New York: Pantheon, 1981). Our definition of a crisis of legitimacy is largely based upon Jürgen Habermas, *Legitimation Crisis* (Boston: Beacon Press, 1973).

3. Robert R. Alford and Roger Friedland, *Powers of Theory* (Cambridge: Cambridge University Press, 1985).

4. In a larger project, of which this article is a portion, we try to develop a more satisfactory approach to regulation by systematically examining the limits of each of these logics and the work of scholars rooted in them. We propose a synthetic approach to regulation and democratic policy-making rooted in Habermas's notion of undistorted communication and the participatory democracy of Benjamin R. Barber, *Strong Democracy* (Berkeley: University of California Press, 1984). Our theoretical approach is applied in case studies of hazardous waste regulation and community and workplace right-to-know laws.

5. Alford and Friedland, p. 432.

6. Katznelson, p. 52.

7. See David Montgomery, *The Fall of the House of Labor* (Cambridge: Cambridge University Press, 1987).

8. Richard Hofstadter, *The Age of Reform* (New York: Vintage Books, 1955).

9. Thomas McCraw, *The Prophets of Regulation* (Cambridge, MA: Harvard University Press, 1984).

10. Montgomery, pp. 252-253.

11. Martin Shapiro, "On Predicting the Future of Administrative Law," *Regulation* 432 (1982).

12. For left criticisms, see Gabriel Kolko, *The Triumph of Conservatism* (Glencoe, IL: The Free Press, 1963). For center criticism, see Theodore Lowi, *The End of Liberalism* (New York: W.W. Norton, 1969). For criticism from the right, see Samuel P. Huntington, "The Marasmus of the ICC: The Commission, the Railroads, and the Public Interest," *Yale Law Journal* 51 (1952).

13. David Vogel, "The 'New' Social Regulation in Historical and Comparative Perspective," in Thomas K. McCraw, ed., *Regulation in Perspective* (Cambridge, MA: Harvard University Press, 1981).

14. Burton Weisbrod, *Public Interest Law: An Economic and Institutional Analysis* (Berkeley: University of California Press, 1978).

15. R. S. Melnick, *Regulation and the Courts: The Case of the Clean Air Act* (Washington, DC: Brookings Institution, 1983).

16. James Q. Wilson, "The Politics of Regulation," in James Q. Wilson, ed., *The Politics of Regulation* (New York: Basic Books, 1980).

17. The cost-bearing interests generally, but not always, participate following the logic of capitalism, while the public interest groups pursue a democratic logic, neither of which is compatible with the agency's preferred logic, *i.e.*, that of bureaucracy. As a result, agency processes are so contradicted that outcomes are often challenged in court by both parties.

18. This discussion is largely drawn from Bruce A. Williams and Albert R. Matheny, "Free to Choose, or Just to Lose: The Politics and Economics of State and Local Hazardous Waste Regulation," a paper presented at the Meetings of the Midwest Political Science Association, 1987.

19. Of course, similar redistributions on a lesser scale often occur in neighborhoods where group homes are proposed, or in areas where prisons are to be located. But these decisions are limited in scope, involve non-technical decision criteria, and present qualitatively more obvious risks.

20. Love Canal was just one of many formative incidents, including the Bhopal disaster, which have brought the risks of chemical production and disposal to the forefront of citizen consciousness. This awareness grows out of a continuing American concern for the environment and a belief that government has not regulated the environment properly, leading as we mentioned earlier, to social regulation such as the *National Environmental Policy Act.*

21. Charles Perrow suggests that there is an underlying bias in the regulatory agenda because only the distribution and redistribution of risks is considered, not whether those who profit from the risks should be permitted to create them in the first place. That is, Perrow points to the underlying "systemic" power, created by the very logic of private control over economic decisions in capitalism, which privileges those who make and benefit from such private decisions. See, Charles Perrow, "Not Risk But Power," *Contemporary Sociology* 11 (1982), pp. 298-299.

22. See Nicholas A. Ashford, *Crisis in the Workplace* (Cambridge, MA: M. I. T. Press, 1976).

23. See *e.g.*, Lowi.

24. See Charles Noble, *Liberalism at Work* (Philadelphia: Temple University Press, 1986).

25. This person was, indeed, the standard's chief architect, then-Deputy Assistant Secretary of Labor, Patrick R. Tyson, who supervised both the development of the standard and the policy of enforcing it. See, P. R. Tyson, "The Preemptive Effect of the OSHA Hazard Communication Standard on State and Community Right to Know Laws," *Notre Dame Law Review 62* (1987), p. 1010.

26. Michael Brown, "Disputed Knowledge and Worker Access to Hazard Information," in Dorothy Nelkin, ed., *The Language of Risk: Conflicting Perspectives on Occupational Health* (Beverly Hills: Sage, 1985).

27. See Bruce A. Williams and Albert R. Matheny, "Regulation, Redistribution, and Federalism," a paper presented at the Meetings of the American Political Science Association, 1985. The states with at least some form of "right-to-know" legislation are Alaska, California, Connecticut, Delaware, Florida, Illinois, Maine, Maryland, Massachusetts, Michigan, Minnesota, New Hampshire, New Jersey, New York, Pennsylvania, Rhode Island, Virginia, Washington, West

Virginia, and Wisconsin. A sampling of the communities with full-fledged "right-to-know" ordinances follows: Cincinnati, Philadelphia, Sacramento, and San Diego.

28. J. T. O'Reilly, "Driving a Soft Bargain: Unions, Toxic Materials and Right to Know Legislation," *Harvard Environmental Law Review* 9 (1985), p. 307.

OUT OF CONTROL AND
BEYOND UNDERSTANDING:
ACID RAIN AS A
POLITICAL DILEMMA

Robert B. Gibson

Ignorance has long been a phantom of the political opera.[1] The great gaps in human knowledge on matters of public importance have been underestimated and their political significances overlooked. They have been wished away. Despite rising public cynicism about the competence and motives of governments, there is a continuing tendency to believe that ignorance is not a major political problem, that there are correct answers to most of our questions, and that the extraordinary scientific and technical advances of the recent past have led us near the point at which properly supervised and directed scientists and administrators, assisted by specialized experts, could identify the right responses to most policy problems.

That these are dangerous fictions is nowhere better revealed than in the evidence of environmental abuse. The case of acid rain, on its own and as the representative of a host of similar industrial malignancies, provides an instructive example.[2] Current concerns with the greenhouse effect, with the development of holes in the ozone layer, and with many kinds of toxic releases are also cases in point. Some of the broad political conclusions regarding acid rain reached in this article could be applied to these problems as well.

Acid Rain as a Political Problem

There is easily enough research evidence to show that acid rain has caused widespread environmental damage, particularly to aquatic ecosystems, and that it threatens to cause much more.[3] We have known for some time that acid rain is a disaster in the making and that to forestall it, immediate and decisive actions are needed.[4] Unfortunately, governments must induce or force those responsible for individual sources of acidifying emissions to carry out costly abatement programs. In each case, the government officials must decide not only *whether* to compel abatement, but also how much, how quickly and despite what costs. These specific, individual case decisions are inevitably both complicated and time consuming. If they are to be justified fully there must be much more complete and detailed information (about acid rain processes, effects and damages and about abatement possibilities and costs) than is required merely to justify a general decision to act immediately and decisively. If the individual decisions cannot be justified fully, then the political challenges multiply. Considered in this context, five central characteristics of the acid rain problem remain worrisome despite initiatives which are now finally emerging.

(1) Acid rain and its effects are exceedingly complex and remain generally ill-understood. A multitude of processes affect the dispersal and transportation of acidifying emissions, their chemical transformations in the atmosphere and their deposition on various receptors. The factors influencing subsequent aquatic, terrestrial, biological and human health effects are, if anything, even more numerous and complex. Many, in fact almost all, of the individual processes and factors are extremely difficult to study because of their subtlety, the complexity of similar and related influences, the weakness of available experimental and analytical techniques, and the costs of research. It should not be surprising, therefore, that many of these individual processes are still very poorly understood. Even less is known about the interrelations among these processes and other influences contributing to or competing with acid rain effects. As a result there is relatively reliable information about only a few of the larger-scale damages which acid rain has caused or exacerbated. There is no adequate basis for describing with much precision or confidence the nature, extent and timing of future damages given various emission scenarios. And there are additional barriers to providing satisfactory estimates of the economic and other costs that will result from a general or partial failure to initiate substantial abatement programs, or the reductions in damages likely to be gained through various kinds and intensities of abatement effort.[5]

(2) There is no prospect that the uncertainties will be overcome. The current weakness of the information base on acid rain processes, effects and costs persists despite the publication of research findings from hundreds of scientific studies and economic analyses, and despite relatively heavy funding of acid rain studies in recent years by governments in affected jurisdictions.[6] This research has thrown light on several murky areas. It will no doubt continue to do so. But relative to demands for a fully detailed understanding of the problem, studies in the foreseeable future can be expected to provide only a modest diminution of ignorance.[7]

(3) Acid rain involves competing interests in separate, even distant jurisdictions. Abnormally acidic precipitation has been identified thousands of kilometres from contributory sulphur and nitrogen oxide emission sources. The many major and countless minor sources are located in and subject to a variety of jurisdictions. While deposition effects vary depending on the vulnerability of receptor areas, the effects are often most serious in areas distant from emission sources. Consequently, abatement efforts in jurisdictions with major emission sources may have limited domestic benefit while environmental protection efforts in areas vulnerable to acid rain damages may be ineffective in the absence of concerted action in upwind source areas.[8]

(4) Abatement options are unattractive to emittors and difficult for regulators to evaluate. Given the uncertainties about acid rain processes, effects and damage costs, there would be problems in attempting to justify specific abatement requirements even if a single regulatory jurisdiction were involved. Emittors resist abatement proposals for obvious reasons. Environmental costs are traditional "externalities" and abatement technologies are expensive. In many cases, even the costs of nearly complete abatement would be far from crippling, and appropriate, well-tested technologies are available. Still, emittors insisted for years in Canada — and still insist in the United States — that abatement requirements are not justified if there is no proof beyond a reasonable doubt that the measurable environmental benefits of individual proposed abatement programs will be greater than the costs of abatement. There should be no action, so goes the claim, if there is not a certainty that the proposed abatement efforts will represent the most economically efficient and socially or environmentally beneficial uses of available funds. The position taken by Dr. Stuart Warner of Inco Ltd. in a 1979 statement to a committee

of the Ontario Legislature is representative of this view:

> The scientific community is gearing up to acquire the necessary understanding of acidic precipitation. We believe it would be inadvisable to make important, regulatory decisions before this information is available. Doing so could result in a net loss to Ontario.[9]

(5) Acid rain is inextricably linked with a host of other environmental abuses. Acid rain is not essentially different from, or obviously more serious than, a number of other problems. The increase in atmospheric carbon dioxide levels, the degradation and loss of foodlands, and the proliferation of ill-tested chemicals, for example, are not much less worrisome. The sulphur and nitrogen oxide emissions which are the chief contributors to acid rain are accompanied by countless other discharges and depositions, unseen leakages, accidental spills and intentional applications of poisons. For all our scientific accomplishments, we have but rudimentary knowledge of the extent, much less the effects, of these individual abuses on local, regional and global ecosystems. Nevertheless, it is the interaction of all these pollutants along with the effects of other kinds of environmental maltreatment (over-harvesting, habitat destruction, species elimination, etc.) that really threatens future existence.[10]

The political challenges posed by environmental issues will be understated when these challenges are addressed with reference only to one high-profile malefaction. Acid rain is in many ways typical at least of the insidious new class of slow, subtle and silent pollutants. Still, it is but one element in the much larger network of environmental poisonings and abuses, the cumulative implications of which are much further beyond contemporary scientific and political understanding than the effects of acid rain.

Political Responses to Acid Rain

The uncertainties about acid rain do not excuse inaction. Although far from complete, the existing body of information on acid rain effects does point unmistakably to needs for energetic abatement of contributory emissions. And the record on other identified environmental hazards shows that additional research almost invariably reveals reasons for greater concern. We do have some useful information on the significance of sources, the nature of transportation, transformation and deposition patterns, and the relative vulnerability of receptors and receptor areas. What is lacking is a satisfactory basis for objective decisions about what priorities to assign to specific abatement needs, or how much abatement to require at individual sources. We are not, and cannot expect to be, certain about what costs and other sacrifices are justified, which efforts are most crucial, or how much abatement will be enough.

Decisions on these matters must be based largely on values and educated guesses. They must necessarily reflect the extent of the decision-makers' willingness to accept and impose uncertain risks or to make sacrifices to avoid these risks. They must inevitably reveal the depth of decision-makers' concerns for people and ecosystems far downwind, for the environment generally, and for future humanity.

It is not surprising, therefore, that the political responses to acid rain to date exhibited the biases and interests favored by the predominant political arrangements, institutions and ideologies.

First Response: Research

In the United States the initial, and in some cases still the only, political response to acid rain has been the ordering of further research into scientific, technological and economic aspects of acid rain and its proposed solutions. There are some legitimate reasons for this. More information would make it easier for dedicated authorities to assess abatement priorities and options, and to argue against those whose narrow interests lead them to deny the existence of the problem or their contributions to it.[11]

The research response does, however, have weaknesses. While further research is not logically an alternative to abatement action, it tends to be used and perceived that way. The well-publicized research programs in Canada, which may well aid negotiators facing domestic pollutors and recalcitrant American officials, also provide the appearance of political concern and action without involving politically unattractive demands for abatement expenditures by powerful vested interests. And insofar as the research focuses on effects of pollutants from foreign sources, it serves the political goal of shifting blame to another jurisdiction. In the United States, the research response was adopted openly as a reason for delay.

The Environmental Protection Authority argued for many years that, given the prevailing uncertainties, immediate abatement requirements would be premature. However, at least some of the proponents of research-before-action must be aware that there will never be enough information on acid rain to supply scientific and economic proof beyond reasonable doubt that each element in a possibly adequate overall abatement program will provide net benefits. For them, research is a gesture intended only to deflect foreign and domestic pressure for abatement action.

It is also noteworthy that acid rain research efforts have been funded at times when environmental protection budgets were shrinking. The money, research talent and other resources devoted to acid rain studies were taken directly or indirectly from other, perhaps more important, work.

Second Response: Abatement Requirements

The most obviously appropriate political response to acid rain is the ordering of abatement action. Nevertheless, drastic reductions have not yet been ordered and achieved in any North American jurisdiction. Even in Ontario, action has been remarkably slow in coming and compliance has been, in effect, bargained over a period of decades. Ontario is the home of several major and some notorious point sources of acidifying emissions, but is also both downwind from emission centres in the United States, and particularly vulnerable to acid rain damage. Ontario has a good record for abatement requirements relative to other jurisdictions, but if action has been slow to come in Ontario it is hardly surprising that it has been slower elsewhere. Media attention and expressed public concerns in the province intensified the political attractiveness of abatement requirements to the point where action was unavoidable.

In the case of the Inco Ltd. smelter in Sudbury, the continent's largest and most infamous source of sulphur dioxide emissions, government officials retreated several times from the demanding requirements of a 1970 Minister's order requiring reduction of sulphur dioxide emissions to 750 tons per day.[12] Representatives of the provincial Ministry of the Environment appearing before a legislative committee examining Inco abatement options argued that they could not, on the basis of existing information, justify compelling the company to reduce its emissions below the then current rate of 3600 tons per day. They also stated that because of the importance of pollutants from sources outside the province it was not clear that further abatement at Inco Sudbury would reduce acid rain damages in Ontario.[13]

The replacement control order issued to Inco in July 1978 accepted the existing 3600 tons per day rate and merely required further research. A subsequent special regulation announced in September 1980 finally ordered abatement to 1950 tons per day by 1983 — a target achievable through application of technology that the company conceded was practicable.[14] In contrast, the Ontario Legislature's Standing Committee on Resources Development called for abatement to 1500 tons per day by the end of 1985.[15] In an October 1981 report, the Acid Rain Sub-Committee of the federal Standing Committee on Fisheries and Forestry recommended that Inco be compelled to cut the emissions to 750 tons per day within five years.[16]

This level, the same as had been ordered in 1970, was not achieved by 1986, though some modest gains were made in the early 1980s. Recalculated on an annualized and metrified basis, the actual emissions in 1986 were 685 kilotonnes per year. In 1988 they were 659 kilotonnes with a production increase. The Ontario Liberal Party, having formed the government of Ontario in 1985 following 42 years of Conservative Party rule, issued new control orders which called for total loadings of 265 kilotonnes per year by 1994. This is very nearly equivalent to the level that had been ordered in 1970. The same target has thus been sought, on and off, for two decades; but now, with engineering work underway, there is at least finally some evidence that compliance will be achieved.

Ontario was no less hesitant to insist on maximum feasible abatement of emissions from other major sources. In January 1981 the provincial Environment Ministry ordered Ontario Hydro to reduce sulphur emissions in the interim and to avoid installing emission scrubbers in new coal-fired plants.[17] The federal Acid Rain Sub-Committee observed that greater reductions in emissions were "feasible and affordable" and recommended that Ontario Hydro be compelled "to utilize the best available technology to control emissions of sulphur and nitrogen oxides at all existing and new coal-fired generating stations."[18] Ontario Hydro's SO_2 output peaked in 1982 at 450 kilotonnes per year. Currently the utility emits 370 and it has been instructed to achieve 175 by 1994.

There are several explanations for the slowness of Ontario's abatement response. Government leaders and officials of regulatory agencies are rarely inclined to take stern action against corporate powers (including both public and private corporations). Often this reflects shared ideology, perceived common interest and close professional association. Sometimes there is also evidence of more direct political coziness. But the hesitancy results as well from the inherent difficulties of regulation where legal traditions are devoted more to protection of private property rights than to preservation of public goods, and where regulators must rely heavily on the cooperation of regulatees.[19] Pollution control orders in Ontario, like abatement requirements in most jurisdictions, are generally the products of private negotiations between polluting companies and government officials.[20] Especially when they are major employers or pivotal actors in local economies, the companies can also threaten economically and politically undesirable cutbacks or closures in response to pressures for costly abatement action.

Ontario Environment Ministry officials, starting with a generally weak bargaining position, confronted the acid rain cases with a troubling lack of firm evidence about the precise processes and pathways connecting emission rates at individual facilities to clearly identified downwind damages. They knew, moreover, that the environmental benefits would be less immediate and perceptible than the costs of abatement and that the beneficiaries would be more dispersed and less well-connected politically than the recipients of abatement orders. This situation remains the case in many U.S. jurisdictions, and is compounded by the fact that the worst damage is in other jurisdictions altogether.

Generally discounting the international bargaining importance of exemplary abatement action, Ontario government officials in the 1970s and early 1980s concluded that stringent abatement requirements in the province would be unfair to Ontario polluters, who would be subject to requirements not imposed elsewhere. They also concluded that, given the significance of foreign emission sources upwind from Ontario, unilateral measures would not ensure a substantial reduction of acid rain damages in the province.[21] This perspective shifted only when it became obvious that American action was stalled and that local political concern was getting very heated indeed.

Third Response: International Negotiations

Environmental protection officials in Ontario and other places vulnerable to acid rain damage were in a sense right to insist that the problem cannot be addressed properly, much less solved, through unilateral abatement actions only in the jurisdictions suffering damages. Concerted international action is needed. To this end Canada, Ontario and some affected American states have initiated legal and even political interventions in other source jurisdictions, have carried out or supported lobbying of decision-makers in Washington, D.C., and have tried to negotiate an international abatement accord.

These efforts have had some salutary effects. Plans to reduce abatement requirements under the U.S. Clean Air Act were forestalled and significant promises were obtained once the Reagan Administration passed the torch. Along the way many legislators were persuaded that acid rain is a problem. But relative to the need, progress has been very slow in coming and even now there is yet to be a sufficiently demanding international accord, nor any certainty that new U.S. legislation will be adequately enforced.[22] This leaves us in essentially the same position we were in a decade ago.

The ineffectiveness of international negotiation efforts may have been due in part to the hesitation of the Ontario government and other advocates of international action to demonstrate sincere concern by promptly enforcing maximum possible abatement requirements within their jurisdictions. But there are more important factors. Corporate and government decision makers in major source areas have exhibited willful blindness even to well-established existing evidence and have demanded, as a prerequisite for action, complete and incontestable information on all acid rain processes, effects and costs.[23] No doubt, they have been confident that such information could not be provided. They may also have concluded that so long as there is considerable uncertainty, so long as the costs of emission abatement are more evident, more immediate and more strongly felt by powerful interests than the damages clearly attributable to particular emission sources, authorities in the United States are unlikely to order and enforce onerous emission reduction requirements. In effect, abatement opponents are relying on a reasonable perception that the international scale and impenetrable complexity of the acid rain problem put it beyond the competence of existing institutions.

Recent political analyses of the situation in the United States suggest that modest advances based on complex cost-distribution formulae may be plausible in the near future.[24] Post-Reagan journalistic commentators generally concur in this, but few are optimistic that there will be a significant reduction in total SO_2 and NO_x emissions. Existing plants will be improved, the costs of those improvements will be widely shared, new plants will be held to a relatively high standard, but total output may yet rise (or fall very slowly) especially if coal use continues to expand. More than that, as Regens and Rycroft put it, "...it may be impossible to implement a standard of technical or economic rationality for agency performance when the policy arena is characterized by ambiguous scientific evidence and high economic stakes."[25]

In a now-standard assessment of the complexity of acid rain politics in the United States, Ackerman and Hassler observed in 1981 that the environmental movement coincided with "...the decline of an older dream — the image of an independent and expert administration creatively regulating a complex social problem in the public interest."[26] That dream evaporated in conflicts among experts over the interpretation of incomplete information, and the lobbying of regulatees against "premature" action. In designing the Environmental Protection Agency, Congress sought consciously to allow imposition of abatement requirements on polluters who used the experts' uncertainties as an excuse for inaction. But the excuse prevailed anyway in the case of acid rain and Regens and Rycroft have noted the irony that the current acid rain policy debate has brought discussion of action in face of uncertainty in the United States back to the same point it had reached twenty years earlier. Some action is now possible, but it is hard to imagine that the fundamental political and administrative logjam will be suddenly and decisively broken.

Lessons Learned

The evident inadequacy of political responses to acid rain is due in part to injustices permitted by the present range and distribution of political power.[27] The concerns of the emittors are not those of the victims (human and environmental) and the power of the former to resist action is greater than the power of the latter to compel it. But the role of ignorance is at least equal to that of injustice. Acid rain is a predictable product of a society which has with unrestrained self-confidence pursued a path of environmental brinksmanship. The society we have inherited has been built on the assumption that enough would always be known to ensure that endless expansion of production and consumption would bring net benefits. This society has institutionalized a willingness always to press the presumed limits of tolerable environmental abuse with an unquestioned conviction that the proper technological correctives would be found and applied should any seriously threatening mistakes be made.

The most obvious lesson of acid rain is that the self-confidence of large-scale industrial societies is unfounded. With acid rain we may well have fallen over the environmental brink. Our present political institutions seem incapable of organizing an effective climb out of the abyss. We failed for decades to begin to foresee the possible effects of massive industrial emissions. And now that the problem has been identified, our continuing ignorance is presenting barriers to an adequately decisive response. Partial correctives are available, but we can only guess the nature and extent of their inadequacy. Moreover, we fail to make full use of the available correctives in part because of failures to appreciate how little we know about the actual magnitude of acid rain damages and how unlikely it is that a few more years of research will provide unquestionably correct answers to the difficult questions about specific abatement requirements.

The second lesson is that acid rain is an unavoidably political issue and that the way it is confronted will always be determined by the nature of political institutions, the ideologies of the politically powerful, and the distribution of political power. Decisions about acid rain have been, and can only be, based partly on an appreciation of the available scientific, technological and economic facts. They must in addition reflect values, interests and preferences. Indeed, given the depth of uncertainty about the "facts" of the matter, these subjective factors necessarily predominate.

In the acid rain case, the values, interests and preferences that have prevailed have been those of government and industry officials. For varying reasons, both the regulators and regulatees in crucial jurisdictions have been committed to the illusions of confidence — to faith in expertise, reliance on technical fixes and belief in the possibility of successful brinksmanship. The regulators, despite evident failures and in the face of growing public distrust, are still professionally and politically inclined to insist that they know best and have things well in hand. The regulatees, who are producers of consumer "goods" as well as environmental threats, feel a similar need to display confidence. Moreover, they obey relatively myopic and narrow economic motives that encourage avoidance of environmental protection costs and favor introduction of new products and activities despite uncertainties about their environmental implications.

The political treatment of acid rain reflects the essential nature of an industrial society devoted primarily to wealth-seeking and managed (to the extent that it is under control at all) through reliance on specialized expertise. The powerful in this society are typically inclined to discount uncertain hazards and to underestimate their own ignorance. It is therefore unreasonable to conclude that what we need is stronger international authority to impose effective environmental protection requirements on recalcitrant governments. What may really be necessary are fundamental changes in social and economic organization and in motivation.

We ultimately need to create societies and economies which are not inherently inclined to produce environmental abuses that require powerful international responses. We may need to reduce the scale of economic activities so that they are governable without extraordinary expertise and are unlikely to result in abuses that have more than local effects. We certainly need to de-emphasize wealth-seeking and to initiate a devolution of power that will encourage ordinary people to enjoy pleasures unavailable to mere consumers.[28] Most importantly, we need to institutionalize reminders that our ignorance is great and that we ought always to err on the side of environmental caution.

This is not to belittle efforts to press existing authorities for action against acidifying emissions, to lobby in Washington on *Clean Air Act* emissions, and to continue to press for even stronger and more universal control orders in Ontario and elsewhere in Canada. We should, however, increasingly see these efforts as part of a larger strategy. It will remain important to seek reforms that would require polluters to prove their discharges are benign (rather than require victims or regulators to prove needs for abatement), to encourage effective public participation in abatement decision-making, and to ensure more rigorous enforcement of environmental protection legislation. But the strategy should not be limited to anti-pollution campaigns, however broadly conceived. We are likely to find that significant overall cuts in acidifying emissions, and in discharges that contribute to global warming, are unlikely without changes in energy policy and practice to promote efficiency and reduce demand.[29] But it will not be enough even to link the acid rain fight with struggles in related sectors to promote environmental stewardship and social justice. Ultimately the lesson of acid rain is that these efforts and others like them should be considered and carried out as steps to the more distant and difficult goal of establishing societies that respect the boundaries imposed by human ignorance.

Notes

1. "Ignorance" refers here not to cases where individuals or groups remain unaware of available information, but rather to cases where the relevant information is not available to anyone or where what exists cannot be comprehended by anyone.

2. "Acid rain" is adopted here as the popular shorthand for wet and dry deposition of acids or acidifying compounds originating from anthropogenic emissions. Sulphur and nitrogen oxide emissions are the chief contributors.

3. For the North American evidence see, *e.g.*, United States-Canada Memorandum of Intent on Transboundary Air Pollution, *Interim Report* (February, 1981), report of Work Group 1, Impact Assessment; for the European evidence see, *e.g.*, L.N. Overrein *et al.*, *Acid Precipitation: Effects on Forest and Fish*, Final report of the SNSF project 1972-1980 (Oslo: December, 1980).

4. See Sub-Committee on Acid Rain, House of Commons, Canada, *Still Waters: The Chilling Reality of Acid Rain* (Ottawa: 1981).

5. A survey of the complexities is provided by, *e.g.*, D. Drablos and A. Tollan, eds., *Ecological Impact of Acid Precipitation*, proceedings of an international conference, Sandefjord, Norway, March 11-14, 1980 (Oslo: October, 1980). The problems posed by the uncertainties are recognized in, *e.g.*, Organization for Economic Cooperation and Development (OECD), *Economic and Ecological Interdependence* (Paris: 1982), pp. 20-21. A more narrowly focused examination of these problems with reference to one category of emission sources is provided in Brian E. Felske and Associates Ltd., *Sulphur Dioxide Regulation and the Canadian Non-ferrous Metals Industry* (Ottawa: Economic Council of Canada Technical Report No. 3, 1981), esp. chs. 2, 9.
    The continuing uncertainties about processes, effects and costs have proved a fertile breeding ground for conflicting scientific and economic opinion. These differences have been exploited, if not initially fostered, by the competing vested interest of emittors and vulnerable recipients. See M. Keating, "U.S. Suppressing Data on Acid Rain, Canadian Charges," *The Globe and Mail* (October 6, 1982).

6. Drablos and Tollan (n. 5 above) contains over 140 scientific papers and is but one of many collections. For ongoing work, see Environment Canada, *A Research Activity Catalogue on the Long Range Transport of Atmospheric Pollutants (LRTAP) and Acidic Precipitation* (Ottawa: February, 1981).

7. It is worth noting here that the limits to knowledge regarding environmental matters is also visible in the case of asbestos. Asbestos is one of the two or three most studied of toxic substances. Yet scientists cannot yet provide the sorts of near-certain information with which policy-makers might be most comfortable. As one recent scientific assessment put it: "[A]lthough much is known about the various asbestos-related diseases...large gaps in our knowledge preclude the development of accurate exposure-response models." This despite thousands of completed studies and a widespread general view that tough action is appropriate. See William H. Hallenbeck, "Can We Really Evaluate the Health Risks Due to Exposure to Airborne Asbestos?" *The Environmental Professional* 10 (1988), p. 333.

8. On the long range transport of these pollutants see, *e.g.*, OECD, *The OECD Programme on Long*

Range Transport of Air Pollutants: Measurements and Findings (Paris, 1977), and United States-Canada Memorandum of Intent, , report of Work Group 2, Atmospheric Modelling. On variable vulnerabilities and the need for concerted action see, *e.g.*, Sub-Committee on Acid Rain, *Still Waters*, esp. pp. 14-16.

9. Dr. Warner's statement is quoted in Standing Committee on Resources Development, Legislature of Ontario *Final Report on Acidic Precipitation, Abatement of Emissions from the International Nickel Company Operations at Sudbury, Pollution Control in the Pulp and Paper Industry, and Pollution Abatement at the Reed Paper Mill in Dryden* (Toronto: October, 1979), p. 25. See also Walter Curlook (president and chief executive officer, Inco Metals Company), "Remarks at the Ontario Ministry of the Environment Public Meeting to Discuss Proposed Control Order" (Sudbury, June 4, 1980).

10. On the limits to knowledge and related difficulties concerning environmental poisons generally see Ross H. Hall and Donald A. Chant, *Ecotoxicity: Responsibilities and Opportunities* (Ottawa: Canadian Environmental Advisory Council, Report No. 8, 1979).

11. See Ontario Standing Committee on Resources Development, *Final Report*, p. 26.

12. The 1970 order was issued in response to the local effects of sulphur dioxide emissions. More distant acid rain effects were not then considered.

13. See Felske, pp. 159-165; Ontario Standing Committee on Resources Development, pp. 37-39, 50; and Ross Howard and Michael Perley, *Acid Rain: The North American Forecast* (Toronto: Anansi, 1980), pp. 133-146.

14. "Practicable" means technically feasible and economically affordable.

15. Ontario Standing Committee on Resources Development, p. 54. Conservative members of the committee (a minority in 1979) dissented from this recommendation and did not propose an alternative.

16. Sub-Committee on Acid Rain, p. 44.

17. See R. Matas, "Hydro foresees 30% Rise This Year in Coal Emissions that Lead to Acid Rainfall," *The Globe and Mail* (May 8, 1981). The refusal to require scrubbers at the Atikokan plant has been a matter of long-standing debate. See Howard and Perley, pp. 129-133.

18. Sub-Committee on Acid Rain, p. 40.

19. On the biases inherent in legal traditions see, *e.g.*, Gordon C. Bjork, *Life, Liberty and Property* (Lexington, MA.: Lexington Books, 1980).

20. On the perceived need for cooperative relations with industry, see Donald N. Dewees, *Evaluation of Policies for Regulating Environmental Pollution*, (Ottawa: Economic Council of Canada, Regulation Reference Working Paper No. 4, 1981), pp. 15-16.

21. See Andrew R. Thompson, *Environmental Regulation in Canada* (Vancouver: Westwater Research Centre, 1981), esp. pp. 33-41.

22. See Ontario Standing Committee on Resources Development, pp. 42-45; and Howard and Perley, pp. 149-155.

23. For example, W. S. White, chairman of American Electric Power, was quoted in *Time* (November 8, 1982): "Acid rain is natural."

24. James L. Regens and Robert W. Rycroft, *The Acid Rain Controversy* (Pittsburgh: University of Pittsburgh Press, 1988). See also Winston Harrington, "Breaking the Deadlock on Acid Rain Control," *Resources* 93 (Fall, 1988), pp. 1-4.

25. Regens and Rycroft, p. 117.

26. B. A. Ackerman and W. T. Hassler, *Clean Coal/Dirty Air* (New Haven: Yale University Press, 1981), p. 1.

27. The examination of environmental issues, like that of other political issues, demonstrates great inequities in the distribution of power. It also shows the tendencies of the powerful (or at least the institutions supported and operated by the powerful) to exploit and victimize the powerless. Skeptics may wish to refer, *e.g.*, to Lloyd Tataryn, *Dying for a Living* (Ottawa: Deneau and Greenberg, 1979).

28. *Cf.* Robert B. Gibson, "The Value of Participation" in P. S. Elder, ed., *Environmental Management and Public Participation* (Toronto, CELA/CELRF, 1975). For a more complete version of this argument, see Robert B. Gibson, "An Examination of the Fundamental Basis for Valuing Political Participation," Ph.D. Thesis, University of Toronto, 1981.

29 See Marbek Resource Consultants Ltd. and Torrie, Smith, and Associates, *Electricity Conservation and Acid Rain in Ontario* (Toronto: Ontario Ministry of Energy, March 1989).

TOXIC WASTE AND THE ADMINISTRATIVE STATE: NIMBY SYNDROME OR PARTICIPATORY MANAGEMENT?

Robert Paehlke and Douglas Torgerson

The emergence of toxic waste problems on the public agenda has been sudden and, in a sense, unexpected. Largely ignored during the rise of the environmental movement in the late 1960s and early 1970s, toxic wastes have more recently been called "the centerpiece of the environmental movement" and "the environmental problem of the century."[1]

The whole complex of environmental problems — identified since the early 1970s — might be viewed as a largely unintended and unanticipated consequence of industrialization: a sharp contradiction to the expectations of order and calculability which animate the conventional administrative outlook. Indeed, the "rationalization" of the world, as described by Max Weber, involved the expansion of industry and bureaucracy, along with a pervasive cultural orientation which simply could not contemplate the difficulties that were to emerge.[2] For those who believed that the world was becoming progressively rationalized, such a lapse in control could hardly be imagined.

The case of toxic wastes is especially instructive in this regard. It seems that virtually no one anticipated the problem as it has emerged. Of course, this does not mean that these problems were in principle entirely unpredictable; they might have been foreseen if sufficient attention had been given to the question of where all the wastes were going. Industrial corporations certainly had little incentive to raise such questions; it was not their business:

> It was corporate managers, in companies large and small, strong and weak, that chose to abandon wastes all over the [U.S.]

countryside. When they have been apprehended, their defence has been that, however bad their practices were, they were established and standard at the time.[3]

Although in retrospect we can see that the generation of toxic wastes has been a major feature of the whole project of industrialization, the problem of what to do with these wastes had not until the 1980s been seriously considered by either public or private agencies. While industrial corporations sought to rid themselves of a nuisance, it has been suggested, "government...viewed toxic waste materials as an insignificant after-effect of industrial production."[4] In the absence of significant government actions to the contrary, the *de facto* public policy became one of permitting countless corporate policies[5] which have together produced what now is, by general agreement, a serious danger to the public and the environment.

The apparent mismanagement of toxic wastes draws into question the ability of the administrative state — and its cloistered decision process — to manage effectively not only this specific problem, but also the complex array of environmental problems generated by an advanced industrial economy. As we shall see, the administrative state has at least at times responded to rising public concern over environmental issues by moving tentatively towards greater openness in the decision-making process. The large question raised by this development is whether advanced industrial processes do not tend to generate problems which, in turn, create pressures for change in the structure and processes of the administrative state.[6] Here, however, we do not consider directly proposals for major structural transformation, but focus instead on the significance of emerging (albeit uneven) tendencies for marginal change toward more open administrative processes.

Before the 1970s, the management of toxic wastes was widely perceived as a routine matter to be handled by experts housed in the apparatus of public and private administration.[7] The burgeoning of the environmental movement in the early 1970s, however, set the stage for a different orientation. With the public and private mismanagement of toxic wastes apparent in the Love Canal episode of 1978, the competence and commitment of administrative experts was publicly questioned.[8] And now, with toxic waste management a matter of political controversy, we have witnessed a dramatic shift "from a closed to an open decision-making context."[9] The widening scope of conflict and the involvement of diverse individuals and groups have, that is, brought toxic waste management out of the insular realm of administration; now there are new participants in the decision-making process. What we have seen, in other words, is a change from a situation in which the issues of toxic waste management "are decided by a small, narrowly constituted elite to one where they are now influenced by a more diverse set of actors."[10]

For the administrators of both public and private organizations, this change can be unsettling. At the very least, the intrusion of new actors into the decision-making process may appear disruptive to the normal pattern of consultation among experts, within and between the public and private bureaucracies. Calm, rational deliberation in the public interest is now displaced by the emotional maneuvering of special interests. Careful plans and efficient operations meet ill-tempered obstruction and delay. Projects urgently demanded by various interests, and presumed as well to be in the public interest, face continual frustration.

Despite such administrative inconvenience, it has been argued, a shift from a closed to an open decision process is salutary for democracy. Reliance upon a closed process of expert decision-making reinforces the anti-democratic tendencies of the administrative state — that is, of public officials deciding among themselves and, perhaps, in quiet consultation with officials of private corporations. The interests of a democratic society, it has been suggested, require that the administrative values of expertise, efficiency, and effectiveness now "be tempered by [the] more democratic norms" of "greater public involvement and a more open decision-making process."[11] Significantly, however, this formulation of the issue takes for granted the questionable idea that effectiveness in the management of toxic wastes really can be achieved through a closed decision process. Whether one believes that a more open process is unavoidable because of political pressures or is desirable because of democratic values, one here remains wedded to the conventional presupposition that it really would be better to leave the whole matter to the expertise of bureaucrats.

Yet if one accepts the generally held view that toxic wastes constitute a major environmental problem, requiring urgent and effective action, then this is certainly a vulnerable defence of democracy. We would suggest the advisability of directly questioning this conventional presupposition of administration. The question might be posed in the following form: would an open, participatory process of decision-making in toxic waste management be not only more democratic, but also more effective, than a closed one?[12]

No one would deny that some dramatic changes have occurred since Love Canal in the management of toxic wastes. While it might be reasonable to speak of the move from a closed to open decision-making process as one key change, the variety of actual developments has of course been more complex. Here we turn to a cursory overview of these developments in North America, focusing first on the United States. Later we will consider Canada, primarily the Province of Ontario.

It is at least an overstatement to speak of a general shift from closed to open processes. The record is mixed. While the process everywhere is certainly now more open in the sense that toxic wastes are now a focus of public concern, it is also the case that — especially in formal procedures — openness is often more apparent than real. While open on the fringes, the official decision-making process has at times been deliberately maintained, at the center, as a closed world.

Toxic Waste Management in the United States: From a Closed to an Open Process?

In a few short years Love Canal became a symbol of environmental mismanagement recognized worldwide. A relatively closed process of environmental protection — a process held jointly in public and private hands — was content to ignore the potential hazards posed by a proliferation of toxic wastes under a thin layer of earth. Only the combination of angry citizens and a determined media brought action. But this action was rarely other than reluctant at all levels of government,[13] and by 1981-82 the process which had seemed in 1979-1980 to be moving in the direction of determined action and greater formal provision for public participation, appeared to be moving in reverse.

The story of toxic waste management in the United States is largely the story of the passage and implementation of three federal bills. Two of these were passed prior to Love Canal (the *Toxic Substances Control Act* and the *Resource Conservation and Recovery Act*), but actually took shape in the administrative apparatus in the climate of the great public concern associated with that episode. The third, the *Comprehensive Environmental Response, Compensation and Liability Act*, was a direct result of that public concern and involvement. The three together, it was hoped, would provide a reasonable legislative basis for approaching the toxic waste problem. But since 1980, and even before, the implementation has clearly been ineffective.

The *Toxic Substance Control Act* (TSCA) was passed by Congress in 1976 and greeted by President Ford as "one of the most important pieces of environmental legislation that has been enacted by Congress."[14] This legislation authorized the Environmental Protection Agency (EPA) to "require testing of chemicals identified as possible risks, scrutinize new chemicals prior to manufacture, regulate chemicals known to present a health risk, and report and maintain data on all chemical substances."[15] The agency was thus set to work on a task of staggering proportions.

Implementation of TSCA has been widely criticized in the press and in Congress and has been resisted at every step by the chemical industry. Indeed, neither openness nor effectiveness has been evident. In 1979 the Natural Resources Defense Council, a major American environmental organization, successfully filed suit against EPA, seeking to force the agency to implement key portions of the legislation. It should be noted that the suit was still found necessary nearly a year after the decision by New York State officials to evacuate the neighborhood built over and around the Love Canal. It should also be noted that TSCA contains provisions which virtually invite citizen groups to take various kinds of action to force agency implementation.[16]

TSCA thus broke new ground in the area of public participation in environmental management. The mid-1970s, of course, were the high point in the introduction of public access and participation into the regulatory processes of American government, a time which also saw the passage of important amendments to the *Freedom of Information Act*.[17] TSCA, for its part, required a wide range of public participation activities. However, the period from 1978 to 1980 saw little actual growth in participation regarding hazardous chemicals. By July, 1980, EPA had initiated regulatory action on only five classes of chemicals among the thousands within its jurisdiction, and citizen groups had achieved a *total* of only $1,500 in funding for intervention.[18] Also, other sectors of the bureaucracy, most notably the Office of Management and Budget (OMB), were coming to resist in principle the funding of public participation.

With the arrival of the Reagan Administration funding for these never-tried participation programs was virtually eliminated. As one official put it (in 1981): "We had a staff of 10 and projected budget of $800,000. Then one day in January 1981 I got word that we were being discontinued. Everything. The citizen participation programs right now do not exist."[19]

Citizen groups were left primarily with the expensive route of court action as an access point to environmental decision-making. The move to an open system was rapidly becoming one of legal form rather than substantive reality. An elected administration openly hostile to environmental protection sought to move quickly against established avenues for openness. One might offer the conjecture that its goal in so doing was, indeed, to lessen administrative effectiveness.

A second piece of environmental legislation, also dating to 1976, has unexpectedly proven to be more central to the management of toxic chemicals in the United States. The *Resource Conservation and Recovery Act* (RCRA) focused principally on solid waste disposal and recycling, but contained sections pertaining to toxic wastes which Congress — it has been said — passed "almost absentmindedly".[20] As Epstein characterizes the situation,

> ...virtually no one...had any notion of what would be required to carry out the mandate of safe disposal of hazardous wastes. Indeed, Congress viewed the problem as a petty oversight resulting from earlier pollution laws, and RCRA as a rather modest mopping-up operation in the triumphant war against pollution.[21]

RCRA, of course, proved to be the principal legislative basis for federal leadership in hazardous waste management in the United States, a leadership which prevailed until the deliberate roll-backs of the Reagan Administration.

As with TSCA, however, the EPA was very slow to move to the implementation phase. The agency went well beyond the April, 1978 deadline for defining "hazardous waste" and establishing standards for disposers, processors and storers of these wastes.[22] The agency took several years to locate existing hazardous waste disposal sites and only by late 1980 (well after Love Canal) did a clear picture of the extent of the problem begin to emerge.[23]

The initial regulations on the identification, generation, transportation, storage, treatment and disposal of hazardous wastes were not issued until May, 1980.[24] Part of the reason for slowness may well have been the realization within the agency of the scope of the problem which lay before it. A study in 1980 estimated that the clean-up of two thousand major existing sites could cost approximately $4 billion.[25] Somehow a problem of this scope had been overlooked by both public and private bureaucracies for decades. When the scope of the problem was finally made apparent by those formally outside the administrative decision-making process, the bureaucracy was almost frozen, locked in a still-closed, public-private consultation process.

By 1984 Congress had tired of the slowness to implement RCRA regulations; it passed amendments which strengthened the law and placed EPA on a detailed schedule.[26] When faced with a requirement to monitor groundwater and meet modest financial requirements by November 8, 1985, two-thirds of the hazardous waste land disposal facilities in the United States chose instead to close. Even though requirements were established to either 'clean close' or carry out 'post-closure' care in such facilities, little compliance has ensued. Indeed, in the period 1985 through 1987, EPA found RCRA hazardous waste site compliance to be between 44 and 57 percent.

However, in RCRA (as in TSCA) there are significant provisions regarding public participation. RCRA emphatically requires public involvement at both the federal and the state levels in all aspects of implementation.[27] But public participation under RCRA suffered the same fate at the federal level as it did under TSCA. The budget and staff associated with public involvement in RCRA were essentially eliminated early in the Reagan Administration. A small budget remained for public information (a one-way flow), but all that really remained of the high ambitions of the mid-1970s for enhanced democracy was the legal requirement of RCRA for public participation at both the state and the federal levels.

In 1980 (the final year of the Carter Administration) a new legislative measure was passed by Congress, the *Comprehensive Environmental Response, Compensation and Liability Act* (CERCLA, also known as "Superfund"). This piece of legislation created an initial federal trust fund of some $1.5 billion to be used for financing retroactive clean-up work on existing waste sites. Additional funds have since been authorized on several occasions. The states were to take legal action to recover from the responsible parties the costs incurred in cleaning up. In the meantime, Superfund would allow action to precede litigation, and was in turn funded predominantly by taxes on the production of selected organic and inorganic chemical feedstocks and crude oil. This method of funding passes the costs of clean-up through to the source and helps to incorporate environmental costs into product costs. It should also be noted that Superfund was created in response to strong public opinion, spurred by environmentalist organizations and the media. At the time an ABC-Harris Poll (July, 1980) found that 86 percent of the American public favored "giving the problem of toxic chemical dumps and spills a very high priority for federal action."[28]

The Superfund legislation encouraged both state and federal "community relations programs," but was much less explicit about the form this would take than were TSCA and RCRA. Indeed, the use of the term "community relations" rather than "public involvement" reflects how much a retreat from "openness" had taken place *prior* to the arrival of the Reagan Administration. Needless to say, even "community relations" were not seriously undertaken at the federal level during the Reagan years. EPA did, however, in consultation with state governments, produce a list of priority sites for cleanup using Superfund monies. Yet considerable controversy arose over the effectiveness and integrity of the process whereby these priority sites were established.[29] Clearly, the process of site selection has not been an open one, and the funds available under the program have generally not been adequate to the enormous task at hand.

But lack of adequate funding has been only one of the problematic aspects of the Superfund program as a whole. When Superfund was reauthorized in 1986 Congress tried to guide EPA more specifically regarding clean-up procedures. As one analyst put it: "Congress was concerned that during the first five years of the Superfund program EPA had wasted taxpayer and private-party money by designing 'cleanups' that would not last and would have to be redone in the future at greater expense. This came to be called the toxic shell game."[30] But two studies (one by the Office of Technology Assessment and one by environmental organizations) concluded that EPA's 1987 cleanup decisions were not improved by the Congressional attempt to limit administrative discretion.[31] EPA, it seems, has reverted to relatively closed bargaining with potentially responsible parties and as a result (or in keeping with this decision) has neither collected private monies for cleanup very often, nor insisted in the end on stringent cleanup standards. A critical assessment of recent EPA behavior concluded that:

> In negotiations EPA has clearly been willing to put the cleanup
> standards to be used at a specific site on the bargaining table, with
> the result that the potentially responsible parties..., realizing that
> an enforcement action against them is unlikely, can bargain EPA
> down from the protective cleanup levels the statute requires.[32]

In summary, during the Reagan Administration federal actions in the toxic waste field were, on the whole, a public scandal. It is, indeed, arguable that a deliberate effort was made to cripple effective environmental management in general — and the management of toxic wastes in particular. At the same time, there were consistent efforts to constrain tendencies towards greater openness and public participation in decision-making. The early Bush Administration has displayed less ideological hostility to environmental protection, but made few dramatic changes as regards toxic waste.

However, even in the face of long-standing hostility, the defense of toxic waste management by environmentalist organizations met with some success in the 1980s — success largely predicated on legal provisions for public involvement and requirements for administrative openness instituted in the 1970s. Several Reagan Administration deregulatory initiatives in the toxic waste area were turned back.[33] We also witnessed a series of public scandals involving the mismanagement of funds and industry influence which culminated in Congress finding EPA chief administrator Anne Gorsuch-Burford in contempt for refusing to release subpoenaed documents.[34] Indeed, virtually the entire "deregulatory team" installed by Reagan was forced to resign by early 1983.[35] Throughout this period, one of the most effective instruments in defence of toxic waste management was court action to prevent delays in implementation.[36]

While the federal government remains the legislative center of toxic waste management, the states have significant responsibilities and some states have taken important new initiatives in the late 1980s. But at the state level performance has been highly uneven. It is fair to say that no state has been entirely successful in coping either with remedial problems or with the ongoing handling of new wastes. Some states have made significant progress, yet many states seem utterly unable or unwilling to cope with the problems they face. Texas allows disposal to continue at what are perhaps the worst possible sites (along its gulf coast). Florida, despite a highly vulnerable hydrogeology and large environmentally dependent industries (tourism, agriculture), proceeded very slowly through the early and mid-1980s. More recently, however, much improved state efforts have ensued, as in New Jersey and California.[37]

The state record on public participation is also mixed. A survey of the thirteen states with serious toxic waste problems indicated that only six had increased budgets for public involvement in the period 1979-1982, though nine had increased personnel. Still, it was concluded that many states "still emphasize a relatively passive citizen role: programs often focus upon informing the public and allowing it some voice in technical planning but restraining it from influence in the full range of technical and policy issues to be resolved...."[38] However, it is the state, rather than the federal, level which is responsible for siting decisions and decision procedures. Thus the states cannot avoid public involvement, whether formal or informal.

In sum, the U.S. was moving in the 1970s towards an open administrative process, but significantly retreated in practice during the Reagan years. Nonetheless, the legal basis for participation remains and has at times been effective in the face of a political regime evidently hostile to environmental protection. Primarily through the courts and the press, public involvement in the 1980s continued to affect the decision-making process and slowed the withdrawal from protective actions.[39] Still, the public involvement which has developed thus far remains largely on the periphery of the administrative world.

Toxic Waste Management in Canada: Ontario's Move Toward an Open Process

The Canadian situation provides a contrast to the American in that the federal level of government has not assumed primary responsibility for directing toxic waste management for the country as a whole. In Canada, federal actions concerning toxic wastes have been principally oriented to research and the regulation of inter-provincial transport.[40] The key responsibility regarding the disposal of toxic wastes is located at the provincial level.[41] The provincial story is complex and has not been treated extensively in the academic literature. Indeed, very little significant research has been done.[42]

It is in Ontario that the most interesting developments have occurred, and it is here that we now focus our attention. Indeed, in turning to Ontario, we are immediately struck by the fact that, whereas the United States presents at best a mixed picture, we have here a rather clear case of a move from a closed to an open process of decision-making. It is in this context, moreover, that we can explore the prospect that a more open, participatory process can promote the attainment not only of democratic values, but also of effective administration.

The management of toxic wastes in Ontario has not been marked by any single dramatic experience analogous to that at Love Canal. Nonetheless, that episode, occurring just across the border in New York State, certainly had an impact on the perception of the toxic waste problem in the province. Indeed, in 1978, soon after New York officials ordered the evacuation of the vicinity surrounding the Love Canal site, the Ontario Minister of the Environment — Harry Parrott — hinted at the possibility that the provincial government might become more directly involved in toxic waste management. At that point, however, the Minister put the prospect in the negative: the Ontario government, he said, "would only consider getting involved in the waste disposal business as an operator if it became obvious private enterprise won't or can't do the job."[43] The Minister thus indicated a determination, for the moment at least, to persevere with the established provincial approach to managing toxic wastes. Within two years, nonetheless, he was to announce government acceptance of responsibility for developing and operating a central facility for liquid industrial waste treatment and disposal. This would be the job of a new public body, the Ontario Waste Management Corporation (OWMC).

The traditional approach to toxic waste management in Ontario was one in which government relied upon private corporations. Indeed, some critics made an impressive case that this reliance amounted to a dependence which undermined the effective management of toxic wastes in Ontario.[44] In keeping track of the volume of waste produced and transported, in monitoring existing waste facilities, and in developing new facilities, the provincial government has been largely dependent upon the information and initiative of private corporations. The government stance has been one of attempting to foster the cooperation of the private sector, taking it for granted that the producers and disposers of toxic waste possessed the competence and commitment to manage the problem effectively. The result, it is argued, was an inadequate set of regulations, coupled with an inadequate policing and enforcement of the regulations which exist. Indeed, an official largely lends support to this view in attempting to explain why the Ontario Ministry of the Environment considered prosecution a last resort in dealing with violations: "It is the function of this Ministry not to close down sites but to try and obtain cooperation...."[45] This orientation, which critics claim is inadequate to the realities of the waste management problem, is also evident in government efforts to promote the development of new waste disposal sites. The counterpart to the cooperative relationships between public and private officials was, critics also argued, a hostility to citizen intervention in the decision-making process.[46]

During the late 1970s widespread doubts developed regarding the adequacy of treatment and disposal facilities in the province. Existing facilities were outstripped by need and in addition a number of private facilities closed, largely due to environmental and health concerns.[47] A series of closures — involving a deep-well site, two incinerators, a solidification plant, and a landfill — continued into the early 1980s. During this period concerns about water contamination had led to a Ministry of the Environment announcement prohibiting the disposal of untreated liquid industrial wastes in landfill sites. The absolute prohibition proved unfeasible — because of the lack of alternatives — but there was nonetheless a major cutback in the use of landfills. At the same time the United States began to restrict the importation for disposal of toxic wastes from Canada.

The development of new disposal sites in Ontario thus was seen by the provincial government to require concerted action. The private waste management industry responded to government requests with a series of proposals which were subsequently abandoned for various reasons — partly, it seems, because of public opposition. In its promotion of private sector initiatives, the provincial government went so far as to join as a co-proponent in two projects. The government stated that it would aid the private companies at public hearings, both through testimony and through financial support.[48] Finally, in 1980, the provincial government abandoned its reliance upon the private sector, announcing that the management of toxic wastes in Ontario was to become the responsibility of a public corporation.[49]

In announcing the Ontario Waste Management Corporation, the government indicated that the mandate of the company would be to construct and operate a major, centralized toxic waste facility in South Cayuga.[50] Local opposition to such a facility was immediate and intense.[51] In accepting the position of OWMC President, Dr. Donald Chant stipulated the condition that the new corporation would have the right to review the selection of the South Cayuga site and, if deemed necessary, to reject it.[52] Within a year, the OWMC had reached the conclusion that the site was "marginal or borderline" and embarked upon a new process of site selection.[53]

Viewed from a conventional management orientation, one of the central problems now facing the OWMC was that of overcoming public resistance to the siting of the new waste management facility. Indeed, as the squeeze in the availability of disposal facilities developed during the late 1970s, officials in both public and private bureaucracies came to identify public resistance to the siting of new disposal sites as one of the chief problems to overcome in ensuring the effective management of toxic wastes. From this perspective, the main difficulty was the NIMBY syndrome: put the wastes somewhere else, *not in my backyard*. Local opposition to the siting facilities — so the argument goes — is based upon an emotional reaction which selfishly disregards the public interest. "There comes a time," as the Minister of the Environment put it in 1980, "...when all but the most biased must accept that something must be done in the broader public interest...."[54] Resistance from local residents and from more widely based public interest groups is thus seen as threatening the public interest by interfering with the timely actions of responsible public and private organizations. From this viewpoint, direct public participation in the decision-making process is seen, at best, as a necessary inconvenience. The role of the effective administrator is to limit the inconvenience and thus to pave the way for rational administrative action.

By examining the actual experience with public participation in toxic waste management, however, researchers associated with environmentally oriented public interest groups have developed quite a different view of the NIMBY syndrome. Through local resident groups, local governments, and more broadly based public interest groups, citizen action has, it is admitted, had a definite impact on the plans of public and private organizations — and upon the toxic waste management system in the province. The argument is, however, that the effect has generally been a salutary one.

Public involvement in toxic waste management has occurred both inside and outside formally established administrative mechanisms. Outside the administrative mechanisms, there are instances of citizens taking on a role of monitoring the operation of disposal facilities and pressing government for more stringent enforcement of existing regulations. In what might be viewed as the emergence of some tendency toward informal citizen monitoring, we find cases of local residents — sometimes in cooperation with local governments — undertaking their own investigations and hiring their own experts. This source of monitoring information, independent of public and private bureaucracies, was apparently important in the series of disposeal site closures beginning in the late 1970s. Together with public pressure, citizen monitoring has elicited some government effort in enforcing regulations and ameliorating conditions.[55]

Within established mechanisms, citizen involvement has generally followed the route of participation at public hearings (required under the *Environmental Protection Act*)[56] on proposals for the siting of disposal facilities. Together with efforts to mobilize public opinion and to press officials directly, formal citizen participation at such hearings—although constrained by severely limited resources—has had an impact. Plans for new facilities have been advanced, only to be regularly abandoned. For public and private officials alike, this resistance to the siting of new facilities has been seen as the most serious manifestation of the NIMBY syndrome—a real danger to the effective management of toxic wastes.

Researchers with environmentally oriented groups have, however, argued that administrative complaints about the NIMBY syndrome overlook the actual reason why public and private officials have suffered setbacks in their plans. The main reason, it is argued, is that the plans themselves have been technically inadequate. As a researcher with the Canadian Environmental Law Association concluded:

> Notwithstanding the views expressed by government and industry that the public is largely responsible for blocking the establishment of new sites, hazardous waste siting proposals have often been rejected on technical, not emotional grounds. Public interveners, despite the lack of adequate funding, have frequently shown that the industry has simply not done its technical homework by the time of provincially required public hearings.[57]

If one accepts this assessment, then it follows that reliance upon official expertise and commitment is insufficient to ensure the effective management of the toxic waste problem. In an important article on "The NIMBY Syndrome," Edward J. Farkas argued this point explicitly. He maintained that an adversarial hearing process open to the public encourages the refinement and improvement of project proposals. Such a process thus promotes a higher level of technical quality in proposals. "In the formalized, adversarial proceedings…," moreover, "objections based on emotion or a NIMBY syndrome are quickly torn apart." The conventional administrative viewpoint, Farkas thus argues, considerably overstates the costs of public involvement while ignoring the benefits—which include a better chance of avoiding "severe environmental contamination" in the future: "Citizen intervention may actually save governmental agencies from themselves, and help them avoid expensive design errors."[58]

Researchers associated with the Ontario Public Interest Research Groups (OPIRG) have, indeed, gone so far as to argue for the regular employment of "public expertise" to counter and complement administrative expertise.[59] Their description of encounters with people in seven local groups—even if perhaps overstated—provides a vivid contrast and necessary corrective to the conventional administrative perspective:

> It is common to find voluminous quantities of technical resource materials carefully filed in their homes. Conversation with these people shows that they have thoroughly absorbed the information contained in those files. When confronted by a possible danger to their community, they have gone to extraordinary lengths to become educated on the topic. Time and again they have proven that it is those who have the most direct interest in the issue who are able to quickly grasp the essence of the problems involved. They, after all, are the ones who know the community and its land best.[60]

These OPIRG researchers argued in considerable detail that there is a consistent pattern in which "citizens in the areas proposed for waste disposal sites have been able to show major shortcomings in [the] plans" which have been advanced.[61] These successes, they concluded, were achieved—despite limitations of money and other resources—primarily because of two factors. First, local residents (unlike administrators) have a direct personal interest in uncovering problems. Also, the residents have an immediate acquaintance with the local terrain and infrastructure. Although lacking the extensive funding and relevant information typically accessible to both public and private officials, citizen groups have thus perhaps been able to counter the administrative monopoly on expertise.

These considerations of the so-called NIMBY syndrome do not deny that citizens (not to mention experts) may become emotional, may overstate their case, and may proceed in a manner which ignores a broader public interest. However, these considerations do point beyond the conventional administrative viewpoint and suggest, at least tentatively, that a more enlightened perspective would regard public participation as not mainly an inconvenience, but as an important resource in the effective management of toxic wastes. This perspective suggests, furthermore, that it may be advisable to encourage more citizen participation both through the development of appropriate administrative mechanisms and through a public policy aimed at increasing the availability of the funds and information needed for effective citizen intervention. It may be advisable, in short, to move toward a more open process:[62] indeed, to one approaching participatory management.

A move towards a more open process occured with the emergence of the Ontario Waste Management Corporation. At the outset, indications were otherwise. There was a clear message from the Minister of the Environment that the decision to proceed at South Cayuga was final; serious public hearings would not be held, and development of the site would proceed expeditiously in the face of an urgent public need.[63] With the appointment of Chant to head the corporation, however, the government accepted the possibility that the South Cayuga site might be rejected and that the public hearing process could become extensive. Both possibilities have been borne out in subsequent developments.

It is difficult to imagine a more astute choice than Chant as a leader to enhance the legitimacy of the corporation and to persuade critical members of the public that the government was determined to deal effectively with the toxic waste problem. Public interest advocates certainly remain critical of aspects of the OWMC.[64] Nonetheless, Chant's credentials are impeccable not only because of his expertise as a toxicologist, but also because of his highly respected reputation as a leading figure in the Canadian environmental movement. Indeed, he was a founder of one of the most prominent of Canadian environmental groups — Pollution Probe at the University of Toronto.[65] Chant has long argued for the value of groups like Pollution Probe,[66] and — shortly before assuming his post at the OWMC — he emphasized the importance and growing sophistication in Canada of environmental non-government organizations.[67]

Under Chant, the policy of the OWMC is that public participation is not only to be allowed, but promoted, in the process of choosing the site and reviewing the plans for the new treatment and disposal facility which the company is to construct. The decision-making process is to "allow for public input...in each critical stage...through financial assistance provided by the Corporation to the participants in the hearings."[68] Already in the case of South Cayuga, indeed, the OWMC took the step — remarkable in light of the conventional administrative perspective — of contracting OPIRG temporarily "to disseminate information on industrial and hazardous wastes" at a Hazardous Waste Information Centre which OPIRG had established in the area.[69]

OWMC used its credibility and the care involved in its site-selection procedure to gain considerable public support for its choice of site (West Lincoln, a choice announced in September 1985). The corporation also provided considerable funding to local opponents so that they could prepare their case for environmental impact assessment hearings. OWMC has also indicated that it will involve community groups and local governments in obtaining independent monitoring of the environmental impacts of the OWMC facility once it is in operation.[70]

The very emergence of the OWMC would have been unlikely without citizen actions challenging administrative plans and, indeed, drawing into serious question the effectiveness and legitimacy of the whole toxic waste management system. The OWMC and its policies on public participation might be interpreted, at least in part, as a response designed to restore legitimacy. However, the establishment of the OWMC remains an act of substantive significance; the clear commitment of the chief administrator and his staff rules out any interpretation suggesting that the corporation now is not serious either about safely treating and disposing of toxic wastes or about the genuine involvement of citizens in the decision-making process.[71] Perhaps the principal cost associated with these twin commitments is, as one would expect, time: OWMC has now been nearly a decade in siting, planning, and gaining approval for its facility.

The corporation will continue for some time at least to be in an adversarial relationship with many citizens — especially residents in the selected community. However, opposition is not universal even in the site community: OWMC has considerable public support and approval is expected. More broadly focused public interest groups have, however, emphasized another issue, one which points to potential limitations of the OWMC — perhaps, indeed, of the administrative state itself. In its organizational mandate, the OWMC is concerned with treatment and disposal. For citizen environmental organizations, this focus is inadequate since it does not come to grips with what is viewed as the environmentally appropriate management strategy: the reduction, recycling and re-use of toxic chemicals.[72] Chant understands the virtues of this strategy,[73] but it remains to be seen how significant a role OWMC will play in promoting this approach. Moving very far in this direction would surely be a more complex and difficult administrative step than that of setting up an agency to deal with disposal.[74]

Conclusion

We have found a mixed record of participation in environmental administration. Environmental politics in the United States has included a concern to build openness into environmental administration. Thus the 1970s saw a range of legal devices and programs which encouraged public participation in environmental decision-making. But the late 1970s saw a growing resistance to this trend develop within the bureaucracy, and the 1980s have seen an explicit, politically-based attempt to eliminate both effectiveness and openness, particularly in the case of toxic waste management. Legal and political avenues are primarily what remain open to the public: court action, legislative review of the administrative process, and — in a few instances — political channels to state governments. By way of contrast, we find few of these avenues for public involvement in the Province of Ontario; in particular, there is limited legal protection for procedural openness in administration. Nonetheless, the OWMC seems to have made a real and continuous effort at openness in toxic waste management. One might be justifiably concerned in this case that an openness based on persons rather than on laws, or at least formal administrative rules, is potentially fleeting. But the American experience suggests that even a legislatively authorized openness is not firmly assured.

Although there are emerging ideas of decentralization and democratization in environmental administration,[75] the conventional orientation still pervades an administrative world primarily devoted to the advance of industrialization. The anti-democratic tendencies of the administrative state, when recognized, are generally deemed regrettable but necessary in the name of effective administration. Environmental policies and agencies established in this context certainly do indicate at least some tempering of the one-time total commitment to industrial advance. What we have questioned, however — in the case of a major environmental issue — is the notion that public involvement in an open decision-making process is necessarily detrimental to effective administration. Some such involvement, at least, has been necessary in giving effective environmental management whatever political priority it has attained. More fundamentally, the potential of public involvement in effective environmental management draws into question the appropriateness of the bureaucratic form itself — of a closed administrative world, populated by official experts.

Notes

1. Albert Gore, Jr., "Foreword," in Samuel S. Epstein *et al.*, *Hazardous Waste in America* (San Francisco: Sierra Club Books, 1982), p. x; and Epstein *et al.*, p. 37. A good recent review of the issue is Charles E. Davis and James P. Lester, *Dimensions of Hazardous Waste Politics and Policy* (Westport, CT.: Greenwood, 1988).

2. See, *e.g.*, Max Weber, "Science as a Vocation," in *From Max Weber: Essays in Sociology* (New York: Oxford University Press, 1958), p. 139.

3. Epstein *et al.*, p. 357.

4. *Ibid.*, p. 181.

5. *Cf.* T. F. Schrecker, *Political Economy of Environmental Hazards* (Ottawa: Law Reform Commission of Canada, 1984), ch. 4.

6. It is interesting that environmentalist approaches to public policy issues often appear to be at odds with the traditional bureaucratic form. This certainly seems to be the case, at least, with the proposal for a "soft energy path." See David B. Brooks, *Zero Energy Growth for Canada* (Toronto: McClelland and Stewart, 1981), ch. 13. A question posed by the environmentalist orientation is, indeed, whether the pattern of industrialization does not create problems which are essentially unmanageable. See J. W. Grove, "Administering the Unadministrable? The Case of Atomic Energy," in O. P. Dwivedi, ed., *The Administrative State in Canada* (Toronto: University of Toronto Press, 1982).

7. See Robert M. O'Brien *et al.*, "Open and Closed Systems of Decision Making: The Case of Toxic Waste Management," *Public Administration Review* 44: 4 (1984), p. 334; Epstein *et al.*, pp. 181ff.

8. See John A. Worthley and Richard Torkelson, "Managing the Toxic Waste Problem: Lessons from the Love Canal," *Administration and Society* 13: 2 (1981), pp. 145-160.

9. O'Brien *et al.*, p. 335.

10. *Ibid.*, p. 334.

11. *Ibid.*, p. 339.

12. Here we focus throughout on effectiveness as a prerequisite for efficient environmental management. It might turn out that really efficient environmental management would require a strategy of socio-economic development which would anticipate environmental problems at the design stage rather than treating them as matters for subsequent "clean-up" operations. This certainly seems to be so in the case of toxic wastes. On the concept of administrative effectiveness, see Douglas Torgerson and Robert Paehlke, "Environmental Administration: Revising the Agenda of Inquiry and Practice," in this volume, n. 3. For a study which deals with toxic waste management and complements our approach, see Edward J. Woodhouse, "External Influences on Productivity: EPA's Implementation of TSCA," *Policy Studies Review* 4: 3 (1985), pp. 497-503.

13. On the slowness to act regarding Love Canal in particular see Michael Brown, *Laying Waste: The Poisoning of America by Toxic Chemicals* (New York: Washington Square Press, 1981) and Adeline Gordon Levine, *Love Canal: Science, Politics, and People* (Lexington, MA: D. C. Heath

and Company, 1982).

14. Richard Riley, "Toxic Substances, Hazardous Wastes, and Public Policy: Problems in Implementation," in James P. Lester and Ann O'M. Bowman, eds., *The Politics of Hazardous Waste Management* (Durham, NC: Duke University Press, 1983), p. 25. (The volume is hereinafter cited as Lester and Bowman.)

15. *Ibid.*, p. 26.

16. See Epstein *et al.*, pp. 273-274.

17. For a discussion of matters relevant here see Walter A. Rosenbaum, "The Paradoxes of Participation," *Administration and Society* 8: 3 (1976), pp. 355-384.

18. See Walter A. Rosenbaum, "The Politics of Participation in Hazardous Waste Management," in Lester and Bowman, p. 186.

19. *Ibid.*, p. 187.

20. Epstein *et al.*, p. 194.

21. *Ibid.*, p. 193.

22. See Riley, p. 35.

23. See *ibid.*, p. 37; Epstein *et al.*, p. 197.

24. See Bruce Piasecki, ed., *Beyond Dumping: New Strategies for Controlling Toxic Contamination* (Westport, CT: Quorum Books, 1984), p. vii.

25. See Worthley and Torkelson, p. 146.

26. See Hawley Truax *et al.*, "Managing the Nation's Waste," *Environmental Action* 20 (1989), pp. 25-32.

27. See Rosenbaum, p. 183.

28. Steven Cohen and Marc Tipermas, "Superfund: Pre-implementation Planning and Bureaucratic Politics" in Lester and Bowman, p. 43.

29. See, *e.g.*, Epstein *et al.*, ch. 9; Ann O'M. Bowman, "Epilogue," in Lester and Bowman.

30. Douglas W. Wolf, "Superfund Implementation: The Polluter Must Be Made to Pay," *Environment* 31 (1989), p. 42.

31. U.S. Office of Technology Assessment, *Are We Cleaning Up? 10 Superfund Case Studies* (Washington, DC: OTA, 20 June 1988) and *Right Train, Wrong Track: Failed Leadership in the Superfund Program* (Washington, DC: Environmental Defense Fund *et al.*, 1988).

32. Wolf, p. 44.

33. See Epstein, *et al.*, p. 251.

34. See Bowman, "Epilogue," p. 252.

35. See *ibid.*, pp. 252-253.

36. Harvey Lieber, "Federalism and Hazardous Waste Policy," in Lester and Bowman, p. 65.

37. See in particular two articles in Lester and Bowman: Bruce A. Williams and Albert R. Matheny, "Hazardous Waste Policy in Florida: Is Regulation Possible?" and Kenneth W. Kramer, "Institutional Fragmentation and Hazardous Waste Policy: The Case of Texas." Information on developments in New Jersey, California and elsewhere was obtained through interviews with public officials in 1988 and 1989.

38. Rosenbaum, p. 191.

39. The American public has often also shown a determination to resist the siting of both landfills and hazardous waste treatment facilities. There are now, in fact, fears in many states that inadequate handling of toxic wastes will continue for want of a location for new, more environmentally appropriate facilities. The administrative problems and opportunities of the so-called NIMBY syndrome are discussed below with regard to Ontario.

40. See Vic Niemela, "Time for Action: Taking First Steps Toward Solving Canada's Toxic Waste Problem" *Alternatives* 10: 2/3 (1982), pp. 3-4; Schrecker, ch. 1.

41. At the federal level the Environment Canada research cutbacks of the early Mulroney years bore a striking resemblance to the cutbacks made by the Reagan Administration at the Environmental Protection Agency. But as the Mulroney years advanced it was easy to sense that the government became much less inclined to confronting environmental interests and perspectives. On the early developments, see Robert Gibson, "The Government Shows Its Colours," *Alternatives* 12: 2 (1985), pp. 49-52.

42. Perhaps the most useful study concerning Canadian toxic waste management is John Jackson, Phil Weller, and the Waterloo Public Interest Research Group, *Chemical Nightmare: The Unnecessary Legacy of Toxic Wastes* (Toronto: Between the Lines, 1982). (Hereinafter cited as Jackson and Weller.) Despite certain limitations and a deliberately polemical style, this volume is based on serious research and provides a helpful foundation for further work. For a collection of articles on the topic (edited by Robert Paehlke), see the "Special Double Issue on Toxic Wastes" of *Alternatives* 10: 2/3 (1982). A forthcoming paper, Robert Paehlke and Douglas Torgerson, "Toxic Waste as Public Business," will compare toxic waste management paractices in three Canadian provinces.

43. "Parrott Promulgates Industrial Waste Program," *Ecology Week* (October 27, 1978). *Cf.* Victor Malarek, "Find Answer for Liquid Waste or We Will, Tory Tells Industry," *The Globe and Mail*, (October 19, 1978), p. 5, where Parrott is quoted: "I'm not going to let the health of this province go down the drain because of the private sector."

44. See Jackson and Weller, chs. 2-3.

45. R. B. Jackson, Legal Services Branch, quoted in S. H. S. Hughes, *Report of the Royal Commission Appointed to Inquire into Waste Management Inc., et cetera* (March 30, 1978), p. 44. An orientation towards negotiation and collaboration is reinforced by the right of companies to appeal regulatory actions. Compromise is often deemed preferable to the risk of having actions refused, weakened, or delayed through appeal to the courts or the Environmental Appeal Board. See David Estrin and John Swaigen, eds., *Environment on Trial: A Handbook of Ontario Environmental Law* (Toronto: Canadian Environmental Law Research Foundation, rev. ed., 1978), pp. 37-39.

46. See Jackson and Weller, esp. ch. 5.

47. The relevant information is summarized in a useful chart in *ibid.*, p. 68.

48. See *ibid.*, pp. 69-70.

49. See the statement of Harry Parrot, Minister of the Environment, in Legislature of Ontario, *Debates*, 4th session, 31st Parliament (November 25, 1980), pp. 4595-4600.

50. *Ibid.* This statement by the Minister of the Environment announced the name of the OWMC and the plan to establish it as a crown corporation. The formal creation of the OWMC as a crown corporation came in 1981.

51. See Phil Weller and John Jackson, "South Cayuga I: Lessons in the Need for Public Participa-

tion," *Alternatives* 10: 2/3 (1982), pp. 5-8. (Hereinafter cited as Weller and Jackson.)

52. Interview with Dr. D. A. Chant, President, Ontario Waste Management Corporation, November 7, 1984. *Cf.* D. A. Chant, "Managing Ontario's Industrial Wastes," address to the Annual Conference, Rural Ontario Municipal Association, Royal York Hotel, Toronto, February 9, 1982, p. 3.

53. D. A. Chant, "Press Conference Remarks...Regarding the Proposed South Cayuga Site for a Secure Landfill," Ontario Waste Management Corporation, November 18, 1981, p. 7. *Cf.* Michael Scott, "South Cayuga II: The Role of the Ontario Waste Management Corporation," *Alternatives* 10: 2/3 (1982), pp. 9-11. (Scott is Director of Communications for the OWMC.)

54. Harry Parrott in Ontario Ministry of the Environment, "Facts," August, 1980, quoted in Jackson and Weller, p. 71. Also see Parrott's statement in *Debates*, pp. 4594-4600 (n. 49 above).

55. See Jackson and Weller, ch. 3.

56. The *Environmental Assessment Act* (1975) created the Environmental Assessment Board (EAB)—in effect reconstituting and broadening the authority of the previous Environmental Hearing Board (EHB). The EAB retained the functions of the EHB authorized by the *Ontario Water Resources Act* (1970) and the *Environmental Protection Act* (1971). See D. Paul Emond, *Environmental Assessment Law in Canada* (Toronto: Emond-Montgomery, 1978), ch. 3. *Cf.* D. S. Caverly and M. G. Jones, "The Evolving Role of the Environmental Assessment Board in Decision-making," in M. Plewes and J.B.R. Whitney, eds., *Environmental Impact Assessment in Canada* (Toronto: Institute for Environmental Studies, University of Toronto, 1977). Under the authority of the older legislation, the Environmental Assessment Board acts as an advisory body. In assessing the practice of the Board under this legislation, Edmond has noted a tendency to limit "hearings to a review of the technical detail, rather than expanding them to generate the information and criteria needed to make important policy decisions" (p. 135). Under the newer environmental assessment legislation, the EAB is constituted formally as a decision-making body—although the Minister of the Environment has the absolute discretion to alter decisions of the Board. As Emond further points out, the newer legislation "by requiring a discussion of alternatives, mandates a review of the broader implications of whether or not development should proceed" (*ibid.*). Moreover, the definition of the "environment" is considerably more comprehensive in the *Environmental Assessment Act* than in the *Environmental Protection Act*. With the exception of two cases which did not reach the hearing stage, waste disposal site proposals have been dealt with under this older, more restrictive legislation. See Jackson and Weller, p. 78. Further on the limitations of the EAB under the *Environmental Protection Act*, see Estrin and Swaigen, *Environment on Trial*, ch. 3: "Nevertheless, it's often the only game in town" (p. 241). *Cf.* n. 63 below.

57. Joe Castrilli, "Hazardous Wastes Law in Canada and Ontario," *Alternatives* 10: 2/3 (1982), p. 55.

58. E. J. Farkas, "The NIMBY Syndrome," *Alternatives* 10: 2/3 (1982) p. 48.

59. Weller and Jackson, pp. 7-8. *Cf.* Jackson and Weller, pp. 71-77, 85-87.

60. Weller and Jackson, p. 8.

61. *Ibid.*, p. 7.

62. *Cf.* D. J. Gambel, "The Berger Inquiry: An Impact Assessment Process," *Science* 199 (1978), pp. 946-952; L. Graham Smith, "Mechanisms for Public Participation at the Normative Level in Canada," *Canadian Public Policy* 8: 4 (1982), pp. 561-572.

63. Indeed, it is doubtful whether any public hearings were actually contemplated. The Minister, Harry Parrott, explicitly ruled out hearings under either the *Environmental Assessment Act* or the *Expropriations Act*. (Most of the land was owned by the Ontario government, but some was still in private hands.) See *Debates*, p. 4596 (n. 49 above). *Cf.* Stan Oziewicz and Gwen Smith, "Ontario Picks Cayuga Farmland for Industrial Waste Dump," *The Globe and Mail* (November 26, 1980) pp. 1, 4. Public hearings are required under the *Environmental Protection Act* for sites intended for hazardous waste; however, a hearing can be denied if the responsible official (Director of the Environmental Approvals Branch, Ministry of the Environment) deems that there is an emergency requiring the immediate disposal of wastes. See Estrin and Swaigen, *Environment on Trial*, pp. 239-240. Parrott was emphatic about the urgency of the problem.

64. *Cf.* Jackson and Weller, pp. 85-87.

65. Douglas Torgerson was on the staff of Pollution Probe at the University of Toronto from 1974 to 1976.

66. See D. A. Chant, "Pollution Probe: Fighting Polluters with their Own Weapons," in A. Paul Pross, ed., *Pressure Group Behaviour in Canadian Politics* (Toronto: McGraw-Hill Ryerson, 1975).

67. See D. A. Chant, "A Decade of Environmental Concern: Retrospect and Prospect," *Alternatives* 10: 1 (1981), p. 4.

68. Scott, p. 11.

69. *Ibid.*

70. See *OWMC and the West Lincoln Community: Managing Change* (Toronto: OWMC, 1987). This initiative was first mentioned to us in an interview with Chant in Toronto on November 7, 1984.

71. This judgment is based upon interviews in 1984-1985 with Chant and OWMC Director of Communications Michael Scott, as well as a previous acquaintance with Chant on the part of both authors.

72. See Moni Campbell, "Industrial Waste Reduction and Recovery," *Alternatives* 10: 2/3 (1982), pp. 59-64; Jackson and Weller, ch. 6.

73. See Chant, "Managing Ontario's Industrial Wastes," p. 9: "Over the past few months, it has become clear to us that if we are to do it right, we must set as our objective the development and implementation of a province-wide, *long-term program*, aimed at not only treating and storing wastes, but assisting in reducing and recycling them."

74. See Ontario Research Foundation, Proctor and Redfern Limited, and Weston Designers-Consultants, *Waste Reduction Opportunities Study* (prepared for the Ontario Waste Management Corporation, 1983), esp. ch. 8.

75. See, *e.g.*, C. A. Hooker and R. Van Hulst, "The Meaning of Environmental Problems for Public Political Institutions," in William Leiss, ed., *Ecology versus Politics in Canada* (Toronto: University of Toronto Press, 1979), pp. 132-133. *Cf.* Torgerson and Paehlke, "Environmental Administration."

CONCLUSION

ENVIRONMENTAL POLITICS AND THE
ADMINISTRATIVE STATE

Robert Paehlke and Douglas Torgerson

In the context of advancing industrialization, the fiction of apolitical administration readily appears plausible. Made in the image of the machine, the administrative apparatus becomes both an achievement and instrument of rationalization — of technological progress in an increasingly mechanized universe: "mechanical technology is impersonal and dispassionate, and its end is very simply to serve human needs, without fear or favor or respect of persons, prerogatives, or politics."[1] Bureaucratic organization emerges as a mechanism especially well suited to promoting a natural and necessary course of development. The administrative state, in particular, can thus appear as a form of governance beyond politics.

The advent of environmental politics has not been able completely to dispel this technocratic illusion, but has challenged it. With the established pattern of development drawn into question, the conventional agenda no longer appears simply as natural and necessary, but stands out clearly as a matter of choice — as something subject to revision. As this agenda comes under scrutiny, attention also turns to the process in which it is formulated and in which concrete policy decisions are made. Here the divide between politics and administration collapses: the two intermingle in a way which violates rationalistic expectations and prevailing canons of administrative legitimacy. The technocratic imagery now appears as a veil, obscuring the normal interplay of forces in the administrative sphere of state and economy. What is drawn into question is not only the historical direction created and maintained by the convergence of these forces, but also the institutional form which they collectively constitute.

Environmental Politics

Environmental politics disturbs the composure of the administrative state. Even though Leviathan endeavors to force environmental problems onto the procrustean bed of conventional administrative thought and practice, the goal proves to be elusive. With the dramatic outburst of environmental concern some two decades ago, officials were generally quick to align their statements with the prevailing sentiment. Just as quickly, however, there emerged among them a sense that environmental problems had either been solved by modest reforms or displaced by more serious and pressing economic difficulties. Environmentalism, many hopefully believed, was going out of style and would not hold public attention for long. It seemed safe for officials to slight environmental concerns, and eventually neo-conservative forces were able to mount a determined assault upon environmentalism and the reforms it had initiated in the administrative state. Nonetheless, environmental politics had been animated by a particular perception of environmental problems — a perception which was strong and pervasive enough to sustain environmental concern in a substantial network of environmental organizations and among a significant proportion of environmental professionals. Once again, it now does not seem safe for public officials to ignore environmental concerns or simply to repeat the clichéd promises of progress.[2]

To say that environmental politics is animated by a particular perception of environmental problems is not to say that this perception is universally shared by all actors in this arena. Indeed, it is a perception which has often been ridiculed by forces committed to the conventional vision of order and progress. Nonetheless, environmental politics has emerged as an identifiable arena of contemporary politics and administration through the impetus of actors sharing a view which challenges the complacent notion that there is nothing new to environmental problems — that these are really just problems like any others and can be handled in the ordinary way.[3]

In a manner necessarily irritating to the administrative mind, environmental problems are deemed both enormously complex and serious — as raising in a dramatic fashion moral issues which once seemed settled and technical questions which few had even imagined. Against the expectations of the administrative mind, this view focuses on problems which may be entirely unmanageable and which, at the very least, call for a thorough revision of administrative inquiry and practice. In its view of the complexity and seriousness of environmental problems, this perception contains a paradox. The problems seem virtually beyond comprehension yet enough is known to demand urgent action.

Environmental problems are perceived as being multidimensional, interconnected, interactive and dynamic. They point beyond the controlled setting of the laboratory or the production process to an ambiguous world where innumerable variables elude identification, much less measurement. The very scope of the unknown seems to expand dramatically with each little bit learned. Yet the problems appear not only extraordinarily complex, but also extremely threatening to particular concerns and, indeed, to the general interests of humanity.

A sense of crisis demands action and innovative directions in problem-solving. No single fact or model demonstrates an emerging crisis, but a litany of difficulties becomes increasingly impressive. Environmental impacts appear largely cumulative, moreover, and it becomes increasingly hard to deny that the maximum sustainable level of imposition of economy on environment has been reached or exceeded. Human populations and activities are encroaching in some way on the habitats of other species on nearly every square mile of land on the planet. Virtually all the best agricultural land now carries human-imposed eco-systems, maintained in many cases through the use of toxic chemicals. Ground water, river water, lake water, and the oceans are laced with chemicals: polar bears carry toxic chemicals in their livers. Precipitation around the world appears altered in both quantity and quality, and the ozone layer has been disrupted. Tropical rainforests seem headed for rapid elimination. Human beings are silently, surreptitiously being killed by unacceptable — and "acceptable" — levels of pollution.

The perception alternates, then, between a sense of human limits and a confidence that human action has at least a chance of solving environmental problems. This ambivalence allows for differing approaches, including the reflex response of looking to established authority as some environmentalists have done. What that approach fails to recognize, however, is that established authority is itself seldom bothered by a sense of human limits and instead typically exudes unshakable confidence in prevailing institutions and their capacity to resolve problems. Of course, this capacity cannot, in principle, be disproven. Problems which seem to be insoluble in the context of established institutions could — however dim the possibility — conceivably be resolved through some unanticipated innovation, or through some unforeseen way of defining the problems. What remains striking, nonetheless, is the unshakable character of this confidence, for its foundation is as suspect as the rationalistic imagery which adorns it: "The achievements of modern science and technology, however impressive, do not of themselves provide solid evidence that the problems which they confront and, in fact, create, can actually be overcome."[4] There is, indeed, reason for doubt. The administrative sphere, while singularly successful in promoting the established pattern of development, has not shown itself to be effective in either restraining or qualitatively redirecting industrialization. The administrative sphere, moreover, craves that which is definite, precise, and calculable—tolerating little in the way of ambivalence. Nonetheless, such ambivalent perception may well be in accord with an organizational form oriented toward a balance between the humility of recognizing limits and the confidence needed for effective action.

While environmental politics is animated by a particular view of environmental problems, it is also characterized by the rather distinctive perspective and interests of those advancing environmental concerns. Environmental politics is a dimension of political life which is different from the politics of left, right, and center. While the center has typically endorsed environmental concern—even reducing the environment to a so-called "motherhood" issue—environmentalism has also been portrayed as a mere extension of the socialist movement or of the earlier progressive conservation movement. Despite the frequently unabashed hostility of neo-conservatism to the environmental movement and its goals, there is also an ambiguous relationship between environmentalism and the appeals of neo-conservatism.[5] Environmental politics, moreover, stands apart from conventional interest-group politics and thus bears a distinctive relationship to the state and the administrative world generally.

The intriguing ambiguity in the relationship between environmentalism and neo-conservatism turns largely on how the two view the administrative state. Both exhibit a notable hostility. For neo-conservatives the goal has been economic recovery and expansion through deregulation, entrepreneurship, and the "magic of the market". Environmentalists, in turn, have often emphasized alternative patterns of development, comprising grass-roots citizen participation and empowerment, responsible individual action, and both public and private decentralized initiatives. For environmentalism, this emphasis in part represents a reaction against the administrative orientation of the earlier conservation movement.

Neo-conservatives are reacting against the seemingly unidirectional growth of the "positive state".

In terms of concrete policy thrusts, neo-conservatism has ironically pursued a course ensuring the continued growth and presence of the administrative state in economy and society. This course has included the financing of megaprojects, direct and indirect subsidies to private corporations, bailouts for companies and industries "too big to fail," grants for technological development, and—especially in the American context—mammoth expenditures amounting to a "military Keynesianism".[6] Nor was such a course really avoidable because neo-conservatism has by no means replaced the prevailing consensus which attributes to the administrative state ultimate responsibility for the economic management of advanced industrial society. A further irony is that neo-conservatism in America, Canada, and Britain has had to make a concerted effort to restrain a seemingly visceral hostility to environmentalism in order to project at least an appearance of environmental concern. One of the most dramatic adjustments in current political life, this change suggests that continuing public support for environmental protection may prove to be a significant chink in the neo-conservative armor.

There is now a real struggle underway for that segment of political opinion which wants to restrain the bureaucratic dominance of contemporary society. Neo-liberals and the traditional left share a heritage which looked hopefully upon the administrative state as potentially an impartial mechanism that could serve the general interests of society. It remains an open question whether they can come to terms with an environmentalist view which focuses upon the limitations of conventional administration. It remains an open question, as well, whether neo-conservatives can adapt to environmentalist doubts regarding economic growth, corporate bureaucracies in the private sector, or the supposed magic of the market. Finally, it remains an open question how different environmentalists will come to locate themselves in terms of the left-right continuum—whether splitting along it or somehow realigning and redefining it.

Besides its unique orientation to the prevailing ideological map, environmental politics also departs from the conventional framework of interest-group politics. The focus of environmental groups, that is, is concerned more with a broad public interest than with a narrow, particular interest. This point is implicit in the literature on "post-materialist" values; and environmentalism is central to discussions of the "new social movements" that challenge conventional politics.[7] Those devoted to environmental politics are not typically seeking economic advantages. Instead, environmentalists see themselves generally as representing a universal human interest (including future generations) or as speaking for other species and especially threatened parts of non-human nature – indeed, more comprehensively, as working in the interests of the planet and its inhabitants as a whole.

The distinctive orientation of environmentalism is significant in the politics of the administrative state. For this realm works smoothly only if those seeking favors are uniformly professional and responsible – if they speak the proper language of precision and instrumentality while standing ready to make the trade-offs necessary for compromise solutions. With their particular perspective and interests, environmentalists often do not measure up to these standards. Yet as they seek concrete results in the policy process, they are bound to interact over time with the administrative state and the corporate world. Then environmentalists do – often in a dramatic and deliberate fashion – become increasingly professional and "responsible." Indeed, participation in environmental impact assessment hearings and other administrative procedures often requires time and expertise. Since environmentalists are hardly less likely than others to need a means of livelihood, they may well become reliant on the continuing success and stability of an environmental organization or network – even if remuneration tends to be meagre. Moreover, with the frankly moral character of its demands, environmentalism can appear overbearing and untrustworthy in a world where one gets along by going along. Environmentalists are pressed to compromise simply in order not to appear uncompromising.

Yet this is not the entire story, for professionalized environmentalists are frequently eclipsed by events and "out-greened" by others.[8] This tension runs through existing groups, and is increased with the entry of new groups and individuals into environmental politics. A significant impetus in this regard arises with the so-called NIMBY syndrome, or – in distinctly different terms – with opposition to LULUs: locally unwanted land uses. Here local residents may generally oppose development which would degrade the recreational amenities of the area. Or landowners could object to particular projects which would decrease the sale value of their property. Clearly, these motives are common to interest-group politics, and there is an arsenal of compensatory devices available in conventional politics and administration. Yet, typically in such situations, there are two elements which resist ready compromise and a smooth resolution to disputes. One is the attachment that people may feel to a place with which they identify. The other is the fact that some who object to a landfill, a toxic waste depository, or an oil refinery do so not only with their particular interests in view, but also with concern for a broader, interrelated context of environmental problems. Indeed, when such opposition resists conventional compromises, more than an immediate difficulty is created for the administrative state. For these situations also direct the attention of a broader citizenry to environmental concerns; face-to-face with particular consequences of industrialization, some are led to perceive broader questions and perhaps to inject a vigorous and uncompromising attitude into environmental politics.

Environmental Administration

In its collision with the administrative state, as we have seen, environmental politics is influenced by an historically unique perception which takes environmental problems not to be ordinary problems, easily remedied or administered in the conventional manner. Environmental politics thereby clearly departs from the earlier politics of conservation and its tendency to align itself with the administrative apparatus of an emerging industrialism. Indeed, at times environmental politics seems moved by an impulse to have done with administration altogether.[9] Yet this impulse would appear to be based in a recognition of the inadequacies of conventional administration in grappling with environmental problems. What the impulse obscures is that administration cannot simply be abolished: the historical possibility is for a form of administration more adequate to the environmental problems which are emerging as we move into the aftermath of industrialization. The at least implicit logic of environmentalism, of environmental politics, is to realize this new kind of administration.

Environmental administration possesses no completed form or systematic program, but is an emerging orientation of inquiry and practice distinctly at odds with the conventional agenda. Exposing the hidden political nature of that agenda, environmental administration is itself constituted as a political goal which, implicitly or explicitly, serves as a common focus of effort for the diverse environmental movement. As a political goal, environmental administration remains somewhat fluid and indefinite, with the precise content of the goal shifting with differing perspectives. Nonetheless, it is possible briefly to characterize an emerging agenda.

As a departure from the conventional approach to administration, environmental administration is not simply administration which deals with environmental matters. Of course, it begins by taking a focus on the environment, thus distinguishing itself from an earlier administrative tendency to focus on the internal operations of a single organization and to take the external environment for granted. By now, however, both the social and natural environments of organizations have increasingly been added on as categories to the conventional administrative form. Environmental administration differs, however, in that its way of seeing the environment promotes a distinctive mode of defining and grappling with environmental problems. Moreover, environmental administration is not in principle restricted to dealing with environmental problems directly; that is to say, it offers an orientation which can deal with a range of economic processes — e.g., manufacturing, services, agriculture, resource extraction, transportation — in a manner which anticipates environmental problems in both planning and implementation. Environmental administration, in other words, departs both from conventional administration and from the pattern of development which it has served.

In order to grasp the idea of environmental administration more fully, we can briefly and provisionally characterize it with an interrelated and incomplete list of adjectives: (1) non-compartmentalized, (2) open, (3) decentralized, (4) anti-technocratic, and (5) flexible. Here we will focus, in turn, on each characteristic.

(1) *Non-compartmentalized*. Environmental administration resists the typical bureaucratic tendency toward compartmentalization. Because it recognizes a pervasive complex of problems, environmental administration has indefinite boundaries and has, indeed, challenged early efforts to confine environmental concerns to a single, often marginal, sub-division of government. The institutionalization of environmental impact assessment, for example, has — despite its limitations — prompted a broad range of government departments and agencies to think environmentally. Even so unlikely an agency as the United States Navy is currently reviewing its administrative structure to include environmental factors more effectively in its decision-making processes. Government printing offices in Maryland, Washington, and Oregon, moreover, procure paper from

recycled sources. During the "energy crisis" of the early 1980's, widely diverse administrative agencies took up or promoted extensive energy efficiency improvements. More and more new government revenue policies have a secondary objective of environmental protection; indeed, environmentalists in Canada have even proposed subjecting governmental budgets to comprehensive environmental impact assessments. Environmental administration is thus not easily confined or isolated.

(2) *Open*. While the hallmark of conventional administration is secrecy in a cloistered decision-making process, the hallmark of environmental administration is openness. The relatively unbounded character of environmental concerns creates perplexities for any effort to neatly mark the boundary lines of the administrative process and to definitively circumscribe the range of legitimate participants. This problem in principle is compounded by the political reality that educated citizens are increasingly reluctant to accept the secrecy of the administrative sphere. Public administrators, and even private decision-makers, are more and more likely to find themselves at a public hearing or in a courtroom, rather than closeted in the offices of a confidential world. The conventional framework of administration is thus challenged by "discursive designs".

(3) *Decentralized*. The slogan "think globally, act locally" reflects a significant ambivalence in environmental administration. For the impetus toward decentralization provides a reorientation, but by no means entirely replaces centralization. Environmental administration is concerned with problems which at once entail pressures toward decentralized, even local, decision-making and toward centralized, even international, decision-making.

Global problems in some cases require common, cooperative global solutions, with little room for wide variations in approach: diverse initiatives here need coordination to be effective. Prompt efforts to stem the depletion of ozone in the upper atmosphere, to take an obvious example, could well be pointless if China should embark upon a program of providing CFC-based refrigerators to its vast population. Some central administration is necessary, moreover, to prevent havens for pollution in areas where authorities are inclined to trade environmental quality for economic opportunities: the air of much of a continent can be fouled from within a single, neglectful political jurisdiction.

Yet the pressures for centralization, seen from the conventional administrative viewpoint, can easily obscure a key distinctive feature of environmental administration, which itself has arisen in significant part from pressures brought to bear by a diverse, mobilizing citizenry. If environmental administration must deal with global problems, so too must it deal with the local and the particular, with peculiar geographical and cultural contexts. Here necessary knowledge and initiative cannot be the preserve of a centralized administrative structure, staffed by remote and anonymous personnel. Knowledge and initiative, indeed, arise from intimate involvement in the context.[10]

Established patterns of centralized power in advanced industrial society, moreover, retain an orientation which typically leaves them unsympathetic to rapid, vigorous, large-scale action for environmental protection. So the political and historical context by itself clearly sets limits to a reliance upon centralization; implicit, though not always recognized, in such reliance is a challenge to established centralized hierarchies which would effectively replace them with new ones. Yet political support for such a change would, paradoxically, itself require decentralized initiative and action.

Obviously, environmental administration anticipates some kind of new balance, integration, or alignment of centralization and decentralization. While some provisional guidelines to approach this relationship could no doubt be developed, especially in the context of specific problems, any comprehensive formula is likely to remain elusive not only because of the obvious complexities involved, but also because of a reason which those wanting such a formula might not recognize: the present relationship between centralization and decentralization has emerged as part of a pattern of historical development, and any proffered formula would be inadequate if it failed to take this context into account. Yet to take this context into account would be to expect the unexpected, to anticipate contingencies which are not repetitive and predictable, but new and surprising. At the very least, one would have to recognize that those who manage and confront Leviathan also find themselves perhaps in a transitional phase — and that the relationship between centralization and decentralization in environmental administration may emerge as something qualitatively different should that time pass: should, that is, the pattern of social and economic life change into one in which massive environmental problems are no longer generated routinely by an enormous complex of centralized hierarchies.

(4) *Anti-technocratic*. As a goal arising from environmental politics, environmental administration emerges in part as an alternative to conventional administration and, by contrast, as a mirror which exposes the surreptitious political dimensions of prevailing practices. What is exposed is the at least implicit commitment to a form of life and historical vision which anticipates a smoothly functioning social system, guided by experts in the administrative sphere. Environmental administration departs from this technocratic commitment, and advances, moreover, with a more or less clear recognition of the interest-group machinations and class forces which actually infuse the administrative state despite its technocratic imagery. Obviously, this frankly political orientation raises questions of administrative legitimacy. The cloistered politics of conventional administration are rejected in favor of the more open patterns of communication deemed appropriate to democratic government and society.[11]

This appeal to democracy, however, is only partly effective. While it may be possible to parody and ridicule the technocratic style and idiom by drawing upon popular sentiment, technocracy is still potent in projecting a mystique suggesting it holds a monopoly on relevant knowledge. A key challenge to environmental administration is to counter this claim by placing expertise in context.

Environmental administration necessarily draws heavily on the findings and opinions of experts. Sciences such as ecology, epidemiology, and toxicology, indeed, provide important foundations for environmentalism as a perspective which informs environmental administration in its challenge to technocracy. But expertise, almost by definition, is specialized and thus insufficient by itself for handling environmental problems. With its features of non-compartmentalization and openness, environmental administration clearly draws attention to the importance of the generalist capable of viewing problems in a broader configuration, of perceiving and judging collectivities, interactions, and relationships across systems. The importance of the generalist suggests, moreover that the boundary between relevant expertise and common sense is often fluid and indistinct.[12] The door is thus open to citizen participation in a process which could educate *both* citizens and experts.

The insufficiency of specialized expertise means that the administrative process needs to remain open to a range of influences and experiences which are typically excluded in conventional practice. This point reinforces the importance of the knowledge and initiative to be gained through a relatively decentralized pattern of interaction involving both citizens and experts. Such a pattern could no doubt prove annoying to those accustomed to a more closed process, and resistance to such innovation is often evident. Yet environmental administration points to the limited effectiveness of a cloistered administrative domain, protected from the trouble of dealing with external concerns: "weak outside scrutiny insulates the regulatory system from substantive criticism that could lead to improved effectiveness."[13]

No doubt there is often a rationale to exclude such influences. For example, there is often concern about the supposedly unwarranted delays occasioned by the NIMBY syndrome. Yet this concern is based upon the assumption that administrative officials have both the competence and commitment to handle environmental problems effectively without external influences. To take a case in point, the failure of the administrative sphere — both public and private — to prevent or effectively respond to the massive Valdez oil spill was followed by a rapid mobilization of local communities attempting, with inadequate and makeshift equipment, to contain the damage.[14] This spontaneous, decentralized response suggests that the initial planning of the damage control system might well have relied upon local knowledge and initiative; and this would have required the active involvement of local communities. Of course, this approach would have elicited concern and many questions from these communities, and the conventional administrative view would take this to be a sufficient reason for the approach to be rejected. It is indeed possible that intense opposition would have been encountered, but it is also possible that this very opposition would have promoted the design of a more effective damage control system — or, indeed, the choice and design of a transportation system which would have made damage on such a scale impossible in the first place. This observation is no doubt relevant to many major projects and LULUs. What often seems to be the danger of unwarranted delay might also be viewed as a necessary trial for projects which would render less likely at least some major mistakes. More broadly considered, indeed, such an orientation to the administrative process would alter its present commitment and enhance the prospect of a pattern of development consistent with environmental concerns.

The technocratic orientation distributes benefits of doubt and burdens of proof in a way which promotes the prevailing pattern of socio-economic development — and does so by appealing to an imagery of expertise, precision, and knowledge while conjuring up a "number" to support any decision. This practice obscures the actual process and its bias:

The "number" selected for an environmental standard only appears to be derived directly from the pure disinterested inquiries of the laboratory; in fact, it usually represents a rough compromise among vested interests, balancing science, politics and economy on the knife-edge of potential catastrophe.[15]

The challenge to technocracy does not propose, of course, to miraculously abolish the uncertainties and perplexities of decision-making. Environmental administration, indeed, is oriented toward a process that would make the problems more visible — dispelling the mystique which supports unbounded confidence that problems generated by the prevailing pattern of development can be overcome. Informed by a different view of environmental problems, the processes of environmental administration tend toward a reallocation of the benefits of doubt and the burdens of proof.[16]

(5) *Flexible*. Conventional problem-solving focuses on a form of analysis which proceeds from a fairly fixed conceptual framework, seeking impatiently to reduce ambiguity and diversity in the subject-matter to something manageable and familiar. What is lost is a sensitivity to those changes and differences which resist ready recognition, much less classification. Following from its non-compartmentalized, open, decentralized, and anti-technocratic characteristics, environmental administration remains flexible in its orientation to problems. Indeed, environmental administration is also flexible in another — perhaps perplexing — sense: it resists precisely the type of characterization we are trying to give it, for it is an emergent phenomenon. Environmental administration is taking shape, and remains to be shaped further. But no one is in a position to offer a comprehensive description or prescription. The very vocabulary now available is inadequate, distorting environmental administration even while describing, prescribing, and emerging along with it. For it would be ridiculous to say, taking the opposites of the terms employed here, that environmental administration possesses no features which could be considered somehow compartmentalized, closed, centralized, technocratic, or fixed. Such a notion of environmental administration would itself be absurdly rigid, yet such a distortion is certainly possible given the prevailing political and administrative context. Obviously, to speak of environmental administration is a task more complex than coming down on one side or another of a polar opposition. Yet the words to grasp and convey the right balance, integration, or realignment are not yet part of the

available vocabulary. To create such a vocabulary is part of an intellectual — indeed political — task which would change the prevailing agenda of inquiry and practice.

Environmental Administration and the Administrative State

To emphasize the interpenetration of politics and administration — in particular, to portray environmental administration as intrinsically political and a goal of environmental politics — is not to deny a distinction. Political and administrative life both contain, in varying degrees, contrary elements of innovation and routine, disagreement and consensus, chaos and order. In politics, the tendency is toward innovation, disagreement, and chaos while, in administration, it is toward routine, consensus, and order. The overlapping of the two domains is fluid, so that any conceptual boundary necessarily remains imprecise and provisional. There is nonetheless a difference between politics and administration, and this difference holds in the case of environmental administration.

The carnival atmosphere which accompanied the rise of environmental politics was bound to be eclipsed by other events. The response of conventional administration was to absorb opposition and smooth over conflict with modest reforms prone to be eroded as public attention lapsed and political dynamics shifted. Still, with these reforms, with a continuing and widespread recognition of environmental problems, and with a self-organizing environmental movement, a significant institutionalization of environmental concern was achieved: the emergence of environmental administration became perceptible and could be deliberately promoted through inquiry and practice. To be sure, there is no central direction and control of this effort. Indeed, environmentalism betrays differences and tensions as some groups tend toward professionalism, compromise, and workable solutions while other groups accentuate an oppositional posture accompanied by direct action and sensational stunts. Both these elements are necessary, though perhaps not sufficient, in the emergence of environmental administration.

Impatience with Leviathan should not obscure what is both obvious and paradoxical: moving beyond Leviathan would also mean initially helping to manage it. This is not to deny that the process could be long, even interminable — that opposition could significantly be absorbed through accommodation. Yet institutionalization has a memory that is more than momentary. Once established and set in motion, an administrative process gains a dynamism of its own and may see something through, especially if there are pressures which will not allow it to forget what it might prefer to forget. Institutional changes which tend to make the administrative process more open and participatory introduce an element of unpredictability which can be denied only through the illusion which the administrative mind fosters of its unbounded capacity to control events. Innovation of this kind, moreover, raises the prospect not only of citizens interacting with experts, but also of citizens *as* experts and experts *as* citizens. The strengthening of this already-present tendency would be a key event in the emergence of environmental administration: Leviathan might then become manageable.

Notes

1. Thorstein Veblen, *The Engineers and the Price System* (New York: Viking Press, 1933 [1921]), pp. 135-136. This book inspired the Technocracy movement of the 1930's; the term *technocracy* has since, of course, come to have a broader application.

2. In the midst of an outburst of environmental concern, the Nixon Administration quickly embraced a series of environmental measures in 1970, in particular with the President signing the *National Environmental Policy Act* of 1969 with much fanfare on the first day of the new decade. Yet the high priority of the environment did not last long. In mid-1971, the President clearly suggested the need for a shift: "We are not going to allow the environment issue to be used sometimes falsely and sometimes in a demagogic way basically to destroy the [industrial] system." By 1973, risk of an environmental crisis had apparently passed: "When we came to office in 1969," Nixon said, "we tackled this problem with all the power at our command. Now there is encouraging evidence that the United States has moved away from the environmental crisis that could have been toward a new era of restoration and renewal. Today...we are well on the way to winning the war against environmental degradation—well on the way to making our peace with nature...." Fuel shortages now placed an urgent new priority high on the agenda— that of securing expanded energy supplies. A key measure in this regard was the construction of the Trans-Alaska pipeline. See Richard N. L. Andrews, *Environmental Policy and Administrative Change* (Lexington, MA: Lexington Books, 1976), ch. 3, esp. pp. 24-25 for quotations. Recently, the final communiqué of the 1989 economic summit in Paris "devoted more space to the environment than to any other subject.... Being politicians, the leaders did not suddenly decide to go green because they liked the color. Powerful public sentiment in their respective countries drove them toward the fine words of their communiqué.... Environmental groups...are right to remain skeptical...." Jeffrey Simpson, "The Greening of the G7," *The Globe and Mail* (July 19, 1989), p. A6. *Cf.* Anthony Downs, "Up and Down with Ecology: The 'Issue-Attention Cycle'," *The Public Interest* 38 (1972), pp. 38-50.

3. The distinctive character of the environmental perspective is emphasized in Robert Paehlke, *Environmentalism and the Future of Progressive Politics* (New Haven: Yale University Press, 1989).

4. Douglas Torgerson, *Industrialization and Assessment: Social Impact Assessment as a Social Phenomenon* (Toronto: York University, 1980), p. 72. Also see ch. 2 generally and pp. 186-189.

5. On the relationship of environmentalism to the major political ideologies, see Paehlke, *Environmentalism and the Future of Progressive Politics*, ch. 7.

6. See Robert Paehlke, "Environmentalism: 'Motherhood', Revolution, or Just Plain Politics?" *Alternatives* 13:1 (1985), pp. 29-33; Robert M. Campbell, "From Keynesianism to Monetarism," *Queen's Quarterly* 88 (1981), pp. 635-650.

7. See, *e.g.*, Vaughan Lyon, "The Reluctant Party: Ideology versus Organization in Canada's Green Movement," *Alternatives* 13:1 (1985), pp. 3-8.

8. See Michael W. McCann, "Public Interest Liberalism and the Modern Regulatory State," Polity 21:1 (1988), pp. 373-400; Ronald Inglehart, "Post-Materialism in an Environment of Insecurity," *American Political Science Review* 75 (1981), pp. 880-900; Claus Offe, "New Social Movements:

Challenging the Boundaries of Institutional Politics," *Social Research* 52:4 (1985), pp. 817-868. Also see Robyn Eckersley, "Green Politics: A Practice in Search of a Theory?" *Alternatives* 15:4 (1988), pp. 52-61.

9. Tension within and among environmental groups became apparent as Pollution Probe in Toronto joined with Loblaws, a major supermarket chain, in developing and promoting "green" products. This involvement with the private sector of the administrative sphere followed from and reinforced a deliberate effort to develop a more professionalized environmental organization. The outcome was conflict within Pollution Probe, the resignation of the executive director, and criticism—at least of Loblaws—by Greenpeace Canada. In response to the controversy, various environmentalists affirmed the need for a diversity of groups. See Craig McInnes, "Environment Groups Face a Crisis of Identity," *The Globe and Mail* (July 15, 1989), p. D2.

10. For a convenient summary of some relevant literature, see Brian Martin, "Self-Managing Environmentalism," *Alternatives* 13:1 (1985), pp. 34-39.

11. For notable efforts to ground such legitimacy in recent critical theory, see Ray Kemp, "Planning, Public Hearings, and the Politics of Discourse," and John Fischer, "Critical Evaluation of Public Policy," in John Forester, ed., *Critical Theory and Public Life* (Cambridge, MA: The M.I.T. Press, 1985).

12. See Douglas Torgerson, "Between Knowledge and Politics: Three Faces of Policy Analysis," *Policy Sciences* 19 (1986), p. 51. No doubt resistance to this prospect is to be expected. Consider in this regard the comment of a citizen dealing with officials in a case involving the problem of radioactive waste: "They got nervous when someone started using the same technological jargon. They were always presuming that no one was going to do that, and...that they would just intimidate everyone, and that everyone would just shut up." Quoted in Donald Alexander, "Eldorado: Local Citizen Activism and the Nuclear Establishment, 1933-1988," M.A. Thesis, Trent University, Peterborough, Ontario, 1989, p. 76.

13. Edward J. Woodhouse, "External Influences on Productivity: EPA's Implementation of TSCA," *Policy Studies Review* 4:3 (1985), p. 501.

14. In an NBC News report of April 14, 1989 from Valdez, Don Molina described Homer, Alaska as a "town under seige," bracing for the oil spill to reach it and with 4,400 people fashioning improvised oil collecting booms. "There are finally some signs of order among the chaos of the clean-up," he added, "the beginning of coordination for all the equipment in place or on the way three weeks after the spill."

15. William Leiss, "Political Aspects of Environmental Issues," in William Leiss, ed., *Ecology versus Politics in Canada* (Toronto: University of Toronto Press, 1979), p. 264.

16. See T. J. Schrecker, *Political Economy of Environmental Hazards* (Ottawa: Law Reform Commission of Canada, 1984), ch. 2.

The Authors

Douglas J. Amy, an Associate Professor in the Department of Politics, Mount Holyoke College, is the author of *The Politics of Environmental Mediation*. He is currently writing a book on the electoral system in the United States.

Robert V. Bartlett is an Associate Professor of Political Science at Purdue University. He is the author of *The Reserve Mining Controversy: Science, Technology and Environmental Quality* as well as numerous articles, and most recently has edited *Policy Through Impact Assessment: Institutionalized Analysis as a Policy Strategy*.

John S. Dryzek is an Associate Professor of Political Science at the University of Oregon. His most recent books are *Rational Ecology: Environment and Political Economy* and *Policy Analysis by Design*. His writings on political theory, public policy, environmental politics and on the history and philosophy of social science have appeared in a number of leading journals.

Robert B. Gibson, an Associate Professor in the Department of Environmental and Resource Studies, University of Waterloo, is the author of numerous monographs and articles on environmental policy and political philosophy, including recent works on environmental assessment law and forest management decision making. He is also the editor of *Alternatives: Perspectives on Society, Technology and Environment*.

Albert R. Matheny is an Associate Professor of Political Science at the University of Florida. He is co-author, with Bruce Williams, of *Democracy, Dialogue and Social Regulation: Being Fair versus Being Right*, and is involved in ongoing research on legal development and professional reform.

Robert Paehlke is a Professor of Political Studies and Environmental and Resource Studies, Trent University. The author of numerous articles and monographs, he recently published *Environmentalism and the Future of Progressive Politics*. He is the founding editor of *Alternatives: Perspectives on Society, Technology and Environment.*

Ted Schrecker is a doctoral candidate and lecturer in the Department of Political Science, University of Western Ontario; previously he taught in Trent University's Environmental and Resource Studies Program. He is the author of *Political Economy of Environmental Hazards, The Pitfalls of Standards*, and numerous articles, and has served as a consultant to various governmental agencies and non-governmental organizations.

Douglas Torgerson is Associate Professor and Director, Administrative and Policy Studies, Trent University; formerly he taught in the Faculty of Environmental Studies, York University. He is the author of *Industrialization and Assessment: Social Impact Assessment as a Social Phenomenon* and articles on the relationship of political philosophy to policy and administration. He is also a former editor of *Alternatives: Perspectives on Society, Technology and Environment.*

Kernaghan Webb (LL.B., LL.M.) is a consultant with the Administrative Law Project of the Law Reform Commission of Canada and teaches environmental law at the University of Ottawa. He is the author of *Pollution Control in Canada: The Regulatory Approach in the 1980s.*

INDEX

Alternatives:

Perspectives on Society, Technology and Environment

An environmental quarterly publishing since 1971, *Alternatives* has provided a critical and rigorous focus on society, technology and the environment. Feature articles are combined with book reviews and a reports section on environmental activities to offer a comprehensive view of environmental thought and practice.

Issues of the journal are often devoted to the in-depth examination of themes such as these: agriculture and ecology; toxic waste management; the politics of acid rain; environmental ethics; confronting bureaucracy; science and survival; environmental protest and ideology; nuclear power; soft energy paths; the conserver society; occupational heath; third world development; northern communities and sustainable development; and saving the Great Lakes.

Authors have included Barry Commoner, Amory Lovins, Hazel Henderson, David Brooks, Peter Victor, William Ophuls, Elaine Bernard, John Livingston, Bernard Rollin, Toby Vigod, William Leiss, Norma Kassi, Dixon Thompson, Donald Chant, Murray Bookchin, and Rose Sheinin.

Subscription information, a list of available past issues, and author guidelines will be sent on request. Those planning submissions are urged to contact the editors in advance, and should note that feature articles are refereed.

Write to:
Alternatives
c/o Faculty of Environmental Studies
University of Waterloo
Waterloo, Ontario, Canada
N2L 3G1